B. H. HAGGIN was born on December 29th, 1900, in New York City. He graduated in 1920 from the Institute of Musical Art (now the Juilliard School), where his instrument was the piano, and in 1921 earned a B. A. from New York's City College. He began in 1923 to contribute articles and reviews to *Freeman, New Freeman, The New Republic,* Marc Van Doren's *The Nation,* and Lincoln Kirstein's *Hound and Horn.* He was music critic of the Brooklyn *Daily Eagle* from 1934 to 1937. Beginning in 1935 he began also to write about classical ballet (he was one of the first American critics to recognize the special qualities of Balanchine). In 1936 he became record critic, and in 1939 music critic of *The Nation,* where his distinctive (often dissenting) column appeared until 1957 (he was one of the few critics to comment publicly on the writings of other critics). From 1946 to 1949 he wrote the column "Music on the Radio" for the Sunday *New York Herald Tribune*; he reviewed records in *The New Republic* from 1957 to 1966 and in *Commonweal* from 1967 to 1969; he reviewed music and ballet in *The Hudson Review* from 1958 through 1972, and in *The New Republic* from 1975 through 1977. From 1957 until 1986, when he retired at the age of eighty-five, he reviewed records in *The Yale Review.* He published twelve books about music (not counting revisions of earlier works) and two about ballet; he gave talks on radio and lectures at several universities, and he contributed occasional pieces to *High Fidelity, American Scandinavian Review, Ballet News, Encounter, Ovation, The Sewanee Review, The Kenyon Review, Vogue, Commentary, The New York Review of Books* and others. He died in New York on May 28th, 1987.

ARTURO TOSCANINI

Contemporary Recollections
of the Maestro

BOOKS BY B. H. HAGGIN

A Book of the Symphony (1937)

Music on Records (1938)

Music on Records (1941)

Music for the Man Who Enjoys "Hamlet" (1944, 1960—Republished in 1983 as *Music for One Who Enjoys "Hamlet"*)

Music in The Nation (1949)

The Listener's Musical Companion (1956)

Conversations with Toscanini (1959, 1979—revised and republished in 1989 in *Arturo Toscanini: Contemporary Recollections of the Maestro*)

Music Observed (1964—republished in 1974 as *35 Years of Music*)

The Toscanini Musicians Knew (1967, 1980—revised and republished in 1989 in *Arturo Toscanini: Contemporary Recollections of the Maestro*)

The New Listener's Companion and Record Guide (1967, 1978)

Ballet Chronicle (1971)

A Decade of Music (1973)

Discovering Balanchine (1981)

Music and Ballet 1973-1983 (1984)

ARTURO TOSCANINI

Contemporary Recollections
of the Maestro

Containing reprints of two titles
CONVERSATIONS WITH TOSCANINI and
THE TOSCANINI MUSICIANS KNEW,
expanded and revised.

by B. H. HAGGIN

Edited by Thomas Hathaway
New preface by Elliott W. Galkin

A DA CAPO PAPERBACK

Library of Congress Cataloging in Publication Data

Haggin, B. H. (Bernard H.), 1900-
  Arturo Toscanini: contemporary recollections of the maestro / by B. H.
Haggin: edited by Thomas Hathaway.
    p.   cm.
  "An expanded and revised edition of the two volumes Conversations with
Toscanini and The Toscanini musicians knew."
  ISBN 0-306-80356-9
  1. Toscanini, Arturo, 1867-1957. 2. Conductors (Music) — Biography. I. Hag-
gin, B.H. (Bernard H.), 1900–   Conversations with Toscanini. II. Haggin, B.
H. (Bernard H.), 1900–   The Toscanini musicians knew. III. Title.
ML422.T67H35   1989   89-1551
785'.092'4 — dc19   CIP
                                                                    MN

All action photographs of Toscanini were taken during the recording session in Carnegie Hall on March 4, 1947, by Robert Hupka copyright © 1963 by Robert Hupka.

This Da Capo Press paperback edition of *Conversations with Toscanini,* originally published in New York in 1959, and *The Toscanini Musicians Knew,* originally published in 1967, brings together in one volume the editions published in 1959 and 1980, respectively, edited and annotated by Thomas Hathaway, and supplemented with interviews, letters, and additional material by the author, and with a new preface by Elliott W. Galkin. This edition is reprinted by arrangement with the Estate of Bernard H. Haggin.

Published by Da Capo Press, Inc.
A Subsidiary of Plenum Publishing Corporation
233 Spring Street, New York, N.Y. 10013

Manufactured in the United States of America

Editor's Acknowledgments

I am indebted to Bea Friedland for Da Capo Press's interest in revising and reprinting these two books, and for her sympathetic cooperation at each stage of the work. To Rose Hass, for advice, editorial help, and time spent obtaining materials and in preparing both books for reproduction. To Victoria Hathaway for transcription and other assistance. To Robert K. Dodson, Clive Giboire, Jeffrey Kraegel, Mark Muday, John Oughton, Ben Raeburn, Karl F. Reuling, Eliot Wagner, and one person who preferred not to receive formal acknowledgment, for editorial assistance of various kinds in preparing this edition. To Shirley Fleming of *Musical America,* and Patricia Reilly of *High Fidelity Magazine,* for their help in securing and reproducing the cover photograph of Toscanini. To Robert Hupka, for once again allowing his own photographs of Toscanini to be reproduced. And to Marshall Beil for advice on various matters.

Regarding *Conversations With Toscanini* in particular, I am indebted to John H. Corbett, Arthur M. Fierro, Michael Gray, and Harvey Sachs, for information, assistance, and advice. Regarding *The Toscanini Musicians Knew,* I am indebted to Milton Katims, for his cooperation and good will in preparing his statement for publication, to Shirley J. Miller for permission to publish the statement by her husband, the late Frank Miller, and to Frank Miller's son, David, for his assistance.

T. H. — 1988

Preface to
Da Capo Edition

Like Arturo Toscanini, B. H. Haggin was brilliant, imperious, and authoritative. Like Toscanini he could be reclusive, irascible, always impatient with mediocrity — and in a profession so tarnished by vanity — contemptuous of self-aggrandizement. No two musicians were more idealistic, and no two shared a more serious creative relationship based upon common purposes of artistic commitment.

Among American critics, none was more insightful or analytical than Haggin in defining Arturo Toscanini as the pivotal figure in the history of modern conducting: Haggin was prophetic in recognizing the extraordinary influence Toscanini was destined to have upon the development of a sophisticated orchestral tradition in the United States. Yet, at a time when the Italian *maestro* was being adulated in print (his is one of the largest bibliographies in the literature about conductors and conducting), Haggin resisted writing his biography — undoubtedly because he realized the dangers of affectation and idealization.

Born in 1900 into a middle-class New York Jewish family (his father was a pharmacist), Haggin completed his formal musical studies in 1920 at the Institute of Musical Art (now the Juilliard School), and a year later received a B. A. from City College in New York (C.C.N.Y.). He looked back at his formal musical education as pitifully inadequate; like Berlioz, he frequently disapproved of the narrow activities and aspirations of music schools. And — again like Berlioz — he constantly criticized critics, especially Deems Taylor, Olin Downes, and Samuel Chotzinoff. In 1940, summarizing the past eighteen years of criticism in New York, he wrote categorically, " . . .there is little to recall with pleasure or respect."

Haggin began his career in 1923. America's musical life was characterized by a conscious dependence upon European eclecticism, groping in its search for musical insights — its audiences more untutored than sophisticated, its composition imitative, its scholarship rudimentary — and its critics all too frequently lacking in professional competence. Haggin, in contrast, provided fresh and factual viewpoints in the press. His observations were perceptive, penetrating, and astute in their recognition of the critic's role as teacher: " . . . whether or not a critic performs a pedagogical function by intention, he does so in practice." Unlike so many others, Haggin was always a serious critic, and always reflected intellectual integrity.

When Haggin's career came to a close in 1986, Toscanini had been dead twenty-nine years. America, with its 1500 orchestras (more than half of all those in the world), and its renowned scholars, composers, and performers, was now recognized internationally for its independent artistic spirit and impressive levels of musical performance and creativity: America had become the most important of musical capitals.

During this period of dramatic development, Haggin and Toscanini provided unflagging leadership and inspiration to the public; for the thirty-two years that their careers overlapped, Haggin consistently wrote in admiration of Toscanini's accomplishments and significance. He agreed with Pierre Monteux's estimate of Toscanini as "*le plus grand de tous*," and hailed him for his ability, more than any other conductor, to fuse poetic insights with fervor and concentration — to create " . . . sharp contours of individual sounds and phrases, transparency of texture, unfailing continuity and perfect plastic proportions of the continuum of sounds progressing in time . . . feeling for purity, simplicity, economy, and subtlety." (The Toscanini Haggin knew responded with praise — and his well-known sense of ironic humor: "Mr. Haggin writes like God.")

There are elements in the Haggin-Toscanini relationship as summarized in *Conversations With Toscanini* which are comparable to those in the twenty-five years of correspondence between Richard Strauss and Hugo von Hoffmansthal — fascinating dialogue about musical repertoire, concepts of interpretation, and activities of performers — discussed spontaneously, uninhibitedly, and always with intensity. Obviously an important aspect of the bond of friendship between these individuals — so dissimilar in background and age, and each typically a tenacious guardian of personal privacy — was based upon their sharing not only congruent ideals and insights, but also similar musical gifts: an extraordinary memory, and an infallible ear.

There is no doubt that Haggin possessed what the French call "*l'oreille*." He could hear harmonic and melodic details precisely, incisively, and analytically. He also had a remarkable ear for timbre: he was capable of being " . . . startled by a splice in Toscanini's recording of Debussy's *Ibéria*, because sound quality . . . that had been marvelously bright and clear, suddenly became less bright, less clear, and less spacious." In contrast, two other critics, well-known for their writings about recordings, found the splice "undetectable," maintaining " . . . it can't be heard."

His prose reflects his ability to translate sounds into a rhetoric at once forceful and feeling. Little wonder that he was able to discuss nuances of instrumentation and intonation with a conductor whose ear was legendary in the profession—who could detect not only a wrong note, or an inaccurate dynamic detail, but a deviant bowing or fingering. Little wonder that Toscanini, who characteristically had little respect for critics, was impressed.

Haggin admired W. J. Turner, whom he praised in 1947 as " . . . the most distinguished critic of our time." But there was also an element of Hanslick in Haggin's writing and beliefs—especially in his old-fashioned insistence upon unity, order, clarity, and balance. It would not be an exaggeration to propose that any of Haggin's books might have been subtitled *Vom Musikalischen Schoenen*. Furthermore, like Hanslick in Germany (and Berlioz in France), he was the most authoritative pioneer commentator about musical aesthetics and music appreciation in his country's popular press. He not only explained and analyzed—he also challenged and stimulated.

In his own words, he was incapable of genuflecting before eminences—too skeptical to worship heroes. Frequently his convictions seemed heretical and disturbing to his readership: the crowd-pleasing pianist Josef Hoffmann he considered as representing " . . . one of the worst examples of the virtuoso career" (he equated virtuosi with acrobats). Prokofieff, he wrote, " . . . goes through elaborate notions of saying a great deal, when he is saying absolutely nothing." Shostakovich's music was " . . . pretentiously feeble, inane, and banal"; much of Brahms, " : . . labored, pretentious and saccharine." Comparably devastating was his judgment of certain eminent conductors: Furtwängler's direction of Beethoven's Ninth Symphony in 1937 constituted "... butchery ... by a tasteless effect-monger"; while Stokowski practiced "... corruption of taste and understanding."

In contrast, he was inspired by articulateness and the complex vitality of creative men—like Shakespeare's vulnerable hero whom he praised by entitling one of his most interesting books, *Music for the Man Who Enjoys Hamlet.* (The book was dedicated privately to Toscanini.) He applauded boldness and imagination, what he characterized as "greatness of mind and spirit." In *The Nation,* Haggin shared his highly personal views with a small readership which contained the intellectual and the elite; this was a public, insightful and inquisitive, capable of enjoying "Hamlet." But his works on Toscanini have reached a far wider readership.

The concept and format of *The Toscanini Musicians Knew* is traceable to Oscar Sonneck's *Beethoven, Impressions of Contemporaries,* which appeared three years after Haggin had begun to write music criticism. Sonneck's study was retrospective, his sources historical; Haggin's was contemporary: in effect he anticipated that genre known today as oral history.

Together with *Conversations with Toscanini, The Toscanini Musicians Knew* fulfills an important function in the Toscanini bibliography. Before these two publications, the literature about Toscanini constituted a corpus of information much of which was oversimplified and superficial: Toscanini the *naif,* the tyrant, the tempestuous conductor feared by his musicians and acclaimed more than any other maestro in history.

The Toscanini Musicians Knew provides readers with first-hand information about his baton technique, and intimate insights about his commitments and his manner of living and working. Until *The Toscanini Musicians Knew,* the writings about him were characterized by one of the members of his NBC Orchestra, that magnificent organization which he conducted from 1937 until 1954 in weekly broadcasts heard coast-to-coast, as the products of "outsiders." Haggin's book is unique because it consists of facts supplied by " . . . insiders—the musicians who actually rehearsed and played with Toscanini"; the compilation constitutes " . . . an authoritative statement by those who experienced his greatness, to give the people in the future a correct idea of what that greatness was."

The Toscanini Musicians Knew provides the major reasons for such eminence. It consists of nineteen interviews with a distinguished selection of musicians with whom the *maestro* worked: conductors Robert Shaw and Alfred Wallenstein; singers Jennie Tourel, Jan Peerce, Giovanni Martinelli, and Alexander Kipnis; and soloists such as Mieczyslaw Horszowski and Felix Galimir, and the various members of his NBC Symphony. In effect, the book might be considered as nineteen variations on the theme of conducting as dramatized by its foremost practitioner of the time. The information ranges far and wide: the characteristics of his time-beating movements; the clarity, compelling predictability and inevitability of the gestures of his baton; his sense of humor and his temper tantrums; his unrivaled powers of persuasion on the podium; and his ability to make the musicians play better than they ever thought themselves capable.

Certainly, as a result, Toscanini influenced the course of musical performance as no other conductor. With his NBC broadcasts, heard weekly for sixteen years, he set standards which inspired subsequent orchestras. In the words of Walter Damrosch, who was the first to conduct an orchestral concert relayed by radio across the United States and who was Toscanini's colleague at NBC,

"Toscanini illuminated whatever he touched. He made the familiar new, and the new familiar and intimate."

All the more important, therefore, in these days of what has been termed "Toscanini-bashing"—minimizing his achievements, rejecting his significances as technician and interpreter, and accusing him of being a media pawn —that Haggin's first-hand accounts should reappear to provide a contrasting perspective. His books document the reasons for the supremacy of Toscanini's authority, and enrich our understanding of conducting as art and craft.

— ELLIOTT W. GALKIN
Baltimore, MD.
October, 1988

CONVERSATIONS
WITH
TOSCANINI

B. H. Haggin

Illustrations by Robert Hupka.

Contents

Editor's Foreword

This edition reprints the first (1959) Doubleday edition of *Conversations With Toscanini,* with these differences: the footnotes on pages 21, 22, and 130 are taken from the 1979 edition. Pages 9 through 163 are otherwise unchanged (including the "A—"on pages 79, 86, and 106 that referred to Charles Munch, the "X—" on page 34 that referred to Sir Thomas Beecham, the "Y—" on page 74 that referred to Artur Rodzinski, and the "Z—" on page 78 that referred to Fritz Reiner—all of whom were still alive in 1959). Of the two "Postcripts" to the chapter "The Broadcasts and Recordings," the first—beginning with the first full paragraph on page 164—is by Haggin and is taken from the 1979 edition. (The order of the words in brackets in the opening sentences of the first two paragraphs has been altered so that these sentences and what follows may stand independently of the material that preceded them in that edition.) The second "Postscript" I provided myself. The new chapter called "Toscanini's Resignation from the NBC Symphony" is also from the 1979 edition. Other corrections and amplifications appear as endnotes. The discographies—both the 1959 and 1979 versions—have been omitted entirely, as it has become impractical to keep such lists up to date in a book. The subject of Toscanini's recorded legacy is discussed in the chapter "The Broadcasts and Recordings."

—THOMAS HATHAWAY
Toronto, 1988

CONVERSATIONS
WITH TOSCANINI

Once, after a rehearsal at which Toscanini had erupted into one of his rages, I heard an NBC Symphony player ask Harry Glantz, the orchestra's first trumpet who had played under Toscanini in the New York Philharmonic: "Was he any worse in his Philharmonic days?"

"Well," said Glantz with a meaningful look, "he was fifteen years younger."

The fact is that Toscanini did mellow in his later years; and it is to this fact, I am sure, that I owe the personal experiences with him that I am about to describe. For from the very beginning of my awareness of his existence—which is to say from January 1914, when I heard my first performance at the Metropolitan, one of *Madama Butterfly* which he conducted—he was for me an awesome figure, known to be formidable to the musicians whom he worked with in the opera house, and remote, forbidding, unapproachable outside of the opera house—unapproachable above all to the press (though one of the newspaper reviewers, Max Smith, was a personal friend). And this impression of him was strengthened in the course of time by the excitement over his sudden, silent, unexplained, and therefore mysterious departure from the Metropolitan in April 1915; the excitement over his return in the season of 1920–21 for a tour with the orchestra of La Scala; the excitement over his coming as guest conductor to the New York Philharmonic in January 1926; the excitement over his departure—again silent and mysterious—from the New York Philharmonic-Symphony in 1936; the excitement over his performances in Salzburg in 1937.

Toscanini's awesomeness was brought home to me personally in one particular way. My piano teacher at the Institute of Musical Art had known some of the wealthy women who were influential in the affairs of New York orchestras; and I had been given permission to attend Mengelberg's rehearsals first with the National Symphony and then with the New York Philharmonic. Some of these women also came to the rehearsals; and Mengelberg seemed to enjoy having a little audience for his lectures to the orchestra on what he called the "princips" of orchestral performance. But with Toscanini nobody was allowed at rehearsals; and one read about the lights being turned on periodically in Carnegie Hall while the staff went through the balconies to make sure nobody was hiding up there. Under these circumstances I didn't even try to get in; but I must have learned things were different in Salzburg, for in 1937, when I was about to go there, I secured, through the kindness of Mr. B. W. Huebsch, a letter from Stefan Zweig to Mme. Toscanini asking permission for me to attend one rehearsal. In Salzburg, in obedience to Zweig's instructions, I presented myself to a specified intermediary who took me to the *Festspielhaus* where we waited for Mme. Toscanini to come out; and I was then presented to her and gave her the letter. She asked which rehearsal I would like to attend, and I said one of Verdi's *Requiem;* and she said I would hear from her at the proper time, a few weeks later, but I never did. By this time I had—as someone who was keeping the AP correspondent in Vienna informed of what was happening in Salzburg—become *persona grata* to the director of the festival; and from him I obtained a pass to the last rehearsal for Toscanini's last orchestral concert. But when I got to the *Festspielhaus* I found a little group of Toscanini relatives and friends standing outside disconsolately: enraged by something that had gone wrong in the rehearsal the day before, he had decreed that nobody was to be allowed in today.

The excitement over Toscanini's return to New York in December 1937 to conduct the NBC Symphony did not make him a less awesome and remote figure for me. And I was therefore wholly unprepared for what happened in Carnegie Hall one Sunday afternoon in March 1940. Sauntering down the aisle, Robert A. Simon of *The New Yorker* stopped to ask: "Do you know Toscanini reads you in *The Nation?*" Amazed, I answered: "No. How do *you* know?" "People who see him have told me," said Simon. "He showed them your article on the Philharmonic and Barbirolli and said: 'See?' "

Actually the article Simon referred to had been not about the Philharmonic and Barbirolli but about how certain critics had dealt with the subject. I had pointed out how

W. J. Henderson's crotchety irritation with the fuss about virtuoso conductors had caused him to insist in the *Sun* that the Philharmonic and the music of Beethoven and Brahms would remain even without Toscanini and even with a conductor of less than stellar magnitude, though he must have known that the orchestra and the music would sound different under such a conductor; and how this had placed a powerful argument in the hands of those who had brought about the engagement of Barbirolli, which had considerably reduced the orchestra's usefulness to the community. I had pointed out further that Henderson had at least—when he had heard subsequently what the Philharmonic and the music actually sounded like under Barbirolli's direction—expressed his disapproval; whereas Lawrence Gilman had written in the *Herald Tribune* concerning Barbirolli's achievements—including a performance of Brahms's Fourth which had torn passion to tatters—that they showed him to be "something better and rarer and finer than a conductor of power and sensibility. He permits us to think that he is akin to those uncommon interpreters who give us a measure of 'that inner standard of distinction, selection, refusal' which an incorruptible artist once defined: who have sifted from experience 'all that seemed beautiful and significant, and have treasured above all things those savings of fine gold.'" And I had said that in this way Gilman had been of great help to the Philharmonic directors—"the help, perhaps, that an orchestra's program annotator should be; but he failed in his obligations to his position as critic, to his readers, to the community whose orchestra the Philharmonic was." All this apparently had been of interest to Toscanini; and his "See?" carried implications of how he had felt about it.

I was pleased of course by what Simon told me; but it wasn't until a year later that it gave me the courage to write Toscanini for what I considered a legitimate purpose: to suggest that he perform Berlioz's *L'Enfance du Christ,* which W. J. Turner had declared to be Berlioz's most beautiful score, but which at that time was never performed. I wrote Toscanini that I addressed my request to him because of the interest in Berlioz he had shown by playing *Harold in Italy* and the *Queen Mab* Scherzo and other excerpts from *Romeo and Juliet;* because it had been in *Harold* as he had performed it around 1930 that I had first understood the special quality of Berlioz's mind, imagination and style; and because what I was asking was something for the entire musical public: it was like asking someone to let the public see a great painting that had been hidden for many years. And I added a request that he conduct and record *Queen Mab.*

Some days later, opening an envelope addressed in an unfamiliar and striking handwriting, and unfolding the letter inside it, I was amazed again to see at the bottom of the sheet, signed very cordially, the name Arturo Toscanini. Evidently under the impression that I had suggested *L'Enfance du Christ* for the broadcast of April 5, he wrote that he was sorry but the program for that date had already been planned as follows: Rossini's Overture to *Il Signor Bruschino,* Mendelssohn's *Scotch* Symphony, and Berlioz's Overture *Les Francs-Juges,* his *Love Scene* and *Queen Mab* from *Romeo and Juliet,* and his Hungarian March from

The Damnation of Faust. And he assured me *Queen Mab* would be recorded.

I wrote to thank him for his kindness in answering me, and to express my hope that he would perform *L'Enfance* at a later time—which he never did.

In November 1941 I wrote to him again. He was to conduct the Philadelphia Orchestra in three programs that season, and Victor had announced some of the performances would be recorded. I told him that I had had his 1936 performance of Schubert's C-major Symphony with the New York Philharmonic recorded off the air, but that the recording had turned out to be imperfect, and that I therefore hoped this symphony would be one of the works he would record for Victor. I hoped also for recordings of Tchaikovsky's *Pathétique* and *Romeo and Juliet,* of Mozart and Haydn, and of course Berlioz's *Queen Mab.* And I wrote that I had learned from his son that he had disliked what I had written about Brahms in my *Book of the Symphony,* but that possibly he would like what I had written about Mozart, Haydn, Schubert, Tchaikovsky in my new book *Music on Records.*

This brought a reply in which Toscanini informed me that one of his first recordings would be the Schubert C-major Symphony which he was going to conduct the following week with the Philadelphia Orchestra, and that he would record also the *Pathétique, Ibéria* and *Queen Mab.* Then, for no reason, apparently, other than the fact that it was in his mind at the moment, he went on to say he had a weakness for Beethoven's Septet, which he had played the preceding season with ten violins, ten violas, eight cellos and four basses, because he had never enjoyed this wonderful music when it was played by seven instruments as Beethoven wrote it. He had, he said, heard many performances of the piece in its original form by distinguished musicians; but the right balance [of strings and three winds] had never been attained. He would, he went on, read what I said about Schubert, Haydn and Mozart with the utmost interest; concerning Brahms his comment was, for the moment, the Italian proverb *acqua in bocca*. And he ended with cordial greetings.

The Schubert C-major opened the first program, which I heard at the Saturday-night concert of the pair on November 15. The performance of the symphony was of course the matter of major interest; but interesting too was the way the orchestra played and sounded under Toscanini's direction. Since 1937 he had been working with the NBC Symphony, and producing with it excitingly beautiful and effective performances but not the sheer incandescence of execution and sonority that he had achieved with the New York Philharmonic; and the reason for this was not, as some have contended recently, that he could conduct orchestras but not build and train them. "You can quote me on this," said an NBC Symphony violinist in happy excitement once after a rehearsal of Debussy's *La Mer*, at the end of which the orchestra had applauded Toscanini: "We come here to go to school!" And the contention—by some who never even heard the Philharmonic under either Mengelberg or Toscanini—that it was not Toscanini but Mengelberg who made of this orchestra an ensemble in the class of Stokowski's Philadelphia and Koussevitzky's

Boston Symphony, is contrary to the facts that I observed. I was a witness, at the daily rehearsals, of the training Mengelberg gave the Philharmonic from 1921 to 1926, and can testify to the discipline and finish of its playing under his direction; but although I did not witness Toscanini's work at rehearsals I did hear that it was only when the orchestra began to play under him in 1926 that it began to exhibit the dazzling virtuosity and tonal beauty comparable with those of the Philadelphia and Boston Symphony—to produce, that is, the razor-sharp attacks, the sharp-contoured phrases, the radiant sonorities and transparent textures comparable with the Philadelphia's lush sumptuousness, the Boston Symphony's refinement of execution and tone. Moreover it was Toscanini who in 1928 chose the players from the Philharmonic and the New York Symphony for the combined Philharmonic-Symphony, and who trained this orchestra to the point where its playing exhibited the incandescence I have mentioned, which can be heard in the 1936 recordings of the Rossini Overtures to *Semiramide* and *L'Italiana in Algeri* and the Brahms-Haydn Variations.

If now it is asked what *was* the reason why the Philharmonic could play in this way and the NBC Symphony could not, the answer is that the Philharmonic was a group of players who had worked together for a number of years, whose only professional activity was playing together as a symphony orchestra, and who—whatever the laxity they permitted themselves with other conductors—maintained in their four or five rehearsals and three or four concerts each week with Toscanini the discipline, cohesiveness, and sensitiveness to his direction that they had acquired in their years of work with him; whereas the NBC Symphony had been assembled only a couple of months before Toscanini began to conduct it, and the nature and conditions of its members' other work largely nullified the training he gave it. NBC did not in 1937 create an additional new orchestra for Toscanini's exclusive use: it had a staff orchestra for its Red and Blue Networks, and the NBC Symphony was set up as a group within that staff orchestra—a group which included a number of players engaged for Toscanini as higher-caliber replacements of previous members of the staff orchestra. The weekly "services" of the NBC Symphony players were therefore not merely the up to ten hours of rehearsal and the hour-and-a-half broadcast with Toscanini: they included also more than that number of hours of rehearsal and performance for the networks' other programs, sustaining and commercial, with conductors unable to hold the players to Toscanini's high technical and musical standards; and he had to work with men who sometimes came to his rehearsal straight from a two-hour rehearsal of dance music, or rushed from his rehearsal to a commercial program under a staff conductor. And later, after NBC had had to sell the Blue Network, the NBC Symphony was made up of (1) a permanent group of about forty-five who were part of the NBC staff orchestra of sixty-five that included about twenty men used in jazz programs, and (2) about forty-five extra men engaged only for the NBC Symphony series, who were not always the same; and members of the jazz contingent also were used on occasion. Hence it was not until 1950, and the transcontinental tour that gave the orchestra six weeks of re-hearsing and playing under Toscanini, that it began to exhibit the precise, finished and sensitive execution, the blending, refinement and beauty of tone, of a first-rate symphony orchestra.

In Philadelphia in November 1941, therefore, after Toscanini's four years with the NBC house orchestra, it was interesting to hear what he achieved with one of the world's great symphony orchestras again—this time with the marvelous instrument Stokowski had created in the Philadelphia Orchestra. One thing that was interesting was the change in the orchestra's playing: instead of the Sto-kowski flood of tonal sumptuousness and splendor it pro-duced the Toscanini radiance, transparency, sharpness of attack and contour. But it was interesting also that play-ing under Toscanini only a few days the orchestra was not sensitized to his direction as the Philharmonic had been after ten years, so that he didn't get from it the miraculous subtleties of inflection and coloring of the Philharmonic's 1936 *Semiramide* performance. And there was in addition a human aspect of the occasion that was touching: Sto-kowski had left the orchestra a few years earlier; and the awe on the face of the very young first cellist, Samuel Mayes, as he looked up from his music to Toscanini during the Schubert symphony, the smiles of all the men at the end of the performance, were evidence of what it meant to them to be playing again under a great conductor, and one who was in addition a great musician.

But what was most important was the performance of the symphony. The work was very dear to Toscanini (he played it at his very first orchestral concert, on March 20, 1896, in Turin); and his treatment of it had always been criticized—one of the things objected to being his faster-than-usual tempo for the second movement. I had always been startled by the first measures and had then gone along easily with the rest of the movement; but at this Philadelphia performance I thought I understood for the first time what was behind that fast tempo: a feeling for plastic simplicity, economy, subtlety, that caused Toscanini often to set a single subtly modified tempo for all the sections of a movement. In the second movement of the Schubert C-major, then, he set a tempo for the opening section that he could maintain unchanged not only for the alternating section but for the catastrophe in the middle of the movement, so that the increasing urgency and tension of this passage was achieved without any acceleration, and in fact a slight broadening at the end gave shattering power to the chords with which the passage breaks off into momentary silence.

It was also objected that Toscanini's performance was not in the Viennese tradition—which led me to question such tradition and its authority. Even if Schubert had himself conducted a performance of his C-major Symphony which conductors of his time had heard and followed as a model for their own performances, which in turn had been followed as models by their successors, and so on down to the present—even if all this had happened I did not believe that what Schubert had done with the symphony would be still discernible in the performances today. But actually the symphony was rehearsed but not performed shortly

after his death; then it was forgotten until Schumann discovered it in 1838 and Mendelssohn played it in 1839;
and these performances represented only the understanding
of the work that each conductor had achieved by his own
study of the score. Did this establish a tradition which could
forbid other musicians—and one of the greatest musicians
of all time—to do the same thing? (I asked this unaware
that Richard Strauss, asking who could maintain today that
Beethoven did or did not want a particular tempo, had
contended there was no tradition determining such matters
and the personal artistic conviction of the conductor had
to decide what was right or wrong.)

Another objection was that this symphony was a Viennese work which should be played with a Viennese relaxation that Toscanini's performance did not have. But
not all the music written in Vienna is alike, and not all
of it is relaxed: the particular relaxed quality of some of
Schubert's music is not in Mozart's or Beethoven's or even
all of Schubert's. A correct understanding of his music includes perception of the power and tension in some of it;
and a correct understanding of the C-major Symphony
includes perception of its sustained tension and momentum
and grandeur, which Toscanini's performance achieved as
no other did.

In addition to the Schubert, Toscanini conducted Debussy's *Ibéria* and Respighi's *Roman Festivals;* and at the
end I went backstage and talked with a member of the
orchestra whom I knew. After a while I caught sight of
Walter Toscanini; and I asked him if I might thank his
father. "Certainly," he replied. "He reads you; he answers

your letters; he doesn't answer *my* letters but he answers *yours*"; and smiling he led me to his father's dressing room. When we got there Toscanini and Mme. Toscanini were standing in the doorway saying good-by to the last visitor, and Mme. Toscanini was about to close the door. "This is Mr. Haggin of *The Nation*," said Walter to his father, who smiled and extended his hand but said nothing; and I thanked him and left.

I went to Philadelphia again for the concert of January 10, 1942, at which Toscanini conducted Haydn's Symphony No. 99, Respighi's orchestration of Bach's *Passacaglia* for organ, excerpts from Mendelssohn's music for *A Midsummer Night's Dream,* and Strauss's *Death and Transfiguration.* When I saw Walter Toscanini at the end of the concert he said: "Father did not know who you were last time. He said: 'Why you did not tell me it was Mr. Haggin of *The Nation?*'" And he led me again to his father's dressing room, which this time was filled with visitors. But when Walter introduced me to him Toscanini again smiled and extended his hand and said nothing. There was an exchange in Italian between Walter and his father; then, as Toscanini was drawn away by someone else, Walter said to me: "Father said about your new book: 'He writes like God: he knows what is good music and what is bad music. *I* do not know what is good music and what is bad music; but *he* knows.'" *

Before I went to Philadelphia for the concert of February 7 I was told I could be present at the recording session the following day. At the concert Toscanini conducted Tchaikovsky's *Pathétique,* a Vieuxtemps Ballade and Polonaise,

* Some readers [of the first edition of this book] didn't understand that Toscanini was speaking facetiously.   B.H.H.—1979

Berlioz's *Queen Mab*, and Debussy's *La Mer*; and the next day I was present during the recording of the *Pathétique* and part of *La Mer*. The occasion provided my first experience of Toscanini rehearsing—of which I remember now only his working out dynamic values and balances in the introduction of the *Pathétique*.

During a break in the recording session, Walter invited me to visit his father in his dressing room, where we found him fanning himself and worrying about the difficulties of recording. "I make *pianissimo* in *La Mer*: in hall is correct; on record is *not* correct! In 1936 I make *Rhine Journey* with Philharmonic. I go to Paris; a commission—Gilman, Betti, Chotzinoff *—listen to record and say is good. In Carnegie Hall is right tempo; when I hear record, is wrong tempo. Last year I am in bed, and a friend telephone to me: 'Maestro, listen to radio.' I listen: is *Rhine Journey*; is good —is right tempo—IS MY *RHINE JOURNEY*! in 1936 is wrong tempo; now is right tempo! Ah, *Dio santo*!" and he hurled the fan at the wall in despair.

The program was repeated in New York two days later— which is to say after the additional rehearsal and playing at the recording sessions—and in Carnegie Hall, which was acoustically even finer than the Academy of Music; with the result that the sounds produced by the orchestra on

---

* In 1936 Lawrence Gilman had been the music critic of the New York *Herald Tribune*; Adolfo Betti the first violin of the Flonzaley Quartet; Samuel Chotzinoff the music critic of the New York *Post*. In 1959 Bruno Zirato of the New York Philharmonic informed me that Chotzinoff had not been a member of the committee that listened to the recordings.

B.H.H.—1979

this occasion ranged themselves with the other wonders
I had heard achieved by human powers in Carnegie Hall—
the sounds produced by the Philadelphia Orchestra under
Stokowski, the Boston Symphony under Koussevitzky, the
New York Philharmonic under Toscanini. But the sounds
were not just sounds: they added up to wonderfully right
and effective realizations of the pieces of music; and it
seemed to me that one reason for the impression of rightness conveyed at every point in the progression of the first
movement of Tchaikovsky's *Pathétique* was the plastic
coherence imparted to the form in sound by Toscanini's
sense for continuity and proportion in the continuum of
sound moving in time; and that another reason was the
fact that the nuances of sonority and tempo with which
he molded this continuum were the ones Tchaikovsky specified in his score to produce the form he had imagined. Or
rather, they were the close approximations to these that a
performer could achieve: the composer's notations could
not convey the imagined form completely; the performer
therefore could not produce it in living sound exactly as
the composer had imagined it; and his obligation was to
produce it to the extent to which the notation did convey
it. About halfway through the first movement of Debussy's
La Mer, after the music has died down into mutterings of
basses and kettledrums, an upward leap of the cellos is followed by a slight swell of the kettledrum from *pp* to *p*
and back, and this by an echoing swell of the horns.
There was no notation that could convey exactly what
Debussy imagined as *pp* and *p* and as the timbres of the
horns; and his notation therefore left room for the differ-

ences between Toscanini's values for *pp* and *p* and Koussevitzky's, the sound of Toscanini's horns and that of Koussevitzky's; but it left no room for Koussevitzky's change of the swell of kettledrum followed by echoing swell of horns to the simultaneous thunderous swell of kettledrum *and* horns. For Koussevitzky a person who wanted the composer's score adhered to was someone who didn't want the music to be alive (the words are his); but it was Toscanini who, by obeying Debussy's directions, gave life to the magical effect of horns echoing over the water, and it was Koussevitzky who, by his change, killed that effect.

In April 1942 the New York Philharmonic ended its centennial season with a Beethoven festival conducted by Toscanini; and I wrote to ask him for permission to attend the rehearsals. He granted it; and so I witnessed the extraordinary thing that happened at the very first rehearsal. It was six years since Toscanini had conducted the orchestra; one expected that it would take inch-by-inch rehearsal to restore the precision and tonal beauty of its playing under him six years earlier; and the members of the orchestra must have expected this too as they sat tuning and practicing passages in the *Missa Solemnis*. Eventually the hubbub died out; there was complete silence as the orchestra waited for Toscanini; and at last he appeared at the side of the stage and, in the tense hush, walked in his absorbed fashion to the podium, stepped onto it, suppressed with a quick gesture the first sounds of a demonstration of welcome, and, with no more than a word of greeting, raised his arm and began to conduct the opening of the *Missa*. And then the extraordinary thing happened: as though the interval had been not six years but one day, the orchestra began at once—in response to the large shaping movements of Toscanini's right arm and the subtly inflecting movements of his left hand—to produce the razor-sharp attacks, the radiant sonorities, the transparent textures, the beautifully contoured phrases which these movements had elicited in April 1936. For minutes at a time he continued to conduct and the orchestra continued to play in this way; only after such long stretches were there halts to go back and correct an imperfect balance at one point or to work out the contour of a phrase at another. And something similar happened at the end of a later rehearsal, when, turning to the finale of the First Symphony, he led the orchestra through it without interruption and produced the performance of six or seven years earlier in all its beautiful detail.

In part, certainly, the explanation of this was Toscanini's powers as a conductor—the movements through which he transmitted his moment-to-moment purpose, the compelling personal force that imposed that purpose through the movements; in part the explanation was the fact that he was conducting an orchestra he had conducted for ten years, and in works they had rehearsed and played together in those years. But I could see that in large part the explanation was the nature of Toscanini's musical conceptions that I mentioned earlier—the plastic continuity and coherence of the shapes he created in the continuum of sound moving in time. That is, in such a progression the timing and force of one sound implied the timing and force of the next irresistibly; and it was the power of these implications, causing the many players in the orchestra to produce the next sound at the same point in time and with the same weight and color, that accounted in large part for the remarkable precision of Toscanini's performances, and for what happened at that first rehearsal of the *Missa.*

Considering these musical conceptions further as musical conceptions, I was struck especially by Toscanini's feeling for the time element in the sound-time continuum; and its manifestations—in his setting of a tempo, his modification of it, his maintenance of proportion between successive tempos—were, it seemed to me, among the most distinctive characteristics of his performances. One heard in the *Missa Solemnis* the rightness of the pace of the *Benedictus* for the blessedness which the music was concerned with, and looking at the score one discovered that this pace was exactly the Andante molto cantabile e non troppo mosso which Beethoven prescribed; but Toscanini didn't get his tempo merely from this direction—he heard it in the music: with the same printed direction, but with not the same musical discernment, Koussevitzky had the *Benedictus* move at an Andante pace so troppo mosso as to be an unsuitable Allegretto. Again, though it was Beethoven who gave only one direction for the entire second movement of the *Eroica* Symphony, it was the necessities of Toscanini's own understanding of the music that caused him alone to establish a single unifying tempo for the various sections. And with no directions at all from Beethoven it was such necessities that produced the subtle modification of this single tempo, the distentions that built up the fugato section of the movement to a climax of shattering power.

A few other incidents of the festival remain in my memory. It was, I believe, after the second rehearsal that Walter Toscanini invited me to visit his father in his dressing room, where we found him radiant. Grasping my coat lapels and giving me a little shake, he said: "My dear Haggin— today I can hope." At a later rehearsal, after devoting considerable time to securing clear articulation of some fast passage-work for strings in the *Leonore* No. 2 Overture, he stopped, undecided, then turned around: "Rachmaninov," he called out, "can you hear?" "I can hear," came the reply from somewhere behind me in the darkened hall; and reassured, Toscanini went on. After the performance of the Ninth Symphony that concluded the festival I went backstage, where I found a huge crowd outside the door of the greenroom. As I stood there Bruno Zirato, at that time assistant manager of the Philharmonic, came out of the room and cast his eye over the crowd; and when he saw me he signaled to me and took me into the room, where Toscanini—wrapped in a blue terry-cloth jacket and fanning himself—stood smiling in the middle of another crowd. When I got near him I thanked him; and he said: "You were not tired to come to all rehearsals?" "If you weren't, why should I be?" I answered. A moment later he asked: *"Qu'est-ce qu'il fait là?"* *—motioning toward Walter, who was surrounded by youngsters in uniform. I looked over their shoulders and reported to Toscanini that Walter was taking the names and addresses of the boys who were

---

* "What is he doing there?"

leaving their programs to be autographed; and he nodded, smiling.

A couple of months later, however, when with other members of the press I attended the final NBC Symphony rehearsal for the American première of Shostakovitch's Seventh Symphony, I was exhausted after only the first half-hour of the pretentiously inflated banalities. "In this symphony I hear suffering of Russian people," he explained two or three years later, when another symphony of Shostakovitch had appeared in which he said he did not hear anything of interest.

By the autumn of 1942 Toscanini had heard the test pressings of his Philadelphia Orchestra recordings and had been dissatisfied with certain sides, which it was expected he would re-record with the orchestra. (But the long Petrillo ban on recording intervened to prevent the remaking of these sides; in addition the processing of the recordings in incorrectly constituted solutions had resulted in many of the sides being afflicted with noisy ticks; and these were made more disturbing by the excessively low volume-level of the recording. As a result of all these things the recordings—of some of Toscanini's finest performances—were never issued.) I was bringing *Music on Records* up to date for a new edition; and since at this time it was expected that the recordings would eventually be issued (the Berlioz *Queen Mab* was in fact already scheduled for release), I wanted to hear them and list them as being in preparation. I wrote to Walter Toscanini, who was with Victor in Camden, asking if I might hear the test pressings; and he an-

swered that he was going to be in New York the following
Monday and would be glad to play for me some that were
at his father's home. Would I come to the Villa Pauline
between eight-thirty and nine.

The Villa Pauline, in the Riverdale section of New
York, was the house Toscanini had lived in since 1937.
Shortly after my visit there in September 1942 he moved
to the house now occupied by the British delegate to the
United Nations; but a few years later he moved back to
the Villa Pauline, which remained his American home
until his death.

The living room of the Villa Pauline was a large central
hall on the ground floor from which a large stairway led
to the upper floors. In it, in addition to Walter Toscanini,
I found Mme. Toscanini and a young man with whom she
was conversing across a small table. She rose to greet me,
went to the foot of the stairway, and called softly: "Tosca";
then she returned to the table and her conversation with
the young man, which they continued for some time, pay-
ing no attention to what else went on in the room. And in a
moment Toscanini came down the stairs quickly, a book
on world government in one hand, a pince-nez in the other,
a smile of greeting on his face.

I had brought with me a recent Victor recording of somebody else's performance of Smetana's *Die Moldau*—excellent-sounding on my phonograph—as a check on the sound
of Toscanini's equipment; and I asked Walter to play this
first. While I listened to the sound Toscanini stood listening
to the performance; and after a few moments he said to
Walter: "Get my *Moldau*." Turning to me, he said: "I put

trumpet at the end because is not clear only with trombones." When Walter put on the record of a broadcast of *Die Moldau* Toscanini stood not just listening but conducting the performance in every detail; and at the end he directed my attention to the trumpets' strengthening of the melodic line. From this I learned that although Toscanini adhered strictly to the composer's text he didn't hesitate to correct what seemed to him a miscalculation in orchestration that kept something from being heard clearly. (It was surprising to learn, some time later, of the many such changes in *La Mer*. "I tell Debussy are many things not clear; and he say is all right to make changes.")

Toscanini then asked Walter to play the test pressing of an NBC Symphony recording of the Prelude to *Tristan und Isolde* that pleased him with its clarity and sonority; but I found the brilliance of the violins excessive and unpleasant; and when one of the sides of the Philadelphia *Death and Transfiguration* was played I found the violins harsh and the bass too heavy. In reply to my inquiry Walter told me the machine was being played with maximum range of treble and maximum intensity of bass; and I suggested trying the next side of *Death and Transfiguration* with treble range and bass reduced somewhat. This made the violins lustrous and sweet, and changed the bass from a huge confused rumble to sounds that were clearly defined and in correct proportion; and when I said I liked this better Toscanini said he did too. I then asked to hear the *Tristan* Prelude with my settings of treble and bass, and found the sound of the violins greatly improved; but Toscanini this time liked the earlier sound better. However, my settings were retained for the recordings that were played for me.

One was the Philadelphia *La Mer,* which Toscanini, as before, listened to standing and conducting the performance. At the end of the first movement, his face registering his delight, he exclaimed: "Is like reading the score!"—which clearly was his idea of what a performance should be. Thus he stated one of his basic principles—that whatever was printed in the score must be audible in the performance. And a moment later, listening to the second movement of *La Mer,* he cried out in anger at not hearing one of the woodwinds, and made Walter stop the record.

When we came to the Philadephia *Queen Mab* Toscanini's face clouded, and after asking Walter to bring him the Wotton book on Berlioz he told me what was troubling him. He was about to open the New York Philharmonic's season with a performance of Berlioz's *Romeo and Juliet* in its entirety; and in preparing for it he had again come up against the problem, for him, of the placing and removal of the strings' mutes in the *Love Scene.* "A man write to me——" he said, leaving his statement unfinished as Walter handed him the Wotton book. "This man," he said, pointing to Wotton's name, "is musician or is musicologist?" And as I was about to answer he went on: "I think must be musician"—making clear in this way his estimate of musicologists. He opened the book to a passage on page 186, in which he had underlined many words, and read aloud Wotton's criticism of the reasoning which had led the editors of the big Breitkopf edition to change the original direction given on page 151 of the Eulenburg miniature score—the direction to place mutes on the second violins, which the Breitkopf edition extended to violas and cellos. Then Toscanini showed me in the Eulenburg score his solution of the problem created, it turned out, not by any lack of explicitness and clarity in Berlioz's directions but by Toscanini's inability to believe that they really represented Berlioz's objectives. On page 147, where Berlioz removed mutes from the cellos, Toscanini removed them also from the violas; on page 151, where Berlioz added mutes on the second violins to those still on the violas, Toscanini placed them on the second violins, violas and cellos; hence on page 161, where Berlioz removed them from the violas, Toscanini removed them also from the cellos; and instead of removing them from the second violins on page 162 as Berlioz did, Toscanini removed them in the first measure on page 161 because at this point the second violins played the same melody as the unmuted firsts and at the same dynamic level. (The man he said had written to him was Jacques Barzun; but actually it was Toscanini who—encountering Barzun's name in the preface of the Wotton book, and interested in what Barzun might contribute on the subject—had originally written to Barzun. And in his gigantically ostentatious book on Berlioz several years later Barzun wrote that Toscanini had explained his solution of the problem "during a conversation sought"— Barzun informed us—"by him." Toscanini's comment on this was a shake of his head and "Vanity, vanity!")

I remember the playing of only one more recording that night—of the 1941 performance of the finale of *Die Götterdämmerung* with Helen Traubel. I no longer recall what brought it to Toscanini's mind, and remember only his saying: "You must hear *Immolation Scene* with Traubel. *Ah, che bella voce, che bella voce!*" * And he continued to exclaim in pleasure as he listened to what was in fact some of the most beautiful singing of Traubel's career.

A few days later the rehearsals of Berlioz's *Romeo and Juliet* began. Toscanini had played three instrumental sections of the work—the one beginning with *Romeo Alone* and ending with *Great Festivity at the Capulets'*; the *Love Scene*; and the *Queen Mab*—a number of times before; but this performance of the entire work, the first in my lifetime, provided a first hearing of two other extraordinary pieces of music: *Juliet's Funeral Procession* and *Romeo in the Vault of the Capulets*. All this music represented not only Berlioz's remarkable musical powers but their susceptibility to poetic stimulation; and Toscanini's approach to it was at all times by way of the poetic situation: "Here speaks the prince," he said of the recitative-like passage for the brass in the *Introduction,* which he worked on for the quality and weight of sound, the inflection, the portamento, that made it the pronouncement of an angered ruler. At the point where Romeo's rush—Allegro agitato e disperato— into the Capulet vault broke off, Toscanini's hushing out- spread arms and *"Grand silence!"* created the silence of the vault in which were heard the soft, solemn antiphonal chords of brass, woodwinds and strings. And concerning the anguished phrases later in this section he reminded the orchestra: *"DI-SPER-A-TO!* You are all *DI-SPER-A-TI!"*

* "Ah, what a beautiful voice, what a beautiful voice!"

After the second performance on Friday afternoon I went backstage; but I had stopped to talk to a friend, and when I got to the greenroom I found everyone gone and the door of the dressing room closed. At that moment the door opened and Toscanini came out dressed for the street and followed by Mme. Toscanini. His mind was still on Berlioz's music; and when I spoke of how extraordinary *Romeo in the Vault of the Capulets* was, he answered with an intense "Ye-e-es!" and added: "One finds in Berlioz's scores some things one cannot understand or imagine—until one hears them from the orchestra; then one hears they are right and beautiful."

For his second week's concerts with the Philharmonic Toscanini's program comprised Haydn's Symphony No. 99 and Shostakovitch's Seventh; and on the morning of the Sunday of the final concert I went up to Riverdale to speak to Walter Toscanini about something. His father had already moved to the other house; and while I was talking to Walter in the large living room off the central hall, the door opened and Mme. Toscanini, in a dressing gown, looked in but withdrew hastily when she saw me. Shortly afterward the door opened again; and this time it was Toscanini, in slippers and a brocaded silk dressing gown over his undershirt and trousers, and with the small score of Haydn's No. 99 in his hand. "You can see," he said, opening the score to the beginning of the first movement after the slow introduction, and pointing, "is written Vivace assai; but X—— play too slow. Is dilettante!" And from this excessively slow tempo he went on to others, of which I now remember only one—that of Pamina's *"Ach, ich fühl's"* in *The Magic*

Flute. Clasping his hands as he acted Pamina's agitation, he exclaimed: "Pamina say 'I lose my Tamino! Where my Tamino!' Must be Andante, but is always Adagio!"

"*Senti*," * said Walter at one point, taking out a handkerchief and patting his father's face with it. "Why are you perspiring?"

"Because I am warm!" Toscanini answered vehemently. "When I talk about music I am not cold!"

A little later Walter told him that the master of the first side of the 1936 recording of Beethoven's Seventh couldn't be used any longer, and Victor asked him to listen to a pressing from the master of one of his other "takes" of that side. As Walter was putting the record on the turntable Toscanini said to me: "I never like first side. Is too slow." And when the sound of the suggested replacement began to emerge from the speaker his face lighted up and he exclaimed: "So is correct!" Astonished by all this, I asked: "But who chose the old side?" Toscanini apparently didn't hear me; and it was Walter who, standing behind his father, pointed at him with a grin. Only later did I remember Toscanini's statement in Philadelphia that the 1936 recordings had been passed on by a committee of Gilman, Betti and Chotzinoff; which meant that Walter was mistaken.

Eventually Toscanini left the room; and when I had finished talking with Walter and was about to leave, his father reappeared, dressed for the day, and invited me upstairs to see the three picture views that were framed by the three windows of his study. We went out onto the

* Listen

35

terrace; and some point connected with his imminent NBC broadcast of Gershwin's *Rhapsody in Blue* came up that caused him to speak with sorrow about Gershwin who had been "very *simpatico.*"

Toscanini also conducted the Philharmonic in a Red Cross concert devoted to Wagner, late in November, with Traubel again as soloist in the *Tristan* and *Götterdämmerung* finales. I remember him, at the beginning of the first rehearsal, working patiently to achieve the accuracy, the balance, the radiance of the opening chords of the *Lohengrin* Prelude; and I remember him, at the end of the last rehearsal, in a rage about something the orchestra hadn't done as he wished in the *Götterdämmerung* finale. When this rehearsal was over, Walter invited me to visit his father in his dressing room, where I expected to find him still raging—instead of which I found him seated on a sofa, his powerful torso bare, the sweat dripping off the tip of his nose, and a look of pleasure on his face as he searched eagerly in the full score of *Die Götterdämmerung* open in his lap. "I am sure," he exclaimed, "Brünnhilde is very unhappy. . . . Yes"—having found what he was looking for, and pointing to it—" *'Verraten'*! * *She is 'verraten'!*" And reading further: "Yes . . . *'Alles, Alles weiss ich.'* ** Yes. . . ."

Shortly before this he conducted the Philadelphia Orchestra in Mozart's G-minor, the Overture and Bacchanale

* Betrayed
** "All, all do I understand."

of Wagner's *Tannhäuser,* and the Musorgsky-Ravel *Pictures at an Exhibition.* I heard the repetition of the concert in New York on November 24, and was surprised by the change in my feeling about the performance of the G-minor. It had always impressed me as too impassioned, and to the performance issued in Victor M-631 in 1939 I had even applied the terms 'tumultuous' and 'ferocious'; but the performance with the Philadelphia Orchestra I now found to be completely and satisfyingly right; and when I went back to the 1939 Victor recording and also to an off-the-air recording of the last Philharmonic performance in 1936, I was astonished to hear the same tempos and the same powerful phrasing and shaping. It was clearly I who had changed (and I discovered this to be true also when I went back to the Beecham performance of the symphony in Columbia M-316, which I had previously considered excellent, and was shocked now by the inappropriate jauntiness of the opening statements—especially the effect of the sharp clipping off of their conclusions—and by the expressive inadequacy of the treatment of the entire first movement).

But on the other hand, listening at this time to the performances of Brahms's symphonies in an NBC Brahms cycle, I knew that in some instances Toscanini had changed in the course of years. Remembering clearly the swift and light-footed progression of the first movement of the Third when he had first played it here in 1929, I was struck by the breadth and weight of the performance now; and there was a similar change in the first movement of the Fourth. These were the first such changes I was aware of in Toscanini's performances; but others as striking, and more significant, were to reveal themselves a couple of years later.

The Brahms cycle included the *German Requiem;* and before the final rehearsal there was the pre-rehearsal hubbub of the orchestra tuning and practicing and the Westminster Choir warming up on syllables like "mi-mi-mi-mi-mi"—all of which Toscanini seemed oblivious of as he talked animatedly with Samuel Chotzinoff, pointing now in this direction at the stage and now in that. At last Toscanini finished with Chotzinoff and went up onto the stage to begin the rehearsal; and it had proceeded for some time when, in a rage at some failure of the chorus, he shouted: "Is not enough to sing 'mi-mi-mi-mi-mi'!" Evidently he was oblivious to no sound.

Several other NBC Symphony performances and rehearsals of that season remain in my memory. The Verdi program of January 31, 1943, offered the exciting experiences of performances which revealed the dramatic power, eloquence and nobility of the early music from *Nabucco* and *I Lombardi* as well as the more familiar *Forza del Destino* and *La Traviata.* The first rehearsal was unprecedentedly late in starting, with the concertmaster Mischakoff's chair conspicuously vacant. At last Mischakoff appeared, followed by Toscanini; and the reason for the delay became evident when Toscanini began to conduct the long instrumental introduction to the Trio from *I Lombardi,* of which the violin solo was played by Mischakoff in an Italian-opera vocal style that he hadn't learned in the conservatory in his youth.

Another Verdi program on July 25 offered the additional

exciting experiences of hearing familiar matters like "*O don fatale*" from *Don Carlo*, "*Pace, pace, mio Dio*" from *La Forza del Destino*, "*Eri tu*" from *Un Ballo in Maschera*, and the entire fourth act of *Rigoletto* emerge "as fresh and glistening as creation itself" in performances in which every detail of the accurately and beautifully played orchestral part was in active expressive relation to what was being sung; the accurately and expressively shaped vocal phrases fitted precisely into the orchestral contexts; and the progression of integrated vocal and orchestral parts was clear in outline and texture, coherent in shape, continuous in tension. (The *Rigoletto* act—with Jan Peerce, Gertrude Ribla, Nan Merriman, Francesco Valentino and Nicola Moscona—was Toscanini's first performance of opera in New York since 1915; and he repeated it—with Zinka Milanov and Leonard Warren in place of Ribla and Valentino—at his Red Cross concert in Madison Square Garden on May 25, 1944.)

The same impression of the familiar pieces being revealed as though newly created was produced at the rehearsal of Tchaikovsky's *Nutcracker Suite* for a Carnegie Hall concert on April 25, and at the rehearsals of a program of "pop" numbers broadcast on April 4. The members of the orchestra sat smiling in pleasure at the phrasing and pacing of the Overture to *Zampa*, the best-known Boccherini Minuet, the *Dance of the Hours*, Liszt's Second Hungarian Rhapsody, *The Stars and Stripes Forever*; and they applauded the exquisite inflection of the long melody of the Haydn Serenade from the Quartet Op. 3 No. 5.

This, I believe, was the first of such programs of "pop"

numbers, which must have impressed less sophisticated listeners as well as the members of the NBC Symphony and myself. That is, it seemed to me that a musically unsophisticated person, listening to these pieces that he knew well, would inevitably be struck by the things that were different about them this time—that listening, for example, to *The Stars and Stripes Forever* he would notice not only the general liveliness and buoyancy but the subordinate melodies or accompanying figures that he had never before heard so clearly outlined and so beautifully modeled; and that in this way he might get an idea of the differences that were possible in performances, and of the particular qualities of Toscanini's performances, which previously he might have thought people only pretended they heard.

At a rehearsal for the June 20 broadcast of lighter classics the tempo of the first part of Debussy's *Prélude à L'Après-midi d'un faune* was strikingly faster than that of other conductors' performances; and happening to be following with the score I discovered what was behind it. Debussy's direction for the tempo of the first part was "Very moderate"; for the middle part it was "First rate of movement"; for the return of the first part it was "Movement of the beginning"; and whereas the usual practice was to play the first part more slowly than the rest, Toscanini obeyed Debussy's directions to maintain the one pace throughout by bringing the first part up to the tempo of the rest. (Years earlier, when he had first played Brahms's First Symphony in New York, he had similarly decided that the Poco sostenuto of the introduction to the first movement must be the same as the Poco sostenuto of the similar passage at the end of the movement. This turned out to be too fast for the proper effect of the introduction; nevertheless in all the three or four performances of the symphony that year Toscanini stuck to this consistency at the cost of effectiveness; but when he played the work again in a later season he took the introduction to the first movement at its traditionally slower pace.)

And there were, finally, the rehearsals of *La Mer* for the broadcast of April 11. At the first, Toscanini worked on the detail of the first two movements; then, finding himself with only a few minutes left, he led the orchestra straight through the final movement in a breathtakingly beautiful and effective performance that caused the orchestra to applaud him at the end. The next day he perfected the detail of this movement and then went through the entire work in a way that impelled the orchestra, at the end, to burst into a storm of applause in appreciation of the imaginative insight and technical powers that had integrated all the bits of color and figuration and all the nuances of tempo into the coherent and magnificent form in sound. It was on this occasion that the young violinist exclaimed to me: "You can quote me on this: we come here to go to school!"

On February 6, 1944, Toscanini conducted the Philadelphia Orchestra in a Pension Fund concert; and I went to Philadelphia for the last two rehearsals. The Beethoven program comprised the *Egmont* Overture, the Septet, the *Pastoral* Symphony and the *Leonore* No. 2 Overture; and at the first of the rehearsals, at which the symphony was worked on, I was bowled over by what the phrasing of the orchestra's great solo flute, William Kincaid, and solo oboe, Marcel Tabuteau, made of the passage of bird calls at the end of the second movement. ("Well," a New York musician replied when I spoke of this, "after all, they've been doing it together for twenty-five years.") The performance of the symphony seemed very fine to me; but after the rehearsal a member of the orchestra whom I knew remarked: "I'm a little surprised at the things he's letting pass," referring to details of execution which an orchestra player's ear would notice but other listeners' would not.

At the final rehearsal the next morning, after a little more work on parts of the symphony, the *Leonore* No. 2 was done; then came the break, and as some of the men started to leave the stage Tabuteau called them back. Turning to Toscanini, he told him of the pleasure it had been for the orchestra to play with him, of its gratitude for his coming to conduct this concert—in token of which it presented him with this scroll; and he handed it to Toscanini who at once, in childlike curiosity, unrolled it and began to read it as Tabuteau continued to speak. Then Toscanini spoke briefly but warmly in reply, ending with the statement that nothing in the future could be certain but "consider me always at your disposition," which the orchestra applauded. And then he went to his dressing room, while the men who weren't needed for the rehearsal of the Septet packed up their instruments and left.

It was therefore in a very happy atmosphere that the rehearsal of the Septet began after the break, with young Samuel Mayes, the first cellist, swaying happily from side to side as he sawed away on his instrument in the Minuet.

But suddenly the sky clouded: in the variation movement a fast passage for the violins was repeated but did not satisfy Toscanini; it was repeated again and still did not satisfy him; he called now on one or two desks of the first violins ("You! you! I hear you!") to repeat it; and then the storm broke. It became evident that he was raging not just about what had gone wrong in the Septet but about all the things he had let pass in the symphony; as for the passage in the Septet, "I play this piece with NBC," he shouted at the violins, "and you are not so wonderful!—no!—you are not so wonderful!—no!—NO!"—a shockingly cruel thing to say to a group which actually *was* very wonderful (its playing in the *Pastoral* had a beauty and finish which the NBC Symphony's did not have in a performance a few weeks later) and which, in the years since Stokowski's departure, had been fighting with gallantry and success to maintain itself as the great orchestra he had made it. The men sat in impassive silence until Toscanini's anger had spent itself and he resumed the rehearsal. At the end of the piece he remained standing on the podium, silent, motionless, brooding; and suddenly Tabuteau was at his side, with an arm affectionately on his shoulder, asking him if he would like another rehearsal of the strings just before the concert that evening. Toscanini brightened: Yes, he would like it; the players nodded their heads vigorously in agreement. And so the rehearsal ended.

I am sure Tabuteau's gesture of affection was genuine. It is my impression that intelligent orchestra players didn't regard Toscanini's rages as mere self-indulgence by a man who could be reasonable and patient but felt privileged to be unreasonable and impatient. I think they understood that he was, in his relation to music, a man obsessed and possessed, and that such a man was not rational and reasonable—not in music nor in anything else; and some of them may have perceived what that remarkably perceptive critic, W. J. Turner, spoke of in a review of Toscanini's concerts in London in 1935. As he had sat watching Toscanini, Turner had been "suddenly reminded of Berlioz's remark, 'Do you think I make music for my pleasure?' I am certain that it is not a pleasure for Toscanini to conduct, but rather that he suffers. It is because of his extreme musical sensibility and intense concentration. Here lies the essence of his superiority." I thought this perception of Toscanini's suffering true even before Toscanini confirmed it in a statement years later. Not self-indulgence, then, but extreme musical sensibility, intense concentration, suffering—these were some of the causes of the rages: "Put your blood!" he roared once at a rehearsal of an insignificant little Italian piece. "*I* put *my* blood!" And they were reasons for intelligent orchestra players to forgive him, as they did.

Late in October 1944 I wrote Toscanini that I was having a copy of my new book, *Music for the Man Who Enjoys "Hamlet,"* sent to him; and that I had thought he wouldn't care for a published dedication, but wanted him to know the book was dedicated to him privately in acknowledgment of my debt to him. To this I received a reply dated November 3, in which he said that I had guessed his feeling correctly—that the dedication of the book on its front page would not have been as dear to him as it was now that it came silently from my mind and heart; and from the bottom of his heart came his best thanks. As for my statement about acknowledgment of my debt to him, he said it made him blush, as he had blushed that day when he had listened to the recording of the *Eroica* that had been made a few years ago. Then he asked when he would have the pleasure of seeing me in Riverdale. He hoped it would be soon—possibly the next week: he wanted very badly to ask me something about my book. And he ended with best good wishes and very cordially.

The recording of Beethoven's *Eroica* he referred to was Victor M-765, which had been made during a broadcast in November 1939; and he had listened to it in preparation for the performance he broadcast on November 5, 1944. The recorded sound of the 1939 performance was the unresonantly dry, flat, hard, tight sound of Studio 8H filled with an audience; the performance itself was one of his greatest. But it was a performance in his earlier expansive style marked by great elasticity of tempo—one which, for rhetorical emphasis, paused for an instant after each of the two forceful chords that claim attention at the beginning of the first movement of the *Eroica,* and which, in the subsequent course of the movement, slowed down momentarily to introduce a new section or broadened out for a climax. And the performance of November 5, 1944, was a striking illustration of the important change in Toscanini's style since 1939—the change away from the expansiveness and toward a swifter, tauter, subtler simplicity involving only slight modification of the set tempo. * But for Toscanini the change was not just a change from one way of playing to another: it was a change to a right way, to the only right way, and from a way, therefore, that had been shamefully wrong. (I might suggest in passing that this habit of mind, rather than the jealousy he was accused of, was responsible for some of his unfavorable estimates of other conductors. His intense conviction at a particular moment that *this* was the right way to conduct a phrase or a movement made all other ways—his own in the past, another conductor's now—appear to him shamefully wrong.)

As for the tendency to swifter, tauter simplicity, it was not without exceptions in the reverse direction: the 1939 Beethoven cycle that included the expansive *Eroica* also included a Ninth whose first movement was faster and less expansive than the first movement in the February 1938 performance; but the first movement of the Ninth recorded in 1952 was slower, and at certain climactic points more powerfully expansive, than the one of 1939; and the *Tristan* Prelude and Finale recorded in 1952 also was enormously slower and more powerfully expansive than the one of 1942.

* Let me make it clear that this later simplification of style was something different from the setting of a single tempo for an entire movement, which I spoke of on page 19. In both the 1939 and the 1944 performances Toscanini set a single tempo for the first movement and again for the second; but in the earlier performance the modifications of the set tempo were expansive, whereas in the later one they were subtle. And I might add that of two performances in the same tempo, one—because of the particular state of Toscanini's mind and emotions at the moment—might exhibit strikingly more or strikingly less power than the other, or might exhibit a tenseness and rigidity which the other did not.

I might add that on occasion the swifter tautness was carried to the point of excessively fast rigidity—as in the Haydn *Surprise* Symphony recorded in 1953; but to this I would have to add that within a week or two of the Haydn performance Toscanini recorded the relaxed performances of Schubert's C-major, Dvořáks *New World* and Rossini's Overture to *William Tell*. Also, the earlier slower and more expansive performance often was more effective than the later faster and simpler one; but not always: the *Eroicas* of November 1944, February 1949, and December 1953 had hair-raising power in their simpler style. And it is interesting that the Scherzo of Mendelssohn's Octet recorded in 1945 was at once faster, more relaxed, and more brilliantly effective than the one in the 1947 broadcast performance issued on Victor LM-1869.

I wrote to Toscanini that it would be a great pleasure to visit him whenever he had time; and a few days after the *Eroica* broadcast I received a note apologizing for the delay—he had been very busy—and suggesting that I come up the following afternoon. When I arrived I found him—ruddy, bright-eyed, genial, his after-lunch toothpick still in his mouth—sitting in a sunny corner of the living room with Mme. Toscanini, who was sewing or crocheting. He rose to welcome me as Mme. Toscanini smiled her greeting; then he led me to an easy chair, sat down on the sofa next to it, and leaned forward to slap my knee as he exclaimed with a smile: "Always fighting!"

Then, "I want to ask you a question about your book. I am stupid in such things. How do you use instrument for measuring?" He was referring to the little cardboard ruler that had been provided with the book to measure places on phonograph records where details I mentioned could be heard. And it was true—as the scratched records and damaged styli testified—that he was very awkward in his dealings with records. We went to the phonograph, and I showed him how I used the ruler to find a place on one of the Victor *Eroica* records. "Is there much difference in records?" he asked; and I showed him in the book the differences in the measurements of the several recordings of the *Eroica.* "And you did all this work!" he exclaimed. "It must be much time." And apparently the measuring procedure still seemed formidable to him, for he said: "I will ask my son; I am stupid in such things."

His mind now reverted to the preceding Sunday's performance of the *Eroica;* and he went to the piano. "I listen to record: the first *accords* are still played with pauses. Sunday for the first time I have courage to play in tempo—so:" and he played the two opening chords in strict tempo. And concerning this tempo: "Forty years ago when I play *Eroica* the first time I hear German conductors—I hear Richter—and I think I must play this German music as they play it—so:" and he demonstrated their slow tempo in the first movement. "But when I play this symphony later I play more and more as I feel; and now I have courage at last to take right tempo—so:" and he demonstrated his tempo of the preceding Sunday, characterizing it, as he played, as "easy . . . easy . . ." "Also in second movement: always I am afraid and play bass part first two times so:" and he played the first appoggiatura note on the beat. "Why—when Beethoven write third time so:" and he played the appoggiatura notes in advance of the beat. "Now I tell *bassi*: 'Play first times so:'" and he played the appoggiatura notes in advance of the beat. "Because Beethoven is very exact—but even Beethoven sometimes write different"; and he cited the pizzicato note that Beethoven wrote now as an eighth-note, now as a quarter, now as a half.

"Germans play everything too slow," he said. The second movement of Beethoven's Seventh, for example: "I have courage to play so:" and he demonstrated his faster-than-usual Allegrotto. "Rodzinski play so:" and he demonstrated the slower tempo. "I asked him: 'My dear, why you do this?' He say: 'Is *marcia funebre.*' I say: 'No, is not *marcia funebre*; is so:" and he demonstrated. "But he play again the same way."

The slow movement of Beethoven's Second was another example; after which Toscanini commented: "Beethoven write only one Adagio—in Ninth Symphony. He put metronome mark 60–3—no, 60; for second part he put 63. Is not much difference; *allóra* * I make so—and so:" and he demonstrated the two tempos of the alternating sections. "But Furtwängler make so:" and he demonstrated Furtwängler's slower tempos.

In Mozart also 2/4 was converted into 4/8, Andante into Adagio. "All German conductors play Mozart Andante too slow"; and he illustrated first with the Andante of the Symphony in E flat, then with the Andante of the *Jupiter*, playing the latter first as an Adagio with dragging accompa-

* then

49

niment eighths, then as a flowing Andante. Concerning the G-minor he had a different complaint: "When I hear G-minor from German conductors the first time, was so:" and he played a jauntily phrased statement of the opening theme of the first movement. But with the Overture to *Don Giovanni* it was again "Always Mozart is too slow": the introduction of the overture should be in the same tempo as when it accompanied the Commendatore's singing at the end of the opera. And there was a difference between the 2/4 time of *Don Giovanni* and the 2/4 of *The Magic Flute*: the right tempo for *Là ci darem la mano* was too slow for Papageno's aria. "When I conduct *Flauto Magico* in Salzburg I am afraid about my tempi; but Rosé [the old concertmaster of the Vienna State Opera Orchestra] say once 'At last!' I tell Bruno Walter 'You will not like my tempi in *Flauto Magico*.' He say 'Is very interesting'; but afterward he make again slow tempi. . . . All German conductors play too slow! Muck! Was terrible! *Orchestra* [the Boston Symphony] was wonderful. But he make program: Haydn Symphony in *re*—the last [No. 104], Mozart [Jupiter?] and Beethoven [First?]; and everything so *slow!* Muck was Beckmesser of conductors!"

I think it was somewhere in all this that Toscanini referred to the excessively slow tempo not of a conductor but of a pianist. "When Serkin play with me Mozart Concerto in B flat [K. 595, which Serkin performed with the New York Philharmonic in 1936] I say I know Schnabel's slow tempo in Larghetto, but I am sure this music should be *alla breve*. And once Serkin send me from Europe photograph of Mozart manuscript of Larghetto: is written *alla breve!*"

Something reminded him of what he had been reading about Wagner's conducting. "You know this life of Wagner by—by—by——" He couldn't remember the name, and went to get the book, which turned out to be the W. Ashton Ellis biography. "You have not read this? Ee-e-e! It describe Wagner's conducting in London . . . is very interesting. Wagner make something which I cannot imagine: Largo in *passage* [the French word] in first movement of *Jupiter* Symphony; but where? Slow movement he play without *sordini* . . . he must play slow movement like Germans— too slow. He make big ritard in last part of Minuet; but where? Is clear, Wagner conduct *a piacere;* * but I cannot imagine what they say he do." And he insisted on my taking the book to read.

Before I left I inscribed his copy of my book with "To Arturo Toscanini" and my signature. And a few weeks later I received his Christmas card, which he had inscribed in similar fashion to me. The printed portion of the card had on one page a photograph of Toscanini looking at a framed picture of Beethoven in his hand, and underneath the first measures of the Andante maestoso section in the finale of the Ninth, with the words *Seid umschlungen, Millionen! Diesen Kuss der ganzen Welt!,* copied out by Toscanini; and on the opposite page his handwritten Christmas and New Year greeting and signature.

* with freedom

51

The *Eroica* of November 5, 1944, was part of a Beethoven cycle which included the Piano Concertos Nos. 1, 3 and 4, and which was brought to an especially notable conclusion with a performance of *Fidelio*. Toscanini didn't often play concertos, and this because of his way of regarding and treating them. A Beethoven or Mozart concerto usually is not something which a conductor puts on a program for itself, and for which he then engages a suitable pianist. It is, rather, something he has to play for a soloist who has been engaged for his box-office drawing power, and something the conductor has little interest in, since its purpose is to show off the soloist, not himself. As a result the performance usually is the product of only enough rehearsal—sometimes a mere single run-through—for the soloist's and orchestra's playing to be geared together in time. A concerto performance in which the orchestral part has been carefully worked out is rare; and rarest of all is the kind of performance Schnabel insisted on—in which the solo and orchestral parts were integrated in every detail of phrasing and style (mostly *his* phrasing and style). Now there were exceptional instances in which Toscanini too began with the soloist—one being Myra Hess's appearance with the NBC Symphony in November 1946, which was his salute to her in recognition of her war work. But in most instances he began with the concerto; and in all instances he treated it as something worth playing for itself: listening to the performance one heard a carefully rehearsed orchestral part in which familiar phrases acquired amazingly new contours and significance, and counterpoints and figurations previously unheard in the mass of sound emerged with startling clarity and impact from the newly transparent textures; and one heard all these things related in a continuous progression which was built up into a coherent and powerful structure. It was an exciting experience; and it remained that even when the structure was built up around nothing—i.e., the characterless flow of sounds produced by Ania Dorfman in Beethoven's Piano Concerto No. 1. Or around something as alien in style as Artur Rubinstein's playing in No. 3. I still remember the occasion when Iturbi, in performances of Mozart's Concertos K.466 and 467 with Toscanini and the New York Philharmonic, was impelled by the orchestra's powerfully phrased playing to match it with a strong inflection of phrase that was in striking contrast to his usual salon-music style in Mozart. But the hair-raising power of the orchestral part of Beethoven's No. 3 had no such effect on Rubinstein, who played with his usual on-the-surface brilliance and elegance, and gave the florid melodic passages in the slow movement Chopinesque inflections. Only Serkin's playing in No. 4—though often unimpressive in its mere fluency, in comparison with Schnabel's strongly inflected playing—had the right over-all character and sufficient vitality to fit well into Toscanini's orchestral framework.

We come, then, to the matter of Toscanini's strange choices of soloists—strange in view of the reason he once gave me for playing concertos infrequently: that he could not operate as a mere accompanist, but had to be satisfied with the soloist's playing of *his* part. In illustration he cited the case of Ossip Gabrilowitsch. In 1935 Toscanini conducted a Brahms cycle in which Gabrilowitsch was announced as the soloist in the Piano Concerto No. 2, a famous specialty of his. A few weeks before the date of the performance I was surprised to see Toscanini sitting in front of me at a concert at which Gabrilowitsch played the same Brahms concerto with the National Orchestral Association; subsequently the Philharmonic announced the cancellation of the work because of Gabrilowitsch's illness; and now Toscanini confirmed my suspicion that he had canceled the work because he hadn't been able to accept Gabrilowitsch's way of playing it. Yet he *had* been able to accept Rubinstein's way of playing the Beethoven No. 3. Nor was this the only instance. His own taste had been evident in the delicacy and purity of Remo Bolognini's style in a marvelously light and winged Philharmonic performance of Mendelssohn's Violin Concerto in the thirties; yet in a performance of this work in the spring of 1944 he had accepted the pretentiously mannered and sentimentally distorted phrasing of Heifetz. He was fanatical about setting the right tempo, about maintaining it once it was set; and his strong convictions about this made him inflexible; yet he accepted Myra Hess's slowing down of the first movement of Beethoven's No. 3 after the orchestral introduction, and a slower tempo in the second movement than he had taken in the performance with Rubinstein. Clearly, Toscanini exhibited most of the time a taste, in the exercise of which he was rigorous and unyielding; but there was occasional inconsistency in the taste itself, and occasional yielding in its exercise. If I am correct in my impression that Rubinstein was not one of the close friends, his case illustrates inconsistency in the taste itself; but the cases of friends like Dorfman and

Heifetz, and of Horowitz, who was married to Toscanini's daughter Wanda (and whose mannered phrasing one would have expected Toscanini not to like) appear to demonstrate that Toscanini's taste could be by-passed by way of his heart. And with Hess his convictions seem to have yielded to her war record.

So with *Fidelio*. Nobody could fuss more than Toscanini did about getting the exactly right singer for a part in an opera; but the Leonore of the broadcast *Fidelio* was Rose Bampton, whose monotonously shrill upper range was not exactly right for this part, and who marred the performance by breaking on the final high note of *Komm' Hoffnung* (a later recording of the aria was substituted in Victor LM-6025), but who was a close friend of the Toscanini family. And I must assume that someone put in an influential word for another singer whose badly accented German made him grossly unfit for his participation in the performance.

What it comes to is that Toscanini, aside from being a great musician, was a human being with the inconsistencies and contradictions—which is to say with the fallibilities and weaknesses—of any other human being. This is hardly surprising; but people who expect, understand and accept the fallibilities and weaknesses in a businessman or an engineer were surprised—and even shocked and outraged—by them in Toscanini, believing apparently that a man who was as great an artist as he must be perfect in all other respects. But I contend that in addition to the reasons for the Toscaninis of this world to behave no better than the businessmen and engineers, there are reasons for them to behave even worse. Not only are their traits of personality and character, like those of businessmen and engineers, conditioned, developed and distorted by the ordinary experiences with family, friends, enemies, teachers, employers; but their lives are subjected to the additional distorting strains of their intensive training and their careers; and sometimes they begin with the unbalance that makes possible a fanatical dedication and concentration during long years of training and then during the years of artistic achievement. If Toscanini had not been, in relation to music, a man obsessed and possessed, willing to endure the suffering caused by his extreme musical sensibility and concentration, he would not have subjected people to the unreasonable, inconsiderate, bad-tempered, sometimes downright cruel behavior described in Chotzinoff's *Toscanini: An Intimate Portrait*; but we would not have had his performances. And having had the performances, we owe him not only gratitude for the experiences he gave us and for his willingness to endure what made those experiences possible, but the same understanding and tolerance of his behavior as we give the businessman and the engineer.

It may have occurred to some to wonder why Rubinstein and why not Schnabel? Toscanini did speak of Schnabel —not on the occasion when he explained his not playing concertos, but on another. Sitting at the piano, he said: "I must ask you—I do not understand why you write so about Schnabel. In Beethoven G-major Concerto [I had written about the piano's opening statement being made by Schnabel 'quietly, deeply, spaciously meditative'] he play so:" and Toscanini astonished me by playing the piano's opening statement with gross distentions that hadn't the slightest resemblance to Schnabel's subtle inflection. "And in Schubert *Moment musical* [I had written that Schnabel played these pieces 'with wonderful feeling for their delicacy and subtlety'] he play so:" and Toscanini astonished me again by playing the best-known F-minor with similar gross distentions that hadn't the slightest resemblance to Schnabel's enchantingly simple and graceful treatment of it. Clearly there was a personal antipathy which impelled Toscanini's ear to hear incorrectly the objective facts of Schnabel's performances. And the antipathy was mutual: "He thinks only *he* is pure!" Schnabel once exclaimed to me scornfully. "I know: I traveled with him one night in the train to Milan."

On January 13, 1945, Toscanini conducted the New York Philharmonic in a Pension Fund concert, repeating the program of his first concert with the orchestra on January 14, 1926: Haydn's Symphony No. 101 (*Clock*), Respighi's *Pines of Rome*, Sibelius's *Swan of Tuonela*, *Siegfried's Death and Funeral Music* from Wagner's *Götterdämmerung*, and Weber's Overture to *Euryanthe*. He had repeated the program also at his final Thursday-Friday pair in April 1936; and it looked as if this was a second and final farewell to the orchestra, which he signalized by writing out the program for facsimile reproduction in the program notes. Far from exhibiting any diminution of his powers, the performances seemed to be the ones of 1926 and 1936 with their wonderful qualities heightened; and this impression was confirmed a few years later when I heard a private recording of the concert and compared the Haydn *Clock* Symphony with the 1929 performance in Victor M-57: the later one was made even more dazzling by the faster tempo, greater energy and sharper inflection.

And again the bond between Toscanini and the orchestra was demonstrated at the first rehearsal—this time in even more impressive fashion than in 1942. Then he had returned to an orchestra only slightly changed in personnel and not at all disciplined by another conductor; now he returned to an orchestra in which Rodzinski had made a considerable number of replacements and which he had drilled for two years. Nevertheless, having first devoted a few minutes to working out the cross-rhythm at the climax of the Wagner piece and the balance of the wind instruments in the opening chords, Toscanini then simply led the orchestra through it without interruption and produced every sound and contour of the performance of 1936—as though there had been no interval of nine years, no changes in personnel, no other conductor. It was, as in 1942, his way of saying: "This is *my* orchestra."

Nor did I hear any diminution of his powers in the performances of Weber's Overture to *Der Freischütz*, Ravel's *La Valse* and the Musorgsky-Ravel *Pictures at an Exhibition* at a benefit concert with the NBC Symphony (there was also the Brahms B-flat Concerto with Horowitz, which I didn't hear). But when I visited him shortly afterward he asked how the performances had sounded, and then told me he had been ill and fearful of not getting through the concert, and had conducted *Pictures* with no knowledge and control of what he was doing.

At this visit his mind was full of Haydn's Symphony No. 98, which he had played during his first NBC season and was preparing to play again. The preparation, as usual, consisted in studying the score, listening to the recording of the 1938 broadcast, and reading what he had found in print about the work—Tovey's comments in *Essays in Musical Analysis*. Mentioning Tovey's demonstration of the remarkable similarity between a passage in the slow movement and a passage in the Andante of Mozart's *Jupiter*, Toscanini went on to say, to my amazement, that he considered Haydn greater than Mozart. "I will tell you frankly: sometimes I find Mozart boring. Not G-minor: that is great tragedy; and not concerti; but other music. Is always beautiful—but is always the same." And what he had in mind became clear when he played the record of the 1938 broadcast of Haydn's No. 98: he sat conducting the performance, signaling to me when something was about to happen, smiling his delight when it happened; and it was evident that what delighted him was Haydn's liveliness of mind—the surprises he contrived for his listeners in melody, harmony, rhythm, orchestration. Above all orchestration: it was also evident that as a conductor Toscanini was delighted most by the variety, freshness and ingenuity of Haydn's use of the orchestra—details like the one Toscanini pointed to in the Minuet, exclaiming gleefully: "Flutes and basses!" Nor was it only Haydn who surpassed Mozart in this respect, he said, but also Rossini—as he undertook to show me with the orchestral ingenuity and variety of the Overture to *La Cenerentola*. And here something characteristic happened: putting on the turntable what he thought was the record with the *Cenerentola* performance, he stood listening with surprise as the scherzo movement of Tchaikovsky's *Manfred* came out of the speaker instead; then, his hands involuntarily beginning to move with the music, he gradually became completely involved with it and conducted it to the end of the record—after which he remembered *La Cenerentola*, found the correct record, and conducted that, pointing out to me the orchestral details that delighted him.

The performance of Haydn's No. 98 that Toscanini broadcast on March 25, 1945, and recorded afterward was, and is, superb considered by itself: only when one compared it with the 1938 performance did one discover that it was less expansive and relaxed, and as a result less effective. Similarly the V-J Day performance of Beethoven's *Eroica*, characteristic and impressive by itself, revealed—when compared with the 1944 and 1939 performances—a shocking lessened energy. And the possibility that Toscanini's powers might be failing was raised by the performances in his regular NBC series the following winter—performances whose extreme rigidity suggested the alarming possibility of a change in his mental processes analogous to the stiffening of the movements of an aging body. I recall in particular a driving, tense first movement of Brahms's Fourth that was in shocking contrast to the slower, relaxed, expansive one three years before; and a Mozart G-minor without the fluidity and energy of the 1939 performance in Victor M-631.

It was not until the fall of 1946 that a lessening of the

rigidity, tenseness and drive and a return of relaxed plasticity began to manifest themselves—most notably and excitingly in the November 3 performance of Mozart's Divertimento K.287 for horns and strings. It was on another occasion that Toscanini remarked to me how difficult it was to play Mozart—how boring the music could be unless one knew what to do between the *p* here and the *f* eight measures later; but the comment was relevant to this performance of the Divertimento, which not only had the old fluidity and grace, but revealed Toscanini's knowledge of what to do between the *p*'s and *f*'s in the profusion of subtle inflection that delightfully enlivened the Allegros, gave exquisite contours to the variation movement, and shaped the Adagio as a grandly impassioned vocal declamation with a cumulative expressive force that was breathtaking. And the broadcast also offered a performance of Mozart's *Haffner* Symphony which—in contrast to the expansively plastic 1929 performance in Victor M-65—exhibited a simplification and clarification that made it grand and apotheosized.

I wrote enthusiastically to Toscanini about the Divertimento performance; and when, shortly afterward, I went up to the Villa Pauline to visit him, he met me at the door of his study with the pocket score of the Divertimento in his hand. "I will tell you why I play this piece," he said. "I listen last summer to Tanglewood—" and he shook his head and rolled his eyes heavenward at the memory of what he had heard. Opening the score and pointing to the bass part, he said: "Koussevitzky use *celli* without

bassi; allóra sometimes violas play lower than bass part."
Also, Koussevitzky's tempo in the variation movement had
been too slow for the prescribed Andante and for the character of the music. But most shocking of all had been what
happened near the end of the Adagio, where Toscanini
showed me in the score the usual indication, which any
musician would understand, for the interpolation of a cadenza: the halt on an anticipatory six-four chord, followed
by a rest for the interpolated cadenza, and a trill to conclude the cadenza and bring in the orchestra for the rest
of the movement. And Toscanini's face now expressed the
horror with which he had heard the Boston Symphony
pause on the six-four chord, break off for the rest, and—
without any cadenza having been interpolated—play the trill
and conclude the movement. "This man is no musician!"
Toscanini exclaimed. "Is *ignorante!*" He had therefore
played the Divertimento correctly for Koussevitzky's instruc-
tion: "I think maybe he listen."

Walter Toscanini, who meanwhile had been searching
among the 16-inch acetate recordings of the NBC broadcasts, now had what he had been looking for—the recording
of the November 3 broadcast of the Divertimento. As he put
it on the turntable his father seated me at his desk with the
score open before me; and standing behind me and looking
over my shoulder he conducted the entire performance as
it came out of the speaker. At one point in the first movement where the first violins swept up to a series of high
A's he chuckled and exclaimed: "Is difficult!"; and when
later in the movement they swept up to an analogous series

of high B-flats he again chuckled and exclaimed: "Is difficult!" *

In the time since the 1944 *Fidelio* Toscanini had broadcast the opening scene of Bellini's *Norma* and the Prologue
of Boito's *Mefistofele* in December 1945, and all of Puccini's
La Bohème in March 1946. And on December 1 and 8 of
that year he broadcast Verdi's *La Traviata*. Only a few days
before the first half Carl Van Vechten had spoken to me of
Toscanini's great period at the Metropolitan: "In those years
he would conduct a *Tristan* or *Götterdämmerung* that was
overwhelming; but the thing to hear was his performance
of early Verdi—of *La Traviata*." And a few days later Toscanini gave millions of radio listeners an idea of what Van
Vechten had talked about. These listeners, for whom *La*

---

* By the time the Divertimento episode got into Howard Taubman's
book, *The Maestro,* it had been transformed as follows: "On another
occasion he confided that he had made a recording of Mozart's
Divertimento for strings and two horns for the benefit of his colleagues, the conductors. . . . In the slow movement he had
always felt something lacking and decided what was needed was
a cadenza for the first violin. After he had made this addition,
Toscanini found a letter from Mozart to his wife which confirmed
his hunch." The letter is not to be found in the Mozart correspondence, and a cadenza, by its very nature, is not something of which
the need is suspected. And reviewing the book in *The Nation* I
pointed out that this incident didn't belong with the stories about
Toscanini puzzling over something in a score and reaching a conclusion about it that was confirmed later by documentary evidence;
that in this instance, on the contrary, the entire point had been the
score's explicit indication of the cadenza by the six-four chord, rest
and trill, which Koussevitzky had not heeded, causing Toscanini
to pronounce him *ignorante.*

But even worse nonsense was to follow. Collecting material for
his book, *Toscanini and the Art of Orchestral Performance,* Robert
Charles Marsh picked up Taubman's statement and picked up mine,

Traviata had been a discontinuous series of sections pulled out of shape by the vocal exhibitionism to which the conductor had meekly deferred, now heard phrases in which even the tenor's or soprano's climactic high notes were part of the plastically modeled phrase-contours—heard whole acts which by such continuity of pace and sonority from phrase to phrase and section to section were made into coherent entities. In 1935 W. J. Turner, attempting to convey the superiority of a Toscanini performance to those of other conductors, used the analogy of a poem of Keats printed clearly on good paper as against the same poem printed in smudged ink on blotting paper, or a first-class photograph made by an expert with the finest materials as against a poor one made with a mediocre camera by a not highly capable person. "The musical impression made by Toscanini when he conducts a work," said Turner, "is incredibly clearer in detail, better proportioned as to parts, and more vivid as a whole, than those made by any other con-

---

apparently with no recognition that mine was a demonstration of the inaccuracy of Taubman's, for he combined the two, omitting Taubman's incorrect statement and attributing to him instead the very statement of mine that corrected his error: "In his book, *The Maestro*, Howard Taubman tells us that Toscanini made this recording for other conductors as a demonstration of how Mozart should be played. Among other things it demonstrated [still, apparently, according to Taubman] that in the slow movement Mozart had clearly indicated a cadenza for the first violin by writing a six-four chord, a rest, and a trill leading back into the melodic line. Haggin reports that when Toscanini heard the Koussevitzky performance, in which the chord, the rest, and the trill were played through exactly as marked, he exclaimed, 'This man is no musician. He is *ignorante!*' "

Such was the writing about Toscanini.

ductor." This was the impression produced by the 1946 *Traviata;* and with its accuracy, clarity and order it had the effect of revelation: one heard the work as one had never heard it before.

I suspected at the time that this performance was slightly different from those Van Vechten heard at the Metropolitan—that in the opera house the performance, although essentially the same in style, had proceeded a little more slowly and with more rhetorical expansiveness, and that in the concert hall, after many years in which Toscanini had been concerned mostly with symphonic music, it was a little swifter and closer-knit. The style of the NBC performance, in other words, was essentially the same, but refined, clarified, and—like that of the November Mozart *Haffner* Symphony—even apotheosized. As for its effect, there were moments which I thought would have gained by the earlier expansiveness, but others which unquestionably gained by the new urgency—notably the first act and the later scene of Flora's party, whose febrile character was excitingly effective and right.

The first act also was tense; and this must have increased the nervousness of Licia Albanese that resulted in her unsteadiness and inaccuracy in *"Sempre libera,"* as against her beautiful singing in the subsequent acts. As for that tension, it should have taught Toscanini something he hadn't known ten years before. When he left the New York Philharmonic, Dusolina Giannini told me he had said he was tired of the routine of four or five rehearsals and three or four concerts week after week—especially the three or four performances of one program; and one attraction of the NBC offer had been that it called for only one performance each week. But the repetitions of the one program with the Philharmonic had had an important value: a conductor and an orchestra may achieve a performance completely at rehearsal; but the first time in public there is likely to be unsettling tension; and relaxed security may come only at the second or third performance. I recall, for example, that when Toscanini conducted the Philharmonic in Beethoven's Ninth in 1936 the performance was tense, driven and harsh-sounding on Thursday and again on Friday, but amazingly relaxed, spacious and beautiful-sounding on Sunday. At NBC there was only the first public performance, in an atmosphere of tension that sometimes made this performance less good than the one at the final rehearsal where conductor and orchestra were at ease; and it was in fact at these rehearsals that one heard some of the greatest of Toscanini's performances. The first act of an opera, then, was likely to suffer from this tension; and the first act of *La Traviata* did.

Thus there were defects in the *Traviata* performance, but not the ones alleged by some critics—not, specifically, the "tempos . . . both fast and rigid" which "thwart [the singers'] efforts." There were fast tempos which were suitable, like the ones in the febrile first act; but there were also tempos—even in the first act—which were suitably slow and plastic; and the beautiful-sounding, plastically and expressively phrased singing of Peerce and Albanese was not that of singers who were being thwarted. Neither, for that matter, was the coarse-sounding singing of Merrill.

66

As a matter of fact the critics I have just referred to, who specialize in opera, object to all the Verdi performances—the *Otello, Aïda, Falstaff* and *Un Ballo in Maschera* as well as the *Traviata*—that Toscanini broadcast and Victor subsequently issued on records. And I may as well deal with their objections at this point.

The performances they approve of are the usual ones in opera houses, in which the singers are allowed to show off their voices at any cost to shape of phrase and continuity of flow; the performances they disapprove of are the ones in which the singers are held by Toscanini to tempo and shape of phrase. They don't of course express their approval and disapproval in those terms: the self-indulgent singing they call "expressive"; the tempos and style that permit it they call "idiomatic"; and in the Toscanini performance presumably unidiomatic tempos "both fast and rigid" "thwart" the singers' attempts to sing expressively and compel them to sing inexpressively. Virgil Thomson made up in his head a Toscanini who was an opera conductor until the age of fifty, when he had to deal with the symphonic repertory without knowledge of its traditions, and solved the problem by "streamlining" the music; from the opera specialists I have referred to one would get the idea of Toscanini as a symphonic conductor who in his old age, lacking knowledge of what is idiomatic in the performance of Verdi, streamlined *this* music. Nor is it only with excessively fast and rigid tempos that he is alleged to have made it impossible for singers to do more than produce the notes without expressiveness: he is accused also of having preferred inexperienced or undistinguished singers who were willing to submit to his tyranny; and to his accusers' ears the performances betray not only the singers' lack of experience and distinction but their terror of him.

Actually Toscanini's NBC performances of Verdi were those of a man who conducted his first *Aïda* in the opera house in 1886 and his last *Falstaff* there in 1937, and whose stage performances—as I can testify concerning the Salzburg ones of 1937 and the Milan Scala ones of 1929—were like the NBC performances in their freedom from the singers' "idiomatic" distortions that Verdi fought against all his life. Presumably the critics who disapprove of the NBC performances would not have liked the similar *Traviatas* and *Trovatores* that Van Vechten heard at the Metropolitan and treasured in his memory; but they could hardly have attributed those performances to ignorance of either the correct style for Verdi or the traditional distortion of that style in the opera house. Toscanini's Metropolitan performances represented his knowledge of what was truly idiomatic and his repudiation of what was falsely "idiomatic"; and what his critics would not have liked in them represented in addition the personal style of performance (what Virgil Thomson called "streamlining") that he brought to all music—to opera at eighteen, to symphonic music at twenty-eight—a style whose outstanding characteristic in opera as in symphonic music was a coherent plasticity that tended in later years toward greater simplicity, economy, subtlety. His beat, then, was never anything but flexible in relation to the music; in relation to the singer it was unyielding only in compelling her to operate within the beautifully plastic flow it created in the music. And this didn't prevent Destinn or Hempel or Fremstad from singing expressively and beautifully.

Nor did it prevent the singers in his NBC performances from doing so: the mediocre, inexpressive singing of inexperienced, intimidated singers who are driven breathless by excessively fast tempos, which the critics have reported hearing, was—and is, on the Victor records—not there to be heard. Some of the singing is poor; but most of it is good, and some of it is superb. Moreover the majority of the principals are Metropolitan stars; and it is two of these, Albanese and Merrill, who do the poor singing in the *Traviata*, and another, Richard Tucker, whose voice is cold and lusterless in the *Aïda*; whereas it is two of the comparatively unknown singers, Herva Nelli and Giuseppe Valdengo—the chief targets of the critics I have mentioned —who, far from being mediocre and intimidated, contribute some of the performances' most beautiful and expressive singing. Nelli, in the third act of *Aïda*, does sound frightened for a moment in the phrase near the end of "O *patria mia*" that rises to high C; but even a greater singer would be frightened by having to sing the difficult phrase all in one breath, as Nelli had to do. And later in the act Nelli and Tucker *are* driven breathless by the excessively fast tempo of the concluding section of their duet; but this is an exceedingly rare exception to the rightness of pacing, fast and slow, that is one of the things in the performances which produce the effect of revelation.

On February 9 and 16 Toscanini gave the radio public its first hearing of Berlioz's *Romeo and Juliet* in its entirety, together with a scene from *The Damnation of Faust*. And somewhere between the *Traviata* and the *Romeo* I was at Toscanini's home, where I listened with him to the test pressings of what I think was the recording of Mozart's *Jupiter* Symphony. For some reason Toscanini was worried about the recorded sound; and in the end I took the records home with me to hear what they sounded like on my phonograph. Within a day, before I could report back, I had a telephone call from Walter, whom I heard repeating to his father my statement that the sound was good. Then Toscanini himself got on the phone to ask me; and I repeated to him that the sound was good. He seemed still unsatisfied; so I asked him if he would like to hear for himself. Yes, he would; and so a day or two later he arrived at my apartment with Walter, who was loaded down with a stack of records.

I first played the older recording of the *Tristan* finale to establish the sound from my equipment, which Toscanini pronounced a little deficient in bass but otherwise good. He kept moving about restlessly, and Walter suggested: "Relax; sit down"; so he sat down, but didn't relax, and soon was on his feet again. I then played the test pressings that had worried him; and he seemed now to be satisfied with their sound. Then Walter began to put on the additional test pressings he had brought along, of which I remember only the ones of Weber's Overture to *Der Freischütz*. After the first side of this recording, as the second side began to be heard, Toscanini, who at that moment was seated at the piano, cried out: "Is wrong record! Is not same tempo as first record!"; whereupon Walter replaced it with another, and his father, when he heard the first measures, exclaimed: "Now is right tempo!"

Later, still seated at the piano, he pointed to the score of Berlioz's *Romeo* on the music rack and said: *"Love Scene is most beautiful music in the world."*

Romeo was followed by Schubert's C-major; and I remember the rehearsal in which the solo horn, Arthur Berv, played his opening statement with the slight emphasis on the first note of each measure that the score prescribes, but Toscanini compelled him to put the heavier and cruder accents on the notes that can be heard in the recording of the performance, M-1167 and LM-1040. It is interesting that in the 1953 performance on LM-1835 Berv plays his opening statement with only the prescribed slight emphasis once more. And the two recordings enable one to hear also that the 1947 performance still retained features of the 1941 performance with the Philadelphia Orchestra—notably the coda of the first movement—but already had some of the changed features of the 1953 performance—notably the coda of the finale.

Another important event of the 1946–47 series was the performance of Beethoven's Overture *For the Consecration of the House* on March 16, which gave most radio listeners their first hearing of this strange and wonderful piece. And most concert-goers too: my own attendance at concerts in New York began somewhere around 1914; but this was the first public performance of the piece for me. Previously I had known it only from Weingartner's recorded performance; and I could appreciate how fortunate radio listeners were in becoming acquainted with it through Toscanini's performance, with its tempos that were so skillfully chosen, as Weingartner's were not, to be right for each section and to connect the sections in a coherent progression.

Since Toscanini was criticized for persisting in playing those little pieces by Martucci and other minor Italians, let me point out that he also persisted in playing parts and the whole of Berlioz's *Romeo and Juliet* when nobody else did; that he did the same with *Harold in Italy*; that he gave my generation of concert-goers its first experiences of Beethoven's *Missa Solemnis*; and that he now did the same with the *Consecration of the House* Overture. He did play some worthless music, but no more, I am sure, than other conductors did. The difference was that he played worthless music mostly by Italians, whereas the others played worthless music by Germans, Russians and Americans; and I don't agree that this constitutes the difference between bad and good program-making.

He was criticized also for not fulfilling his obligation to living composers; but it should be remembered that he began his almost-thirty-year career as a symphonic conductor in this country at the age of sixty, and that as a young conductor in Italy he did conduct what was new and modern. In opera he conducted the first performances at La Scala of Strauss's *Salome* in 1906 and Debussy's *Pelléas et Mélisande* in 1908; and in the season of 1925–26 he prepared a stage production of Stravinsky's *Petrushka* there which illness prevented him from conducting. And as one of the most active symphonic conductors in Italy he played Strauss's *Till Eulenspiegel* in 1902, *Death and Transfiguration* in

1905, and *Don Juan* in 1906, Debussy's *Faun* piece in 1905, *Nuages* in 1906, *La Mer* in 1912, and *Ibéria* in 1918, Stravinsky's *Petrushka* in 1916, Dukas's *Sorcerer's Apprentice* in 1904, Glazunov's Symphony No. 6 in 1904, Sibelius's *En Saga* in 1905. Even at the Metropolitan he conducted Dukas's *Ariane et Barbe-bleu*. At sixty he may have felt the obligation to living composers was one for younger conductors; and since there were others capable and willing to assume the obligation, it wasn't a bad division of labor to have Stokowski, Koussevitzky, Rodzinski and Mitropoulos handling contemporary works and Toscanini restricting himself to standard repertory. Even so Toscanini did play Shostakovitch's First and Seventh Symphonies, Khabalevsky's Second Symphony and his *Colas Breugnon* Overture. And at the age of seventy-one, astonishingly, he played Barber's *Essay for Orchestra* and *Adagio for Strings,* at seventy-three Roy Harris's Symphony No. 3, at seventy-five Copland's *El Salón México,* and during a couple of years thereafter pieces by Creston, Gould, Gershwin, Gilbert, Kennan, Griffes, William Schuman and Siegmeister.

On the day in April 1947 that I was to visit Toscanini I happened to see someone from Victor who mentioned a few bits of information and gossip. One piece of information was that Toscanini was dissatisfied with the sound of the timpani on a couple of sides of the recording of Tchaikovsky's *Romeo and Juliet;* another was that Victor had induced him to record the Mozart *Haffner* with a reduced orchestra in NBC's Studio 3A, which was smaller than 8H. As for gossip, there had been an NBC Symphony rehearsal of Strauss's *Death and Transfiguration* at which Toscanini had let the orchestra go on playing to the end of the introduction before he exploded in anger at its inaccuracy; and the engineers had recorded this episode and more of the rehearsal, including further explosions. On a later occasion the recording had been played for Toscanini, who had exclaimed: "That's me!" and covered his face with his hands.

As I waited downstairs that afternoon while the maid went up to announce me I could hear the piano being played. The playing stopped; and a few moments later I heard my name called by Toscanini. I looked up and saw him at the top of the stairs, smiling down at me. "Come up," he said; and when I did he led me to his study and sat down again at the piano. In February he had broadcast a scene from Berlioz's *Damnation of Faust;* and it was this opera that he had been playing on the piano now. "I would like to play this next year: is so beautiful! I hear it played by Y——: was terrible!—such tempi!"—and he gave examples at the piano. "But what tenor? Is extremely difficult, tenor part." Turning a few pages of the score, he pointed to a long-sustained high B-flat (I think) and said: "Is very difficult to sing this note. I hear it once in falsetto"; and he proceeded to sing the aria in his croaking singing voice, accompanying himself with piano chords that were sloppily broken between the two hands. "Is so beautiful! And *Romanza* of Marguerite," which he also sang and played. "But what soprano or mezzo-soprano? I think maybe Tourel, because is very important to have somebody who can sing words properly. But is five years since she sing with me in *Romeo and Juliet,* and I do not know how she sing now." I suggested finding out; and I also suggested Ramon Vinay for the tenor part.

Then, "I want to play for you record of Tchaikovsky's *Romeo and Juliet,* because in this place"—and he played a passage on the piano—"timpani are too weak, and I want to put in more timpani"—by which he meant that he wanted Victor to dub a new side from the old one and at the same time dub in additional live timpani sound. He then played the test pressing of the Tchaikovsky *Romeo* for me, putting on each record himself clumsily while I watched apprehensively, and once putting on a wrong record with the Khabalevsky *Colas Breugnon* Overture. Seated this time, he conducted the performance as always, giving entrances, anticipating points, smiling his pleasure at what he heard, exclaiming once: "Is good, crescendo of *violini,* no?" And he pointed out the unsatisfactory timpani sound: "Only *celli* and *bassi* are clear." "But I hear the timpani," I said. "Yes, but is weak." I pointed out that if the two sides were dubbed to put in additional timpani sound there would be a loss of some of the beauty of all the other sound, as there had been from the similar dubbing of one side of Haydn's No. 98—which he didn't remember. As I spoke he nodded his understanding, but not, it turned out, his agreement; for when I finished he said: "But I cannot let people say I do not know right sound of timpani."

There being nothing more to say about this, he remembered the recording of the Mozart *Haffner,* which he hadn't listened to yet. "First movement and finale of old *Haffner*

are good," he said, "but not Andante and Minuetto: tempi
are too slow." Then he played the new first movement,
but stopped the Andante after a few moments: "Is wrong
take. There is another take with right tempo." Finding the
other, he was pleased by it, and by the rest of the recording.
"When Bruno Walter conduct *Haffner* at La Scala I do
not understand slow tempo of Minuetto. I ask Casals: 'Is
correct, Minuetto so slow?'" And I gathered that Casals
had fortified him in his conviction that his own faster tempo
was right.

"Can you hear is small orchestra?" he asked. "No," I
answered, "but I can hear it is a small studio." At which
he told me how difficult it had been to play in that studio,
which he didn't like and wouldn't record in again. (Actually
he did record the Haydn *Clock* Symphony there too.
According to my Victor informant, RCA [of which Victor
and NBC were subsidiary companies] had insisted on
Victor using NBC's Studio 3A for certain reasons; and
the result was two of the most atrocious Toscanini recordings ever issued—with harsh sound and an acoustic deadness that struck the ear a blow after a loud chord. And
later the LP dubbings were made unlistenable by Victor's
"enhancement.")

Next he played the test pressing of the Schumann
Manfred Overture. "You like *Manfred* Overture?" he asked.
"Very much," I answered. "Is beautiful music!" he exclaimed. "But Downes say is not good music! Ah, *Dio
santo!*" And he played on the piano a passage from a
Beethoven sonata that Downes had said Schumann bor-
rowed. I no longer recall the passage, but remember saying,

as Toscanini nodded agreement, that Schumann might be echoing something but certainly made it his own.

With this, Toscanini stopped playing records, which he said tired him. Looking about him in search of something, he exclaimed "Ah!" and picked up from his desk the pocket score of Mozart's Divertimento. I had asked him in a letter whether he would transfer his markings into another copy of the score for me (my score of Berlioz's *Romeo* has Toscanini's markings for the placing and removal of the strings' mutes in the *Love Scene*); and he now said: "Here is score of Divertimento. I do not have cadenza; I will find it at NBC. Is here cadenza"—as he pointed to the faint traces of some musical notation that had been written in the score and then erased—"but I make different one which must be at NBC. I will find it and send it to you." I explained that I had wanted him to transfer his markings from this copy to another. "No, you take this one."

Then we sat down to talk; and he asked: "You work hard this year?"—referring to the fact that I had begun that year a weekly column on radio music for the Sunday *Herald Tribune*. "Yes," I answered. "There have been two articles to write each week instead of one; and I write very slowly." He nodded as I spoke, and said: "Is better so. Is better to make slow and *good*, as to make fast and not good."

Walter Toscanini arrived; and his father told him that we had listened to the Tchaikovsky *Romeo*, and that the timpani must be reinforced. Again I pointed out the loss in the other sound from dubbing; and he answered: "You have better ear; I will not hear it." I repudiated this amazing statement; whereupon it turned out that he had meant my ear for recorded sound; but I insisted that he would hear the loss, and suggested that he play the finale of the Haydn No. 98, in which he would hear the loss in the first side as against the second. But it was still impossible for him to let the *Romeo* go out with the timpani not right. So we agreed that the thing to do was to make the dubbings and let him decide then whether he preferred the dubbed sides or the originals.

There were questions and comments about performances he had heard. "Did you hear broadcast of Santa Monica Orchestra with Rachmilovich? I do not know anything about this conductor; but I listen—I hear—strings—whole orchestra—is good. I am glad to hear young conductor who play good." And to Walter: "You must tell Chotzie *
to bring him to NBC for summer concerts." On the other hand another conductor, who had been highly recommended to him, "make terrible tempi." And Z——, who formerly "was cold, but conduct correct [illustrated by precise conducting gestures], now stop beating time [illustrated], then make big movement [again illustrated]. And tempi in *Ibéria*! [Toscanini put his hand to his head in pain.] He play second movement so slow that this *passage* [the chromatically descending and ascending passage soon after the beginning] is so [illustrated at the piano]. *Dio santo!*" Then something reminded him of Sibelius's Seventh Symphony: "I listen with score. Sometime you must show me where is music. *I* cannot hear any music in this piece."

* Samuel Chotzinoff.

Had he, I asked, heard the De Sabata recording of Mozart's *Requiem,* which I thought was so remarkable. He nodded as I spoke, and answered: "Is good performance. De Sabata is good but sometimes nervous conductor." (But on another occasion he used a term of disapproval instead of "nervous" for De Sabata's violent gesticulation. Mentioning that he had been accused of not doing enough for young conductors, he said: "I always invite young conductors to come to my rehearsals. De Sabata come to my rehearsals—but then on podium is Pagliaccio!")

"Did you hear A——?" he asked. "Only a little of the *Coriolan* Overture and *Daphnis and Chloë,* which I didn't like," I said. "Did you hear Berlioz *Fantastique?*"—referring to the performance with which A—— had created a sensation. "No." "I hear only part of last movement on record," said Toscanini. "Is in double tempo. Is easy to make exciting in double tempo. But is so fast, *tromboni* cannot play correct this *passage* [he played it on the piano]; also violas here [he played the passage on the piano]." Walter had found the record, an acetate made in Carnegie Hall during the performance; and when he played it Toscanini pointed to the inaccurate playing of the trombones and violas. "Is easy to make exciting in double tempo," he repeated at the end, "but not easy to play correct." And I believe it was on this occasion that he said of the work itself: "I never like *Fantastique:* is for me not good music. Only last two movements are good music. Once, in Lago Maggiore, at night, I hear on radio *Fantastique*—I do not know who conduct—is so beautiful I think maybe is good music. I look in score: is not good music. I never know who is conductor of this performance!"

Toscanini's mind reverted to Berlioz's *Damnation of Faust;* and we all discussed my suggestion of Vinay. Toscanini now remembered the matter of time. He added up the time required by the scenes that would make up the first broadcast and found that they would fit into the available hour; but the second part turned out to be too long; and Toscanini speculated whether the program following the NBC Symphony would give up a quarter of an hour this one time. He began to figure out the time again, while Walter remarked to me: "What my father does not understand is that there must be a decision *now,* because singers must be engaged before they get involved with other activities." Tourel was mentioned again, and Toscanini repeated: "I must have somebody who can sing words. Is not enough, beautiful voice: must be expression. No singer understand that."

The subject of singers with nothing but voices, and their musical excesses in the display of those voices, reminded him of a De Lucia record which he asked Walter to play. While he was getting it his father played on the piano some of the phrases as De Lucia distorted them; and when the record was played Toscanini sat laughing at them. But Caruso's name caused him to hold his head in his hands: "He sing with me at La Scala in '99, and I write to Boito: 'You must come to La Scala to hear *Elisir d'Amore* with young tenor who sing like angel.' But in 1901 is already change; and in New York——! I tell him: 'Yes, you make much money—but no! *no! NO!!'* "

80

It was now late in the afternoon, and Toscanini left us for a few minutes. When he returned he had changed from his maroon smoking jacket to his usual black suit. He was driving down to dinner with Mr. and Mrs. Vladimir Horowitz, his son-in-law and daughter, and offered me a lift. While we waited for the car he showed Walter a book—with a long inscription by him—that he was taking to little Sonia Horowitz. "Is very good," he said to Walter, his face expressing his delight over it.

In the car I asked him about Schuch, a former director of the Dresden Opera, whom someone had mentioned to me; and his face lighted up: "Oh yes! Is *good*! Is *good* opera conductor! He came to La Scala—is good conductor of Italian opera. I also hear him in Dresden—I hear *Oberon* —I remember overture is very beautiful, and I am *sure* is change in strings. When Busch come to La Scala I say: 'Look in score of *Oberon* and tell me if is change in strings.' "

What about Nikisch? "Is good conductor—but make performance for public [he made gestures of acting]. And sometimes he do not look at score." Then with increasing intensity: "When I conduct I am always prepared. I do not stand before public to show I am Toscanini—never! Always I try to do my best. And always conducting is great suffering for me. At home, with score, when I play piano, is great happiness. But with orchestra is great suffering—*sempre, sempre!* * Even when I listen to record I am afraid horn will not play correct, clarinet will make mistake—*sempre, sempre!* Last week they play for me record of rehearsal

* always

8 1

of *Tod und Verklärung*. I do not know why they make this record. All my life I have bad temper: is impossible for me to understand why orchestra cannot play correct. But when I hear this record I am ashamed."

Later he asked again about my work; and as I described how I had made things harder for myself by undertaking to give a lecture which I had given before, but which I had now found had to be changed, Toscanini nodded and smiled his understanding. He asked how long I had been writing for the *Herald Tribune;* and I said since the preceding October. "I read some interesting things in these articles," he said. "Do you also read the *Nation* articles?" I asked. "Oh yes! . . . People write to you?" "Yes," I said, "from all over the country; and it's a great pleasure—especially the letters from young people, sometimes very extraordinary young people, and from small places." His face had been expressing his own pleasure at this; and he said: "You write about this man . . . [he groped for the name] is professor . . . in university . . . here"—and he pointed northward from Ninety-fifth Street where we were at the moment. "Columbia?" I suggested. "Columbia, *sì?*" "Lang?" "Lang, *sì*." He was referring to a *Nation* article in which I had, among other things, quoted from a letter in which a reader cited the factual record of the number of performances and number of seasons, against Lang's statement in his *Music in Western Civilization* that Auber's opera *La Muette de Portici* was forgotten shortly after its initial success. "In that article," I said to Toscanini, "the letter I quoted was from one of those young people—from Greensboro, North Carolina." He nodded; then, pursuing his own thought, he said: "The musicologists—they know everything——" "Except music," we concluded in unison.

I visited Toscanini again in mid-October 1947; and on the way upstairs to his study I heard him playing over and over again the little ascending scale of the woodwinds at the beginning of Beethoven's *Consecration of the House* Overture. It turned out that he was going to broadcast the piece again on the twenty-fifth, and was preparing as usual by going over the score and listening to the recording of the performance of the preceding March. He showed me in the score the places that were creating problems and difficulties—the bassoon part in one tutti, for example, about which he said, shaking his head dejectedly: "I try everything, but I am afraid I will never hear these bassoons." And then with the score open before us we listened to the recording of the earlier performance.

I remember only one other matter that came up that morning. In July NBC had announced that in October the NBC Symphony broadcasts would be moved from Sunday at five to Saturday at six-thirty; and I had written in the *Herald Tribune* that if NBC was right in contending that a greater number of stations would carry the program at the new time, this was only because the time had little commercial value—which was to say that it was a time when people were at dinner or preparing for dinner or on the way out to dinner, and in any case not able to listen to the radio. In September I had discussed the matter again in the *Herald Tribune*, quoting readers in the Midwest and West who had written me that the broadcasts, if carried live, would reach those areas at earlier times when some people were at work. Moreover, in mid-October Toscanini had not yet begun his broadcasts, and the orchestra was still playing under its summer conductors. I was therefore amazed, when Toscanini mentioned the matter that morning, to discover he was under the impression that several million more people were listening on Saturday than had listened on Sunday.

I think this was one of the times I was asked to stay for lunch; and I remember the servant attempting, without success, to coax Toscanini to take some veal in addition to the few vegetables that were all he ate.

With the *Consecration of the House* Overture Toscanini, on the twenty-fifth, played Beethoven's Seventh; and I recall the performance of the finale at a rehearsal. His movements at rehearsal were more uninhibitedly vigorous than they were in the presence of an audience at a concert; and the climax of the last crescendo had him stamping his feet—with results that caused one member of the orchestra to exclaim: "I've got to get back into my skin." On the other hand the first measures of Mendelssohn's rarely heard *Tale of Lovely Melusine* Overture were played, at a rehearsal the following week, with an inflection so exquisite as to bring tears to my eyes. And Mendelssohn's pieces for *A Midsummer Night's Dream* were played with an exquisite plasticity and grace, and on occasion an elegantly impassioned animation, which I found equally moving.

A Mozart program included the Divertimento K.287

again and the Bassoon Concerto K.191, both of which were recorded. I imagine the concerto was written for some bassoon-player Mozart knew; and I would suspect that Mozart used the occasion to amuse himself—not only obviously with the tootling and braying he gave to the solo instrument, but subtly with the comments he gave to the orchestra—comments which go unnoticed in the usual performance, but which claimed delighted attention with the life they had from Toscanini's inflection.

And a subsequent Handel-Vivaldi-Bach program had one wondering why, if Toscanini played a Handel concerto grosso with a small chamber group, he played a Bach suite with all the NBC strings; why, with this mass of strings, he didn't use a piano that would have been heard instead of a harpsichord that was inaudible; why he played an uninteresting little violin concerto of Vivaldi instead of one of the many lovely works of this composer that he might have played; and why he played the monstrous Respighi transcription of Bach's *Passacaglia* for organ.

The climax of the fall series came on December 1 and 8 with the performance of Verdi's *Otello*. The art which manifests itself in astounding fashion in as early a work as *Macbeth,* in the vocal and orchestral writing of the *Sleepwalking Scene*—this art achieves in *Otello* a sustained incandescent invention that fills in moment after moment with marvelously wrought details of melody, harmony, figuration and orchestration. And this sustained operation of Verdi's powers was given overwhelming effect by the similar sustained operation of the powers that kept the progression unfailingly beautiful in sound, clear in outline and texture, and continuous in impetus, tension and force. In this performance Toscanini had an all but perfect cast; and so one heard—and still hears on Victor LM-6107—not only the orchestral part superbly played but the vocal parts with the tonal beauty and remarkable expressive inflection and coloring of Valdengo's singing, the loveliness and purity of Nelli's, the fine singing of Vinay at the times— notably in the third act—when he achieved delicacy without disturbing effort, and ringing sonority without a disturbing quaver.

At the rehearsals of the orchestra alone Toscanini filled in the singing—with no vocal beauty but with much expressive force. I still remember his delivery of Iago's *"Non so"* * in reply to Otello's question what had happened, after the drunken brawl in the first act. And I remember also his stopping the orchestra in the third-act duet of Otello and Desdemona to say: "You must understand this situation: these are her first tears."

Before I visited Toscanini early in February 1948 I asked to hear some of the recording of the broadcast of Berlioz's *Romeo and Juliet* a year earlier. But when I arrived Toscanini had an acetate recording of A——'s entire performance of the Berlioz *Fantastique* with which to demonstrate to me that other parts were as bad as the finale. "I pay for recording, to have proof!" he exclaimed—proof that the march movement, which he proceeded to play for me, also was whipped up in tempo in a way that was exciting but that

* "I don't know."

86

converted the *March to the Scaffold* into a march of triumph—something he regarded as not just a musical but a moral transgression.

With this demonstrated, Toscanini sat down with me at the piano with the score of *Romeo* open before us, to listen to the recording of the broadcast. I listened and read; he conducted, gave entrance cues, sang, and occasionally pointed to something in the score, exclaiming: "This is *honest* performance: you can read it in score!"

Later, as he was putting away the score, he looked at me with a smile and said: "Now, Haggin, what would you like?"

"Anything you would like to hear," I answered.

"No"—still smiling—"what would you like—what would you like to have?" And as I stared at him uncomprehendingly he added: "You come only to see me?"

"Yes, of course," I managed to answer, so shocked that I didn't until later apprehend what he was telling me in this way; but then I did see what a revealing incident this was. My meetings with Toscanini were few and infrequent and limited in scope; and I didn't get to know him as his intimates did; but I did get to know him as *I* did—meaning that I think I learned some things about him which I feel sure of, no matter how they may appear to someone else. Those who have read the description of Toscanini's behavior in the Chotzinoff book may find it hard to accept the idea of his essential innocence; but I am thinking of a child's innocence which is sometimes retained up to the point where the young person comes face to face with some of the brutal and evil realities of adult existence and resorts to defenses and counterattacks that may be unpleasant. I got an impression of such innocence in Toscanini; and I find it understandable that coming face to face with a world of hard-eyed people who all wanted something from him—for whom he was in one way or another an object of exploitation—he occasionally dealt with them in the ways described by Chotzinoff. Even with friends? Even with friends: apparently he sensed what sort of friends some of them were. And to me it is significant that Chotzinoff in his book describes Toscanini as unfailingly courteous and considerate to servants.

After the playing of the Berlioz *Romeo* recording and the incident I have just described there was the usual chatting about what we had heard. Ansermet had been conducting the NBC Symphony for the first time; and Toscanini pronounced him "best conductor of NBC"—which I took to mean the best of the guest conductors the orchestra had had. "Is good musician. When he play *La Valse* is different from my *La Valse,* and Chotzinoff say is not good. But I say: 'No. Is not like my *La Valse*—but is good.'" As for the music Ansermet had played, Stravinsky's *Symphonies pour instruments à vent* had impressed him as the work of a mathematician (it may have been on this occasion that he said he had stopped playing Stravinsky because "he call Beethoven fake"—clearly a misconstruction of whatever Stravinsky had said). Nor had he cared for Debussy's *Jeux.* Ansermet had also played Debussy's *Gigues;* and this visit may have been one of the several times when I asked Toscanini whether he had ever played *Gigues* and *Rondes de printemps,* the companion pieces of *Ibéria,* and each time, nodding and smiling reminiscently, he answered: "Ye-e-es, Debussy send me score," and nothing more. Late in March *Rondes de printemps* was announced for a Debussy program, but didn't materialize.

Since he was to play Tchaikovsky's *Manfred* in a few weeks this work was in his mind, and he told me why he liked it best of Tchaikovsky's music. "Is not one note banal. Not like Fifth—Fifth is banal: second movement—ah-h-h, *Dio santo!*" He mentioned that he was going to play Beethoven's Ninth at his last broadcast. And the opera next year would be Verdi's *Falstaff.*

At some point I asked him his opinion of Frieda Hempel, whose recordings had given me an impression of her as the greatest singer of her time. "Was good Eva in *Meistersinger,*" he said; and he remembered also her Page in *Un Ballo in Maschera,* her singing in Beethoven's Ninth. The soloists in this performance of the Ninth at the Metropolitan—Hempel, Homer, Karl Jörn, Putnam Griswold—were "best I ever have; and was good orchestra." This reminded him of the rehearsal at which the Metropolitan orchestra "play like pig" and he swore at it in Italian. When, subsequently, the Italian was translated, the orchestra was offended and said it wouldn't play for him until he apologized. To the mediator who came to see him Toscanini explained that he couldn't apologize because "orchestra play like pig." But he proposed the solution that worked: "I go to rehearsal and smile and say '*Good* morning.'"

I had been asked to stay for lunch; and when Toscanini

and I seated ourselves at the table Walter Toscanini wasn't there. "Is good," Toscanini commented, "but not punctual. Only once was punctual: I was married June 21; he was born March 21."

Of the further talk at lunch I remember only a few fragments. At one point Toscanini spoke of Puccini as not having been "sincere" in relation to the words as Verdi had been—except in the finale of *La Bohème*. At another point the name of Cleofonte Campanini came up; and Toscanini spoke highly of his ability as a conductor: "Had taste in Italian opera, but could not read score. First rehearsal is good; but he make more rehearsal and make worse," and he chuckled. Koussevitzky's name also came up: Toscanini thought he should have stopped conducting, and suspected that "he conduct because I conduct. I will conduct until I am ninety!"—this with an emphatic jab of his arm toward the floor. And Koussevitzky's actions as a world figure elicited from Toscanini the comment "I am not great man! Is enough to be a man!"

He was driving down to NBC for a rehearsal of the soloists for the Ninth Symphony; and I drove with him part of the way. I remember only mentioning something done by his extraordinary first cellist, Frank Miller, and Toscanini's face lighting up as he agreed that Miller was a fine musician—and, he added, his first viola, Carlton Cooley, too.

On March 6 Toscanini broadcast the only performance of Mozart's Symphony K.543 in E flat that he ever gave with an American orchestra. It was a performance, on the one hand, filled with the exquisite inflection he so well understood how to put in between the *p*'s and *f*'s; but a performance, on the other hand, sacrificed to a cause—the cause of the true Andante. The common error of taking Andante to mean slow, and of playing a Mozart Andante, in effect, as an Adagio, had become an obsession with Toscanini; and instead of playing the Andante movement of the E-flat Symphony as a true Andante in terms of its substance, he made the performance a demonstration of a true Andante in terms of the 2/4 time signature—with results that can be heard on Victor LM 2001, which reproduces the performance that was broadcast: the Andante in terms of the two beats in each measure was much too fast for the proper flow and articulation of the substance. The obsession about even slow tempos being too slow caused him also to play the Adagio introduction of the first movement a little too fast for the music to have the majesty it should have. And the obsession about everything being too slow produced an Allegretto tempo in the Minuet that was too fast for the music to have its proper grace.

On March 20 the owners of television sets wherever the NBC telecast was carried by local stations were able not only to hear but to see Toscanini and the NBC Symphony perform a Wagner program. Like the OWI film of performances of Verdi's Overture to *La Forza del Destino* and *Hymn of the Nations,* the telecast followed the usual film practice of shifting back and forth between conductor and players. The moments in which one saw Toscanini at close range as his first-desk string-players saw him, and not only observed but felt the intensity of his involvement, were moving and exciting; and some of the goings-on in the orchestra were interesting. But because Toscanini was not kept uninterruptedly in view, the listening spectator did not witness what was so fascinating in the Toscanini operation—the related continuities of his activity and the performance it produced.

The continuity in the performance I have referred to many times: it was, first, one of impetus and tension, which caused the progression of sound, once started, to keep going with unfailing momentum and cohesive tension from one sound to the next; it was, in addition, one of shape, produced by changes of sonority and pace that were always in right proportion to what preceded and followed, so that the timing and force of one sound strongly implied the timing and force of the next, giving the flow naturalness and inevitability in addition to its coherence. This continuous flow of the performance was produced by a continuous activity—a continuous exercise by Toscanini of the utmost attentiveness, concentration and control. Once he started the progression going, he marshaled it along, watched over it, controlled it to make it come out as planned. The marshaling was done with those large, plastic, sensitive movements of his right arm (extended to the point of his baton), which delineated for the orchestra the flow of sound in much of its subtly inflected detail and literally conducted the orchestra from one sound to the next in that flow—the effectiveness of these movements being due to their extraordinary explicitness in conveying his wish at every moment, and to the compelling personal force they transmitted. The left hand meanwhile was in constant activity as the instrument of the apprehensive watchfulness that showed itself on Toscanini's face—now exhorting, now quieting, now warning, now suppressing.

The moment-to-moment relation of the continuities of activity and performance was, I have said, fascinating to watch. And moving in addition was the absorbed, unselfconscious operation of extraordinary powers that gave Toscanini's conducting the appearance of a natural act like a bird's flight, in which the powers operated with complete adequacy for each momentary situation but with no more than adequacy—an economy that was a form of honesty in relation to the material and situation and gave the operation a moral quality.

In this first telecast some of the shifts from Toscanini to the orchestra were well chosen and timed; but sometimes the camera reached the player late, or even too late; it also did some aimless wandering about, and some picking out of players who weren't doing anything that called for this attention; and it failed sometimes to pick out a player who was doing something of great importance.

The April 3 telecast of Beethoven's Ninth was in all respects better. There were longer images of Toscanini's conducting; some of the shifts from him to the orchestra or chorus or soloist were made by a slow dissolve which carried his movements into the playing or singing they were related to, so that the playing or singing became a continuation of his activity; and in some instances the image of Toscanini conducting was kept superimposed on the image of the players or singers. There was less aimless wandering of the camera, and better marksmanship wherever it was aimed. Nevertheless the horn solo in the Trio of the Scherzo was missed both times, and this after the kettledrum joke in the *Ritmo di tre battute* section of the Scherzo had also been missed both times; and I was fuming about all this during the return of the Scherzo, when suddenly there was Toscanini signaling the drummer for the first *forte* statement of the three-note figure, then the drummer playing the figure *forte,* and again *forte,* and again *forte,* and then —after an unexpected extra measure—an unexpected *mezzoforte.*

What remains in my memory is one image: of Toscanini, at the end of the first movement, lowering his arm and at the same time lowering his eyes in momentary relaxation of bodily and mental tension, then raising his eyes which flashed an electrifying signal to the orchestra as he raised his arm for the second movement.

The performance of the Ninth on this occasion was in Toscanini's later, less expansive style, of which it provided one of the finest, most effective examples. Unfortunately he had undistinguished soloists in the finale.

But he was even more unfortunate in the benefit performance of Verdi's *Requiem* in Carnegie Hall on April 26. In the unaccompanied passage for soprano and chorus just before the concluding fugue, Herva Nelli became separated from the chorus in pitch by an ever widening gap. One expected Toscanini to stop and begin the section again; but he went on, providing a striking example of his iron self-discipline in public in the face of mistakes by his musicians or annoyances from the audience, as compared with his lack of self-control at rehearsals. The commotion at the opening *Fidelio* of the Salzburg Festival in 1937—caused by the presence of the Windsors—was such that I expected him to throw down his baton and walk out; but he went on conducting the performance.

Six of the broadcasts in the fall of 1948 were devoted to a Brahms cycle noteworthy for the fact that the performances of the Haydn Variations and the Third and Fourth Symphonies exhibited once more the repose, the relaxation, the steadiness, and as a result the spaciousness and grandeur they had not had two or three years before. Especially impressive in this way was the concluding passacaglia movement of the Fourth, whose effect—the cumulative force and impact of the series of varied repetitions of the initial eight-measure statement—depends on maintaining the tempo of this initial statement throughout the series of variations, as Brahms directs. This effect is destroyed by the usual practice of changing the tempo in each variation and slowing down enormously in Variations 10 to 15; but Toscanini achieved it in impressive fashion by maintaining the single tempo, with only subtle modifications, throughout the movement.

The relaxation, spaciousness and clarification continued to be evident in the performances of other music in the remaining two broadcasts of the fall series, including one of Strauss's *Don Quixote*. "That," remarked an NBC musician after the final rehearsal of the Strauss piece, "is something we'll never hear the like of again." He was referring to the marvelous clarity of the detail in the complex texture, the plastic beauty of the form in sound; and actually these were heard again in the performance Toscanini broadcast in November 1953, which was issued by Victor on LM-2026. But my musician was right: I have never heard a performance by another conductor that had this clarity and plastic beauty. However I did hear a performance—by Bruno Walter with the New York Symphony in the twenties—which made me laugh more with its sharper pointing up of the fun in the piece. And listening to a recording of Toscanini's performance in 1938 I was amazed by the greater energy it exhibited right from the opening high-spirited statement of the oboe and flute. This lessened energy showed itself in some other performances of the later years, but not in all.

Toscanini was followed by Ansermet, and Ansermet by Guido Cantelli. Listening to Toscanini in those years, and marveling at his continuing powers, one had realized that some day there would nevertheless be an end, and had wondered if there would ever again be the accidental coming together of the particular musical taste, technical capacities and personal characteristics that had combined to produce this unique way of operating as a conductor and its unique results. And so it was exciting to hear in Cantelli's performances with the NBC Symphony an operation similar to Toscanini's in attitude, method and result. The performances, like Toscanini's, shaped the works strictly on the lines laid out by the composers' directions about tempo and dynamics in the score; the shaped progressions resembled Toscanini's in their purity of taste and style, their continuity and organic coherence, their clarity of outline, texture and structure. There were of course differences too: as against the power creating a continuous tension in the flow of a Toscanini performance, one heard in Cantelli's perform- ances a youthful lyricism and grace. These qualities of youth the performances exhibited, but not the immaturity about which some critics felt safe in pontificating to show their keen discernment ("That degree of musical culture and experience which can settle, almost instinctively, on proper tempi and sonorous values for such works as the Mozart are not yet his," observed Irving Kolodin out of the implied fullness of his own musical culture and experience, con- cerning a beautifully paced and phrased performance of Mozart's Divertimento K.287): the performances certainly would change in time, but each as it was produced then emerged as a completely, satisfyingly achieved entity.

The performances also resembled Toscanini's in their precision of orchestral execution and sonority, their bril- liant virtuosity; and if anyone points out that Cantelli was, after all, conducting a virtuoso orchestra, the answer is that such an orchestra plays in that way only for a virtuoso conductor. One heard in the performances the authority of directing mind and hand that was evident at rehearsals: the authority of the kind of knowledge of everything in the score and everything going on in the orchestra, of one's purpose and the means of achieving this purpose, that commands the respect and response of an orchestra like the NBC Symphony. And Cantelli's musical and technical equipment, his fanatical personal dedication, won this re- spect and response not only from the conscientious musicians in the orchestra but from the hard-boiled specimens of the genus New York orchestral player.

I believe that in a letter to Toscanini at this time I included the question whether I might attend Cantelli's rehearsals; and when he telephoned he said: "Yes, come to rehearsal. You must hear this young conductor." I had missed the first rehearsal, but got to the second, at which Cantelli worked with the orchestra on Hindemith's *Mathis der Maler*. He did so under several handicaps, one of which was the awareness of Toscanini himself listening in the sixth row behind him. But if this contributed to Cantelli's nervousness and tenseness, it also was a help: the demands of a high-strung, fanatically dedicated person, the fact that he was a young man facing the orchestra of the world's most celebrated conductor, his handicap of not knowing a word of English—all these created not only tenseness in Cantelli but tense situations with the orchestra, which Toscanini's presence prevented from developing into anything worse.

Toscanini's presence also provided the orchestra with amusement. At the first rehearsal he had been given the score of *Mathis*, which he soon knew by memory; and thereafter, completely unconscious of what he was doing, he sat conducting the piece—beating time, signaling entrances, and all the rest. And the same thing happened a week later at the rehearsals of Bartók's *Concerto for Orchestra*.

The program of Toscanini's first broadcast after Cantelli's engagement constituted an additional compliment to the young conductor: a recognition that this time Toscanini was returning to an orchestra which had been kept at the high pitch of technical performance that enabled him to play Berlioz—and not just the *Roman Carnival* Overture and *Harold in Italy*, which require the utmost precision in execution and balanced sonority, but the terrifyingly difficult *Queen Mab* Scherzo, with its feathery string *pianissimos*, glints of woodwind color, and magical sounds of distant horns. And it occurred to me this time that in addition to the imagination, the ear and the technical powers there was one other characteristic of Toscanini that made him so effective a conductor of Berlioz—one related to an outstanding characteristic of Berlioz himself. Nothing that happens in Berlioz's music is perfunctory: when an instrument enters or an inner voice moves, the activity is something attentively, purposefully, freshly thought—this fresh thinking from point to point being responsible for much of the music's ever-amazing originality. In whatever happens one is aware of Berlioz's mind working; and this activity in the music makes it excitingly alive—as it was especially when conducted by Toscanini, in whose performances too one heard nothing done perfunctorily, everything done with attention and energy by a mind unceasingly active.

The spring series was made notable by a Beethoven *Eroica*—in the simpler, swifter, tauter style—that was hair-raising in its energy and power; and on the other hand by a Schubert *Unfinished* remarkable in the way its steady tempos created an almost superearthly quiet and calm in which both the dramatic force and the serenity of the work were achieved. And the series ended with a performance of *Aïda*, on March 26 and April 2, whose accuracy, clarity and order caused this much-battered work also to sound as though it were newly created. Not only did it give artistic validity and effect to the surviving formulas of the earlier Verdi style, but it allowed one to hear beautifully realized the exquisite harmonic and orchestral details with which *Aïda* is enriched, and which Verdi's subtilized craftsmanship elaborated into the fluent idiom of *Otello*.

Except for Tucker, whose voice was powerful but cold and lusterless, the cast was excellent, with Nelli and Valdengo again, and a newcomer, Eva Gustavson, who revealed in the second broadcast the luscious contralto voice that nervousness clouded with tremolo in the first. Nervousness also made Nelli's voice weak and breathy in the first broadcast (portions of the rehearsals, in which Nelli and Gustavson were at ease, appear to have been substituted in Victor LM-6132, with passages that were re-recorded in 1954). And an additional reason for the nervousness on this occasion was the fact that the performance was televised. It was, in fact, filmed, and could be shown again.

The *Aïda* performance was still in Toscanini's mind when I visited him in April. In fact, the first thing he did was to give me a photostat of the passage in the letter in which Verdi added the low B-flats at the end of "*Celeste Aïda*" that are heard in the performance in LM-6132. "I do not know why Verdi did not change the published score," said Toscanini. "Is impossible to sing high B-flat *pianissimo*— only in falsetto, which is not correct style in this work."

I spoke enthusiastically about certain exquisite details in *Aïda*; and Toscanini, who was seated at the piano, played not only the ones I mentioned but others—among them the violins at the beginning of the Nile Scene and the alternations of major and minor in the dance in the Temple Scene. Verdi, he said, was a great artist in addition to being the great melodist that Bellini and Donizetti were—and that only the Italians were, not the Germans. This he demonstrated by first pounding out on the piano the endless sequences at the beginning of the *Liebestod* in *Tristan und Isolde*, breaking off with a vehement *"Dio santo!"*, and then playing *"Spirito gentil"* from Donizetti's *La Favorita*, with his face registering his pleasure.

I said I thought Aïda was the most taxing soprano part in the operatic repertory; and he agreed that it was very difficult, especially if the soprano sang the long phrases in *"O patria mia"*—and here he played the one near the end that rises to high C and the concluding phrase that rises to A—in one breath as they are marked, and as Nelli had done.

What about the next opera—what about *Falstaff?* "I would like very much to perform this opera, and I would also like to perform it in little theater in Bussetto in 1952 and to record this performance. But it depend on singers." He mentioned one baritone he had found unsuitable; another who "could sing—but is lazy." And once more he said: "In this opera pronunciation of words is most important."

And *The Damnation of Faust?* "Is no tenor. The high B-flat—though it could be in falsetto, because is the style."

Cantelli also was very much in Toscanini's mind. "I love

this young conductor," he said, his face glowing at the thought of Cantelli. "I think is like me when I was young." Nevertheless he had rejected the NBC suggestion to drop Ansermet the following year and give an additional four weeks to Cantelli. "Ansermet is good conductor; and I do not want people to say I bring only Italian conductor."

He thanked me for the copy of W. J. Turner's *Beethoven* I had sent him, and agreed that there were wonderful things in it. I told him about Turner's other writings, including his remarkable pieces about Toscanini's concerts in London. Toscanini said he hadn't met Turner there: "I meet man who write about Wagner"—meaning Ernest Newman. I then told him how, when I had met Turner in London in 1937, he hadn't pretended an interest he didn't feel; how surprised, therefore, I had been in 1943 by a letter from him congratulating me on my writing in *The Nation*; and how pleased and moved I had been to receive this appreciation that was so completely unexpected. "Yes! And so spontaneous!" Toscanini exclaimed, his face lighting up.

I asked him about a statement concerning the appoggiatura that I had found marked by him in Lilli Lehmann's autobiography, which he had lent me. I remember his answering—illustrating at the piano with the opening section of the Overture to *Don Pasquale*—that there had to be variety in the treatment of the appoggiatura, "and this is matter of taste, which conductor must have." And he cited the appoggiaturas in the aria in the second act of Gluck's *Orfeo*, which "Bruno Walter make always the same." The German manner of treating the appoggiatura that he considered wrong was, he said, started by Mahler. "Was crazy man! Fourth Symphony [which presumably he had heard on the radio a day or two before] is terrible!"

I also asked him about a Sunday article of Olin Downes in the early thirties—a report of a conversation with Toscanini, in which Downes quoted him as saying that Berlioz's orchestration was original but not good—that of a genius but an amateur, compared with Wagner—and that it was nonsense to say Rimsky-Korsakov's editing had spoiled Musorgsky's *Boris*—that on the contrary, without Rimsky we wouldn't have had *Boris*. He didn't recall this conversation and remembered only meeting Downes when he conducted the Scala Orchestra in Boston. "Then he was all right; but later—*Dio santo*! I do not understand this man, who write this much [indicating with his fingers a volume a half-inch thick] about my performance of *Otello,* and then praise Metropolitan *Otello.* . . ." Then, coming back to Musorgsky's *Boris,* he conceded that Rimsky's correction of the consecutive fifths in the Simpleton's song had spoiled the passage, but insisted that the editing as a whole had made the work a success. I cited Rimsky's own statement in *My Musical Life* that the Musorgsky original had been a success when it had first been produced. "Yes," said Toscanini, "but only in Russia."

The Metropolitan *Otello* reminded him of Tamagno and *Otello.* "I ask: 'You sing always so?' He say: 'Yes, I sing always so.' I ask Verdi, and is not true."

"To get Tamagno," he continued, "we must take Calvé in opera called *Messalina.* When she sing this opera for me composer play piano; and I ask him: 'You are satisfied?' He say: 'Yes, I am satisfied.' Calvé tell me when I may come to hotel for rehearsal; and I tell her we make rehearsal in theater. She leave the same day"; and he chuckled.

It must have been the discussion of *Boris Godunov* that reminded him of Chaliapin. "We ask him, but he will not sing at La Scala. After I am gone he sing there"—this with another chuckle. "He sing in first *Mefistofele*. When I hear him in *Mefistofele* later I would not speak to him. But later I hear him in first *Boris* in Paris, and I go to him and say I must embrace him."

And it may have been on this occasion that he told me the story of his first orchestral concert in Turin, to show that "Toscanini was always Toscanini. I make rehearsal in pit; then I say I must have rehearsal on stage because in concert orchestra will play on stage. Manager say is not necessary; I say I will not conduct concert. This man was like father to me; but when is time for concert I am in bed. Manager come to hotel; but I stay in bed." And so the concert was given only after Toscanini had had his rehearsal on stage.

He remembered that I had written him about a photograph—one of him rehearsing with the Philadelphia Orchestra—which Mason Jones, the great first horn of the orchestra, had asked me to take to Toscanini to be autographed. I had brought it with me and gave it to Toscanini, who examined it closely, compared it with one on the piano, and then said: "È *bella*," which was true. He now addressed himself to what turned out to be the formidable operation of autographing it—which is to say that first he had to find the bottle of white ink, then the pen, and then he began to

make stroke after stroke of the inscription with an intensity
that was awesome, revealing, and moving.

I said there had always been a great mystery about his
leaving the Metropolitan in 1915, and asked him if he would
tell me why he left. "I could be millionaire," he said, "but
I am somebody who could say no. In 1915 I find impossible to stay in Metropolitan: is no discipline. With me, yes;
but with other conductors, no. I say to Gatti-Casazza: 'You
need position; you stay. I do not need to stay; I go.' Later
Otto Kahn come to me: 'Maestro, what I hear? Is impossible
to believe you leave Metropolitan.' I say: 'When are performances of *Un Ballo in Maschera* and we must have
five musicians to play on stage you say why we do not
take five musicians from orchestra. I know: they tell me.
In this theater I cannot work.' I go to Italy. In Milan I
give concert for charity: I invite all musicians and singers
for nothing; and Mr. Kahn send $1,000, but I do not an-
swer him. For five years I conduct for charity and do not
make a penny. After war they ask me to come back to
La Scala. I do not want to go; but they say I must. I begin
with five operas; next year twelve; and I conduct ninety
performances in season. Then other conductors conduct
more and more, and I conduct only fifty performances.
Then I feel I cannot take responsibility for season, and I
resign."

He described the system of rehearsal: the productions
of the first year required only one or two rehearsals the
second year; and rehearsal time went to the new productions. "At Metropolitan when I repeat *Götterdämmerung*
second year I have only [two?] rehearsals."

Toscanini's reference to Mahler as "crazy man" is the last comment of his about another conductor that I recall; and with the record of my experience in this matter all in I will say what I have concluded about it. It has been alleged that Toscanini spoke only ill of other conductors, and that this was evidence of the jealousy that showed itself further in his treatment of some of the eminences who were associated with him—notably Stokowski, Bruno Walter, Mengelberg. But in my experience Toscanini did *not* speak only ill of other conductors: he spoke well of Ansermet, whose enormous success with the press and the public should on the contrary have aroused the jealousy attributed to him; he spoke with especial warmth of Schuch, the one-time director of the Dresden Opera; he spoke of Nikisch as a good conductor, but criticized him for his occasional insufficient study of the score and for the acting on the podium that others have told me Nikisch indulged in; similarly he spoke well of De Sabata but disapprovingly of his violent gesticulation. And here we come to the point of the matter: in my experience, whenever Toscanini spoke ill of a conductor he did so on the basis of something the conductor had done that seemed to Toscanini dreadfully, shockingly, intolerably wrong. With Muck and certain others it was their wrong tempos; with A—— it was the achieving of excitement by whipping up tempo; with Koussevitzky it was the musical ignorance exemplified by, among other things, the failure to interpolate a cadenza where it was indicated in the score.

Concerning Stokowski and Walter at NBC I can report no statement by Toscanini; but in the spring of 1943 one of the serious musicians in the orchestra told me repeatedly about Stokowski's "line" of the moment, which was to exhort the orchestra not to be bound by the printed score, but instead to be creative, to improvise. This musician and others in the orchestra took Stokowski's "line" to be directed against Toscanini's principle of strict adherence to the printed score; and its consequence in practice was that the orchestra played with less than the absolute technical precision Toscanini demanded of it. For Toscanini, then, Stokowski was someone who not only advocated the violation of a principle Toscanini believed in, but, as a result, did not hold the orchestra to what Toscanini regarded as the proper technical standards.

Something of the same kind happened with Bruno Walter. In Salzburg in 1937 the American composer and conductor Hermann Hans Wetzler reported to me Toscanini's remark to him: "When Walter comes to something beautiful he melts. I suffer!" Nothing more perceptive was ever said about Walter; but it didn't keep Toscanini and Walter from being professionally associated for several seasons in Salzburg and from being warm personal friends, or keep Toscanini from inviting Walter to conduct the NBC Symphony. What ended all this, I was told at the time, was that during one of the periods when Walter was conducting the NBC Symphony in the broadcasts, Toscanini had to rehearse it for a concert in Newark, and was enraged by the technically unprecise playing, for which he held Walter responsible.

As for Mengelberg, his musical distortions and vulgarities must have been extremely distasteful to Toscanini; but his departure from the New York Philharmonic, I was told at the time, resulted from his talking against Toscanini to the orchestra, which caused Toscanini to request the Philharmonic to choose between Mengelberg and himself.

And as for Mahler, the Toscanini remark I have quoted must surely have had additional musical causes beside Mahler's treatment of the appoggiatura; but it also characterized Mahler as a person; and all accounts describe Mahler as a morbidly unhappy, tormented and "difficult" man, whose behavior might have seemed "crazy" to Toscanini.

When I visited Toscanini late in October 1949, I found him playing an NBC recording of a broadcast of the *Love Scene* from Berlioz's *Romeo and Juliet*. He was to broadcast the piece that week; also, Leonard Bernstein, who was going to conduct excerpts from *Romeo* that season, had come up the day before to ask Toscanini about his tempo in the Victor performance of the *Love Scene*; and they had compared the Victor *Love Scene* with the one from the 1947 broadcast of the entire work, and had found that the Victor was in fact faster. "I say is possible one day I am stupid," said Toscanini, who told me that in addition to playing the usual instrumental excerpts Bernstein was going to end with *Romeo in the Vault of the Capulets*. "I say is impossible to finish concert with *piano*; but he want to play this piece." And possibly it gave Toscanini the idea of playing it too; for a little later he said: "I will play all *Romeo and Juliet* next year again, because I am the only one who conduct this work." It was in this accidental way that works were suggested to him for performance; and it wasn't surprising, therefore, that in the end they weren't performed—as Berlioz's *Romeo* wasn't the following year.

Later in the fall Toscanini broadcast Beethoven's *Eroica* again, presumably in order that he might record it for Victor. All through 1948–49, someone at Victor told me, the company hadn't approached Toscanini about recording, having concerned itself with Horowitz, Heifetz, Rubinstein, Iturbi, Mario Lanza and other greats. And so some of the outstanding performances of that year—including the *Eroica* and Schubert *Unfinished* of the spring series—had not been recorded. This had led me, in May, to write a letter of protest to David Sarnoff, president of RCA, who had replied that the *Eroica* would be recorded before Toscanini's departure for Europe. Unfortunately Toscanini had then slipped in the bathtub, injuring his arm; and the recording sessions had therefore been canceled. And so it was in November that Victor recorded an *Eroica* of less intensity and power than the one of the preceding February, though impressively powerful considered by itself.

Still later there was a rehearsal of the Prelude to *Parsifal* which caused one of the men in the orchestra to exclaim afterward that nobody but Toscanini could have conducted the piece beating not the usual eight but a slow four to the measure—a subtly inflected four that was hair-raising in the sustained power with which it filled out the intervals of time with life and continuity in the flow of the sound. (In April 1954, at the first rehearsal for his tragic final broadcast, he would attempt something similar with the Prelude to *Lohengrin*, and not be able to bring it off.)

During a few rehearsals in the spring series, for the first and only times, I stood behind the percussion section in the passageway between the stage of Studio 8H and an unused control room, from where I could see Toscanini's face—attentive, alert, apprehensively watchful in all directions—as he marshaled the playing along. And observing him in operation in this way I noticed one thing more. I had been aware of the cohesive tension in the musical progression forward; now I became aware of the lateral tension which held the ninety-odd players in precisely right relation to each other, and the strands of continuing sound in the precise balance that produced the transparency of texture characteristic of his performances.

A few moments of one of these rehearsals that I had occasion to describe at the time may be of interest. Winthrop Sargeant, then a writer for *Life,* had described, in *Time-Life* style, how a rehearsal began: "Toscanini glances quickly over the assembled orchestra and, without further preamble, the baton descends like the knife of a guillotine." And Sargeant had also contended that Toscanini didn't use with an orchestra the explanatory technique of other conductors—that where they "will describe what they wish to obtain and the method to be pursued in achieving it, Toscanini will produce the effect . . . by setting up in the player's consciousness an emotional reaction which automatically produces it." Among the rehearsals I attended from 1942 on there were some at which Toscanini said good morning or afternoon, waited for the orchestra to become still and attentive, and "without further preamble" began to conduct. But more often I saw him do what he did on March 2, 1950, when, after his good morning, he picked up the score of Tchaikovsky's *Pathétique*, found the fourth measure after letter M in the third movement, explained to the flutes and clarinets that in this measure he wanted them to break off the held G-sharp in order to attack the subsequent descending scale with an accent, and had them do this for him several times; then found the similar measure at letter Z and had the strings and woodwinds play it in the same way; then began to conduct the movement from the beginning, but stopped after the second measure because the strings had not been precisely together, began again, stopped again, and told the violas: "You make the bow jump too high," illustrating by bouncing his baton on his finger; then began again and—the violas now being precisely together with the violins—went on, but stopped after the third measure to tell the oboes and bassoons they were not playing an accurate two against the other woodwinds' three, and got this measure played correctly; and so on thereafter. And I don't recall a rehearsal without its explanations and discussions with the first-desk string-players of methods of bowing that would produce the phrasing or accentuation or lack of accentuation Toscanini wanted. *

A few weeks after this rehearsal of the *Pathétique* an amusing incident occurred during a rehearsal of the second

---

* But Marsh—on the basis of experience unknown to me—writes, in *Toscanini and the Art of Orchestral Performance*, that unlike Rodzinski, whose knowledge of English made him "able to analyze difficulties and tell the men how to cope with them," Toscanini had an orchestra "simply [play] for many minutes at a time, going over works again and again until [he] was satisfied."

movement of Debussy's *Ibéria*. In the eighth measure the horn plays a motif which rises to D-sharp; two measures later the cellos mutter the same motif, but with D-natural instead of D-sharp; and on this occasion when the horn played the D-sharp Toscanini stopped, told the player he should have played D-natural, and began the movement again. This time again the horn played D-sharp; and again Toscanini stopped and told the player he should have played D-natural, and began the movement a third time. By now the atmosphere was tense; and when the horn played D-sharp again I was prepared for an explosion—instead of which Toscanini continued to conduct without a word: he had evidently remembered that it was D-natural for the cellos but D-sharp for the horn.

The spring series ended with the performance, on April 1 and 8, of *Falstaff*. From the way Toscanini spoke of this opera it seemed to be the one he cared about most; his performance of it had been one of his most famous achievements; and this one too was dazzlingly and enchantingly swift and light and clear. It is one of the performances in which some critics have reported hearing inexpressive singing that betrays the singers' inexperience in their parts and their terror of Toscanini; but listening to it again after a few years, when it was issued in Victor LM-6111, confirmed my original impression of the excellent singing of the entire cast except the tenor who sang Fenton, and made me freshly aware of the beauty and expressive inflection and coloring of Valdengo's singing, the powerful dramatic projection of Cloe Elmo, the technical and musical security of Teresa Stich-Randall's use of her exquisite lyric soprano. It was possible to argue that a weightier voice than Valdengo's would have been even better for Falstaff, and a less youthful one than Guarerra's better for Ford; but not to say, as one critic did, that the performance was accurate but had very little more to recommend it.

And *Falstaff* was followed by the transcontinental tour which began with the concert in New York's Carnegie Hall on April 14 and ended with the one in Philadelphia's Academy of Music on May 27. During this season the years of work under Toscanini had begun to be audible in the orchestra's playing, as the men themselves realized: "You know," I heard one of them exclaim, "we're beginning to sound like a symphony orchestra!" And the truth of this statement was demonstrated right at the start of the New York concert—in the performance of Rossini's Overture to *L'Italiana in Algeri,* which had a precision and finish, a refinement of tone and subtlety of nuance, a sensitiveness to Toscanini's direction, that made it possible to think one was hearing the Philharmonic in 1936. However the performances at this concert—including the Beethoven *Eroica* and Debussy *La Mer*—didn't reach the heights of the ones at later concerts, after the weeks in which Toscanini and the orchestra continued to rehearse and play the works they had prepared for the tour. I was told of an especially wonderful *Eroica* in Pasadena; and at the final concert in Philadelphia I heard a *La Mer* that was phenomenal as a realization of the piece, as an exhibition of virtuoso orchestral performance, and in the relaxed ease with which conductor and orchestra operated. The NBC Symphony had become one of the world's great orchestras; and it remained that to the end.

That year a collection of my *Nation* articles had been published under the title *Music in the Nation;* and when a copy was sent to Toscanini I wrote him that he was to consider this book too as dedicated to him. I had a telephone call from him, in the course of which he said he had been reading the book: "What you say about me is too much. But why is not inscribed?" I explained that the copy he had received had come from the publisher, and that I was inscribing to him a special leather-bound copy which the publisher had given me. And when I sent it to him I said I had been thinking of what he might do now with the first copy of the trade edition, and it had occurred to me that he might inscribe it to me.

I didn't see him that spring until the day he was to leave on the tour, which I believe was Easter Sunday. I had volunteered to Walter Toscanini to put into order, while his father was away, the 16-inch acetate records of the NBC broadcasts, some of which were in a closet next to Toscanini's study, and the rest piled high in complete disorder everywhere in the room. And on this Sunday morning I went up to discuss with Walter how the job was to be done. While I was talking to him and to the secretary, Miss Eugenia Gale, in the study, Toscanini appeared—not in his usual sober black, but very natty in light gray trousers, gray shirt, and tan shoes with gray cloth tops.

"Did you hear *Falstaff?*" he asked, his face lighting up.
"Yes, it was very beautiful," I answered.

"Ah," he said, "for me is *most* beautiful opera!"

At this moment a messenger delivered a parcel of test
pressings on which Victor wanted his approval before he
left. "Yes," said Toscanini, "I want to hear. Find G-minor:
I want to hear finale." Walter found the record and began to play it; but Toscanini interrupted: "They change
machine; *allóra* is different sound and I cannot hear." So
we moved to his bedroom, which now had the equipment
he was accustomed to. The room was in a state of great
disorder and commotion with preparations for the trip;
nevertheless the record was played; and as we stood listening I noticed the two copies of my book on a table. After
the finale Toscanini asked for another record of the G-
minor, which couldn't be found; then he remembered
wanting to hear the first movement of Schubert's *Unfinished,* "because first time oboe play too loud: must be
piano and is *forte.*" The record was found and played;
Toscanini stood conducting and listening intently, and
pointed as the oboe began its first statement *forte*; and
when the oboe played the repetition of the statement *piano*
he pointed again and said: "So is correct—*piano*. I want
to hear second time"—meaning the second take, which
couldn't be found.

The playing of test pressings ended, Walter and I returned to the study to resume our discussion of what to
do with the NBC records. After a short time Toscanini
reappeared, holding in his hand the first copy of my book.
Handing it to me with a trace of a smile, but saying noth-

ing, he again left the room. And when I opened the book to the first blank page I saw that he had originally written his name diagonally across it, and had now added below his name an inscription to the author of the book who, he wrote, had made him blush many times as he had read it.

I saw Toscanini again a few days after the final concert of the tour in Philadelphia. I had written him enthusiastically about the *La Mer,* and had reproached him for the terrible thing he had done to me by playing Brahms's First in place of the Fourth that had been announced. And I went up to Riverdale to report to Walter Toscanini what had been accomplished with the NBC records. I hadn't been able to complete the job, and continued with it after Toscanini left for Italy; and I found not only some of the wartime glass-based acetates broken, but a large number of records in varying states of deterioration caused by the sulphuric acid in the paper of the envelopes. It was this deterioration that led Walter Toscanini to transfer all his father's recordings from disc to tape; and unfortunately the first Victor engineer who did the work for him had ideas about beefing up Toscanini's Victor recordings with echo chamber and peaking of treble, and seems to have been able to persuade Toscanini to substitute his in some instances monstrously falsified "enhanced" versions for the originals.

When I walked into the office on the top floor I found Miss Gale and a man checking the names on the photographs (amusing ones of Toscanini seated in the ski lift at Sun Valley) that Toscanini had inscribed to the members of the orchestra in remembrance of the tour. As I stood talking to Walter Toscanini his father entered the room, and with barely a nod to the visitor whom his nearsighted eyes didn't recognize he addressed himself to Miss Gale. But at that moment he heard and recognized my voice; and with a smile he came over to shake hands with me.

"I will tell you why I play Brahms First in Philadelphia. Somebody ask for Brahms Fourth in Washington; *allóra* I play First in Philadelphia. But why you do not like First? Is beautiful music. Of course Fourth is better—finale has wonderful harmony [I think that by 'harmony' Toscanini meant writing for winds]. But First is beautiful too. You write once—a word—'bombastic'! But no-o-o!" I said it was the first movement that I found bombastic. "Oh no-o-o! Is beautiful!" And the second movement I found excessively sentimental. "Oh no-o-o! When is played too slow, yes; but in right tempo is beautiful! And Third Symphony——" I said I didn't like the third movement of this one. "Oh no-o-o! In right tempo is beautiful!" And he demonstrated by singing it to me, as everyone in the room grinned.

"Brahms's symphonies," Toscanini went on, "are first after Beethoven. Schumann? You like Fourth, but——" and he caricatured the principal theme of the first movement. I reminded him of the slow movement. "Yes, is beautiful, but——" and again he caricatured the first movement. "I play only one symphony of Schumann, the—the——" "The Third?" I suggested. "Yes, the Third. And Second has beautiful Andante, but——" and he caricatured the first movement. "Schumann: no! Schubert? Is not like Mozart, who write too easy—without work. (Beethoven: you can hear how he worked!) But no harmony." [One would suppose he said Schubert *was* like Mozart in the ease of his writing; but I have given what my notes have. His thought on Schubert isn't clear, especially from a man who played the C-major Symphony at his very first orchestral concert and so many times thereafter.] Mendelssohn? No. *Italian* Symphony? I object as Italian to saltarello finale. When I play cello I play once in E-flat Quartet, and I hear is weak: I never play Mendelssohn again—until I hear movement with theme like *Parsifal*——" "The *Reformation* Symphony?" "Yes, *Reformation* Symphony."

Later, "Tonight I record *La Mer*. And tomorrow Brahms Fourth, because in Washington orchestra play beautifully, and I think this performance should be recorded." "Yes," I said, "but the performance of *Ibéria* is more important to record." "Ye-e-es; but I want to record Brahms Fourth because orchestra play so beautifully." "Yes," I persisted, "but *Ibéria*." He also persisted; and this impasse too was not resolved.

"After tour," he said, "I am not tired. But for one broadcast I am tired. Three rehearsals and one broadcast I am more tired as six weeks of tour." This led to a discussion of the reason I mentioned earlier in this book: the tension of the first public performance at the broadcast, as against the relaxed feeling with the repetitions after a first performance.

At this point Miss Gale told him he would have to inscribe three more photographs, and gave him the names. With a rueful smile he said: "After writing so much I *am* tired." I said I had brought along a photograph which I liked especially, and I wondered whether he would agree. He watched with interest as I extracted from the envelope a photograph of him at a rehearsal, demonstrating something to the cellists, with his left hand holding his baton as though it were a cello and his right hand holding an imaginary bow. "Oh ye-e-es," he said. "I remember this. Where is it?" "It must be either Vienna or Salzburg," I said. "Yes, Vienna or Salzburg." "I wonder if you would be kind enough to sign it for me." He didn't answer but merely took the photograph from me and left the room. I resumed my conversation with Walter; and after some time Toscanini reappeared, holding the photograph in his hand and exclaiming: "I look everywhere—in letters—in books—in telephone book —everywhere, but I cannot find your first name!" So he had inscribed it to B. H. Haggin.

Again he left the room; and a little later he reappeared with a paper which he gave to Miss Gale and discussed with her briefly. Then, as he turned from her he said with a smile and a shrug: "I am supposed to have bad character." Another shrug: "Is not true—but they say." And he left.

That night I went to the recording session in Studio 8H. This was the first reassembling of the orchestra since the tour; and so there was a happy atmosphere in the place and much excited talk. The performance of *La Mer* that was recorded was the phenomenal one I had heard in Philadelphia a few days before, but with its sound in the Academy of Music now altered in Studio 8H. I didn't stay for the recording of Saint-Saëns's *Danse Macabre,* but went again the next night for the recording of Brahms's Fourth, and was dumbfounded when I was told that not Brahms's Fourth was to be recorded—but Debussy's *Ibéria!*

When the first movement had been recorded a break was announced for playback. There was a delay; and Toscanini left the studio, while the men of the orchestra drifted off the stage and stood around on the floor in groups. Then the playback began; and it had proceeded for only a few measures when Toscanini came rushing into the studio in great agitation, gesticulating with his right arm in protest, and exclaiming: "Is wrong tempo! Machine play too slow!" Actually he had played the movement in a delightfully lilting tempo which—I was assured by members of the orchestra—was the one in which he had played it the several times on the tour; but listening from the outside of the performance, so to speak, he had now found it too slow. The orchestra was quickly reassembled and rehearsed in a faster tempo; the movement was then recorded a second time; and this performance satisfied him. And the intense feeling about playing too slowly continued—not only for the recording of the rest of *Ibéria,* but for the remaking of the first movement of Schubert's *Unfinished.*

My meeting with Toscanini the day before left me with every reason to suppose I would see him again in the fall; but my letters the next year brought no answering telephone call or invitation to visit him, and for reasons that remained undisclosed to me I never had an opportunity to speak to him again. There was the possibility that something I wrote angered him; but this seemed improbable when I received one of the Christmas cards he sent out from Italy the year after his retirement. On one page was a photograph of

Toscanini looking at an opened score with a photograph of Verdi nearby, and reproduced underneath this the theme of the closing fugue of *Falstaff* with the words *Tutto nel mondo è burla l'uom è* copied by Toscanini; and reproduced on the opposite page was his handwritten Christmas and New Year greeting, signature and date.

ADDENDA

REHEARSALS AND
PERFORMANCES OF
THE LAST YEARS

Though I had no further meetings with Toscanini I continued to attend rehearsals. He was inactive in the fall of 1950, for reasons which were at first reported to be anger at the transfer of the broadcasts from Studio 8H (which NBC had converted into a television studio) to Carnegie Hall, and from Saturday at six-thirty to Monday at ten, and which were later reported to be trouble with a knee. I cannot say whether these reports were correct; but I can say why they were believable. The men of the orchestra told me they hated Studio 8H because they couldn't hear each other; and one of the pleasures of the tour had been the experiences of playing in several fine auditoriums in which they said they had heard details in performances that they had never heard before. But Toscanini, they said, liked Studio 8H because standing on the podium *he* could hear everything very clearly. In addition, I was told, he felt that just as Carnegie Hall was the Philharmonic's place, 8H was *his* place; and I remember hearing about recording sessions scheduled for Carnegie Hall which at the last minute he insisted on transferring to 8H. These were the reasons I knew about that may have caused him to object to the move to Carnegie Hall, which one would have expected him to welcome since it was so good for the broadcasts. Monday at ten also was better for them than Saturday at six-thirty: it was a time when music-lovers were free to listen not only in the East but in other parts of the country where it was nine and eight (if, that is, the broadcasts were carried live). But we have seen that when NBC sold the Sunday-at-five spot it convinced Toscanini that more people listened Saturday at six-thirty; and he now insisted on NBC's moving the broadcasts back to that time. As for the knee trouble, there was visible evidence of it when he did resume conducting—in the fact that his left hand frequently grasped the railing around the podium, presumably to relieve the strain on the left knee.

Toscanini may have been unhappy in Carnegie Hall, but for the orchestra and the listener the place was a pleasure. I retain in my memory the beautiful sound of Beethoven's Fourth at the rehearsals for the performance of February 3, 1951—in particular the silken, luminous sound of the violins; and my reason for remembering it is that on this occasion the performance had to be broadcast from a tape which transmitted a muffled falsification of the sound I had heard, and which was the source of the recording later issued by Victor.

I remember also certain rehearsals in the fall. Toscanini returned from Italy with his knee trouble gone, his powers operating with amazing energy; and the virtuosity of the orchestra and its sensitiveness to his direction made possi-

ble an almost casual achievement of the magic that is
so difficult to achieve in Berlioz's *Queen Mab*. They
also made it possible for even first readings to exhibit
the precision and tonal beauty that I remember hearing
at the first rehearsal of Dvořák's Symphonic Variations;
and at the first rehearsal of the Prelude to Act 3 of *Die
Meistersinger* the integrated sound of the brass section,
plastically shaped and sensitively inflected like the sound
of one instrument, took my breath away.

And yet when the performance of Rossini's *Semiramide*
Overture recorded by Victor in the fall of 1951 was issued
a few years later and was compared with the 1936 Philharmonic performance, it was astonishing to hear the NBC
Symphony's playing—seemingly unsurpassable—surpassed
right at the start, in the slow introduction, by the subtleties
of attack, inflection and coloring of the Philharmonic horns,
and later, in the Allegro, by the energy of the Philharmonic
violins in their soft opening statements, the sensitized response of the full orchestra. Nor was this all. Nothing,
seemingly, could be more effective than the pacing and
shaping of the piece in the 1951 performance; and so it
was astonishing to hear how much more effective the Philharmonic performance of the introduction was with its
relaxed expansiveness involving great elasticity of tempo,
than the NBC Symphony performance with its faster,
tighter simplicity involving only slight modifications of
tempo. But the most striking and significant difference occurred at the point in the Allegro where the long concluding crescendo of the exposition breaks off for the series of
violin statements leading to the recapitulation: in the 1951

performance these violin statements were inflected not only without the breadth but without the force and sustained tension they had in the 1936 performance, revealing once again the lessened energy that had manifested itself a couple of times before—in the V-J Day *Eroica* when it was compared with the 1944 performance; in the 1948 Strauss *Don Quixote* when it was compared with the 1938 performance. And let me emphasize that such occasional lessened powers and effectiveness in the later years were something one became aware of only when the performance was compared with an earlier one. If one listened to the 1951 Verdi *Requiem* or the 1953 Beethoven *Missa Solemnis* without comparing it with the 1940 *Requiem* or *Missa,* one was aware only of phenomenal powers operating to produce a performance that was wonderfully right, effective and beautiful, and playing by the orchestra that was something to marvel at.

Nor did the later performance always reveal lessened powers and effectiveness when compared with the earlier ones: the opposite also happened on occasion, as the performance of the *Tristan* Prelude and Finale that Toscanini recorded early in 1952 demonstrates. For more than thirty years we have been able to get an idea of the Toscanini *Tristan* that Carl Van Vechten called overwhelming only from Toscanini's performances of the Prelude and Finale. I recall that the performance of these two excerpts was in fact overwhelming the first time in 1926; it was overwhelming each of the numerous times thereafter; and most overwhelming, it seems to me, is the performance that comes off LM-6020. For comparison of this performance with

earlier ones preserved on records reveals that the performance changed in the course of time, and that the change
was of an unusual kind: whereas tempos generally tended
to become faster in Toscanini's later performances, in
the *Tristan* Prelude and Finale they became much slower,
giving the music increased expressive force. I retained from
the first performance in 1926 a recollection of a marked
and exciting acceleration in the Prelude soon after the direction *Belebend* in the score; and this is confirmed by
the records with the performance broadcast in 1938, the
one recorded in 1942, the one at the Red Cross concert in
1944: in these performances the Prelude, after the intro-
ductory statements, proceeds with great slowness and weight,
with powerful inflection and tension of phrase, with tremendous expressive force, until in the eleventh measure after
Belebend it begins to accelerate rapidly to a much faster
tempo in which it continues thereafter in exciting fashion,
broadening out momentarily for the climax of the *meno
forte* passage, then resuming its rapid course in the final
crescendo, and broadening out again in the last two measures of this crescendo for the climax of the piece. But in
1952 the acceleration after *Belebend* is slight, so that the
piece continues with slowness, breadth and powerful inflection—which is to say with more powerful expressive effect than in 1938—broadening out tremendously at the climax of the *meno forte* passage, then resuming its slow and
powerful course in the final crescendo, and broadening out
even more tremendously for the climax of the piece. And
the 1952 Finale also is enormously slower than the one of
1938—with, consequently, more breadth and power, and

with increased expressive effect of exaltation and trans-figuration.

These changes—and others concerned with smaller de-tails—are not only fascinating in themselves but moving in what they tell us about Toscanini. The *Tristan* piece was one of those Toscanini played most; but even after many performances his mind continued to work at it, to change it for increased esthetic and expressive effect; and the next performance, down to the last, was not a perfunctory routine act but a fresh application of attention and energy. *

Fascinating and moving in the same ways are the changes in the great performance of Schubert's C-major early in

* But Marsh, in *Toscanini and the Art of Orchestral Performance*, writes concerning the *Tristan* performance in LM-6020: "In Alma Mahler's biography of her husband, we learn of Mahler's misgiv-ings about Toscanini's performances of *Tristan*...I share Mahler's reservations. The performance (there is no reason to believe it has changed in the intervening years) is over-refined, the antiseptic souvenir of passion rather than its full-blooded actuality. In *Tris-tan* this will not do, although it is easily understood when we see that these two works rank fourth and fifth in frequency in Toscanini's repertory: they have had all the life played out of them." But Marsh, intent on associating himself with Mahler, pays too little attention to what Alma Mahler actually says about the Tos-canini *Tristan* of 1909—that "the nuances in his Wagner were dis-tressing. His style has been simplified since those days"; and he therefore doesn't perceive that in his disapproval of the "over-refined...antiseptic" Toscanini *Tristan* which he had invented he is not sharing *her* disapproval of the nuanced Toscanini *Tristan* she reports having heard in 1909, and is instead disagreeing with her evident approval of what she describes as Toscanini's simplified later style in Wagner. Nor does Marsh perceive that the disap-proval she reports is her own, not her husband's; and as it hap-pens, Bruno Walter, a more truthful witness than Alma, reported Mahler's telling him, after hearing Toscanini's *Tristan*, that al-though it was different from theirs it was very beautiful.

B.H.H.—1979

1953, recorded on LM-1835—the changes one discovers when one compares it with the great performance with the Philadelphia Orchestra in 1941. Toscanini played this work at his very first orchestral concert in 1896; and one would think that by 1941 his mind had achieved finality about it. But the changes in 1953 make it clear that he had continued to think about it, and in this thought to be concerned with an esthetic end—the esthetic beauty, for him, of a movement played in a single tempo with only slight modifications that are the more effective for the steadiness from which they depart. This single tempo in the Allegro of the first movement is—again in surprising reversal of his tendency toward faster tempos in later years—slower in 1953 than in 1941, and is accelerated only a little in the *Più moto* coda, which means that it has to slow down only a little for the concluding proclamations of the theme of the introduction. But for this satisfaction Toscanini sacrifices the greater momentum created by the faster 1941 tempo in the Allegro, and especially by its greater acceleration in the coda, where from measure 589 the canonic series of overlapping statements of winds, then violins, then low strings are bound together by the fast tempo into a single large-spanned utterance that is tremendously exciting. On the other hand, the single steady tempo in the finale is faster in 1953 than in 1941, with only a slight acceleration therefore in the coda, and only a slight broadening in the groups of four *sfz* unison C's. Thus the movement has all the momentum it has to have; but on the other hand the slightly more relaxed tempo in 1941 accelerates more in the coda, only to take one's breath away with the enormous slowing down and distention of the four unison C's, which creates each time a hair-raising tension that is released in the answering tutti in fast tempo again. Listening to the two performances one may decide that the earlier one was even greater than the later one; but one cannot fail to recognize that the later one was in its own way one of Toscanini's greatest.

And in the fall of 1953 there were other great performances—the wonderfully clarified Strauss *Don Quixote,* Berlioz *Harold in Italy* and Beethoven *Eroica,* and a Beethoven *Coriolan* Overture with breadth and distentions that gave it a power beyond any I recalled. I heard the rehearsals of *Don Quixote,* and still remember the orchestra's great first cellist, Frank Miller, seated out in front, grunting audibly (in the empty hall) with the effort of his huge body that produced playing extraordinary in its elegance of style as well as the tensile strength of its tone and the cohesive tension of its phrasing. But these rehearsals were my last: a letter from Walter Toscanini regretted having to inform me that nobody was to be allowed henceforth at the Thursday afternoon and Friday morning rehearsals, but that I would be on the list of guests invited to the Saturday afternoon dress rehearsal (the broadcasts had been moved to Sunday at six-thirty). He didn't say why; and it was not until late in the season that events suggested what the reason may have been.

After an interval of four years there was again, on January 17 and 24, 1954, a performance of an opera—Verdi's *Un Ballo in Maschera.* Concerning this it was no less con-

siderable a critic than Virgil Thomson who wrote that
the "almost circus-like showmanship" of the orchestra performance had made demands of volume and bravura which
the singers had been unable to meet, with the result that
in Carnegie Hall "they were pretty thoroughly overpowered" and "were obliged so consistently to force their
volume that much of the singing I did hear was both ugly
in sound and only approximate in pitch." I was in Carnegie
Hall too, and can testify that in some of the climaxes the
singers *were* overpowered by the orchestral tuttis that have
overpowered the singers in every performance everywhere,
but that in the more lightly scored passages at other times—
which is to say most of the time—the orchestral accompaniment was beautifully adjusted to the singing, whose every
piano reached me at the back of the hall without the
slightest forcing. If there were occasional unlovely vocal
sounds and deviations from pitch it was because Robert
Merrill's baritone had become rough and coarse and Herva
Nelli simply didn't always sing squarely on pitch.

This review, I might add, was typical of Thomson's performances with Toscanini. He was a brilliantly perceptive
critic when his mind operated on the real facts before him;
but there were occasions when it was concerned not with
real facts but with others that existed only in his head,
and when he applied to them general ideas with no more
basis in reality; and Toscanini's performances were such
occasions. It is anyone's privilege not to like a Toscanini
performance; but the performance and the reasons for dis-
liking it must be real. When some Germans objected to
the luminous clarity and grace of Toscanini's *Meistersinger*

or his Brahms as being unsuitable for music they contended called rather for breadth and solidity, they were applying understandable and valid criteria to correctly heard performances. But what Thomson did for almost fifteen years was to apply imaginary ideas to imaginary Toscanini performances. The *Ballo in Maschera* he objected to was largely imaginary; and an example of imaginary ideas was the business of the marriage of historical and literary with musical culture in the Great Tradition of Wagner, Von Bülow, Nikisch and Beecham that, according to Thomson, was lacking in Toscanini's conducting, but that I suspect was lacking also in Wagner's, Von Bülow's, Nikisch's and Beecham's. Toscanini's actual style of performance, which gave a piece of music plastically coherent shape, Thomson described with the term 'streamlining,' which was incorrect; and this term was part of numerous schematizations by pure invention—e.g., "when one memorizes everything, one acquires a great awareness of music's run-through. One runs it through in the mind constantly; and one finds in that way a streamlined rendering that is wholly independent of detail and even of specific significance, a disembodied version that is all shape and no texture. Later, in rehearsal, one returns to texture; and one takes care that it serve always as neutral surfacing for the shape. But shape is what any piece is always about that one has memorized through the eye and the inner ear." Actually, Toscanini away from the podium did not keep running through pieces of music in his mind, but kept reading them in the score, and in this constant study of the printed score was concerned always with texture—i.e., with this bassoon part or that viola part buried in the tutti that must be made clearly audible in the performance.

What Thomson started, others continued: I was told of one insignificant young commentator on the radio whose way of making himself appear big was to talk about Toscanini's lack of culture. The writing about Toscanini was always one of the forms of exploitation of him: formerly the way to show one's understanding was to praise him, today it is to find fault with him; and the attacks reveal as little understanding of the Toscanini operation and what it produced as did most of the praise.

It was interesting, one Sunday afternoon in March 1954, to listen to the broadcast of Cantelli's performance with the New York Philharmonic of the Mozart Divertimento K.287 that Toscanini had played, and to listen later in the day to the broadcast of Toscanini's performances of Verdi's *Te Deum* and Vivaldi's Concerto Grosso No. 11 from *L'Estro Armonico*. For the two broadcasts threw into sharp relief the difference between the two conductors. The relaxed flow in the fast movements of the Mozart piece had lyricism and grace, as against the powerful impulse that had operated in Toscanini's treatment of them; and to the Adagio also, which Cantelli made a beautifully shaped and eloquent vocal aria, Toscanini's power had imparted a largeness of span, a tension, a grandeur that had made its expressive effect overwhelming. And that power, creating a continuous tension in the flow of sound, and doing this in the quietest music no less than in the most forceful, was impressively evident in the lovely slow movement of the

Vivaldi concerto no less than in the Allegros and in the *Te Deum.*

One heard the power being exercised in those pieces on that Sunday—exercised to hold the members of the orchestra in precisely balanced relation to one another, and to keep every sound in the progression in coherent relation to the next. But the next Sunday one heard that the power was *not* being exercised in the performance of Tchaikovsky's *Pathétique,* in which there was no continuity of impetus and tension, and one sound was not in coherent relation to the next. When I asked a musician in the orchestra about this he confirmed my impression: "He was all there in the rehearsal, but not in the performance." And so there was this to prepare me for what happened at the first rehearsal for the final broadcast on April 4.

I heard all three rehearsals as they came over a line from Carnegie Hall. At the first one, on Thursday afternoon, Toscanini began with the Prelude to *Lohengrin,* and announced: "I will conduct *alla breve"*—meaning a slow two to the measure instead of the usual four. It will be recalled that he had done something similar in the Prelude to *Parsifal* four years earlier, beating instead of the usual eight to the measure a slow four with sustained power that had filled out the intervals of time in exciting fashion. A member of the orchestra had exclaimed on that occasion that nobody but Toscanini could have done this; but now at the rehearsal of the *Lohengrin* Prelude it became evident that even Toscanini no longer could do it: after a few measures there was discord and confusion, the playing stopped, and I heard an apprehensive murmur go through the orchestra. "I conduct *alla breve*," Toscanini repeated; and again the performance broke down in discord and confusion after a few measures, and I heard the murmur go through the orchestra. This time, as I recall it, Toscanini first demonstrated by singing the music as he beat time, then began again to conduct, but stopped to tell the violins to play the opening A-major chords without vibrato, which he said was suitable for *Inferno* but not for *Paradiso*. And I think the next time he began he was able to keep the performance going to the end.

When, some time later, I asked a musician in the orchestra about the breakdowns, he explained: "He didn't beat a two-to-the-measure that we could follow; and he himself began to follow our playing in four to the measure—which threw us off completely." Nor was this incident the only one of its kind that season. And so it suggested a possible reason for the decision not to allow anyone at rehearsals.

The *Lohengrin* Prelude was followed by the Prelude to *Die Meistersinger*; and I remember my surprise that Toscanini did nothing about the nerveless, poor playing. Then *Dawn and Rhine Journey* from *Die Götterdämmerung*, in which there were several stops for corrections that I don't remember, and one stop for something that was to have great importance two days later. The place was the entrance of the kettledrum in the passage immediately after the off-stage horn calls; and Toscanini contended that the timpanist had come in too soon. "It's the same part I always play," said the timpanist. "Maybe," said Toscanini. "All right, I'm always——" I didn't catch the timpanist's last word but presumed it was "wrong." Eventually the passage was played in the way Toscanini considered correct, and the piece was completed.

My notes for the rehearsal on Friday morning have "power all there" next to the Overture and Bacchanale of *Tannhäuser*, and again next to the *Götterdämmerung* piece; and that suffices to describe the different playing I heard that morning. There was one stop in the *Rhine Journey*, but not at the point where the trouble with the kettledrum had occurred the day before.

And so we come to Saturday afternoon's dramatic dress rehearsal. Power was all there again in the performances of the *Lohengrin* Prelude, the *Forest Murmurs* from *Siegfried*, and the *Götterdämmerung* piece as far as Toscanini got in it. My notes record his stopping at one point in the *Dawn* portion and shouting: "Staccato! Staccato! *Ignoranti, tutti!*" And they record his stopping in a fury at the point where the trouble with the kettledrum had occurred two days before. While Toscanini raged I heard Frank Miller call out to the timpanist: "Make it thirteen measures' rest instead of twelve." Twelve was right, and the timpanist had waited that number of measures; but Toscanini mistakenly thought it should be one more; and Miller was telling the timpanist to do what would seem right to Toscanini. "*È vergógna! Vergógna!*"* he shouted. And when the passage was repeated, as he thought, correctly, he stopped again and exclaimed: "*Finalmente!*" Then, in bitter anger: "*L'ultima prova!*" ** There were long moments of silence;

* "It's a shame! A shame!"
** "The last rehearsal!"

then I heard a murmur in the orchestra which told me something had happened; and when it swelled into conversation I realized that Toscanini was no longer on the podium. I heard a voice from a loud-speaker in Carnegie Hall announce the end of the rehearsal and ask the audience to leave but instruct the orchestra to remain on the stage. Time passed; then I heard the voice from the speaker again, this time dismissing the orchestra. The rehearsal was not completed.

To my ears, as I listened to the broadcast the next day, power was not exercised in the performances of the *Lohengrin* Prelude, the *Siegfried* excerpt, the *Götterdämmerung* piece, and the *Tannhäuser* Overture and Bacchanale. Nevertheless, when the climax of the Bacchanale had subsided into the quiet concluding section, I was unprepared for the shock of hearing the discordant evidence of instruments making wrong entrances. It lasted only a couple of moments; but it created an apprehensiveness about what was happening in Carnegie Hall; and these fears were seemingly confirmed when the performance suddenly was cut off, the voice of Ben Grauer announced that "technical difficulties" had necessitated an interruption of the broadcast, and a recorded performance of Brahms's First Symphony came over the air. I had witnessed the inconceivable: a Toscanini performance that had broken down. But suddenly the Brahms stopped and I was hearing the conclusion of the Bacchanale, which apparently had *not* broken down. The piece ended, was applauded, and was followed by a nerveless playing of the notes of the *Meistersinger* Prelude, which concluded the broadcast.

From musicians in the orchestra I learned some of the things that had happened in Carnegie Hall. As early as the *Forest Murmurs* Toscanini had failed to beat a couple of changes of time signature, but with no bad consequences because the orchestra had played correctly. In the Bacchanale, when the orchestra had become aware that he was no longer conducting—his face showing his mind not to be in contact with the performance, his right arm gradually dropping to his side, his left hand covering his eyes—it had managed to keep going past the few wrong entrances, playing correctly after that; and Toscanini had begun to beat time again. Then, in the *Meistersinger* Prelude he had seemed to summon all his strength in the grim determination to beat time through the piece; and he had accomplished this, but not the conducting of a musical performance. (Actually he did not beat time to the very end of the piece, but was already off the podium when the orchestra was playing the final chords.) And through other sources it became known that when Toscanini had stopped conducting in the Bacchanale, Cantelli, in the control booth, had lost his head and insisted on the performance being taken off the air.

It seemed clear that at this tragic broadcast Toscanini had suffered a recurrence of the failing of his powers that had manifested itself now and then during that season. But it is possible that the failing this time was caused by the emotional strain he was under, which may also have been responsible for the happenings at the dress rehearsal the day before. One source of the strain was of course the fact that this was the end—the last rehearsal, the last broadcast;

another was the heart attack suffered by Mrs. Walter Toscanini, whom Toscanini was very fond of. Emotional strain, or lessened strength, or both were evident in the signature—formerly sharply energetic, now wavering, blurred, unclear—on his letter of resignation, which NBC sent out in facsimile with David Sarnoff's reply. It was reported that throughout the day of the broadcast Toscanini had been undecided whether to conduct the concert; and it would have been better if he had not conducted it.

Two eyewitnesses have given different and astonishingly incorrect accounts of the happenings of those last two days. Vincent Sheean, in *First and Last Love* (Random House, 1956), has it that Toscanini at the broadcast broke down at precisely the point in the Bacchanale at which he had ended the rehearsal the day before—when in fact he didn't conduct the Bacchanale at all at the dress rehearsal. And Chotzinoff, in *Toscanini: An Intimate Portrait,* writes concerning the performance of the Bacchanale that the anxieties Toscanini had aroused before the broadcast were "routed" by what he observed from the control room—"the powerful gyrations of his baton, the mystic behavior of his left hand, and the subtle conspiratorial expressions of his eyes and lips." But then, says Chotzinoff, Toscanini faltered, and the orchestra "tried desperately to coalesce and reach the end in unity . . . The attempt, beset by self-consciousness and fear, was a failure. In the soft cacophony that ensued, the Maestro ceased conducting and put his hand to his eyes. The men stopped playing and the house was engulfed in terrible silence . . ." The facts are that the orchestra

continued to play and succeeded in finishing the Bacchanale, after which the hall was filled by the audience's
applause.

This is not the only instance of inaccuracy in Chotzinoff's
book. Telling how in November 1937 Toscanini cabled
from Italy a request to be released from his contract because he had received a report that the high cost of the
new orchestra and its conductor was causing some NBC
employees to lose their jobs, Chotzinoff writes: "I wired
that, far from causing one man to lose his job at NBC,
his engagement had led the company to take on, besides a
full symphony orchestra, a number of people to meet the
increased demands of the engineering, publicity, and press
departments." Actually NBC did not take on a full symphony orchestra for Toscanini in addition to its staff orchestra: what it took on was a number of replacements
and additions for the group that was set up within that
staff orchestra as the NBC Symphony. (Moreover the staff
men who were replaced presumably did lose their jobs.)

Nor is such inaccuracy all that can be objected to in
the book. Its stories about Toscanini's inconsiderate or bad-
tempered treatment of the people around him may be more
accurate than Chotzinoff's account of the breakdown of
the performance of the *Tannhäuser* Bacchanale and the
silence in Carnegie Hall at the final broadcast; but whereas
other reviewers of the book found the stories damaging to
Toscanini, I find them damaging also to Chotzinoff. That
is, I don't think it was admirable of Chotzinoff to accept

mistreatment he didn't have to accept, and later, with Toscanini still alive, to reveal this mistreatment to the world and
thus violate the privacy that Toscanini had expected a friend
to preserve.

THE BROADCASTS
AND RECORDINGS

Replying on March 29, 1954, to Toscanini's letter of resignation, David Sarnoff wrote: "For the last seventeen
years radio, television and the phonograph have done their
best to transmit with the utmost fidelity your self-effacing,
incomparable re-creations of the great music of the past
and present . . . Happily, these instruments have recorded
and preserved for us, and for posterity, the great music
you have interpreted so faithfully and magnificently."

Actually, Toscanini's first performances with the NBC
Symphony on Christmas night 1937 went out over the air
with the unnatural sound of the orchestra in NBC's acoustically dead Studio 8H—sound that was unresonantly dry,
flat, hard, and made airlessly tight by the audience which
filled the studio. And the broadcasts continued to go out
with this sound (of which an example was preserved by
the Victor recording, M-745, of the 1939 broadcast of
Beethoven's *Eroica*) until the season of 1941–42. Then a
shell was installed which changed the unfilled studio from

acoustically dead to harshly reverberant; but with an audience present the sound was still flat and tight, and still very different from the spacious, luminous, warm sound which the orchestra exhibited at an occasional benefit concert in Carnegie Hall.

The sound in Studio 8H filled with an audience couldn't be good; but an engineer named Johnston found the one location for the microphone that produced the best the studio was capable of. In 1947 his successor, attempting to do better, tried other locations and combinations of microphones that produced worse—the shallower sound and lessened clarity of texture that were strikingly evident on an occasion when I heard NBC recordings of these broadcasts compared with recordings from the Johnston period.

For thirteen years, then, Toscanini's performances were sent out over the air with the unnatural sound they had in Studio 8H; then in the fall of 1950 the broadcasts were transferred to Carnegie Hall. Here CBS engineers had worked out a microphone pickup for the New York Philharmonic which placed the orchestra at a sufficient distance from the listener's ear for the sound to be heard properly spaced out and balanced and beautiful. But although the over-all sound of the NBC Symphony came over the air from Carnegie Hall with a naturalness and warmth it hadn't had in 8H, the NBC pickups placed the listener's ear close to the orchestra, where the sound crowded in on him, violins got to be strident, solo woodwinds were louder than tuttis, and other balances so laboriously worked out by Toscanini were similarly destroyed.

Inevitably the question arises: what did Toscanini think and say about the sound of the orchestra in Studio 8H? The only reliable report I ever had about this was that standing close to the orchestra he liked hearing every instrument so clearly. Probably he was less aware than the audience of the unresonant dryness of the entire sound; but if he did remark on this he probably was told that this sound in the studio was what was needed to produce the right sound out of the listener's radio—to which the answer was that the right sound of the New York Philharmonic that came out of the radio was the natural and beautiful sound of this orchestra in Carnegie Hall, whereas the unnatural sound of the NBC Symphony in Studio 8H came out of the radio unresonantly dry and flat.

Which brings us to the question: what did Toscanini think and say about this dry and flat sound produced by the NBC recordings of the broadcasts that he listened to afterward? I never heard him comment on it; but I did hear his comments on other recordings, and I would guess that he felt about the ones of the NBC broadcasts as he did about those others: if he heard every instrument he should hear, played as it should be played, he was satisfied; and dryness or harshness of string sound apparently didn't trouble him when it came out of a loud-speaker. My guess, in other words, is that this was one of the instances in which Toscanini justified his own deprecation of his ear for recorded sound—one of those in which he exhibited the peculiarities and the inconsistencies of his attitudes, perceptions and responses in this matter. And instead of waiting I will mention at this point the most striking instance.

Listening in the spring of 1955 to the recording of Debussy's *Ibéria* (LM-1833) I was startled at No. 48 in the second movement when the sound that had been marvelously bright and clear suddenly became less bright, less clear and less spacious. When I spoke of this to the man at RCA Victor who had had charge of the recording, and to Walter Toscanini who handled his father's communications with Victor in these matters, each acted as though it was news to him; but some months later I encountered in a review by Roland Gelatt in *High Fidelity Record Annual* 1955 and in Marsh's book similar statements— which seemingly represented information from Victor—that Toscanini had approved release of the recording only after a passage in the second movement had been replaced by a splice-in of the same passage taken from a broadcast in 1938 (Gelatt found the splice-in "undetectable to my ear" and Marsh said it "cannot be heard"). The reason for Toscanini's insistence on the splice-in was, I would guess, its slightly more plastic treatment of the music; and for this slight difference he ignored the striking inferiority in recorded sound. Not only that, but in 1947 he hadn't been content to have the timpani clearly audible in the recording of Tchaikovsky's *Romeo and Juliet,* but had insisted on dubbing in more of their sound to make them audible in exactly the right degree, even at a cost in lessened beauty of the rest of the sound; whereas now with the *Ibéria* recording he insisted on a splice-in in which the sustained F-sharp of the basses couldn't be heard at all.

This way of dealing with recorded sound was part of an inadequacy in dealing with recording in all its phases. His scratched records and damaged styli were evidence of his awkwardness with the end products; the failure to record the great Philharmonic performances between 1930 and 1936 resulted from his dislike of the procedures of recording. Thus, it was reported, he disliked having to begin to conduct a "take" of a side in obedience to the engineer's signal; and for the 1936 sessions, therefore, it was arranged that the turntable and cutting head would be set in operation and he would begin to conduct the "take" when he felt ready—this being the reason for the silent grooves at the beginning of some of the sides. However at the 1942 session in Philadelphia that I attended he no longer objected to beginning a "take" of a side when the red light flashed on.

One consequence of this out-of-phase relation with recording was that the Victor people had to operate at recording sessions with little or no help from Toscanini. Another was that Toscanini didn't accept on records what he accepted at concerts. I described earlier how he recorded the first movement of Debussy's *Ibéria* as he had played it repeatedly on the 1950 tour but vehemently rejected the performance as too slow when he heard the playback; I mentioned also his rejection of a side of the Philadelphia Orchestra recording of Debussy's *La Mer* because a woodwind couldn't be heard at one point: in these incidents he exhibited his unwillingness to accept and to let the public hear in a recorded performance the unsatisfactory details of tempo, dynamics and balance that he had to accept and let the audience hear at a concert. And because he insisted on having in his recorded performances the complete freedom from imperfection that he rarely achieved at concerts, we lost recordings of beautiful performances—like the Philadelphia *La Mer* and Schubert C-major—merely because at one point an oboe wasn't exactly as strong as it should be or a wind chord wasn't perfectly balanced. I am speaking of his general practice: his occasional inconsistency in this matter was illustrated by his insistence on the *Ibéria* splice-in in which the sustained F-sharp of the basses couldn't be heard, and by his acceptance of a number of 1941 recordings in which the treble that gave brightness and luster to the upper range of sound was not balanced by the bass that would have given sufficient power and solidity to the lower range.

And another consequence was that intent on accuracy and balance of dynamics, Toscanini missed or ignored dryness, flatness, coarseness and other such defects in the sound. Victor could issue only what he approved; and it had his approval of the poor-sounding recordings it issued.

The first and most notorious of these were the ones of Haydn's Symphony No. 88, Mozart's G-minor, Beethoven's Fifth and *Eroica* made in Studio 8H before the installation of the shell. It has been an astonishing experience for me to hear what they sound like played with the best reproducing equipment of today: completely unresonant, dry and tight, but accurate in timbre, clean and not unpleasant; and that is true even of the *Eroica*, which is the poorest because the studio was filled with an audience. But played with even the best equipment of the late thirties and the forties they were harsh and unpleasant; and on less than the best equipment *Nation* readers reported finding the *Eroica* unlistenable.

These first recordings contributed to making '8H' a dirty word among music-lovers; but the fact is that some of the better Toscanini recordings—for example the marvelously beautiful *Ibéria*—also were made in Studio 8H. At one session there in 1945 Toscanini recorded Sousa's *The Stars and Stripes Forever*, which came out with its tuttis coarse, their texture not cleanly defined in quiet, and lacking depth and spaciousness; and at the same session he recorded Gershwin's *An American in Paris*, which came out insufficiently bright but warm, spacious, clear and clean. For the Gershwin piece the principal microphone was placed at Johnston's optimum position, with a fill-in on each side, and the chairs in the studio were pushed back to increase the resonance; the Sousa recording, on the other hand, was the product of a multiple-microphone pickup which had one principal microphone on each side in front of the orchestra and one in the rear of the studio—which is to say, none at Johnston's optimum position. For the *Ibéria*, in 1950, the microphone was at the Johnston position and the chairs were pushed back; for the *La Mer* the day before, the microphone was a few feet back of the Johnston position and the chairs were only partly pushed back—the result being the lessened sharpness of presence and impact of the sound as compared with that of the *Ibéria*. However, the different sound of the Mozart G-minor and Schubert *Unfinished*, even with the microphone in optimum position, demonstrated that microphone-placement was not the only factor, and that another was the turning of knobs in the control room.

Nor were all the poor recordings made in Studio 8H. In Carnegie Hall, Victor produced in 1940 the fine-sounding Brahms Piano Concerto No. 2 and *Immolation Scene* from *Die Götterdämmerung*, but in 1941 a Tchaikovsky Piano Concerto No. 1 that was thin, shallow, harsh and noisily clouded with reverberation; as late as 1949 it produced the dry, compressed and otherwise poor Beethoven *Eroica* of LM-1042, as late as 1952 a Beethoven Ninth without the spaciousness and luster of the Beethoven *Pastoral* a few months earlier. As for the causes of good and bad, Carnegie Hall too had an optimum position for the microphone, which, on one of the occasions when Victor used it, produced the superb sound of the 1953 Respighi *Pines of Rome*; but for the 1947 Tchaikovsky *Pathétique* the microphone was placed further back and higher and draperies were placed over the side boxes and the parquet, the result being the lower volume level and lack of spaciousness and luster of this recording. For the more lightly scored Mendelssohn *Midsummer Night's Dream* music the microphone was placed even further back and higher, making the sound even weaker and dimmer. And I recall watching one of the two microphones behind Toscanini being raised very high at one of the sessions for the 1953 Beethoven *Missa Solemnis*—which may have contributed to the insufficient weight and prominence of orchestra and soloists as against chorus in the recording; though this result may have been achieved also by the twisting of knobs in the control room that balanced what was picked up by the microphones behind Toscanini and the one in front of the chorus. Only such twisting of knobs controlling the balance of treble and bass could have produced the 1941 *Lohengrin* and *Traviata* Preludes, Brahms First Symphony, and *Rhine Journey* from *Die Götterdämmerung* that were lustrous on top but—for lack of sufficient bass—without depth and solidity down below.

Nor, for that matter, were all the bad recordings made in 8H and Carnegie Hall. In 1946–47 Victor had Toscanini record Mozart's *Haffner* and Haydn's *Clock* Symphonies with a reduced orchestra in NBC's Studio 3A, whose acoustical deadness and smaller size produced two of the most atrocious Toscanini recordings ever issued, with harsh tuttis and the acoustical deadness that struck the ear a blow at the end of a loud chord.

I have been discussing the recordings as they were made originally, and pointing out that a number had preserved Toscanini's performances with less than the "utmost fidelity" Sarnoff spoke of. But by the time he spoke a number were changed from what they had been originally. In the days before recording on tape, what was engraved on the wax or acetate couldn't be changed: when Toscanini, in 1947, insisted on the timpani being strengthened at one point in the 78-rpm Tchaikovsky *Romeo and Juliet*, the only way to do this was to record on a new side the sound from the original side together with additional live timpani sound at that point—a transfer which would cost the original sound some of its bloom. But there was no such loss when sound was transferred from tape; and in a tape recording, therefore, changes—like the stepping up or cutting down of the treble or bass end—could be, and regularly were, made while the recording was being transferred from the original tape to the disc master from which the stampers for the final disc records were processed, or from the original tape to a tape master which preserved the changes and became the source of the disc master. In a tape recording of the *Romeo and Juliet*, then, the timpani could have been strengthened very easily and with no loss to the rest of the sound—either by merely stepping up the bass end, or if necessary by introducing the additional live timpani sound —during the transfer from tape to disc master; but in addition it would have been possible to substitute a section of the tape of another "take" in which the timpani were sufficiently strong; and changes were in fact made in these ways in the tape recordings of Toscanini's performances (the splicing together of parts of continuous performances has been objected to as producing a synthetic performance which is a musical falsehood; but it seems to me musically preferable to the old synthetic assemblage of unrelated four-and-a-half-minute sides which was "false" in the same way). The superb recorded performance of the *Tristan* Prelude that I heard at Toscanini's home in September 1942 was not issued because the recording hadn't caught the last quiet plucked G of the basses; but in a tape recording the G would have been spliced in and the recording saved.

Not only could a new recording be modified on tape, but it was possible to go back later to the original tape of an already issued recording and make new tape and disc masters incorporating changes in the sound; and Victor did in fact issue new "enhanced" versions of Toscanini recordings under the old record numbers, with nothing to identify them but new stamper numbers after the serial numbers on the vinylite (stamper numbers like 5s or 12s after numbers like E2RP-1234). Moreover, by first transferring it from the disc to a tape it was possible now to modify even the sound that had originally been recorded on wax or acetate; and "enhanced" versions were in fact issued of Toscanini 78-rpm recordings that had been transferred by means of tape to LP. Finally, in addition to the changes that improved the sound—changes which used the new RIAA recording curve, better cutting heads for less distortion, variable groove-width for full dynamic range— some were possible that made the sound worse; and the "enhancement" with echo-chamber resonance, peaking of treble, and cutting down of bass did in fact damage a number of Toscanini recordings, making the defective ones even worse and spoiling the ones that were beautiful and in no need of improvement.

To add echo-chamber resonance to the unresonantly dry and flat sound from Studio 8H filled with an audience might seem a reasonable and necessary thing to do; but when it was done to the *Otello* it gave us the solo voices trailing fake reverberation in endless empty halls, and those voices not only inflated with a brash resonance which alters timbre but afflicted at times with an edge of buzzing distortion. Similarly it might seem reasonable to add brightness and echo-chamber resonance to the unresonantly dry and compressed sound of the Beethoven *Eroica* issued in 1950 on LM-1042; and when, in the spring of 1953, I heard the new version that was issued in the limited edition (LM-6900) of Beethoven's nine symphonies, the more agreeable sound seemed better. But in the spring of 1955 I had occasion to listen to all the "enhanced" versions of Toscanini recordings; and this time when I compared the *Eroica* issued in 1953 with the one issued in 1950 I realized that what was unresonantly dry in the 1950 version was the true sound of violins, which in the 1953 version was made false by the electronic silkiness and gloss from the echo-chamber resonance, and that the notes of low strings, the forceful chords, the drumbeats that in the 1950 version were cleanly defined, compact, solid, were less so in the 1953 version. By 1955, moreover, Victor had substituted a further "enhanced" version for the original on LM-1042; and I found that in this one the larger amount of echo-chamber resonance changed the violin sound into a liquid stream of electronic gloss, and produced a similar liquefying and blurring all the way down, dissolving the solidity and clean definition of chords, drumbeats and bass notes into a mush of heavy rumble. In addition, with bass cut down and treble peaked the sound was brighter but shallower, and the timbres of some of the instruments were altered: the horn sounded more like a trumpet; the trumpet's sound was sharpened, and sometimes spread or split; the change from dark to light and from dry to glossy made the cellos unrecognizable; the gloss similarly falsified the sound of the clarinet, the bassoon.

Thus, even when the sound was defective the echo-chamber resonance and peaking of treble made it even worse. This was true of the LP dubbings of the lusterless

78-rpm Tchaikovsky *Pathétique* and dim Mendelssohn *Midsummer Night's Dream;* it was true even of the LP dubbings of the atrocious Studio 3A Mozart *Haffner* and Haydn *Clock:* in every instance the original sound was preferable despite its defects.

But the damaging "enhancement" was not inflicted only on defective recordings that invited attempts to improve them. It was inflicted also on LP dubbings of 78-rpm recordings that were sufficiently bright and clear—the Mozart *Jupiter,* Beethoven *Leonore* No. 3 and *Consecration of the House* Overtures, Rossini Overtures, Berlioz *Romeo and Juliet* excerpts (except *Great Festivity at the Capulets'*), Tchaikovsky *Romeo and Juliet.* And it was inflicted on some of the tape recordings that were beautiful reproductions of Toscanini's performances. Though the Debussy *La Mer* had less sharpness of "presence" and impact than the *Ibéria,* it offered nevertheless a breathtaking reproduction of the tonal subtleties and splendors that I had heard in 8H on June 1, 1950, and therefore provided no justification for the electronic tampering that produced the falsifications and the blowzily confused "brilliance" of the first "enhanced" version issued on a later LM-1221, or the even worse falsifications and confusions of the further "enhanced" version issued on LM-1833. Nor did the superb *William Tell* Overture on LRY-9000 and LM-1986 need the brightness and gloss that were added on LRM-7054. And there was no justification for the varying amounts of damage inflicted on other good recordings: the Beethoven *Pastoral* and Septet, the Brahms Fourth and Brahms-Haydn

Variations, the Wagner *Lohengrin* Prelude, *Parsifal* excerpts and Prelude to Act 3 of *Die Meistersinger*, the Tchaikovsky *Manfred*, Smetana *Die Moldau*, Strauss *Don Juan*.

Moreover, the "enhancement" was inflicted not only on old recordings but on new ones issued the first time. The sessions for the "pop" numbers that Toscanini recorded in the summer of 1952 were two occasions when the microphones were placed effectively for Carnegie Hall; and the result was the marvelously beautiful sound—warm, lustrous, spacious, solid, cleanly defined in quiet—of the *Dance of the Hours* first issued on LRM-7005, the slow introduction of the *Mignon* Overture first issued on LRM-7013; nevertheless it was this sound that was made thin and shallow in the Allegro part of the *Mignon* Overture, and given a shallow, blowzy "brilliance" in the *Carmen* Suite on the reverse side of 7013. Similarly Musorgsky's *Pictures at an Exhibition* was first issued on LM-1838 with the magnificent sound of the original tape (which I happened to hear) distorted and falsified by excessive peaking of treble that produced the ear-piercing trumpet sound at the beginning, the snarling sound of the brass in *Catacombs*, the harsh, raucous sound of the full orchestra elsewhere. And it must be added that the *Dance of the Hours* that escaped "enhancement" on LRM-7005 came off the later LM-1834, *Toscanini Plays Your Favorites*, with cellos made bright and glossy, bass less solid, plucked bass notes softened and spread like bass-drum beats.

There is no doubt about Toscanini's having heard and approved the recordings that were issued with "enhancement" right from the start, like the Musorgsky *Pictures* on LM-1838, the *Carmen* Suite on LRM-7013: Victor had to have his approval of a new recording. And concerning the Musorgsky *Pictures* I was told at Victor that he had rejected the original unedited tape of the recording; that a letter from Walter Toscanini had transmitted his father's criticisms and requests of changes; and that Toscanini had approved the edited tape with the "enhancing" changes made by the Victor engineer who was then working for Walter Toscanini and was the originator of most of the "enhanced" versions of the recordings.

I don't know whether Victor had to have Toscanini's approval of new "enhanced" versions of old recordings, and whether he heard and approved all of them. But the engineer involved insisted to a friend of mine that Toscanini approved the "enhanced" *La Mer;* and I would suppose he heard some of the others.

Certain Victor engineers have contended that Toscanini didn't like "enhanced" sound, citing his rejection of an "enhanced" Verdi *Requiem* that was submitted to him. But evidently he did like the sound of other "enhanced" recordings that he accepted; and this appears to be yet another matter in which he was inconsistent. *

Part of the responsibility for the damage to the recordings, then, was Toscanini's. And one can say, I think, that part of the responsibility was the reviewers'. If they had objected, Victor might have retreated; instead, Victor was encouraged to proceed by the approval and even the en-

* It was revealed later that changes in the sound of Toscanini's recordings were not usually submitted for his approval. See the section "Recordings Postscript" at the end of this chapter.

T.H.—1988

thusiastic praise, exemplified by the review in *High Fidelity* which found that the "enhancement" of the Debussy *La Mer* gave the Studio 8H recording "the atmosphere of a concert hall," which was "a real improvement," but added that electronic trickery couldn't give this recording or the *Ibéria* on the reverse side the "clarity, brilliance and presence" of the Musorgsky *Pictures*.

In the spring of 1955 additional Toscanini recordings were in process of "being brought up to Victor standards," as the Victor executive phrased it. And it was therefore a surprise to find in the *Toscanini Omnibus* (LM-6026) issued in August 1955 the *Carmen* Suite with the "enhancement" removed. But on the other hand the record offered the *Mignon* Overture with bass restored in the Allegro but with the sound made unpleasantly sharp by an excessive boost in treble; it offered the *Don Pasquale* Overture—first issued on LRM-7028 with reverberant but true and agreeable sound—now also made unpleasantly sharp by the boost in treble; and it offered a *Forza Del Destino* Overture beefed up at both treble and bass ends.

The first hope that the damage to the recordings might be undone came when Victor, that summer, removed from work on Toscanini's recordings the engineer responsible for most of the "enhanced" versions, and assigned Richard Gardner to work with Toscanini in Riverdale on recordings to be derived from his broadcasts—i.e., from Victor's own tapes of the broadcast performances of the final season and NBC's tapes and acetate discs with the performances of earlier seasons. Gardner was one of Victor's most skillful engineers, with a keen ear for musical sound; and in River-dale he had working with him another excellent engineer, John H. Corbett, formerly of NBC, who had taken over the transferring from discs to tapes for Walter Toscanini's private collection. In addition Gardner was opposed to "en-hancement"; and in an article in *High Fidelity* on his work with Toscanini he reported Toscanini's explanation of how the addition of artificial echo damaged the sound, and promised that henceforth the recordings would repro-duce only the sound that Toscanini had heard in Studio 8H or Carnegie Hall. But the recordings couldn't reproduce the sound Toscanini had heard; they could reproduce only the sound that the microphone or microphones had picked up in the studio or hall, which was in various ways and degrees different from what he had heard. In Carnegie Hall, at the broadcast of November 10, 1951, Toscanini had heard the antique cymbals produce sounds of the required delicacy in the last section of Berlioz's *Queen Mab;* but the microphones, as placed and controlled by NBC's engi-neers, had picked up the excessively loud sounds of the an-tique cymbals that were reproduced by the recording derived from the broadcast and issued in LM-6026. And Tosca-nini, who wouldn't have tolerated those loud sounds in Carnegie Hall, had accepted them in the recording. More accurate, therefore, was Gardner's statement to me that henceforth we would be given sound on records exactly as Toscanini *wanted* it (my italics)—taking into account, Gardner added, the limitations of the source material and the state of the recording art—to which, judging by some of the recordings that were issued, I think he should have added the state of Toscanini's ear for recorded sound.

Gardner also told me his assignment was to work on new recordings, not on old ones; and we got the beautiful-sounding Strauss *Don Quixote* on LM-2026 and Berlioz *Harold in Italy* on LM-1951 processed from Victor's own tapes of the broadcasts in November 1953, and the good-sounding Cherubini Requiem Mass in C minor on LM-2000 processed from NBC recordings of the broadcast in February 1950. We also got recordings processed from earlier broadcasts, in which we heard the limitations and defects of the source material, the imperfect state of recording technique, and possibly the peculiarities of Toscanini's ear for recorded sound. The thin, shallow, nasty sound of the Kodály *Háry János* Suite on LM-1973 processed from the 1947 broadcast may have represented only the poor quality of the source material. But in the Mozart Symphony K.543 on LM-2001 processed from the 1948 broadcast the ear-piercing violin sound could be made normal and agreeable by drastic reduction of treble—which seemed to indicate excessive peaking of treble in the transfer from NBC disc to Victor tape; and the record reproduced the third and fourth movements with a gritty distortion and stridency that I was able to ascertain was not in the sound produced by the tape master—which indicated something badly done somewhere between that tape and my record.

But with the new recordings we did after all get a number of new versions of old ones. In some of these—the Beethoven symphonies reissued in LM-6901 and on the single records under the old numbers; the Beethoven *Leonore*

No. 3 Overture reissued on LVT-1025; the Tchaikovsky *Manfred* reissued on LVT-1024; the Rossini Overtures to *The Barber of Seville, La Cenerentola, Il Signor Bruschino* and *La Gazza Ladra* reissued on LM-2040—the "enhancement" was reduced (presumably the state of Toscanini's ear dictated the putting of the fake gloss on the beautiful sound of the Beethoven *Pastoral*). And in the *Forza del Destino* Overture reissued in *Verdi and Toscanini,* LM-6041, the "enhancement" was removed entirely. But the Mozart Divertimento K.287, first issued in 1950 on LM-13 with no doctoring of the sound dubbed from the excellent 78-rpm original, was now reissued on LM-2001 with a boost at both treble and bass ends—the violins over-bright and glossy, the bass heavy and soft. And in addition to the Rossini overtures I just mentioned, LM-2040 offered the superb *William Tell* Overture with peaking of treble and with reduction of bass that lessened its solidity, and the *Semiramide* Overture (originally on LRM-7054) damaged even more in the same way. For the rest, the Act 2 of Gluck's *Orfeo* reissued on LVT-1041 was less strident in the tuttis than it had been on LM-1850 but had less solidity, requiring the stepping up of bass; and the Smetana *Moldau* and Dukas *Sorcerer's Apprentice* were reissued on *Toscanini Conducts,* LM-2056, without the "enhancement" of the later LM-1118, but with a slight tipping of the balance toward the treble end.

These were the changes I heard in the old recordings that were reissued on records with new numbers. I asked Victor whether any changed versions of other old recordings —with "enhancement" either added or removed—had been issued under their old numbers since 1955; and the answer was that there had been no changes in *any* of the old recordings except the Beethoven symphonies. I am sure I heard the changes I have reported in the few recordings I have mentioned.

RECORDINGS POSTSCRIPT

1979—B.H.H.

[In the season of 1953-54 Richard Gardner] remarked with a grin one day that it might interest me to know Walter Toscanini had taken exception to my statements in *The Nation* about the Toscanini recordings. I was no longer in contact with Toscanini in this period and therefore had no opportunity to learn what he thought of the "enhanced" versions or even whether he heard them. I knew that he heard the original tape of a recording, since Victor had to have his approval of a recording before issuing it; but I did not know whether Victor had to have his approval also of the edited working tape made for the processing of the records, and of each new working tape for a later release, and whether, therefore, he had heard these working tapes. I was inclined to think they did *not* require his approval and he therefore had *not* heard them, since I found it difficult to believe he would have approved the monstrously falsified *La Mer* on LM-1833 if he had heard it. But this was mere speculation; whereas Gerhardt, the RCA technician whom Walter Toscanini had engaged in 1950 to transfer the acetate recordings of Toscanini's broadcasts to tape, asserted as fact—to someone who reported his statement to me—that Toscanini had approved the "enhanced" *La Mer*. And this was the basis of my statement on page 116 that Gerhardt "seems to have been able to persuade Toscanini to substitute his in some instances monstrously falsified 'enhanced' versions for the originals"—which in time I discovered was not true.

The copy of [my letter in 1955 to Victor's Adminstrator of Recording, A. A. Pulley], in which I asked about the changes in the recording of Musorgsky's *Pictures*, has my notations of what he told me on the telephone: that after being informed by Walter Toscanini that his father had not approved the original tape of Musorgsky's *Pictures*, Pulley had received a letter in which Walter wrote that his father had found the sound to be "logy and heavy" and had requested that echo-chamber resonance be added and whatever else be done that would brighten it; and that subsequently the edited tape representing what Pulley referred to as "conferences with Gerhardt" had been approved by Toscanini. And this, it turned out, was one instance of what Pulley described as standard practice. Since Victor dealt with Toscanini through Walter, what happened was that Gerhardt told Walter what he wanted to do with the sound of a recording, which Walter then communicated to Victor as what his father wanted done, and which Victor then told Gerhardt to do. This left me certain, now, that Toscanini not only had not heard and approved the falsified Musorgsky *Pictures* which Victor was told he had approved, but *had* approved the superb original *Pictures* that Victor was told he had not approved.

Thus I discovered that it was not Toscanini but Walter whom Gerhardt had persuaded to substitute his "enhanced" versions of the recordings for the originals. And I thought I understood not only why he had been able to persuade Walter to do this, but why Walter had objected to my unfavorable comments on the substituted versions. As someone musically ungifted Walter did not benefit from being the son of a musical genius; and as the son of an enemy to Mussolini he lost his rare-book business in Milan and had to come here to make a new start. Since he had been interested in the recording process, and had even attempted to record his father's performances, he made this new start with RCA Victor—initially to learn the record business, but, as it turned out, to assist the company and his father in their dealings with each other. And very early, with his interest in the recording process, he was able to do one thing for them which gave him a feeling of personal achievement. That is, perceiving that his father rejected recordings which, when played back to him on the poor reproducing equipment of the '30s and '40s, did not produce what he had heard in the performance he had conducted, Walter got a Victor research engineer named Snepvangers (who later worked on the long-playing record introduced by Columbia) to assemble components of a sound system which created in Toscanini's living room an approximation, in quality and volume, of the sound he was accustomed to hearing about him as he conducted an orchestra—with the result that he was satisfied by recordings he might otherwise have rejected, and approved them for release. On the other hand, with the interest in the recording process that caused Walter to be impressed, ten years later, by Gerhardt's ideas for electronically "enhancing" the sound of his father's recordings, but without the musical gift that would have enabled him to recognize the damage this "enhancement" inflicted on them, he used his position to have Gerhardt's versions issued in place of his father's originals. And this time Walter's own feeling of personal achievement was increased by the all but unanimous approval of the record-reviewers—after which he could not read with anything but shock and anger my dissenting report on what he had achieved.

In 1966 RCA Victor planned—to commemorate in 1967 the hundredth anniversary of Toscanini's birth—a reissue of the Toscanini recordings with their true sound, which was to be obtained by newly transferring without modification the sound from the original metal parts of the 78-rpm recordings or the original tapes of the LP recordings to new working tapes for the new Victrola records. I first heard about the project, in the fall of 1966, from Richard Gardner, who reported unhappily that he had been assigned to it not to work independently, as he had always done previously, but merely to operate the controls as directed by the editor in charge of the project, a man named [Robert] Zarbock; and that Zarbock, ignoring instructions, was directing him to introduce treble-boosts into the newly transferred sound. And in fact when the first group of new Victrolas appeared in 1967 the treble-boost made the violins in Debussy's *La Mer*, on VIC-1246, glistening and silky, the brass brighter and sharper—all attractive to the ear, but false. To obtain the true sound of the violins and brass one had to be able to cancel the treble-boost (with a first-class treble-control that would not also remove some of the brightness of the original sound).

Moreover, in a few instances Zarbock did not make the new transfer from the original recording; and what happened in one of these instances is worth reporting as a demonstration of how the actions of individuals behind the façade of a corporate entity can defeat that entity's intention. One morning late in October 1966 Gardner telephoned to ask me to come down to RCA Victor in the afternoon, when Zarbock and he would be making the new transfer of Beethoven's Eighth, and assured me—when I inquired—that the invitation had Zarbock's approval. Zarbock was pleasant when we met; and I took a seat facing the LC1A speaker, with Gardner at his controls and Zarbock at his desk behind me. There were three tapes, said Gardner; and the first that he played part of was a working tape made by an editor named [Daniel] Slick, which produced sound that was compressed, shallow and lusterless. The second, said Gardner, had nothing to identify it; but the overwhelmingly beautiful, spacious and solid sound it began to produce was unquestionably that of the original tape; and amazed and delighted I swung around toward Gardner, whom I found grinning *his* delight. We turned expectantly to Zarbock, and were dumbfounded by his grim face: he heard echo-chamber resonance, he said. Gardner and I protested that it was the natural resonance of empty Carnegie Hall; but Zarbock was adamant. Gardner then suggested that we listen to the third tape, another working tape of Slick's which produced much the same sound as the first one. Finally Zarbock consented to make a test transfer of a passage from the original tape. I heard him murmuring instructions to Gardner—the result of which was that the violins which earlier had been radiant and sweet were now strident. I said this to Zarbock, who replied that their sound had to be changed in this way on the working tape for the final record to produce what I had heard before from the original tape. I forebore to dispute this with Zarbock or to embarrass Gardner by asking if he agreed with it, and merely asked Zarbock if he would let me hear the test pressing of the record. He promised that he would, but never did; and two months later Gardner told me sadly that Zarbock—determined to have his way—had remade the Beethoven Eighth using the Slick working tape. (When I heard the record eventually it produced sound that was agreeable but without the spaciousness and lustrous beauty of the original that Slick had removed.) I reported the episode to Roger G. Hall, at that time Manager of Red Seal at Victor, and asked him to have Gardner play for him the three tapes I had heard. He did not have Gardner do this; and concerning the three tapes that he alleged were played for him he wrote that the first was the one he, like me, preferred; but that the second—only slightly different from the first, and offering better definition—was the one chosen by Zarbock for reasons as persuasive as ours for the first; and that the third was the Slick tape that all of us, including Zarbock, disliked.

Though the announced intention had been to offer on the new Victrolas the true sound of the original mono recordings for the music-lovers interested in Toscanini's performances, the Victor sales division persuaded the company to begin, early in 1968, to issue the recordings both in their original mono sound on VIC records and in "electrically reprocessed stereo" sound on VICS records for stereo-lovers, most of whom, I would have thought, would not be interested in Toscanini even in pseudo-stereo sound. The retail dealers stocked only the VICS records; and though the early Victrolas issued only in mono were available on VIC records, the later ones were available only on VICS's.

The new Victrolas were issued in England first by Decca; but in 1972 RCA in England began a *Toscanini Edition* with its own remastered versions of the NBC Symphony recordings. I heard only a few that a reader lent me—the Mendelssohn *Italian* Symphony and Schubert *Unfinished* on AT-101, the Rossini overtures on AT-108, the Debussy *La Mer* and *Ibéria* on AT-111, and the Berlioz *Harold in Italy* (not reissued in the American Victrola series) on AT-112—which produced sound that was more clearly and cleanly defined in quieter aural space than that of the American Victrolas. The Debussy pieces were amazingly improved not only in this respect but in the greater spaciousness of the sound. After a couple of years, and a final group of releases that I was told were very poor, the series was terminated.

By that time German RCA had begun its *Toscanini Edition* with its own remastered versions, of which I heard only the superb-sounding Brahms Second on AT-132. From someone I considered reliable I learned that the quality of the German versions depended on the source material obtained from American RCA and what was done with it. Generally, he said, the remastering of tape material produced excellent results—e.g. the Beethoven *Pastoral* Symphony on AT-133, the Beethoven Fourth and Fifth on AT-128, the Brahms Second on AT-132, which offered the best sound my informant had ever heard—but the remastering of pre-tape (i.e. pre-1950) material produced poor results; and he remarked that "the Germans often can't leave a good-sounding tape alone," in addition to making poor material worse with bad equalization, filtering and artificial resonance.   B.H.H.—1979

1988—T.H.

The Germans were not the only ones who could not leave well enough alone. Italian RCA put out its own *Toscanini Edition* in which even the post-1950 recordings were variously altered. This edition followed an earlier Italian series, which was described as having been "half-speed mastered" without saying that the records had also been rechanneled for fake stereo and re-equalized to alter the quality of the sound. From Japanese RCA there was a comprehensive LP set of all of Toscanini's commercial records, some of them reproduced with good sound, some with the high frequencies cut back drastically to reduce surface noise. From the Franklin Mint, by arrangement with the Toscanini family, there were two subscription boxes of selected remastered records, including a few pieces not previously available commercially, but also including a disproportionate number of comparatively insignificant pieces in place of the central masterpieces of Toscanini's repertory. Of the recordings Toscanini had made with the BBC Symphony in London between 1937 and 1939, those that formerly had been on 78s— Beethoven's *Leonore No. 1* Overture, his Symphonies Nos. 1, 4, and 6, Brahms's *Tragic Overture*, Mozart's Overture to *The Magic Flute*, Rossini's Overture to *La Scala di Seta*, and the Weber-Berlioz *Invitation to the Dance*—were issued first on poor-sounding Seraphim records, then on better-sounding Seraphim and English World Record Club discs, and finally in an EMI box that contained as well several Toscanini BBC Symphony recordings that had never been issued before, not even on 78s: Beethoven's *Prometheus* Overture and Symphony No. 7, Cherubini's Overture to *Anacreon*, Debussy's *La Mer*, Mendelssohn's Nocturne and Scherzo from the music for *A Midsummer Night's Dream*, and Mozart's Symphony K. 385 (*Haffner*).

The first digital transfers of Toscanini's recordings were made to LP by American RCA in the early 1980s. The 1953 Schubert Ninth Symphony sounded better than before, but Mozart's G minor and *Jupiter* Symphonies sounded worse. The first digital transfers to be released on compact disc were undertaken by Japanese RCA, working from copies of the American master tapes; but the results were spoiled by the decision of the Japanese not to use the tapes as they came, but to subject them to further processing that made the CD's sound strident.

The American public's response to the Japanese CD's was so negative that in 1986 RCA in the United States initiated its own CD series. The first three releases—Beethoven's *Eroica* (the recorded performance of 1949—not the concert performance of 1953 in the Victrola series) and his First, Second and Seventh Symphonies, Berlioz's *Harold in Italy*, *Roman Carnival* Overture, *Queen Mab* Scherzo, and *Rákóczy March*, Wagner's *Tristan* Prelude and *Liebestod*, the *Siegfried Idyll*, Act I, Scene 3 of *Die Walküre* (with Traubel and Melchior), and the *Ride of the Valkyries*—were dramatically better than any of the preceding LP versions. One reason was the greater clarity, spaciousness, and amplitude of reproduction possible with the digital medium itself; the other was the decision of the producer not to reprocess the sound of the original master tapes. However, he did decide on his own to use whatever "takes" he himself preferred, even if they were not the ones Toscanini had approved. He failed in some instances to make seamless joins between the separate "takes" making up a movement (Haggin never mentioned, although he must have known it, that with the sole exception of the *Missa Solemnis* in 1953, Victor continued to record Toscanini, even on tape, in isolated four-to-six-minute stretches, as in the days of 78s). And the producer could not refrain from making the beautiful sound that was characteristic of digital transfers even more beautiful by imposing artificial reverberation on it—subtly in some instances, not so subtly in others.

In the fall of 1986, RCA assigned the project to Arthur Fierro, a musician who had been Walter Toscanini's administrative assistant. His first CD—Beethoven's Ninth

Symphony—was excellent. And from the superb sound of his next CDs—Brahms's Fourth Symphony and shorter works, Beethoven's Third Piano Concerto (with Rubinstein) and Violin Concerto (with Heifetz), Bizet's *Carmen* Suite, Rossini's *William Tell* Overture, and other "light" pieces—it became clear that he was having more success than anyone in recent years determining the best surviving source material and closely replicating on today's equipment the equalization curves peculiar to RCA's custom designed tape-recorders of the 1950s. Moreover, in Beethoven's Third Piano Concerto he rectified the unsteady pitch of the original 78s by using a tape of contemporary NBC acetates of the broadcast. However, even Fierro could not resist adding some reverberation to Brahms's *Liebeslieder* Waltzes and *Song of the Fates*, and artificial stereophonic separation to Sousa's *The Stars and Stripes Forever*.

The effect of all this was to provide listeners for the first time with recordings that were actually what RCA said they were: close approximations of the sound Toscanini had heard and approved when the first reference tapes and acetate reference discs were played back to him. The fact that this should be occurring only in the mid-1980's, thirty and more years after the records were made, was not lost on Haggin, who had objected to the falsifying of Toscanini's records all those years. "It's very ironic," he remarked when he heard four of the CDs a few months before his death in 1987, "that this should finally be happening when I'm on the way out".

It remains only to add that with the expiration in Europe of the copyright over Toscanini's broadcasts, many of these, too, are now being issued by independent companies on compact discs that are good-sounding or not depending on the source of the material and on whether or not it has been tampered with by the engineer who transferred it.

T.H.—1988

TOSCANINI'S RESIGNATION
FROM THE NBC SYMPHONY

1979—B.H.H.

The letter of resignation that NBC issued in facsimile had Toscanini addressing David Sarnoff as "My very dear David", and beginning with the statement that "seventeen years ago you sent me an invitation to become the Musical Director of an orchestra to be created especially for me." Since Toscanini knew the orchestra had not been created especially for him, the statement created doubts about the entire letter, exemplified by the questions of the NBC Symphony cellist Alan Shulman some years later, when he was giving me his recollections of Toscanini for *The Toscanini Musicians Knew*: " *Did* he resign? Did he do it of his own volition? Did *he* write that letter of resignation?" Shulman evidently was one of those who had not been convinced by Chotzinoff's account in 1956 of the circumstances leading to the letter, in the mélange of fact and fiction laced with malice that constituted the "intimate portrait" of Toscanini in his book. According to Chotzinoff, Toscanini had informed him, only a few days before the first rehearsal of *Un Ballo in Maschera*, that he no longer remembered the words of this opera and therefore requested him to cancel the project; but a day or two later he had informed Chotzinoff that he now remembered the words and could prepare and conduct the performance. This in fact he had done. But, said Chotzinoff, it had been clear to the Toscanini family that the time had come for him to stop; and Toscanini had agreed. At his request a letter of resignation had been prepared (presumably by Chotzinoff); and though weeks had passed without his signing it, during the week of the final broadcast he had "summoned the resolution to put his name to it and send it off."

But Guido Cantelli, who had seen Toscanini constantly during the season of 1953-54, when he had been in New York for engagements with the NBC Symphony and the New York Philharmonic, had reported to Jerome Toobin— manager of the former NBC Symphony when it continued on its own as the Symphony of the Air—what Toobin later told me: that in the fall of 1953 Walter Toscanini had informed his father, at Chotzinoff's request, of NBC's decision to discontinue the NBC Symphony broadcasts at the end of that season, and of Chotzinoff's suggestion that his father might, for appearances' sake, wish to resign; and that as a result there had been terrible scenes at Riverdale. It had been in the fall of 1953 that Walter Toscanini had written me about the decision at NBC to exclude everyone from his father's rehearsals, and that I had begun to hear of Toscanini's occasional confusion at the rehearsals, which had provided a possible reason for the exclusion. And so it had

178

looked as if Toscanini's failing powers had led NBC to the decision Chotzinoff had communicated to Walter.

It was not until 1966 when I was recording Alfred Wallenstein's recollections for *The Toscanini Musicians Knew*, that I learned what Sarnoff had told him in private conversation in the fall of 1953: that Sarnoff and Chotzinoff had driven up to Riverdale to offer Toscanini a contract for the season of 1954-55, but had been intercepted in the driveway by Walter, who had requested them not to offer his father the contract, adding that he would not let him sign it. Presumably Walter had not told his father Sarnoff and Chotzinoff were coming; and not daring to tell him he had prevented them from offering him the contract, he had told him instead that NBC had decided to discontinue the broadcasts and suggested his resignation for appearances' sake. And presumably he had done this because of the family's belief that another season would be too much for Toscanini's diminishing physical strength.

But now we have the letter dated 16 May 1953, in Harvey Sachs's excellent new biography, in which Toscanini writes to a friend:

> I am not well, and no one believes me, the asses, but I'm not the same as I was. My eyes have worsened so much that I can no longer find glasses which can help me. My legs and my memory fail me. I sleep little and badly, tormented by tragic, commonplace or fearful dreams. All in all, a poor unhappy man— and they have had the bad taste to force me to accept another year of concerts. And I, imbecile that I

am, and tired of hearing myself bothered, have given in. The American public will again have to have the patience to put up with having an old man of 86 before its eyes.

It turns out, then, that when Walter Toscanini acted as he did in the fall of 1953 it was with the knowledge that his father himself realized that he should reject the offer of another year of concerts but could not keep himself from accepting it. Walter may have felt that this justified his preventing Sarnoff from offering his father the additional year; but evidently foreseeing that his father might be angered by an intervention he considered presumptuous, Walter did not tell him what he had done. He must also have foreseen how his father would react to what he did tell him—i.e. that for Toscanini NBC's decision to end the broadcasts would be a decision to dismiss him, and as such an indignity without precedent, the shock of which would produce terrible scenes; but evidently Walter was not disquieted by the thought of the rage that would be directed not at him but at NBC. And he may not have foreseen what NBC musicians thought were in some degree consequences of this shock: the confusions at rehearsals, and the momentary breakdown at the final broadcast.

In addition to what Toscanini felt about the indignity to himself there was his grief and fury over the ruthless dismissal of his orchestra. David Walter, another member of that orchestra who gave me his recollections of Toscanini, related that whereas at the previous post-season parties for the orchestra in the '50s Toscanini had been "his old affable, congenial self ", at the last such party in 1954 "he didn't come down to join us; and eventually Ghignatti and Cooley went upstairs to see him. They reported that he was in tears, exclaiming 'My poor orchestra! My poor orchestra!'—feeling that he was responsible for the disbanding of the orchestra, and that he couldn't face us." And Ghignatti, after a subsequent visit, reported Toscanini's referring to Sarnoff and Chotzinoff as *"animali"*.

One can understand, therefore, why the weeks passed without Toscanini's being able to put an unusual shaky and blurred signature to the letter, prepared by one of the *"animali"*, that had him addressing the other one as "My very dear David" and beginning with the statement about "an orchestra to be created especially for me", which he knew to be untrue.

B.H.H.—1979

The texts of the two letters on the following pages:

November 3—1941

My dear Mr Haggin
Yes, it will be one of my first records Schubert's C major
Symphony which I am going to conduct next week with the
Philadelphia Orchestra . . .
Also the Tchaikovsky Pathetic and Iberia and Reine Mab, too.
I have a weakness for Beethoven's Septet which I performed
last season with the N. B. C orchestra with ten violins, ten
violas—eight celli—and four basses—because I never
liked and enjoyed this wonderful music with the seven
instruments as it is written by Beethoven . . . I heard many
performances of this Septet in the original form and played by
distinguished musicians but the balance was never attained. I
shall read what you say about Schubert—Haydn—Mozart with
the utmost interest.
And about Brahms? For the moment "acqua in bocca" as the
italian proverb says. Cordial greetings from
               Arturo Toscanini

November 3—1944

My dear Haggin . . .
      Yes! you were right—you guessed my feeling—The
dedication to me of your last book on its front page would
have not been so dear to me as it is now that I know the
dedication comes silently from your own mind and heart—and
from the bottom of my heart comes to you my best thanks.
      And you wanted to add: "in recognition of what I owe
you" as a complement of the dedication! Dio mio!! You make
me blush as I blushed to day hearing the record of the Eroica
made a few years ago, pur troppo!
      When shall I have the pleasure to see you at Riverdale? I
hope soon—may be next week . . . I want very badly to ask you
something about your book . . .
      With my best good wishes very cordially
               Arturo Toscanini

November 3 — 1941

My dear Mr Haggin

Yes, it will be one
of my first records
Schubert's C major symphony
which I am going to con-
duct next week with the
Philadelphia Orchestra ...
Also the Tchaikovsky Pa-
thetic and Iberia and
Reine Mab, too.

I took a weakness for

Beethoven's Septet which
I performed last season
with the N.B.C. or-
chestra with ten violins,
ten violas—eight celli—and
four basses—because I
never liked and enjoyed
this wonderful music
with the seven instruments
as it is written by Beethoven ... I heard many
performances of this
Septet in the original
form and played by

November 3 – 1944

My dear Happin ...

Yes! you were right —
you guessed my feeling —
the dedication to me of
your last book on its front
pages would have not been
so dear to me as it's you
that I know the dedication
comes silently from your own
mind and heart — and from
the bottom of my heart comes
to you my best thanks.

And you want to add:
"in recognition of what I
owe you" as a compliment of
this dedication! Dio mio !!

you make me blush as I
blushed to day hearing the record
of piacevola made a few
years ago, pur troppo!

When shall I have the
pleasure to see you at Riverdale? I hope you may
be next week ... I want
very badly to ask you something
about your book —

With my best good wishes
very cordially

Arturo Toscanini

To B. H. Haggin

Cordial remembrance of

(June 19th) Arturo Toscanini
1950

ENDNOTES

T.H.—1988:

(Page 28—Toscanini's Philadelphia Orchestra recordings:)

In 1963, four years after *Conversations With Toscanini* first appeared, Toscanini's record of Schubert's Ninth Symphony with the Philadelphia Orchestra was issued by RCA at last on LP; and in 1976 the entire series of Philadelphia recordings was issued in a boxed LP set. The liner notes to the 1963 Schubert LP explained that the recording had been withheld in 1942 because wartime materials and human error in the factory had resulted in "mechanical imperfections which neither the Maestro nor the company could accept". Only "through 750 hours of work," the note-writer said, "and the miracles of new electronic transfer techniques", had Walter Toscanini and his engineer John Corbett succeeded in 1962 in "restoring the recording...to its original state". What this writer said in a general way about the Schubert, the note-writer for the complete set in 1976 reiterated in graphic detail: concerning the first 78-rpm test records, he stated that on all of them "upper string partials had been wiped out; general playback level was almost below audibility in *pp* passages, with musical content being masked more often than not by a crossfire of clicks and pops against a background of generally heavy surface noise".

Haggin had heard some of those first test pressings himself with Toscanini and Walter at Riverdale in 1942, and he had heard no such defects. By 1962 he had heard many of the other test pressings in the series, and while he heard by then that the surface noise was louder than normal, he heard nothing like what was described in the LP notes and nothing that justified withholding the records all those years: "What Corbett's skillful and patient work had achieved," Haggin wrote in his notes for Sol Schoenbach's recollections in *The Toscanini Musicians Knew*, "was not to make audible a sound that had not been audible before, but to reduce the accompanying noise as much as it could be reduced without loss in...the beautiful sound."

Haggin's corrective statements raised two unanswered questions: why were the records ever withheld if they were only slightly damaged; and why was the extent of that damage exaggerated later. Because the unreleased albums have had—ever since the 1940s—a notoriety that has been sustained by what has been written about them on all sides, I will tell here what I have been able to learn about them since Haggin's death.

In the first place there was not one reason the records were initially withheld but several, and not one party to the decision but three: Victor, Walter and Toscanini himself. It appears—from copies of the correspondence between Walter Toscanini and Victor that were given out to different people over the years, and from the correspondence between Walter and Haggin—that although Victor rejected some sides, it was Toscanini who would not approve certain others—not because of mechanical noises, but because momentarily either the orchestra had not played well, or the microphones had not picked up a note or an instrument or a section as he wanted it to be heard. Specifically, Walter wrote Victor at various times in 1942 and 1943 to say that his father wanted the *fortissimo* at the start of the *allegro vivo* of the first movement of the Tchaikovsky *Pathétique* strengthened by recopying that side electronically at a higher volume; he wanted the last side of Respighi's *Feste Romane* recopied with less bass response in order to give the upper strings more intensity in relation to the brass; he wanted a woodwind imbalance in one passage on the second side of the first movement of the Schubert Ninth Symphony corrected—either by over-dubbing live sound or by remaking the side with the orchestra—and he wanted to record an entire side of the third movement over again with the orchestra; he rejected the first side of the second movement of Debussy's *La Mer* because a woodwind was inaudible at one point; and he rejected all of Debussy's *Ibéria* for musical reasons and wanted to record it again.

Walter *was* unhappy about gritty noises on certain sides, and about the higher than normal level of overall background noise. But in at least one case—that of the *Pathétique*—he said that if the volume level of one side were raised, the set could be released. As for Victor, since a letter from Walter in 1944 refers to earlier communications in which David Sarnoff (Chairman of RCA) and Charles O'-Connell (Victor's Music Director) had urged him to get his father to make up his mind about the *Pathétique*, it appears that in this instance Victor, too, was willing to gamble that the public would ignore noises it might not put up with normally on expensive new records for the sake of hearing Toscanini's performance with this unique orchestra.

Concerning the strengthening of certain passages or instruments Toscanini wanted, Walter, contrary to what Haggin had been given to understand, did not contemplate holding new sessions with the Philadelphia Orchestra in every instance. He asked Victor to make many of the corrections electronically in the manner described above. Walter's correspondence, and the fact that apparently Toscanini did not approve any dubbed records either, indicate that the attempt was not successful. Why make-up sessions were never held with the orchestra after the union ban on recording was lifted in November of 1944 is not known. One explanation that suggests itself is that newly recorded sides, which would have been undamaged, would have called attention to the noisiness of the others. However, the main fact is plain: some of the records were rejected by Toscanini himself for reasons that had nothing to do with mechanical defects. Walter told Haggin expressly in a letter in 1962, just before the first of the records finally *was* released, that it had been his father who hadn't been able to make up his mind about the records because he couldn't hear certain things on the equipment of the 1940s—things Walter described as negligible and of only a moment's duration—which he said could be heard on the equipment of the 1960s.

On the other hand, four albums were withheld by Victor. One was Richard Strauss's *Death and Transfiguration,* which Toscanini approved musically, but about whose surfaces Walter complained, and of which Victor appears to have rejected two or more sides. Another was the Mendelssohn *Midsummer Night's Dream* music, of which Toscanini rejected one side for musical reasons (the vocal number, "You Spotted Snakes"; this was to be omitted and the rest of the set issued without it) while Victor's Quality Control Department rejected the rest. The third was the Schubert Ninth Symphony, of which Toscanini objected to two sides for musical reasons, while Victor rejected others because of mechanical defects. And the fourth was Berlioz's *Queen Mab* Scherzo, which was approved by Toscanini, scheduled for release by Victor in 1942, but which I find Walter asking Victor to "repair".

As for the surface noises themselves, I can testify that there were some, although not equally in every set or on every record within a set. I have heard tape transfers of many of the test pressings of each album that were made at various times over the years, and I have heard tapes taken directly from some of the metal molds themselves. There is on all of them a light but audible background hiss; and there are on some of the records momentary crackling noises. I have found no reason to doubt that these things resulted, as has been said, from incorrectly formulated chemical solutions in the factory that marred the smooth surfaces of the metal masters as they were being made from the wax recording discs. Because the microphone levels at the recording sessions had been set lower than was usual, these defects were more audible than they might have been otherwise.

But I can testify also that the magnitude of these defects was exaggerated by the critics Victor and Walter enlisted to justify to the public the company's successive decisions—first to abandon the records, and years later to release them. As against the contention in the LP album notes that the 78-rpm surfaces had been so noisy that *pianissimo* passages were almost inaudible, Haggin's statement was the correct one: "the surface noise was stronger than the usual surface noise from 78-rpm records; but it didn't prevent one from hearing the musical sound: one's ear separated it from the musical sound, which was clearly audible and marvelously beautiful." As against the contention in the LP notes that all the records were afflicted with continuous loud crackling and popping sounds, I can say that a few sides were afflicted for some moments with light crackling noises like the sound of static. The one exception was *Death and Transfiguration,* several of whose later sides gave off such noises all the way through (on two sides as well, the loudest fortissimos were broken up momentarily by distortion).

Haggin was perplexed that it should have been claimed that the records were too noisy to release, since he and Toscanini had listened together in September of 1942 to parts of *Death and Transfiguration, La Mer,* and the *Queen Mab* Scherzo without being disturbed, and since later he himself had obtained test pressings of the Schubert, Mendelssohn and Berlioz that were not too noisy to listen to with pleasure. The explanation is threefold. Concerning *Death and Transfiguration,* Haggin and Toscanini listened that day to only the opening sides, which are quiet. Second, the unobtrusive noises in the other works, which did not disturb them as they listened, were nevertheless noticeable enough for Victor reasonably to anticipate complaints from that part of the public that had demanded refunds or replacements in the past because of similar defects. And third, Walter, beginning with the very first test pressings of the Philadelphia records, had complained with equal vehemence to Victor about minor noises he let pass and about worse noises he did not. He expanded what had been a genuine complaint about a few sides in some sets (particularly in *Death and Transfiguration*) into an exaggerated complaint about every side of all the sets. I have not found anything in the correspondence to suggest that Walter did this with any motive (although I have been told by Arthur Fierro, Walter's Administrative Assistant in the 1960s, that the vehemence of his letters to Victor at this time expressed his frustration at the carelessness and indifference with which Victor—and Charles O'Connell in particular—were mishandling all his father's recordings in this period). Walter's undifferentiating descriptions of the Philadelphia recordings are simply consistent with what his letters reveal to have been his well-intentioned but careless, generalizing, over-excited manner of speaking about most subjects.

The proof that even the records Victor and Walter would not approve were not as noisy as they were said to have been is that they did not sound that noisy on the LP records of 1963 and 1976 (and the LP's were not as clean as the 78s). Both sets of LP album notes claimed that John Corbett, the engineer who transferred the 78s to tape for Walter Toscanini in the early 1960s, had spent 750 hours on the Schubert record alone to make it quieter. Comparable efforts were said to have been expended on the others. In fact Corbett did little to lower the noise level beyond reducing stylus friction as he transferred the records to tape. The only exception was that from his tape of the Schubert, Corbett, using a razor blade, afterwards cut out bits containing the worst clicking sounds. But the fact that the two sets of test pressings I have heard, with nothing removed, do not have many more clicks than the resulting LP made me wonder if Corbett could really have spent 750 hours (or 804, as Walter claimed) preparing it. So I asked someone who had been at Riverdale when the Schubert was being worked on, and he told me that Walter had exaggerated the time Corbett had spent actually working on the records by adding on the time he had spent driving back and forth to Victor's facilities in Camden, and so on. He had done this for two reasons, my informant told me: to catch the public's attention with a colorful story at a time when the advent of stereo had caused sales of Toscanini's monophonic records to decline steeply; and to distract certain fanatics from the fact that he was releasing records Toscanini had not approved—the idea being to claim that surface noises had caused Toscanini not to hear things which the invention of spliceable tape and the expenditure of hundreds of hours now made it possible to hear after all.

Thus it seems that there is not one factor—noisy and damaged surfaces—that by being shown to be true or false reveals a single explanation of why the Philadelphia records were withheld at first and then released twenty years later sounding marvelous. Instead there were several factors. Some of the albums sounded marvelous from the start. Some had a few sides with mechanical defects that, while they do not spoil the music, might have disturbed a person listening

to a new record in the 1940s more than they would someone listening now to what he knows is an old record. Some
sets, defective or not, were approved by Victor for release.
Some—the *Midsummer Night's Dream Music,* Schubert's
Ninth Symphony, and *Death and Transfiguration*—were
rejected by Victor's Quality Control Department because of
mechanical defects on a few sides. Others were withheld because Toscanini (as Haggin observed elsewhere in this book)
"insisted on having in his recorded performances the complete freedom from imperfection that he seldom achieved
at concerts." And while Victor had helped make the records
legendary in the 1940s by not releasing them, Walter confused the legend in the 1960s by not telling the public the
simple truth he told Haggin in a letter in June of 1962—that
his father had been responsible for preventing the release
of at least some of the records in the 1940s (the *Pathétique,
La Mer, Ibéria, Feste Romane* and to some extent the Schubert
Ninth) because on a few sides he had not been able to hear
certain momentary things that he would have been able to
hear on the modern equipment of the 1960s. Instead—for
whatever good reasons—Walter put out a more dramatic
story about enormous mechanical defects on all of the
records that had made quiet passages almost inaudible,
something which Haggin knew—and reported—to be untrue.

It must be added, however, that Haggin was mistaken
when he wrote in 1979 that the poorer sound of the other
pieces on the LP records of 1976 in comparison with the
Schubert LP of 1963 represented deterioration in the metal
masters in the thirteen years in between. Corbett had trans-

ferred all the Philadelphia records to tape at the same time in the early 1960s. With the exception of the Schubert symphony and *Death and Transfiguration*, he appears from the files to have worked from shellac and vinyl test pressings, not from the metal masters. And as far as I have been able to discover, Corbett's tapes, not the test records or the metal masters, were used for the 1976 LPs. This set may not have been made as skillfully as the earlier Schubert LP. But the fact is that the sound of the 78s varied, too. The Schubert symphony and *La Mer* sounded best. The *Pathétique* was almost as good, but because the master for the last side had been entirely destroyed in the factory in 1942, a slightly hollow-sounding replacement was dubbed from an acetate long-playing backup disc made at the recording sessions. In *Feste Romane* and *Death and Transfiguration* the strings had less presence than in the others, and *Queen Mab* sounded dimmer than all of them.

As a footnote to all of the above, the likelihood that it was Toscanini who compelled Victor to abandon some of the Philadelphia records makes his own, angry reaction to their suppression seem more ironic than it did when Haggin reported it in 1979 in the belief that Walter and Victor had been solely responsible for the decision about all of the records: "Walter Toscanini told me that Victor wanted to abandon the Philadelphia Orchestra recordings and have his father make new ones with the NBC Symphony (for Victor there was no difference between a Toscanini performance with the Philadelphia and a Toscanini performance with the NBC Symphony) and that 'we are trying to get father to forget the Philadelphia recordings'—which I understood to mean that the decision was Victor's and the task of persuading Toscanini was Walter's. He didn't tell me why Victor wanted to abandon the Philadelphia recordings, and I could only conjecture (erroneously, as I learned only recently) that it didn't want Toscanini's name to promote what was now a Columbia orchestra, and was willing to sacrifice the recordings to prevent it...I remember Toscanini commenting bitterly about it, 'I worked like a dog!'"

(Page 29—Toscanini's American residences:)

The estate Toscanini occupied for a few years from 1942 on is called Wave Hill, and it now houses a Toscanini collection of recordings and other material. The larger Toscanini archive assembled by his son is housed at the New York Public Library at Lincoln Center. The house that was called the Villa Pauline has been demolished.

(Page 72—Petrushka:)
Toscanini was to have staged *Petrushka* on a ballet double bill with Stravinsky's *Le Rossignol* .

(Page 80—Caruso and Toscanini:)

Caruso made his La Scala debut with Toscanini in December, 1900 in *La Bohème*; the production of *L'Elisir* took place in February, 1901.

(Page 101—Errata:)

Busseto, not Bussetto; 1951, not 1952.

(Page 105—Toscanini, the Metropolitan Opera Co. and La Scala:)

Toscanini did wire Otto Kahn to thank him for his dona-
tion to the Milan charity concert, but he did not refer to
Kahn's invitation to return to the Metropolitan Opera Company. One reason for staying away that he did not tell Haggin was that Metropolitan soprano, Geraldine Farrar, with
whom he had been having an affair, had demanded that he
leave his wife to marry her. (Cf: Sachs, *Toscanini,* page 129)

Concerning Toscanini's reasons for leaving La Scala in
1929, he said himself a few months afterward that "It's
operatic conducting that wears me out; and I must repeat
that the only reason for my departure from La Scala is the
need for a less turbulent life." (*Ibid.* p.196)

Concerning the number of rehearsals for
Götterdämmerung in Toscanini's second year at the
Metropolitan: as he only conducted the opera in his first
season, he may have been thinking of another work when
he spoke about the matter to Haggin.

*(Page 137—Exclusion of guests from Toscanini's rehearsals in
1953:)*

In 1973 Haggin was led to conclude, by a statement made
by the president of the Arturo Toscanini Society, that his exclusion from the rehearsals in November of 1953 had had
nothing to do with Toscanini's occasional lapses and confusions of mind that season, but everything to do with Walter Toscanini's anger at Haggin's criticism of Victor's

"enhanced" Toscanini recordings, for which Walter turned out later to have been responsible.

"[The president] of the Toscanini Society...," Haggin wrote in his "Postscript" to the 1979 edition of this book, "— angered by my criticism of his selection of Toscanini performances for distribution to the society's members—included in a bulletin to those members, in August 1973, an account of our disagreements in which he wrote: 'We have been told by a source in a position to know [Haggin assumed this to be Walter] that this critic's invitation to Maestro's rehearsals in Carnegie Hall near the end of Maestro's career were withdrawn because of his interference in matters which did not concern him'—presumably at the rehearsals. Since I had done nothing there but observe and listen, it occurred to me to look up the letter in which Walter had informed me with regret of NBC's new rule excluding everyone from the rehearsals; and finding it was dated 23 November 1953, I looked up my *Nation* article of that week, and found that I had described and denounced in that article the damaging of Toscanini's recordings with 'enhancement'—a matter which did concern the critic who reviewed recordings for readers of *The Nation*. Thus I discovered at last that it had been Walter who had excluded me from the rehearsals because of what I had written about the recordings."

The issue of *The Nation* containing Haggin's article was dated November 28th, five days later than Walter's letter. Since *The Nation* appeared a week before the date on its cover, Walter *could* have seen it two or three days before he wrote Haggin about the rehearsals. But the more significant coincidence of dates is between Walter's letter to Haggin of

November 23rd and Toscanini's concert of November 22nd, the day before. Toscanini had cancelled his first two concerts that season; he had expressed anxiety about this one, the first one he did conduct; and in the performance itself he had made several mistakes, one of them serious. These factors, and the fact that Walter wrote Haggin immediately afterwards with apparently genuine regret, seem sufficient to contradict the Toscanini Society president's allegation. They seem instead to support Haggin's initial conclusion at the time of the letter: that he and others had been excluded from the rehearsals after the November concert because Toscanini had begun to exhibit occasional failures of mind which the family did not want outsiders to witness.

(Page 145—Erratum:)

For M-745 (1939 *Eroica* recording) read M-765.

(Page 146—NBC broadcasts moved to Carnegie Hall:)

In fact, Toscanini cancelled his first concerts that season and did not conduct in Carnegie Hall until January, 1951.

(Page 146—Toscanini's NBC broadcasts and recordings:) In the 1979 edition of this book, Haggin added the following observations:

Moreover comment on the broadcasts must include the fact that NBC, in the fall of 1947, moved Toscanini's broadcasts from Sunday at 5—a time when people were at leisure and could listen, and therefore a time which NBC could sell to Ford Motor Co. for another program—to Saturday at 6:30, which was not salable precisely because it was the time when people were busy with dinner and children and could not listen; the fact that whereas, in December 1947, NBC in New York added the required fifteen minutes from 6:15 to the 6:30 hour for Toscanini's broadcast of the first half of Verdi's *Otello*, its affiliated station in Rochester broadcast—in place of the first fifteen minutes of *Otello*—the regularly scheduled Answer Man program; and the fact that some of NBC's affiliated stations in major cities did not carry the Toscanini broadcasts live from New York, but scheduled at other inconvenient times recordings of the broadcasts on discs which, readers reported, occasionally were defective, or were played in incorrect order, or, as played, did not begin with the first grooves.

As for the Toscanini recordings, record companies always have claimed, like Sarnoff, that their recordings preserved the art of great performers for posterity, always without mentioning that this art would be preserved only as long as posterity bought the records in quantities which justified their continuing to be manufactured by the companies and kept in stock by the record stores. Actually, since the public buys mainly the recordings of the currently active performers whom it reads about in reviews of performances and publicity stories, the recordings of performers who are no longer active and written about are bought in decreasing quantities that eventually result in their being withdrawn from the catalogues. This happened even to the recordings of someone as famous as Toscanini; and an additional factor in his case was the advent of stereo, which made his mono recordings—even the ones with good mono sound—uninteresting to the large public that cared more about the latest in sound than about the greatest in performance.

It happened to some of the Toscanini recordings most important and treasurable for posterity—the ones he made with the New York Philharmonic in his final season with that orchestra in 1936, of their performances of Beethoven's Seventh, Brahms's Haydn Variations, Rossini's Overtures to *Semiramide* and *L'Italiana in Algeri*, and Wagner's Prelude to *Lohengrin*, his *Siegfried Idyll*, and *Dawn and Siegfried's Rhine Journey* from *Die Götterdämmerung*. They are important because they preserve the phenomenal operation of the Philharmonic under Toscanini's direction, which he never duplicated with any other great orchestra; because they preserve this operation in performances which document his style of that early period—relaxed, expansive, articulating and organizing and shaping the substance of a work with much elasticity of tempo, and molding the phrase with much sharp inflection—as against the style of the later NBC Symphony years that was simpler, tauter, swifter, setting a tempo that was maintained with only slight modification, and giving the phrase only subtle inflection; and because they preserve these performances in sound of extraordinary fidelity and beauty. Equally important and treasurable for posterity—even with their less realistic and beautiful sound—are the recordings Toscanini made with the New York Philharmonic in 1929, of their performances of Haydn's Symphony No. 101 (*Clock*), Mozart's Symphony K. 385 (*Haffner*), the Scherzo from Mendelssohn's music for *A*

Midsummer Night's Dream, Rossini's Overture to *The Barber of Seville,* and the Preludes to Acts 1 and 3 of Verdi's *La Traviata* .

Additional documentation of Toscanini's more effective and impressive earlier style is provided by his first recordings, in 1938 and 39, with the NBC Symphony, of Haydn's Symphony No. 88, Mozart's Symphony in G minor, Beethoven's Symphonies Nos. 3 *(Eroica),* 5 and 8, the Lento and Vivace from Beethoven's Quartet Op. 135, Rossini's Overture to *William Tell,* and Paganini's *Moto Perpetuo.* These document also the extraordinary energy and fire of the performances of those first years, in which Toscanini was stimulated by the exceptional capacities and responsiveness of the many young string virtuosos in the orchestra, and they were stimulated by his awesome powers, magnetism, and dedication.

So much for Sarnoff's claim that the RCA recordings would preserve Toscanini's performances for posterity. And disputable also, in the second place, was his claim of their "utmost fidelity"—as disputable when made for the recordings as when made for the broadcasts. B.H.H.—1979

(Page 148—Dubbed section of Ibéria *record:) In 1979 Haggin was able to add:*
In 1958 Mohr read to me a letter in which Walter, in 1952, had informed Victor of his father's request of the spliced-in passage. B.H.H.—1979

(Page 149—Toscanini's New York Philharmonic recordings:)

Although no records were issued between 1929 and 1936, actually Victor did attempt to make records of some of Toscanini's Philharmonic concerts, notably of Beethoven's Fifth Symphony in 1931 and 1933. And Victor gave Haggin another reason in 1933 why Toscanini rejected even these records, which had not required the recording procedures he disliked: he disapproved of certain aspects of the performances themselves when he heard them played back.

(Page 151—The bad-sounding 1939 Eroica *recording:)*

A letter from Walter Toscanini to Victor states that the 1939 *Eroica* was approved by a Victor committee while Toscanini was out of the country over the summer, and that Toscanini was furious when he returned and discovered that the mechanical defects had not been fixed as he had expected them to be.

(Page 154—Editing in the days of shellac records:)

A letter from Walter Toscanini to Charles O'Connell, Victor's Music Director, requests him to dub in the one missing note in the 1942 *Tristan* Prelude—something which, when done at the end of a side where it would not be superimposed on the rest of the record, was possible to achieve without loss in sound quality. On the testimony of Walter in subsequent letters, the reason the correction was never made was that O'Connell never got around to it.

(Page 161—Toscanini's opinion of the "enhanced" versions of his records:) In the 1979 edition of this book, Haggin said that the engineer Gardner subsequently told him of several incidents in which Toscanini had exhibited his dislike of what was being done to his Victor records:

[These were] his having rejected, because of its "enhanced" sound, the first version of the recording of Verdi's *Requiem* derived from the 1951 broadcast; his having compelled Victor to withdraw the already issued recording of Strauss's *Death And Transfiguration* after he had listened to a copy he was planning to take to Geraldine Farrar and heard with outrage what had been done to the sound he had approved. From this I learned that Toscanini, after approving the original tape of a recording, normally did not listen to the subsequent working tape; and I felt certain that he hadn't even heard the "enhanced" *La Mer*, much less approved it as Gerhardt claimed.   B.H.H.—1979

(Page 162—Concerning the recordings Gardner derived from Toscanini's broadcasts:) Concerning one of them Haggin wrote the following in 1979:

Of the recordings produced by Toscanini and Gardner from broadcasts the Berlioz *Harold in Italy* was issued by Victor in the summer of 1956 and the Strauss *Don Quixote* in the fall; but months and years passed without the release of one especially important and impatiently awaited recording that Toscanini was known to have approved before his death in 1957—the one of the Berlioz *Romeo and Juliet* he had broadcast in 1947. The reason was that Munch—who was still conducting the Boston Symphony and recording for Victor—had made a recording of Berlioz's *Romeo* which Victor wanted to protect from the competition of Toscanini's recording. In 1960, when Toscanini's 1953 Beethoven *Eroica* was issued, the word from Victor was that it was about to release his *Romeo,* which nevertheless it did not do. And the next word from Victor, early in 1962, was that it would release the Toscanini *Romeo* if it could obtain good enough source material of the 1947 broadcast (but the true reason for the further delay was revealed in the fall of 1962, when Victor issued Munch's remake of his *Romeo* in stereo: this new Munch recording now had to be protected from the competition of the Toscanini recording). B.H.H.—1979

(Page 166—Walter Toscanini loses his rare-book business in Italy:)

Walter was not just the son of an enemy to Mussolini, he was himself an active opponent to the Fascist regime.

(Page 177—Toscanini's resignation from the NBC Symphony:)

Haggin was the first to have pieced together all the known factual circumstances of Toscanini's resignation, from the recollections of those who were near Toscanini at the time. Harvey Sachs's account in his biography of Toscanini, which appeared three years before Haggin published his own description of what happened, was based largely on what Haggin had told him. However, in Haggin's account it is not easy to follow the order of events or his reasoning about their effect on Toscanini.

While Toscanini had told friends in 1953 that he wanted to retire, he had not been able to bring himself to do so for two reasons. First, as Sachs records him saying in 1951, he was fearful that life without work would be "unbearable". Second, he knew that NBC would disband the orchestra as soon as his name could no longer be used to attract sponsors. This fact had been in the air as a rumor since 1951. It was taken seriously enough by the musicians of the orchestra that some of them began leaving to take other positions as the opportunity arose, fearing that otherwise they all might find themselves looking for jobs at once. Toscanini's wish to postpone the break-up of his orchestra, some people told Sachs, was the reason he continued conducting as long as he did.

Haggin appears to have been right in supposing, then, that Walter felt he had to intervene to keep his father from again giving in (Toscanini's words) when Sarnoff came to Riverdale in November of 1953 with a contract for a further series of concerts the next season. (The significance of Toscanini's letter to a friend on May 16th, 1953—"I am not well...and they have had the bad taste to force me to accept another year of concerts"—seems to be that NBC, which had no scruple about jettisoning the orchestra once Toscanini was gone, also had no scruple about keeping the eighty-seven year old conductor on his feet as long as it could.) Walter's interception of Sarnoff in the driveway may not itself have galvanized his father's determination to retire, but it served at least to keep him from committing himself to another year. It also precipitated Sarnoff's and NBC's long-impending decision to terminate the orchestra and the broadcasts. And it was this decision that prompted Chotzinoff to suggest a reason for retiring that Toscanini finally felt compelled to accept: the fact that otherwise it would appear as though he were being pushed out.

The sequence in which Haggin relates the separate stories of Sarnoff's, Walter's and Chotzinoff's actions (characteristically, he gives them in the order in which he heard them—to enable readers to follow his successive efforts to puzzle out their significance) does not make it plain that (as far as one can tell) it was only after Sarnoff had been prevented by Walter from signing Toscanini to another year that Sarnoff made his long-held intention to disband the orchestra official, and that it was after he had done so that Chotzinoff asked Walter to relay Sarnoff's decision about the orchestra to his father, adding his own suggestion that Toscanini might want to resign beforehand for appearances' sake.

Haggin also believed that Walter probably concealed Sarnoff's contract offer from his father, and that what he did tell him—that the broadcasts were to be discontinued—would have caused Toscanini to infer that he was being dismissed, something that would have constituted "an indignity without precedent, the shock of which would produce [the] terrible scenes" Haggin heard that Cantelli had witnessed, and which might possibly have caused Toscanini's subsequent lapses and confusions of mind as well. But it is not known that Walter did not tell his father of Sarnoff's offer, or that Toscanini felt he had suffered the personal indignity Haggin speculates he did. What is known is that he was so upset over what was being done to "my poor orchestra" that he couldn't face the players at the end-of-season party; that he felt personally responsible; and that it was because of what Sarnoff and Chotzinoff had done to a great orchestra, not because of what they had done to him, that he referred to them later as "*animali*".

It remains only to observe—since some of the musicians who spoke with Haggin for *The Toscanini Musicians Knew* expressed regret that Toscanini had been made to retire while he still had much to offer—that had Sarnoff not disbanded the NBC Symphony, Toscanini could have retired and the orchestra still would have been there for him to guest conduct as his strength allowed.

ADDITIONAL ENDNOTES

T.H.—1988

(Page 106—"Concerning Stokowski . . . I can report no statement by Toscanini":)

In fact Stokowski was the un-named conductor whose performance of Franck's D minor Symphony Toscanini objected to on pages 26-27 of *The Toscanini Musicians Knew.*

(Page 117—"I play only one symphony of Schumann . . . the Third":)

Actually Toscanini played the Second and Fourth Symphonies, also.

(Page 125—Broadcasts transferred to Carnegie Hall:)

John Corbett told me that one cause of Toscanini's anger was the indignity of NBC's having made the decision without consulting him, as though he were just another employee.

(Page 152—The poor-sounding 1949 Eroica:)

When it was re-issued on compact disc, the recording was revealed to have been better made than it had sounded on LP.

(Page 172—The release in 1988 of previously un-issued BBC recordings:)

Also released was Elgar's *Enigma Variations*; but Mozart's *Haffner* Symphony and the *Midsummer Night's Dream* excerpts were not included after all; nor for that matter were Toscanini's BBC performances of Brahms's Fourth Symphony and various other short pieces, which exist.

INDEX

INDEX

INDEX

INDEX

Characteristics of performance: attacks, sonority, texture, phrasing, 16; single tempo for entire movement, 19, 40–41, 46 n., 131–32; plastic continuity and coherence, 23, 25–26, 92–93, 109, 134; right tempo, and coherence in change of tempo, 26, 95; occasionally alters scores to make every part audible, 29–30; what is printed in score must be audible in performance, 31, 87, 134–35, 147; fidelity to score, 40–41; change from early expansiveness to later simplicity, 45–46, 127–28, 131–32, 204; exceptions in reverse direction, 46–47, 128–30, 132; rigidity on occasion, 47, 60; clarity and shape in concertos, 52–53; integration of solo and orchestral parts in concertos, 52–53; occasional lessened energy, 60, 96, 127–28; return of relaxed plasticity, 60, 95; knowing what to do between *p* here and *f* eight bars later, 61; the Toscanini style in opera: accurate singing, coherence, flexibility and subtlety, 63–69, 85–86, 100; misrepresentation of that operation by critics specializing in opera, 66–69, 113, 133–34; tenseness in one–time–only broadcasts, 65–66; tempi, 66, 67, 69, 76; expressive rightness sacrificed to the cause of the true Andante, 90–91; the Toscanini operation: relation between

his gestures and what one heard, 92–93, un–selfconscious operation of extraordinary powers, 93, economy of gesture that was a form of honesty, 93, mind unceasingly attentive and active, 99, control exercized to keep entire orchestra in balance, 110, clarity and balance of texture, 110, 134–35, 136; Thomson's misrepresentation of these qualities as "streamlining," 134; occasional lessened effectiveness of later performances, 127–28; the opposite, 128–30, 132; tempi that became slower over time, not faster, 128–30, 131; repetitions of pieces never perfunctory, 130–32; powerful phrasing creating large–spanned utterances, 131, 132, 135–36; power exercised and not exercised, 135–40

Changes in performances of: Beethoven's *Eroica*, 45–46, 60, 99, 109, 128, Ninth Symphony, 46, *Missa Solemnis*, 128; Brahms's Symphony **No.1**, 40–41, **No.3**, 37, 95, **No.4**, 37, 60, 95, *Haydn* Variations, 95; Haydn's Symphony **No.98**, 60, **No.101** (*Clock*), 57–58; Mozart's Symphony **K.550**, 60; Rossini's *Semiramide* Overture, 127–28; Schubert's Ninth Symphony, 71, 130–32; Strauss's *Don Quixote*, 96, 128; Verdi's *Requiem*, 128; Wagner's *Tristan* Prelude, 128–30; changes documented

them is commercially significant, 203–204; New York Philharmonic records, 204–205;
Victor attempts to record New
York Philharmonic concerts
in **1930s**, 206; mechanically
faulty **1939** *Eroica* issued over
Toscanini's protest, 206;
Berlioz's *Romeo* withheld
twice to protect Munch's versions, 207–8
Broadcasts: times changed from
Sunday at five to Saturday at
six–thirty, 83–84, 126, 202–3,
to Monday at ten, 125, to Saturday at six–thirty, 126, to
Sunday at six–thirty, 132;
un–natural sound in Studio
8H, 119, 125–26, 145; location
of broadcasts changed from
Studio 8H to Carnegie Hall,
125, 146, 202, 212; Toscanini's
opinion of the sound of Studio 8H and Carnegie Hall,
125–26, 147; muffled sound
of **1951** Beethoven Fourth
Symphony broadcast from
tape, 126; Studio 8H's altered
sound after installation of
shell, 145–46; microphone
placement in Studio 8H and
Carnegie Hall, 146, 151–52,
158, 161; broadcasts faultily
relayed from discs by some
stations, 203; first fifteen minutes of *Otello* not aired by all
stations, 203
Comments, on composers and
music: Italians as against Germans as melodists, 101;
Beethoven, 118, Beethoven's
inconsistent notation, 49,

Septet, 14, Seventh and Ninth
Symphonies, 49; Bellini, 101;
Berlioz, 31–32, 34, *Fantas-
tique* Symphony, 79–80, *Romeo*, 33–34, 71; Brahms and
First, Third and Fourth Sym-
phonies, 117; Debussy's *Jeux*,
Gigues, and *Rondes de Prin-
temps*, 88–89; Donizetti, 101;
Haydn, 59; Mahler's Fourth
Symphony, 103; Mendelssohn
and E–flat Quartet, *Italian* and
Reformation Symphonies,
118; Mozart, 59, 117–118, dif-
ficulty in playing Mozart, 61,
his concertos, 59, tempos in
Mozart, 34–35, 49–50, 51, Pi-
ano Concerto **K.595**, 50–51,
Symphonies **K.543**, 48,
K.550, 50, 59, **K.551** (*Jupi-
ter*), 48–49, *Don Giovanni*, 50,
The Magic Flute, 34–35, 50;
Musorgsky's *Boris*, 103;
Puccini's sincerity in relation
to words, 90; Rossini and
Overture to *La Cenerentola*,
59–60; Schubert, 117–18;
Schumann and Second, Third
and Fourth Symphonies, 117,
212, *Manfred* Overture, 76;
Shostakovitch and Seventh
Symphony, 28; Sibelius's Sev-
enth Symphony, 78; why
Toscanini stopped playing
Stravinsky, 88, *Symphonies
pour instruments à vent*, 88;
Tchaikovsky's *Manfred* and
Fifth Symphony, 89; Verdi,
101, *Aïda*, 100–1, *Falstaff*, 115;
Wagner: finale of *Die
Götterdämmerung*, 36
On conductors: reasons for un-

225

INDEX

ACKNOWLEDGEMENTS

In the production of the first edition of this book I was indebted to

Walter Toscanini, for verification of a number of dates and programs and information about his father's early repertory; and for his permission to publish the texts of two of his father's letters, which, however, were not published in the first edition (1959) of this book because the necessary permissions of others were not received.

Several members of the NBC Symphony, and other persons who also had to remain nameless, for information about some matters I discussed.

Robert Hupka, for making available to me a few of his photographs of Toscanini in action.

Robert E. Garis, Roger Dakin, Margaret Nicholson and Charles B. Farrell, for editorial assistance.

In the production of this second edition I am indebted to

Ben Raeburn of Horizon Press, for his wish to bring out the new edition, and for yet another collaboration of a kind that is unique in my experience.

Robert Hupka, for again making his photographs available to me.

Mary Ann Youngren, for her comments and suggestions on the new material.

Wally Toscanini (Countess Castelbarco) and Walfredo Toscanini, for their permission to publish the two letters of Arturo Toscanini; and Emanuela di Castelbarco, for her assistance in this matter.

Thomas Hathaway and Michael Gray, for information about records in German RCA's *Toscanini Edition*.

"Once he started the progression going, he marshaled it along...
with those large, plastic, sensitive movements of his right arm
(extended to the point of his baton), which delineated for the
orchestra the flow of sound in much of its subtly inflected detail
and literally conducted the orchestra from one sound to the next.
...The left hand meanwhile was in constant activity as the instrument of the apprehensive watchfulness that showed itself
on Toscanini's face—now exhorting, now quieting, now warning,
now suppressing."

THE
TOSCANINI
MUSICIANS
KNEW

B. H. Haggin

Contents

Contents

Editor's Foreword

This new edition duplicates the text of the second edition published in 1980 by Horizon Press, omitting only those Notes — about recordings — that no longer apply. New are the statements by violist Milton Katims and cellist Frank Miller, who gave interviews for the first edition that were not published for reasons that are explained in my introductions to each. New also are the corrections and amplifications in my own endnotes at the back of the book. And an index has been added where there was none before.

— Thomas Hathaway
Toronto, 1988

Relevant Dates in the Toscanini Career

1885–Graduated from the conservatory in Parma as a cellist.

1886–Conducted his first performance of opera—*Aida*—in Rio de Janeiro.

1895–Became conductor at the Teatro Regio in Turin, where he conducted the first Italian performance of *Die Götterdämmerung*.

1896–Conducted his first orchestral concert, which opened with Schubert's Symphony No. 9, in Turin.

1898–Became principal conductor at La Scala in Milan, where he conducted Strauss's *Salome* and Debussy's *Pelléas et Mélisande*, among other new works.

1908–Began to conduct at the Metropolitan Opera in New York.

1913–Conducted the Metropolitan Opera Orchestra, Chorus and soloists in Beethoven's Ninth Symphony at his first orchestral concert in New York.

1915–Left the Metropolitan and returned to Italy.

1920–Conducted the La Scala Orchestra in an American tour.

1921–Became musical director of La Scala when it reopened after the war.

1926/7–Conducted the New York Philharmonic as guest conductor.

1928–Became a principal conductor of the New York Philharmonic. Selected players of the Philharmonic and the New York Symphony for the New York Philharmonic-Symphony.

1929–Resigned from La Scala.

1930–Conducted the New York Philharmonic-Symphony in a tour of Europe.

1930/1–Conducted at the Bayreuth Festival.

1930–Conducted the Philadelphia Orchestra as guest conductor.

1933/4/5/6/7–Conducted the Vienna Philharmonic in concerts and operas in Vienna and Salzburg.

1935/7/8/9–Conducted the BBC Symphony in England.

1936–Resigned from the New York Philharmonic-Symphony.

1936/7–Conducted the Palestine Symphony.

1937–Began to conduct the NBC Symphony broadcasts.

1940–Conducted the NBC Symphony in a tour of South America.

1941-42–Absented himself from NBC for the season, except for a few war-bond concerts.

1941/2–Conducted the Philadelphia Orchestra as guest conductor.

1942–Conducted the New York Philharmonic-Symphony in a Beethoven series in the spring and additional concerts in the fall.

1944–Conducted the Philadelphia Orchestra the last time, in a pension fund concert.

1945–Conducted the New York Philharmonic-Symphony the last time, in a pension fund concert.

1946–Conducted the inaugural concert in rebuilt La Scala.

1950–Conducted the NBC Symphony in a transcontinental tour.

1952–Conducted the Philharmonia Orchestra in London.

1954–Conducted the NBC Symphony's last broadcast, his last public appearance.

Foreword—1980

When this book was first published in 1967—only ten years after Toscanini's death, and, as it happened, on the 100th anniversary of his birth—there was already need of the correction the book provided of the inventions about him by writers acting the sharp-eared challengers of what they contended was the myth of his unique stature. And after thirteen more years of such writing that have left people today wondering what to believe about Toscanini, there is even greater need of the testimony of musicians who rehearsed and performed with him—their descriptions of the ways in which his powers in the conducting of an orchestra and the performing of a piece of music exceeded any they had encountered in other conductors they had worked with.

—B.H.H.

Introduction by B. H. Haggin

In the spring of 1962 my friend Mel Evans told me the idea he had had once for a book about Freud that would have been made up of what those who had known Freud and worked with him remembered of their experiences. Evans thought such a book about Toscanini—containing what the musicians who had played and sung with him remembered about him as a conductor and a person—would be valuable and fascinating; and to convince me he began to improvise stories he imagined these musicians telling. I said I couldn't see how one would make a book out of hundreds of anecdotes; but Evans urged me not to reject his idea until we had been able to ask one of the musicians what he thought of it.

At that point I recalled an incident at the Manhattan School of Music two weeks before. As I was inching my way toward the exit of the auditorium through the crowd that had come to hear Nadia Boulanger speak, I saw a man smiling at me in recognition; and when I reached him I said: "Please forgive me. I know your face, but I can't remember your name." "After seeing me day after day, week after week, all those years!" he answered reproachfully. "And after I bought ten copies of your book on Toscanini! Without even getting a discount!" And

9

more in the same vein, until at last he revealed that he was David Walter of the NBC Symphony's bass section, whom I had seen at Toscanini's rehearsals.

I now telephoned to Walter, who was quite willing to meet Evans and me at lunch, where we asked him what he thought of Evans's idea.

"All the books about Toscanini until now," he said, "have been written by outsiders, only one of whom"—with a nod in my direction—"gave any sign of understanding. And I think it is very important to have a book by the insiders—the musicians who actually rehearsed and played with Toscanini—so that there will be an authoritative statement by those who experienced his greatness to give people in the future a correct idea of what that greatness was." (This was a year before the appearance of This Was Toscanini, *with the illuminating text of Samuel Antek of the NBC Symphony and a large number of the marvelous photographs of Robert Hupka.)*

And he began right then and there to tell us what he remembered, continuing with one fascinating or moving recollection after another, until it occurred to him to ask what time it was. "Four o'clock!" he exclaimed. "I have a pupil waiting for me!" And he rushed off, after arranging to talk to me again the following week.

"You see?" said Evans.

"I do and I don't," I answered. "The stories are marvelous; but I still can't visualize how to make a book out of hundreds of stories."

I hurried home to write down all I remembered of what Walter had told us; and the following week I took notes as Walter talked for two hours more. And then the problem of how to handle this material was solved when I read in The New Yorker *the monologues of a number of actors that Lillian Ross had made out of her interviews with them. What each musician told me in answer to my questions, I would make into such a*

monologue; and the book would be the series of these monologues.

I proceeded in this way with the material Walter had given
me, and gave him what I produced. He substituted a better word
or phrase here and there; cut out a few statements he thought it
better not to make in public; and authorized me to publish the
corrected text, which now follows.

Statement by David Walter

In 1940 Toscanini had become dissatisfied with the bass section that Rodzinski had picked for the NBC Symphony in 1937; and auditions were to be held. At that time I was principal bass in the Pittsburgh Symphony under Reiner; and I was among the principals of a number of orchestras who were invited to audition. But as it happened I played in the NBC Symphony even before I auditioned.

On April 1, 1940, I received a call from NBC: the principal bass was ill from the shots he had been given for the coming South American tour, and a man was needed to complete the section. I couldn't make it that day; so they got a bass-player named Smith. A man was moved up from second stand to first, and Smith was put in at second stand. It was a rehearsal of Tchaikovsky's *Pathétique*, which as you know begins with a fifth—E and B—played by the basses; and when they played it Toscanini stopped them and said "Out of tune!", and called on them to play one stand at a time. The first stand played and satisfied him; and he went on to the second. But Smith was so terrified to find himself in this exposed position that he couldn't draw his bow across the strings; so there was only the B from the other man. *"Ma che è questa!* What is this!" said Toscanini.

"Play!"; and he started again. This time Smith's hand shook so badly that he produced an unsteady sound. There was a violent exclamation from Toscanini, and another start; and this time Smith's bow flew out of his hand and landed where he couldn't reach it; so again the B came out without the E. And at that point Toscanini blew up and walked out.

The next day I was able to accept the NBC call; and when I got there well ahead of rehearsal time I found the entire bass section in the room off Studio 8H carefully tuning their instruments—after which they practiced the opening passage of the *Pathétique* with the bassoon who had the melody. When the rehearsal began the basses played their fifth perfectly, and Toscanini exclaimed: "*Ecco!*"—which I didn't understand until I was told what had happened the day before. And this was my introduction to Toscanini.

I stayed with the orchestra to the end of the season; and it so happened that in that month there wasn't a single outburst of the famous Toscanini temper, so that I began to wonder about all those stories about this gentle old man. And early in May I formally auditioned for him. I began by playing something I thought would have special impact on him—the *Agnus Dei* of Verdi's *Requiem*, in which all the violins, violas and cellos play with only one bass. When I played this bass part Toscanini came and stood near me; and at the end he asked: "Are you American?" I said yes; and he said with a smile: "You play like European"—which I later figured out to mean that he heard evidence of the kind of musical training, particularly in *solfège* and *cantabile* style, that European bass-players got from the start but ours often didn't. Then I played the recitatives in the last movement of Beethoven's Ninth; and Toscanini moved over to the piano and began to play the orchestral part with me. He kept going past the recitatives, so I had to keep going with him; and luckily he stopped just as my memory was about to give out (the orchestra's personnel manager had taken away my music).

13

I was accepted, and joined the orchestra officially in time for the South American tour, which began in June.

On the ship Toscanini walked the decks day and night, and was always approachable and affable and talked freely with the men. He was amusingly observant: once when a poker game broke up at 3 in the morning we found him on deck, and he asked: "It went well?" And he was touchingly human: one cool day we were all on deck in thin short-sleeved sport shirts; and Toscanini, who also was in such a shirt, said solicitously to Bachman, who was of course considerably younger: "Go, Bachman, put on your coat." "What about you, Maestro?" said Bachman. "Oh, I am younger than you," said Toscanini. And I remember a later incident: one of the men was killed by a bus the last day of the tour; and the news was kept from Toscanini until a couple of days before the ship got to New York. When he was told he became terribly upset, feeling that he was responsible for the man's death—that if he hadn't made the tour the man would be alive. As a result we didn't see him again for the rest of the trip; and he canceled the party that had been planned for the last day.

I mention these incidents to show that at this time he was close to us, whereas in later years he became more distant. One reason for this was the deterioration of his sight. I recall an incident involving our solo bassoon, Kohon, whose wife died, and who had to put in a substitute for the rehearsal on the day of her funeral. The substitute sat only a few feet away; but Toscanini didn't see that it wasn't Kohon sitting there; and he said: "No, my dear, no, no, NO! You are not the old Kohon; you do not play like the old Kohon today. No, no, NO!" But in addition, in those later years the entourage that made itself Toscanini's protector against the intrusion of the outside world included his orchestra among the intruders. So at the few parties for the orchestra that he gave in the fifties it was a pleasure to see him his old affable, congenial self again. But I must add that the last party, after his retirement, was very different. There were to be three such parties; and about a third of the men were at the first one. He didn't come down to join us; and eventually Ghignatti and Cooley went upstairs to see him. They reported that he was in tears, exclaiming "My poor orchestra! My poor orchestra!"—feeling that he was responsible for the disbanding of the orchestra, and that he couldn't face us. And the other two parties were canceled.

But to get back to the ship on the way to South America: Toscanini, as I said earlier, talked freely to us, and not only about music. We discovered he was a man who had read a great deal—principally an enormous number of the *fin de siècle* novels that were called romances. I might add that he was also a man who could appreciate the attractiveness of the lady harpist who was with the orchestra on this tour. And so it was exciting to discover that he was a rounded human being.

But of course much of his talk was about music; and the men egged him on with questions to get him to tell the endless and fascinating stories about operas and composers and perform-ances—operas we had never heard of, or this performance in November, 1902, or that one in May, 1905, in which, no matter how much had been good, he remembered the contralto or the second oboe or the seventh cellist who had been terrible. "Did you conduct in England, Maestro?" "O-o-oh, ye-e-es! Oboes were very bad!" What about the premiere of one of the Puccini operas—the soprano, the tenor, the baritone? Toscanini de-scribed the soprano, shook his head over his recollection of the typical example of the species *tenori* that he considered the lowest of all, but broke out into a furious denunciation of the baritone. Someone managed to ask what had become of him. "Ah, poor man," Toscanini said sadly, "I think he died in 1915." Someone asked: "Why do you get so excited about him after so many years?" "Because," Toscanini answered vehemently, "I am angry when I remember what he did to Puccini!"

15

I had a demonstration of that extraordinary memory when we got to Buenos Aires. Ricordi had put on an exhibition of Toscaniniana, among which was a photograph of Toscanini taken many years before that fascinated me: it showed him in his prime, in a proud stance, his mustache fiercely pointed, and wearing a terrifically high collar. I was able to buy a copy, and found the courage to ask him to sign it. He took it from me, examined it with great interest, and said: "Yes, I remember this photograph. It was taken by good photographer, in April, 1913—no, *May*, 1913."

In Rio we rehearsed Beethoven's Seventh. I got to know the Seventh from a popular recording when my family bought its first phonograph in 1929; and later I played it as a student and professional with various conductors; but now when I heard for the first time all the different things in Toscanini's performance I was so excited that I could hardly contain myself. I remember in particular the shock of the second movement. It is often referred to as the *slow* movement; and you know the usual slow tempo [Walter sang the opening of the movement in this tempo]. So you can imagine the effect on me when Toscanini began the movement in *his* tempo [Walter demonstrated Toscanini's faster tempo]. He set a tempo that conformed to the meaning of Beethoven's direction, *Allegretto*, not to the traditional preconception of 'slow movement'.

This was the first of countless demonstrations of his respect for the composer's text. The printed score didn't tell you everything; but Toscanini believed it was what you had to start with; and he made you think of the exact meanings of the words you found there—for example the word '*andante*', which most people think means 'slow', whereas its literal translation is 'going', and its meaning in music is 'with flowing movement'. I remember his stopping us once at the beginning of the second movement of Beethoven's *Eroica*: "Is written *Marcia funebre*. You play *funebre*; I want *marcia!*" And this exactness extended to everything else in the score—dynamics, time values, phrasing.

For example, he was bothered by the usual execution of *fp* which made the *p* almost inaudible. The *p*, he insisted, meant *p*: if the composer had meant *pp* he would have written it. "*Piano, ma voce,*" he would say, meaning a *piano* that was full-bodied. He also insisted on the difference between *f* and *ff* in Beethoven—for example the *f* of this passage [bars 109-112] of the first movement of the *Eroica*, and the *ff* of its more heavily scored repetition. The same with time values. He insisted on a precise execution of the basic rhythm of the first movement of Beethoven's Seventh:

with a short sixteenth-note and a little pressure on the eighth, instead of the usual unprecise

He insisted on exactness in the rhythm of the Funeral Music in Wagner's *Götterdämmerung*:

on which he based the plastic melodic phrase. And the exact delineation of rhythm all the way through the opening statement of Strauss's *Don Juan*:

gave that statement an effect I have never heard in other performances, which are careless about the triplet and the dotted eighth and sixteenth in the second measure. I must add, however, that the exact execution Toscanini insisted on from each woodwind at the beginning of Ravel's *Daphnis and Chloë* Suite achieved something different from the usual impressionistic effect of the passage played without this exactness. I would say what was most outstanding in Toscanini's work was his organization of time and rhythm and dynamics into form; and this made him, in my opinion, most effective in music with clearly delineated rhythmic and formal structure, as against music which made its effect with color. In other words, he was a classicist rather than an impressionist. And so he did well with Ravel's *Bolero*; and if he had played modern music I think he would have done well with Bartók's *Concerto for Orchestra* and Stravinsky's neo-classical works.

But to get back to his exactness about everything in the score: although every marking had to be observed, this had to be done with flexibility and imagination. The opening phrase of Mozart's G-minor was marked with only *p*; but this didn't mean one played it in an anemically unmodified *p*: one made the modifications in the *p* that were necessary to give the phrase a singing quality. The Scherzo of the *Eroica* is marked *pp*; but when we played it with Toscanini it wasn't a light and delicate scherzo: it had an energy and bite that made it a *heroic* scherzo. And the horn passage of the Trio wasn't suave and graceful: it was powerful and noble.

A marking meant one thing in one work, and a different thing in another. I remember the first time I played in Beethoven's Ninth with Toscanini—how surprised I was by the violins statement of the theme of the slow movement, which is marked *mezza voce*, but which this time had a full-bodied sound it hadn't had in other conductors' performances. The movement is marked *Adagio molto e cantabile*; and the violins played the theme in a *mezza voce* that was *cantabile*. And Toscanini's *Adagio molto* actually was a little faster than that—a *con moto* tempo that gave the theme cohesiveness and a structure it hadn't ever had before in my experience: for the first time I heard a long integrated melody instead of the usual series of melodic fragments; and this meant that when the variations on the theme came later in the movement I could hear them as variations. There are those who talk about musical architectonics; but Toscanini produced it without knowing the word.

What he did was to make you sharply aware of the differences in the size of a *forte*, the strength of an accent, the rapidity of a *crescendo* or *decrescendo*, in different works. Even the most expert orchestral musician became more alert and sensitive playing with him. And so without being at all didactic, Toscanini was, in effect, a great teacher.

This was in addition to having extraordinary powers as a conductor. Even for a good conductor whom he respects and likes, the average player does about fifty percent of what he is capable of; but with Toscanini you felt you had to do your best every moment. I have known only two other conductors who made you feel that way: one was Cantelli, the other is Casals. Actually you did more than your best for Toscanini: he got you to extend yourself, so that however well you played, with him you found yourself playing better. In Rossini's Overture to *Cenerentola* there is a fast passage for the basses that is extremely difficult to finger; and in most performances one or two men may make an enormous effort and play it accurately; but with Toscanini the section played it perfectly, and in his faster tempo.

One of the reasons for this effect on the player was Toscanini's superb knowledge of what he was doing. And another was his tremendous involvement in it—emotional and physical. Conductors—particularly older conductors, but even younger ones—will spare themselves; but Toscanini didn't: he fully conducted a *forte*; he fully conducted a *fortissimo*; and he didn't relax even for a *piano*. He simply didn't know any way of easing up: at the time he was having trouble with his right arm he continued its large sweeping movements even when they caused him to grimace and curse for pain. And this affected and inspired the player. There are climaxes in Tchaikovsky in which the basses are asked to saw away *ff* for forty or fifty measures. If the men don't care they make a great show of effort but actually play *f* at most; if they care they arrange to spell each other: one man at a stand plays *ff* for ten measures, then eases up while the other man plays *ff* for ten measures. But with Toscanini fully conducting *ff* throughout the passage, every man in the section played *ff* in every one of those forty or fifty measures. With Toscanini doing his utmost, you couldn't do less.

Those large sweeping movements of the right arm that I mentioned were one of the means of getting you involved as intensely as he was: they swept you on. I should add that Toscanini's conducting movements didn't beat time in accordance with the traditional skeletal configurations of time-beating in conducting manuals; they delineated the musical flow, and in doing this broke the prison of those configurations. And so while they were the most expressive movements and gestures of any conductor, they didn't always answer the orchestral player's well-known question, "Where's the beat?" Nor did they give you all entrance cues, but only the ones that were musically important; which meant that at times you *had* to count measures attentively to know when to come in.

I said before that you were affected by Toscanini's knowledge of what he was doing; and I should add that you were affected also by his knowledge of what *you* were doing. He made you feel that he knew you and knew your part so much better than you did that you couldn't dare to do less than your best. I remember an occasion when he flashed an angry look in the direction of the basses at one point, and afterwards there were five men, each of whom was sure *he* had been the culprit Toscanini had caught in the error and glared at.

You played beyond the limit of your ability—out of fear of his knowledge and fear of his anger, but also out of fear of not fulfilling yourself. So men took their parts with them to practice them at home, and came to rehearsals early to practice them some more. I remember arriving for a rehearsal and finding the woodwinds practicing those enormously difficult passages in the Scherzo of Tchaikovsky's *Manfred*, which usually have to be taken a little more slowly then they are marked; with the result that at the rehearsal the passages were played brilliantly in the right tempo.

Working with him was therefore always very exciting; but what I recall as most exciting were the first years, and on the other hand the last ones, when he seemed to get his second wind. I think of the last Beethoven performances, which not only were less dramatic and more introspective, but had new details that represented new thought and analysis. When we did the Seventh the last time he told us he had been up all night with the score, and mentioned specific details of our earlier performances that he now realized had been mistakes: "I was stupid; *you* were stupid; only Beethoven was not stupid!" That this man, at this age, should feel there was still something to look for and learn in a piece of music he had played so many times—this not only was moving, but inspired you to do more work yourself.

It meant that although he was old in years his mind and spirit were young; and that was the way he felt. This could be amusing. I remember his helping Ansermet up the steps of the podium and saying to someone afterwards: "Poor man, he has aged." And there was the incident at Sun Valley, which we visited on our transcontinental tour in 1950. We had a barbecue in the afternoon, with superb food and lots of liquor; and we were sitting with Toscanini afterwards, very relaxed, when one

of the men said: "Maestro, you are looking wonderful today"—
as in fact he was: some of the men had been afraid to take the
ride on the ski-lift even once; but he had insisted on taking it
twice; and he was still in a glow of excitement. "No," he answered mournfully, "I am old man." And he went on to remind
us of the Italian saying that a man lived only to the age of his
mother—which meant that he, at eighty-two, had only a couple
of years left. "But Maestro," the man persisted, "think of Verdi,
who lived to be eighty-seven. Surely you can expect to live as
long as he did!" "Verdi!" Toscanini exclaimed. "He was sick
old man! I am strong; I will live longer than Verdi!"

One more thing I must speak of is Toscanini's concentration. When he was going over a point of phrasing with Mischakoff or one of the solo winds, he was completely oblivious to the
talking around him; and as a result we got to be known as the
noisiest of orchestras. Once, however, he did notice the noise,
and exclaimed: "Eh! . . . Why you talk?!! Ah, you are *uomini
senza gentilezza . . . senza educazione . . . senza cultura . . .*"

This mixture of languages was habitual: being multilingual,
he would begin a sentence in one language and finish it in
another. "*Bitte, cominciamo*"; or "*Non tedeschi!* You play like
Germans!" Or "You are *primi violini,* but you play like *prime
donne*"—followed by a crescendo of excoriation which halted
momentarily as he searched for a climactic epithet, and then
shouted: "*Farmacisti!*"—a reference to the insignificant Italian
village apothecaries who applied leeches and so on.

His language when he became angry could get violent and
coarse. But I would like to say that the outbursts of rage have
been made too much of. They provided colorful stories; but
they have given people a false idea of what went on at rehearsals.
The fact is that most of the time Toscanini worked with the
orchestra with quiet and superb efficiency. And on one occasion
we learned how his outbursts were to be taken. As his words got
angrier and angrier he tried to break his baton between his

hands; and it bent but wouldn't break. "DOLAN!!!" he roared to the orchestra's librarian, who brought another baton. This one broke easily; and the storm was over. One of the men ventured to express concern over his getting so upset; but Toscanini reassured him: "Don't worry; is good for my blood." After that, whenever he got into a rage we would say: "It's all right; it's good for his blood." Though I recall a different comment once when I commiserated with the tympanist, a very gentle older man, about the way Toscanini had shouted at him. "Yeah," he answered, "if he hadn't been right I'd have told him off."

There were men in the orchestra who would have preferred a peaceful existence without Toscanini to the strenuous one with him. We had a guest conductor once—an unassuming man who made no demands and let us off from rehearsal early; and one of our principal wind-players said: "That's a conductor you could live with." But speaking for myself—and I know others would agree—I can say that when I was worn out at the end of a Toscanini rehearsal I didn't mind, because it had been an endlessly fascinating and exciting and instructive experience.

Alan Shulman

HAGGIN:

Listening again to the 1937-38 and 1938-39 NBC Symphony broadcasts when they were rebroadcast in 1963, one was struck by the extraordinary energy and fire of these early performances —which represented the energy and fire not only of Toscanini himself in those years but of his orchestra. Until then he had conducted orchestras made up mostly of middle-aged players; now he found himself conducting an orchestra which included a large number of young players—notably the brilliant young string-players who had been induced to leave the concert stage and string quartets for the part of the NBC staff orchestra that was to play with Toscanini as the NBC Symphony. Those early performances document their outstanding talent and their youthful vitality, which delighted and stimulated him, as they in turn were delighted and stimulated by his unique powers, magnetism and dedication. One of the youngest to join the orchestra in November 1937 was a cellist, Alan Shulman, who had been graduated from the Juilliard School only four months earlier, but had been playing in the Kreiner String Quartet since 1935. He was able to describe the Toscanini operation of those first NBC years; and since he remained with the orchestra until

24

*the end, he was able also to speak of the tragic happenings of
the last year.*

*What follows (like all except one of the subsequent mono-
logues) is put together from the words spoken into a tape-
recorder. I haven't used Shulman's every word; but the words I
give are his.*

SHULMAN:

For our first broadcast, on December 25, 1937, we had three
or four rehearsals. We had been prepared by Rodzinski, who
had started coaching us in September: four or five rehearsals a
week, just going through the literature. We had a preview
concert with him, then three or four concerts with Monteux;
and then Maestro came. At his first rehearsal everyone was on
tenterhooks until he came in, dressed in his black work jacket,
and said "Brahms"—the First Symphony—and we went to work.
It was electrifying: we were like racehorses that had been training for six months and suddenly were on the track for the race.
You must realize that all I had had before this was training with
Stoessel and Barzin, and that this was my first experience in a
professional orchestra; and as the second youngest player I was
in awe of the big shots: Mischa Mischakoff, our concertmaster;
John Wummer, the first flute; Robert Bloom, the first oboe;
Albert Stagliano, the first horn. So for me this first rehearsal
was an overwhelming experience.

What struck all of us, and what we talked about, was
Toscanini's total honesty, his total dedication, his subordination
of himself to the composer's demands. Instead of the composer
prostrating himself at the base of *his* pedestal, *he* prostrated
himself at the base of the *composer's* pedestal—unlike many
conductors around. And this continued through the years. He
would say to us, "Be honest!"; and he himself had this honesty,
this sincerity: he tried to get as close as one could to the truth
in a piece of music.

There are a couple of incidents I remember that illustrate this honesty and humility in relation to the composer and his music. One occurred at a rehearsal of Beethoven's *Eroica*. So many artists—when they've reached the heights of success he reached—begin to take things for granted; and that's when they start slipping back. But this was where Maestro's unique integrity came into play—when he said: "I have been conducting the *Marcia funebre* for fifty years, and I conducted *male*. Please, may we repeat it—not for you but for me." He meant what he said—no question about that: he had studied the score again and found things that hadn't been revealed to him before; he felt he hadn't done justice to the music; therefore he felt he must repeat it. Not to be blinded by the glare from his own halo, but to be willing to look at a score again and find new perspectives—that was the greatness of Maestro.

The other incident occurred in October 1941. For reasons I'll tell you about later, he sat out the season of 1941-42, and NBC got Stokowski in to conduct us. At that time Emanuel Vardi was playing in the viola section of the orchestra and had quite a friendly relation with Maestro, who had come to Vardi's Town Hall concert. Vardi played my *Theme and Variations*; and Maestro came backstage and congratulated us. So one day in the fall of 1941 Vardi said, "Let's go up and pay Maestro a visit." I said, "Nonsense; we'll never get in." Vardi said, "What have we got to lose?" So we drove up to Riverdale on a sunny afternoon in October. We told Maestro we had come unofficially to pay our respects; and he was a most gracious host. We talked about a number of things; he played test pressings of the Beethoven Septet for us; and at one point he said: "Did you hear the Philharmonic broadcast yesterday?" We said no. And he said: "I listened, and heard the Franck Symphony. I was so angry I wrote a letter. I didn't mail it, of course. But the first sentence was 'Blessed are the arts which can survive without the aid of interpreters.' " This to me is a classic, because it represents his whole philosophy as a musician.

There was an honesty too in his dealing with us. As it happened he didn't blow up that first day: it was not until the second or third rehearsal that we got our first experience of the famous Toscanini temper. But that wasn't important: what *was* important was that he was fair: he knew his scores; he came prepared; he knew what he wanted and how to go about getting it; and he wasn't satisfied until he got it—he wouldn't compromise for half. But once he got it, that was it; and this made him the least demanding of any of the conductors we worked with—by which I mean that he believed in not wearing his orchestra out. We were scheduled for a two-and-a-half-hour rehearsal; and if after the two and a half hours he hadn't achieved what he wanted he had no qualms about keeping us overtime until he was satisfied; but if he was satisfied at the end of an hour he would dismiss us.

In contrast to this there was the incident of a well-known guest conductor's rehearsal of the *Eroica*. It was after we had done a Beethoven series with Maestro, including the *Eroica*; and at this rehearsal, after the first movement Harvey Shapiro and I put a sheet of paper alongside our music and marked on it every time the guest conductor stopped in the second movement. It was fifty-seven times! Maestro had come in after the first fifteen or twenty minutes and sat in the balcony of Studio 8H; and after a while he began to pace back and forth; but by the time we reached the end of the *Eroica* he was running—he was so angry. And we heard later that he went to the dressing room and gave the guest conductor hell for wearing out the orchestra needlessly.

It wasn't hard work if we could satisfy him: it was when we *didn't* satisfy him musically that it was hard. We'd turn a phrase, and it wasn't exactly right; so we'd do it again—and possibly a third and a fourth time—until we hit it; and then it was as though the clouds broke and the sun came through, and he'd smile, and with the tension broken the whole orchestra would relax and breathe again. Because when we didn't get it after two or three attempts we were building toward an explosion. And at such times he was capable of great cruelties—though I'm convinced he wasn't aware of them as such. His dedication to his art was so intense that he couldn't think of anything else, including human feelings; and so he rode roughshod over many musicians. When things went well it was heaven; when they went badly it was hell, and we ran scared. But one thing I must say: if we didn't deliver at a rehearsal there could be an explosion; but if there was a slip-up at a performance—this was the human factor, it could happen to anyone, and there never were any post-mortem recriminations, not even a mention of it. This to me was evidence of understanding and tolerance; and I point to it because all the public heard about was *in*tolerance and temper.

At the concerts there was electricity in the air. The man was supercharged; and it permeated the atmosphere, creating an aura of excitement that we didn't feel with other conductors. A concert can be a concert, or it can be a concert plus an event; and with Toscanini we had the double feature. But it was the dress rehearsals that were absolutely extraordinary: in that atmosphere of quiet and intense concentration we were hynotized, and the ninety-five men functioned as one. At the concert the presence of the audience made it impossible to have that quiet and concentration; and Maestro may even have felt subconsciously that some of the subtleties and the effort they cost would be wasted on the audience. In any case I felt that something was lost at the concerts; and this feeling was shared by many of us. Also, as you say, his movements were less energetic and expansive at concerts than at rehearsals, and the audience may have created a constraint that kept him from letting himself go all out as he did at rehearsals. And maybe it was easier to conduct in a work jacket than in formal clothes.

When you ask about the characteristics of his performances I think of the clarity he got—clarity of texture, clarity of architectural detail. I think too of his linear sense: his phrases were marvelous arcs, which added up to architecture on a grand scale that was commensurate with the concept of the creator of the work. I think of the flexibility—the forward motion, and yet the repose. The ability to milk every note of the phrase, with an Italian warmth, but also with intelligence and good taste. And the electrifying, incisive rhythm, which is something you don't hear today. I've heard musicians talk about Furtwängler; and I've heard his old recording of Tchaikovsky's *Pathétique* with the Berlin Philharmonic, which is very beautiful. But the tempi are a bit on the slow side; so I don't feel the excitement of the march in the third movement. Whereas my God, when Toscanini finished that movement you'd want to jump out of your seat, and the audience always broke out into applause—they couldn't help it: it was electrifying. And it didn't run away. That was another thing Maestro had: his remarkable sense for pace—for the judicious selection of tempi. We played Strauss with conductors whose way of achieving excitement was to take it at virtually unplayable speeds, in which we didn't play half the notes. Toscanini took it a third slower, in tempos in which we could play all the notes; and it sounded twice as fast because it was rhythmically alive. Then his ability to set up dynamics. He would say a *piano* in Verdi is not like a *piano* in Beethoven: you see four *p*'s in Verdi, and you play one; you see four *f*'s in Verdi, and you play one. And his sense for the different styles of music of different periods—though I must say I didn't feel he had it for Bach. We didn't do much Bach with him—only a couple of the suites and the Brandenburg Concerto No. 2, I believe; and I didn't get from it the feeling for the style that one would get from—well, possibly from Scherchen. But Beethoven —Brahms—Mozart!

His Mozart was dramatic: he played the G-minor Symphony differently from other conductors, and he was criticized for it; but I think he felt the G-minor was different from other Mozart symphonies—that it was the writing not of Mozart the symphonist but of Mozart the operatic composer. And it is: the opening phrase of the first movement is operatic: it's *Don Giovanni.* Before Maestro started it, his eyes flashed around so that he'd have contact—this was one of the remarkable things— so that he'd have contact with the entire orchestra before that baton came into play. And with the incisive up-beat we knew what the tempo was going to be: with that little movement it was impossible to go wrong. Also at the end of the slow introduction of Strauss's *Death and Transfiguration,* just before the *Allegro molto agitato* begins with the terrific whack on the tympani: he sustained the long chord while his eyes flashed from left to right so that he had complete communication with every member of the orchestra; and when we went into the boom! of the *agitato,* half the audience jumped out of their seats from the impact.

I've wondered how much schooling he had in music, and whether what he did wasn't the result of natural instinct that developed as he went along. Now that you remind me I remember he *was* a graduate of the Conservatory of Parma and did have a professional musical training; but I always had the feeling that he relied mostly on his innate musical sense, and that he could do no wrong because what he did was so perfectly natural. He used to say: "*Naturale.* Don't force. *Canta, canta.*" He got every instrument in the orchestra to approximate the human voice—to sing. Once when he wanted something very soft he shouted: "*Lontano!* Far away! In Brooklyn!" Another time he said "Graceful! Graceful!" and then—this has been told many times—he pulled a silk handkerchief from his pocket and let it drift gently to earth like a parachute. Or he would say "*Una carezza*" and caress his cheek. And when he couldn't get what he wanted he would say: "Why couldn't they have been *farmacisti?* Why couldn't they have been shoemakers? Why did they have to be musicians?"

What performances stand out in my memory? The Wagner. Wagner programs were physically exhausting; but there was a *Stimmung* he achieved that was just beyond description. And of course the Beethoven. And the Brahms—the Debussy— actually *all* the standard repertory.

I don't think he had any appreciation of modern or contemporary music. He played it because he felt he had to; but with all due deference to his magnificent control of the orchestra, when we did something like the suite from *Petrushka* he was not at his best. A tricky rhythm could throw him off; and with the 5/8 and 7/8 and so on at the beginning of *Petrushka* he occasionally threw us a curve. Since you say the performance of *Petrushka* sounds perfectly secure, I may be imagining things; but I'd like you to check with other members of the orchestra. My feeling was that although his integrity compelled him to try to play this music he wasn't a hundred percent sold on it in his own mind, and so it didn't come off. If Cantelli had lived he would have done with contemporary music what Toscanini did with the standard repertory. When Cantelli did Bartók's *Music for Strings, Celesta and Percussion*, with its many parts in the opening fugue, it was with a feeling for balance and clarity of detail that made it nothing short of fantastic. Toscanini had this feeling for Beethoven, Brahms, Tchaikovsky, Debussy—but not for contemporary music; and so he played only a handful of things—the Shostakovich First, the Kabalevsky Second and *Colas Breugnon* Overture, Roy Harris's Third. The Shostakovich Fifth was offered to him: he took one look at the score and threw it down. But during the war he did the Shostakovich

Seventh—which was not as good a work as the Fifth—because he was emotionally affected by the siege of Leningrad. And a remarkable thing happened, which left us flabbergasted, and which I've never forgotten. He probably didn't care for the work as a piece of music, and played it for emotional reasons; but at our first reading of our parts he stopped us in a huge tutti and said: "*Contrafagotto*, what are you playing?" And it turned out that the contrabassoon was playing a B-natural in his part instead of the B-flat in Toscanini's score. Maestro's ear was one of the three great ears I've encountered in my years of playing under conductors: the others were Monteux's and Cantelli's.

That reminds me of an incident with Rodzinski. I don't know what we were rehearsing—it may have been a modern work—whatever it was, Rodzinski began to ride Robert Bloom's tail, and Bloom didn't like it. So at one point, when Rodzinski said, "Out of tune," Bloom put him on the spot by asking: "Maestro, what is it—sharp or flat?"; and all Rodzinski could answer was "Adjust yourself."

When I talk about Maestro I may sound like a bobbysoxer on Sinatra; but the fact is that I have yet to see his equal. If Cantelli had lived he might have attained that stature; for he certainly was well on the way, as his few records make evident. That was why Maestro sat in the hall during Cantelli's rehearsals beaming like a proud father: if he had had a son who was musically endowed, this was what he would have wanted him to be. You know, Cantelli was sent to a concentration camp because he refused to be conscripted into the Italian army; and he said: "The Germans took my stomach," so that he could only drink milk, and he weighed only ninety-five pounds. It was sheer dedication and will power that enabled him to carry on. He would work from 8 until noon in his hotel room, have a glass of milk, start again at 12:30, and go on till 5; and by that time he had memorized Stravinsky's *Rossignol* or Bartók's *Concerto for Orchestra*. He was accused of choreography on the podium, as another conductor is today; but with Cantelli there was nothing premeditated or stagy about it: he felt the music that intensely, and his bodily movements were an integral part of what he was doing. He was very remarkable; and his death is one of the great tragedies of our time.

To get back to Maestro, actually there were things he did occasionally that I took exception to. For example, the Trio of the Scherzo of Beethoven's Seventh: taken in the same tempo as the Scherzo it felt a little hard-driven. You're right: it *was* *meno*; but for me it wasn't *meno* enough. Then the occasional tampering with scores. True, it was mostly in the whipped cream stuff: I think he made some emendations in the *Skaters Waltz*, and I don't think the orchestration was the original. Also, I was shocked by what he allowed Harry Glantz to do at the end of *Stars and Stripes Forever*. I love Harry and he's a magnificent trumpet-player; but at one performance on the 1950 tour he took us all by surprise by standing up, with the rest of the brass following suit, in the grand finale, as if it were a performance in Radio City Music Hall; and the Old Man was amused and smiled and let Glantz do it every time after that. The Old Man also let Vito change the harp cadenza at the beginning of the *Waltz of the Flowers* in the *Nutcracker Suite,* improving on Tchaikovsky's harmonies. And I'll tell you one thing that disturbed me terribly as a composer: the completely out-of-character cadenza that Maestro wrote for Mozart's Bassoon Concerto. You didn't know it was Maestro's cadenza? Well, now you know. It wasn't good, and had absolutely nothing to do with the work, but just ambled on and on. Incidentally, Leonard Sharrow was upset too by the fact that he was allowed only one 'take' for the recording. After they recorded the Mozart Divertimento there was about three quarters of an hour of the session left—time enough for one take; and so there was only one take.

This attitude was the thing that bothered me in recording, and I believe was responsible for Toscanini's hating recording.

He felt it never did justice to his tonal palette and balances; and he was right; because when it came to balancing the orchestra I remember that Charles O'Connell, the recording director, was concerned with only one thing—that the session didn't go overtime. So everything was great: "Sounds fine, Maestro." Then the Old Man would listen to the playback and say: "I don't hear the oboe; I don't hear the second bassoon"; and they'd say: "Oh, but it sounds different upstairs. It's wonderful, Maestro." But when he got the test pressing he still didn't hear the second bassoon; and so he came to detest recording. For us, of course, even if the bassoon can't be heard there is the nobility of concept, the rhythmic force, the tremendous drive.

Another thing that disturbed me very much on the tour was the playing of *Dixie* in the South. Maestro was criticized for this by some of the press; but it really wasn't his fault: a management executive had the idea of doing it and talked Maestro into it; and after the rebel yells it got the first time in Richmond he persuaded Maestro to do it in the other cities.

That tour was fabulous: the ovations we got all over the country! We played in some horrible barns: in Austin we played in the university gymnasium, which seats 6,500 and didn't offer the best acoustics. But in a few places—the Lyric Theater in Baltimore, which is an old hall but has damned good acoustics, the War Memorial Opera House in San Francisco, the Opera House in Chicago—we gave outstanding concerts. There were many incidents, and the visit to Sun Valley, a promotional thing on the part of the Union Pacific Railroad, where they took that marvelous picture of the Old Man in the ski-lift.

The South American tour of 1940 also was fabulous: the ovations there—for example when we played in the Teatro Colón in Buenos Aires and the Teatro Municipal in Rio de Janeiro—were simply unbelievable. An interesting thing happened in San Paulo: the boxes were conspicuously empty, because there was a large pro-Mussolini group of Italians in San

Paulo, and they stayed away. But the rest of the house went crazy. And there were amusing incidents. After a concert on July 3 in Montevideo some of us went to a night spot and didn't get to bed until 3 in the morning. A rehearsal was scheduled for 10; and Edgar Lustgarten and I, who shared a room, left a call at the switchboard, but they didn't call us. When we awoke it was a quarter of 11; and we were horrified. We dressed and rushed downstairs, and found the men of the orchestra coming back into the lobby. We said, "What happened?" And they said: "Maestro called us to play *The Star-Spangled Banner* on July 4 and then dismissed us."

Just before we got back to New York Chotzinoff read us a letter Maestro had written to us in his own hand. A little of it was printed in *The Times*; and I'll read it to you from the clipping, which is dated July 24, 1940: "You have never played so well, so inspired. We have never been so linked before. We must be proud of what we have done. While writing I feel sad at heart, and it will be always so when beautiful things come to an end." The rest was just as warm; and he told us he was looking forward to conducting us again in November.

But it was soon after he resumed work with us that the incident occurred that caused him to leave us for a year. It took him some time to discover that the orchestra NBC said it created for him played in other programs under other conductors; and it made him angry because it affected our work with him. On a Friday in December 1940 we were scheduled to rehearse from 5 to 7:30 in Carnegie Hall for a performance of the *Missa Solemnis* the next night. There was a concert of the Chicago Symphony in Carnegie Hall that afternoon, after which the platform had to be set up on the stage for the chorus in the *Missa*; so the rehearsal didn't start until 5:30, which meant it would go on to 8. But thirty-five men of the orchestra had to play with Frank Black in the Cities Service program in Studio 8H at 8; and they had to leave at 7:30 if they were to pack their instruments, get to 8H, change their clothes and be ready for the broadcast at ⁿ And since this was the first time we were doing the *Missa* with Maestro he was really out to work. So 7:30 came, and he kept right on working; then it was 7:32, and 7:33; and at that point the personnel manager stood behind Maestro and signaled to the men one by one to sneak out. I saw Carlton Cooley, right under Maestro's nose, get down on his hands and knees and crawl out; and it was only after a number of men had done this that the Old Man's eye caught the movement of the bassoon that one of the men was holding as he crawled out, and he discovered what had been going on. He was so infuriated that he threw down his stand and walked out. He conducted the performance the next night and finished the season; but a couple of months later when the conductors for 1941-42 were announced he was not among them, and we learned that Stokowski was going to conduct us instead.[1]

Were we aware of any change in his work in later years? Certain things were played faster; and I think the reason was that he was afraid of being accused of growing old. Yes, the *Tristan* Prelude did get slower and broader; and this was true also of the Prelude to *Lohengrin*: it got so broad that the violins ran out of bow. But in the Beethoven symphonies the tempi picked up—in the scherzi especially: you probably know that from comparing the recordings. As for whether we felt any lessened energy in the later performances, I would say he may have been so absorbed in his thoughts that he forgot he was conducting; because as time went on he stopped less frequently for corrections. No doubt the orchestra was better-trained and able to satisfy his demands; but time must have taken its toll. And yet when I think of that last broadcast—it was a traumatic experience I'll never forget—when he faltered in the *Tannhäuser* Bacchanale and Frank Miller began to conduct from the first

---

[1]All superior numbers refer to Mr. Haggin's comments in his Notes, beginning on page 209.

cello chair, and then Maestro began to beat again[2] and took us through the Prelude to *Die Meistersinger*, but as though something in him had snapped and he was saying: "I don't really care anymore; let's get through with this"—I find it hard to understand, because a couple of months later we did some remakes for Victor, and he came in like a house afire. It was incredible; and we said: "My God, he's a rejuvenated man!" Yes, there had been disturbing incidents throughout the season; and it may be that his mind was beginning to waver. But I wonder whether all through that last concert the thought that this was the grand finale wasn't preying on his mind. And I wonder too: *did* he resign? did he do it of his own volition? did *he* write that letter of resignation? These are things we don't know.[3]

A day or two after those last recording sessions we were invited to his home in Riverdale for a party. We got there at 5; and there was the usual abundance of food and liquor—but no Maestro to greet us as he always did. He was in his room upstairs; and at about 6:30 one of the men went up to investigate, and reported that Maestro was crying and saying: "How can I face my poor orchestra?" And we never did get to see him.

The other day I happened to hear our recording of the Brahms *Haydn Variations* on the air; and looking back the fifteen years to when we made it I marveled at it. We hear wonderful orchestras; but their playing doesn't have that added dimension Toscanini gave—that electrifying rhythm, that dynamic quality.

I would sum it up by saying that he drove a hard bargain with himself and with his musicians; but when it came off—which was ninety-nine times out of a hundred—it was Utopia.

Fred Zimmermann

HAGGIN:

I wanted, of course, to get to musicians who could talk about the Toscanini of the New York Philharmonic years. And as it happened, David Walter said to me: "The man you must talk to is my teacher, Fred Zimmermann. When I was studying with him in the thirties, he was playing bass in the Philharmonic with Toscanini, and was raving about him. He's a first-rate musician—and, by the way, also a fine painter—and very articulate." Zimmermann did prove to be an impressive musician, who had a great deal to tell—some of it surprising after Walter's introduction.

ZIMMERMANN:

I remember my first Philharmonic rehearsal with Toscanini in 1930 very clearly. We were all seated, practicing and tuning up, when the orchestra manager, Van Praag, came on stage, clapped his hands, and disappeared again backstage. Everyone stopped playing and talking, and we all sat in absolute silence until Van Praag reappeared, pointed toward the podium, and Toscanini walked on in his black rehearsal jacket, his head bent and his stick at his side. He hopped onto the podium, nodded

38

to the orchestra, slapped the stick on his stand—and my first rehearsal with the Old Man began.

I remember how surprised I was that he was so short. And we hadn't played five minutes when he began to shout instructions and criticisms, and I was surprised again by his voice: it was so hoarse and loud. The shouting continued throughout the rehearsal; and I dismissed it from my mind that day as something unusual and temporary; but I soon learned that it was part of Toscanini's behavior at rehearsals. He didn't break any sticks that first day; but I found later that this also was part of the pattern.

It was my first symphonic experience: before that I had played in the Barrère Little Symphony; and it was quite a change from Georges Barrère, a soft-spoken, gentle man, to this volcano, this hurricane, whom no one could control, and who couldn't control himself. What Toscanini wanted, he wanted forcefully; he expressed himself forcefully to get it; and any failure to realize the ideal in his mind aroused impatience and anger.

What he demanded wasn't anything trivial, and yet it wasn't anything extraordinary. It was really very simple, what he asked for: that we play what was in the score—an eighth-note that was an eighth-note, a *pianissimo* that remained *pianissimo* to the end of the phrase—and that we watch him. And he was easy to follow: his beat was very clear and precise. We knew that 'one' was here, and 'two' was here, and 'three' was here, and 'four' was up here; when he subdivided we knew where he was and we were at every point; we knew when he was going to go into a circular movement and out of it; we knew that when he reversed the circle the phrase had ended and a new phrase was beginning. It was all very clear, very precise; and it was very beautiful: he had the most elegant way of holding and moving that stick. So it was almost impossible to make a mistake if one watched him. Also he was consistent: the way he rehearsed the

39

work was the way he played it every time that week. He came to the first rehearsal with a conception of the work complete to the last detail; and it didn't change.

This didn't mean it was the same two years later. A great thing about the Old Man was that he kept thinking about what he had done, questioning it, changing it. When we played Beethoven's *Missa Solemnis* there was a place where the basses couldn't produce the *pianissimo* he wanted. It got to the point where we were playing with only a few hairs of the bow, so that it was hard for me to hear myself or the man next to me, and we were sure we couldn't be heard out front. Some years later Toscanini came back to the Philharmonic and did the *Missa Solemnis* again; and when he came to this *pianissimo* passage he turned to the basses and said: "*Bassi,* I remember. I am sorry. I make mistake: no one could hear you. Now play *your pianissimo.*" It was wonderful that he had questioned his judgment in this place when he had taken up the score again—that he questioned his conception of the form of a piece, and studied the score all over again as though it were a new piece. Once during Beethoven's Fifth he shouted: "Don't you study this symphony? I study for weeks: every night I study this score!" This was part of his power: the drive he had to penetrate further and further into the score.

It was unfortunate that he was so volatile and volcanic: it often got in his way. *He* knew exactly what he wanted, and assumed that *we* also knew. But sometimes we didn't know; and when he lost control of himself he became inarticulate and communication stopped: there was no longer direction, but only cries of "No! No! No!" and the breaking of the baton. I remember our playing the first measure of the finale of Brahms's Second, and his beating the stick on the stand and shouting: "No! No! No! Again!" So we played it again. "No! No! No! Again!" So we played it again; but we still didn't know what was wrong— whether it was the half-note or the eighth-rest, too long or too short. And it went on and on. Another time he glared at the basses and said: "You are stupid, eh? You are stupid? Answer me!"; and we nodded our heads. "You are jackasses? Answer me!"; and we nodded our heads again. Many embarrassing and painful minutes were wasted, instead of the correction that could have been made immediately. What had happened was a slight oversight: in a *decrescendo* passage in the *Bartered Bride* Overture one of the notes had an accent that none of us had ever noticed or played. When we played the passage Toscanini stopped us. *"Bassi,* you play what? *Come è scritto?* What is written?" "Yes." "Ah, so play again." We played it again—and again; and after several playings he said: "Is not accent on this note?" And then he stormed at us for not noticing the accent ourselves. That was thirty years ago; and every time I play those two bars I have a trauma—I hear the Old Man shouting.

But what I liked about Toscanini was the fact that he made the same demand of himself as he made of us. And he was as angry when *he* made a mistake as when *we* failed to observe something printed in the part. When we were doing D'Indy's *Istar* he got lost almost every time in the transition to the 5/4 section: he worried about it when he came on stage, and worried himself into not getting into the 5/4 section correctly. This happened the night of a performance; and he was so distraught that he dug his fingers into his thigh violently, never looked at the orchestra, and at the end of the performance ran off the stage and didn't return for a bow. On several occasions when things didn't go well he turned to each section, saying *"Primi violini:* stupid! *Celli:* stupid! *Bassi:* stupid!"—but also "Toscanini: stupid!" And it was the same when things went exceedingly well: he blew kisses to the sections and said "Bravo, *primi violini!* Bravo, *secundi violini!"* and so on, finally patting his cheek and adding "Bravo, Toscanini!" I remember too, after the slow movement of Beethoven's Ninth, his putting his score to his lips and saying "Bravo, Beethoven!"

Another thing I liked about him was that there were no recriminations, ever. I remember hearing one of the men say to him after a concert: "Maestro, I'm sorry about the mistake I made this evening"—and Toscanini answering: "Oh, this evening is past; it doesn't mean anything anymore. But tomorrow morning . . ." Tomorrow morning everything would have to be exactly as it was printed in the score.

That was the great thing in the Old Man. He said: "We have an obligation. *I* have it; *you* have it." It was an obligation to the composer, to the music; they were of primary importance; only they mattered. And this obligation must be fulfilled always. I remember someone getting impatient and saying: "But this is only a rehearsal!" "Only a rehearsal!" said Toscanini. "This is where we play for ourselves! *Now* we play, not tomorrow night!" And at the concert too it was all for us and all for the music; and that made it wonderful to play with him. We felt his love for the music, his excitement; and we not only conformed to his view of the music—*his* Bach, *his* Wagner—but we reacted to his excitement with our own excitement about the music and the performance.

And there were marvelous performances. The one that stands out in my memory is the Schubert Ninth: it was a heavenly experience. After the concert I just couldn't bear to go into the subway; and so I walked for blocks and blocks to my home with the sounds of the performance ringing in my mind. Wagner too: it was deeply stirring, deeply spiritual; and being a part of it was a transcendent experience.

But we paid for it! Playing for Toscanini was a most rewarding musical experience; but it was also terribly trying. He created tension, apprehension, anxiety and fear in the players; and this kept them from functioning at the maximum of their capacities. It was difficult for them to have full control of those capacities when he was constantly shouting at them; and I feel certain that the performances would have been even greater in an atmosphere more conducive to maximum achievement.

But one thing I can say is that in this trying behavior there was no personal animosity. In all the time he was there he never fired anyone, never showed any personal dislikes, any personal favoritisms. This sort of integrity was wonderful to see: it was only the music he was interested in. And he was an easy man to play for if you had the skill to conform to his demands. If you could do this you received enormously valuable orchestral training—in discipline, in attention, in observing every detail of the printed score. It was training in playing with strict accuracy and restraint—in a classical style that represented Toscanini's great musical integrity.

He had this musical integrity to a degree that I would almost say inhibited him. That is, I felt sometimes that his classical style prevented him from letting himself go in ways called for by the music. Strauss's *Ein Heldenleben*, for instance: there are human voices talking in parts of it—the tubas' "Doctor Barta", for example. This is music for someone with the freedom to bring poetic imagery into play—the way Kleiber did with Berlioz's *Fantastique*—with the voices of the witches in the last movement and the March to the Scaffold. I couldn't imagine Toscanini getting into the metaphors of such program music, which he probably didn't like (maybe that was why he never played the *Fantastique*). It is true, as you say, that he did play some program music; but he played it purely as music: he gave it a classical shape and form. And I didn't think he was happy with *Ein Heldenleben*; because when we rehearsed it he didn't stop and yell: we played straight through it from start to finish, and then he put down his stick and walked away without a word. When he loved something he had a lot to say.

But on the other hand there was his Wagner: this was expressive, imaginative, poetic music; and in it the Old Man was a great poet. He played Wagner with an understanding of the mood, the situation, the problems of the characters, their reactions to these problems. And he controlled the singers, keeping their expressiveness within the limits of good musicianship, good taste. It was intense, but within the boundaries of good taste.

But of course Wagner was nineteenth-century music, and Toscanini was a nineteenth-century man. He was so deeply involved with the music of his own generation that he was incapable—esthetically or emotionally—of stepping into the twentieth century. Yes, he did play some twentieth-century music: his *Petrushka* was marvelous; and his Debussy—I've never heard the end of the first movement of *La Mer* sound as he made it sound; and we always looked forward to playing it with him. But I'm thinking beyond Debussy and Stravinsky—of very modern works: he didn't play Bartók, for instance. Yes, he played Shostakovich; but some of the avant-garde composers he didn't touch: I doubt that he ever even looked at a score of Webern.

But everything we did with him was a great experience that I will always cherish; and I'm glad it came at a time when I was young enough to take what it involved. It was difficult—very difficult at times. He made it difficult for us, and difficult for himself; but it was more difficult for us because he could express himself and we couldn't. I remember a solo wind-player getting exasperated by Toscanini's prolonged shouting at the man next to him, and saying to the Old Man: "Oh, be quiet!" Toscanini turned to him and said: "I wasn't talking to you, you jackass!" The player answered: "Yes, I am a jackass—I am a young jackass, and *you* are an old jackass. *I* can still learn; *you* cannot"; and he packed his instrument and walked out. Afterwards Toscanini sent for him, and there was a reconciliation. Then there was the incident with the harpist Cella, whom Toscanini ordered out after an argument. "I will get *another* harpist!" Toscanini called after him; and Cella, at the door, turned and shot back: "He'll be one of my pupils!"—and slammed the the door behind him. Toscanini stood hitting his leg with his stick angrily at first, then more slowly as he continued to reflect on Cella's retort; then he rested the point of his stick on his forehead as he thought; and you could see on his face what was going through his mind: he was not going to have a pupil of Cella replacing Cella. And Cella was back the next day. On the other hand there was the incident with a solo wind-player who got angry and walked out. At the door he turned and said: "*Good-by!*" "Good-by!" said Toscanini, adding: "When the Pope dies they elect a new one." This time it was not Toscanini but the player who was given something to think about (he was back the next day).

As for my personal impressions of Toscanini, he never came through to me as a person. He was kept insulated; and we never had a chance to talk to him as the NBC men did later on. What I knew was that he came to work, worked hard, and left; that he made enormous demands, which we had to learn to satisfy; that he was very severe; and that he was great. I'd love to be able to play one more rehearsal with him, and one more concert with him.

HAGGIN:

When I told David Walter about Zimmermann's anger over Toscanini's misbehavior, he said: "Interesting. He must have changed his mind. In those days he used to say: 'It's too bad he behaves that way; but if that's the way he has to behave to get those performances, okay.'" At the end of our session Zimmermann had said he would continue to think back and see if he could recall anything further about Toscanini, and asked me to telephone him in a couple of weeks. When I did, he said he wanted to correct his over-emphasis of certain unpleasant but essentially unimportant aspects of Toscanini's work with the orchestra. So I went to see him again; and this time he pushed aside the tape-recorder, and I had to make notes, from which I wrote up what follows.

ZIMMERMANN:

What I said last time was what first came to mind when I began to think back to those years with Toscanini in the thirties. But as I continued to think back I realized that those first recollections had been concerned far too much with something of minor importance. He called us stupid; but the important thing was that this man who called us stupid was a great musician— one with a genius for re-creation. He was a man with unique equipment who could look at a score and imagine the final realization in sound of all those little dots, and who knew the difference between *these* dots that were Schubert and *those* that were Rossini. He was a man who had an ideal in his mind and was intensely serious about it, completely involved, obsessed, as he had to be. And he wanted the same complete involvement from us. But it wasn't *always* possible for us to put our personal problems and worries out of our minds and be as completely involved with Beethoven as he was; and this was something he didn't realize and take into account. All he was aware of was the sublime ideal in his mind; he had no awareness of the human factors that kept us from producing it for him; and so he didn't understand our not producing it, and became impatient. Also he was very quick, and expected us to be quick too. "You are late!" he would say. "I was seven-month baby: I couldn't wait." And when we weren't quick, *that* made him impatient. When he became impatient he made us tense and anxious, and therefore less able to produce what he wanted; but this too was something he didn't realize; and he became more impatient and angry.

He was impatient also because what he asked for was, he thought, very little: only that we do what was marked on the printed page—observe every marking of durational and dynamic value; make the *crescendo* that was marked, without an acceleration that was not marked, and the *decrescendo* that was marked, without a retard that was not marked; make only the accents that were marked, and make no accent when playing up-bow on a secondary beat; keep a prolonged *pianissimo* at a constant dynamic level. But all this was for him a truth to which we had a moral obligation: he demanded of us the truth that was on the printed page. And any failure to produce it was a moral transgression which called forth his fury and statements like "You are lazy!" and "You are *anti-musicale!*" (Another statement I remember, when he couldn't get what he wanted, was "You conspire against the music!" And when a scale passage wasn't cleanly executed he would say: "You eat the notes!")

Not only the musical phrase that came out different from what he expected upset him: *anything* that wasn't as he expected it to be upset him. Once, in a temper, he dug his hands into the pockets of his jacket so violently that he tore them away. He made a tremendous effort to control himself, turning his back to us and saying: "No, Toscanini, no! *Calmo—calmo —calmo!*" Then he began to conduct again; but the passage went no better; and in renewed anger he started to dig his hands into his pockets again, but found they weren't there, since he had torn them away. This new frustration made him so furious that he began to tear the jacket itself to pieces. Another time he attempted to break his stick; but this one only bent and wouldn't break; and this made him so angry that he began to bite it. A musical phrase that wouldn't come out as it should; pockets that weren't where they should be; a stick that wouldn't break as it should—all these were things that upset him.

This was an inability to accommodate himself to the external realities that were different from what was in his mind; and it resulted from the intensity of his involvement with what was in his mind. Serious involvement is essential in an artist; and I'm not saying Toscanini was the only one who had it: Kleiber also had it; and Beecham (even though he began the rehearsal with a joke); and others. But in Toscanini it had an extreme intensity. I used to be fascinated by his intense concentration as he stood on the podium before a performance, with the point of his stick resting on his forehead or his chin, never moving, until suddenly and quickly the stick snapped into the air, his eyes gathered in the players, and the performance began. And before a rehearsal sometimes he would stand motionless for a moment in intense absorption, and then hit the stand violently with his stick before raising his arm to begin.

It was the same with his ability to balance the orchestra in a chord—by having the clarinet play this much louder, the bassoon this much softer—and to get the chord to be in tune and precise in ensemble (for this there was the frequent injunction "Together!"). Again I'm not saying or implying he was the only one who could balance the orchestra, but merely that in this he was extraordinary, even uncanny. I've never encountered an ear like his.

His beat too was the most beautiful I've ever seen, and functionally the most explicit and efficient (I remember his saying: "I conduct *so*" as he made a big movement, and "You play *so*" as he made a small movement). Those circular movements that were unique with him—a creative act in conducting—were a wonderful way of conveying the continuity in the music: they kept going the way the music did. This *going* all the time was what one felt in his performance—a going *toward* something—toward the end, where the whole thing was wrapped up and tied up in a package, a completed shape.

As I said last time, he was a great teacher, to whom I owe a great part of my orchestral training. But of course I learned from others too. When we played *Till Eulenspiegel* with Toscanini it was a piece of music with a coherent shape; but when we played it with Kleiber I discovered that there was also a human story in it: this wasn't just music; it was Till encountering a pilgrims' march; and this was Till's hanging. Right at the start of my experience as an orchestral musician I found myself in two different worlds; and I learned from both. Later I learned things from other conductors; and with them I had important musical experiences that I didn't have with Toscanini. For instance, with Kleiber I learned to know the music of Alban Berg, which Toscanini didn't play. I don't mean this as a criticism of Toscanini: it was enough that he understood and performed the music of his own time; others could perform Berg.

And in some things Toscanini was ahead of his time. I mean the early days when he was a young man conducting in Italian opera houses where the audience was accustomed to get arias repeated, and he defied the audience and refused to repeat the aria and walked out. From the beginning he was different from the others—a man of great musical integrity and great courage.

William Carboni

HAGGIN:

I asked Zimmermann to find out if any other New York Philharmonic musicians would tell me what they remembered about Toscanini; and he reported that William Carboni would. I called him up; we arranged time and place; and when he arrived he turned out to be another musician I had seen for years at the NBC Symphony rehearsals.

CARBONI:

I first knew about Toscanini from my father, who used to go to all the operas in Philadelphia and New York and took me as a kid to hear Titta Ruffo and Caruso. He talked about Toscanini and music; and that's how I got to play the fiddle. I remember the last concert Toscanini gave with the Philharmonic in 1936: I hitch-hiked to New York and stood all day to hear it in the gallery; and I never thought I would play with him. I came to New York; and in 1940 I played in the substitute orchestra at NBC while the NBC Symphony was in South America with Toscanini; and when they came back I had an audition with the Old Man—the best audition I ever had. I played in Studio 3B—with my wife—a Brahms sonata for viola

—and that was all. Spitalny, who was sitting next to Toscanini, asked him if he wanted to hear me play any Strauss or Wagner; and Toscanini said no: if a man could play a Brahms sonata alone he certainly could play in an orchestra. Then he came over to me and patted me on the shoulder and said, *"Bene, bene,"* and put his arm around my wife; and she said it was the most exciting thing—she just found herself in his arms—you know? An old man! Seventy-something! And so I was in: I was in the orchestra. The best audition I ever had: I didn't have to read a lot of stuff.

Then I remember the rehearsals with the Old Man: two and a half hours—and they seemed like nothing. You know what the two and a half hours can be with some conductors: you go crazy; it never ends! But with Toscanini it was as though you had just sat down and played a few notes—and it was time to go home! Because you were never bored. And it was as though he had a built-in time clock that told him when the two and a half hours were at an end. He would pull out his watch—you remember?—but he didn't have to. He rarely was off; and if he did keep us five minutes overtime he was apologetic about it. It was because he knew how to apportion time in a rehearsal— knew what he could do in the time, and never began something he wouldn't be able to finish within the time available.

You got a beat—you watched him—and you followed him. When he looked in your direction you just *had* to play—you couldn't just sit there. Did we feel the force of his presence? Always—always! As soon as he walked in it was just like a magnet: you could feel the magnetic lines pulling you.

Others may have had finer stick techniques—meticulous stuff, dividing everything; but I don't think the Old Man was interested in that. He was interested in the line of the music; and it would come out by singing: he was singing all the time, and he made you sing on your instrument. Of course his beat was always clear in its placing of everything in the measure:

within the meter it was delineative. Sometimes in big climaxes it would go round in circles; but you still knew where you were. And he could make a beat last forever when he was prolonging something: you'd think his arm was a mile long. He didn't have to stop and talk when he came to a change of tempo or change of meter: he was prepared; he knew *before* what he wanted to do; he didn't have to talk about it; he *did* it; and you watched him and followed him. There are conductors—Cantelli was another—who don't *have* to speak; and very few like the Old Man in that respect. You watched his arms and made the *crescendos* where *they* made them. *He* was excited; so *you* would get excited: in the Verdi *Requiem* your hair stood up.

I remember that many times we went through a slow movement, and he wasn't satisfied with it and said, *"Da capo"*; and we did the whole thing through again; and this time we began to get a feeling of line, of continuity—instead of stopping every two bars, with some conductors, and never getting to play the thing through. And I remember once, during a Brahms cycle, we went through a symphony from beginning to end at the first rehearsal. The Old Man stood there like a child: we had done what he wanted; he had nothing to say; and we still had two more rehearsals. So he said: *"You* know it; *I* know it: go home— I'll see you at the concert."

What he stopped for was little things—to get them exactly the way he wanted them. And it was when things didn't go that the tantrums came—especially when he was excited. If he knew something was difficult, he was patient—*very* patient. But something wrong that was stupid or careless infuriated him. He couldn't stand any sloppiness or casualness, because *he* wasn't that way. I remember his saying *he* was sweating and wet, and *we* had to be too: *he* was giving everything he had, and *we* had to give it.

I loved him even when he yelled, because he never yelled at *me,* after all: he yelled at the whole viola section; and when you're taking only one twelfth of it that's all right. But when you're a solo clarinet or English horn taking all of it, then it's hard; and it was very hard on some of the men.

As for what the Old Man had that made you give everything—and what Cantelli had—a lot of conductors you don't look at: they don't have the personality or the magnetism to hold your attention; so you play with your head buried in the music, you see only by peripheral vision the beat going up and down, and as a result you fall in where you shouldn't, or you don't make the retards where they are wanted. But the Old Man and Cantelli got what they wanted because you were always watching them; you had to look at them; and when you looked you saw what they wanted and you had to do it.

In an orchestra there are always some men who don't care and don't give their utmost—who give just the bare minimum, just enough to get by. The Old Man got more out of most of the men than they would ordinarily give to a conductor; and they gave it because they looked at what was up there and they *had* to. That red face—that violence—it could kill anyone! It was like nature—like a raging sea, or a thunderstorm: it's bigger than you, and you don't buck it—you have to go along with it. You couldn't hold back with the Old Man: he made you do what he wanted. So he got more out of most players than they were willing to give; and they didn't like it: they complained that he was a tyrant, that he worked us too hard; but if they had given at the beginning, he wouldn't have had to. The Old Man knew he had to; he knew that if he allowed the men an inch they would take a yard. He told Cantelli: "Never say *bene, bravo*—never, never! Always say it's not good enough, and maybe you'll get something." Once in a while he might say, "*Non c'è male*—not bad"—once in a while. Generally it was "All right, but it could be better." But after the rehearsal—or when you'd go out to his home—he was sweet, like a child. I loved the Old Man; and I think everybody did.

You knew that as a man he had principle and character: what he felt was right was right; and you could kill him but it would still be right. It was like a cat: you can't make a cat do anything; he's got courage and guts. A dog will try to win your affection; the Old Man wouldn't—with anybody. He was a man; and I think he had the feeling that Beethoven was the same kind of man: I remember his saying once, "Beethoven was real man"—meaning no fooling around there: solid; and that's the way *he* was. You knew he couldn't be pulled or swayed by management—that if NBC didn't do what he liked he'd stay home: for $6,000 a concert he'd tell them to go to hell.[1] Someone else would be influenced by the money; but it didn't influence him; and so you had respect for him—great respect for the Old Man. At rehearsal breaks he would talk to everybody, and get carried away and talk about programs he did long ago—always friendly, sweet and kind; but you knew flattery would get you nowhere. And I think he was hardest on himself. Were you there when he slapped himself in the face? We had played something; and he said: "I listen to this performance; and I was *stupido!*" and boom! he knocked himself in the face. It would have knocked anybody else over.

You knew when he came in to do a work that he had studied it and really worked it over—that he knew it and knew what he wanted. He was not like the conductors who let the orchestra carry the ball, and remember by what it does: he was always *leading* the orchestra; he knew what he wanted, and you knew that he knew. He never came to a rehearsal unprepared—never. Everything was prepared thoroughly—including new works he didn't know. He got the score of the Shostakovich Seventh on Wednesday, and by Friday he had the whole thing memorized. (By the way, did you hear the story about that symphony? Just before the Old Man died his son was playing records for him; and one of the things he played was the Shostakovich Seventh. The Old Man asked what it was; and when Walter told him, he said: "Did I play that?" Walter said yes; and the Old Man said: "I must have been crazy." He was a little intolerant of modern stuff; but he was old. He always said let a young guy like Cantelli do new music: *he* did enough of it when *he* was young.)

Another thing you knew about him was that no matter what happened at a performance he would never bat an eye—never; never show anything to the public or on his face. But when he played the piece the next time, two or three years later, he'd say: "You remember when you played . . . ?" (That was when he was in good humor.) And he had no favorites: he would bawl out anybody; because the only thing he cared about was the music. One of the men came from the same town as the Old Man, Parma; and they were friends; but once when he played badly the Old Man said: "If I see you on the street in Parma I go on other side!"

What I remember about his performances? The way he looked when he walked out on the stage—his meticulous appearance, with his shoes and pants and everything just perfect. Even before he came out, everybody's eyes were watching that corner for his entrance; and when he walked out he was ready, set, and all extraneous things had to be forgotten. You could tell what the music was doing by his face. I often think of the start of the Brahms Second or the Brahms Fourth: how quietly and peacefully the Old Man would begin it, letting the music play itself; and here his face—his skin—was white. Then, when the music became excited, his blood went up, his face got red, and he was singing away, yelling at the top of his lungs, his whole being 'gone'. That's when, if anything went wrong, everything was at the top, and the top blew off. What happened in quiet music was all right—nothing to get excited about.

The beginning of the Brahms Second was an example of his repose—his letting the music flow, instead of pushing it. And there was also the clarity. I remember a thing like Strauss's

55

Heldenleben, where there are passages of sixteenth-notes that go on for bar after bar after bar; and with some conductors you get time to play only fifteen and a half sixteenths, and you lose the rhythm and begin to fish for the notes and can't find them. With the Old Man the tempo was exactly straight, and there always seemed to be room for the last sixteenth: you could play all of them. It was always possible to play more notes with him than with anybody else. Other conductors, when they come to the concert, get excited and play the music faster, thinking that way it is more brilliant. But when the Old Man took a tempo at a rehearsal you knew that when you played the piece at the concert it would be that tempo.

I don't think the concerts were as good as the rehearsals, in many cases. I remember I'd feel sorry for the Old Man: I knew the way he worked at things at rehearsals; and many times they didn't go that way at the broadcast. He tried and gave his utmost; but I remember his saying it never went off at the concerts the way it did at rehearsal; and I think this hurt him inside, and I felt sorry for him. One reason for the difference was the strain and tension on everybody's part at the broadcast, because at NBC we played a program only once, whereas other orchestras would have played it two or three times. Also I think he was basically a shy man and may have been bothered by the audience, even though he didn't have much respect for it, judging by the remark he'd make once in a while: "Anything you do is good enough for them."

The performances I remember? The *Otello:* it was immense! Also the *Aida*—and the *Requiem.* And I'll tell you a performance that stands out in my memory—the *Skaters Waltz:* beautiful! And other things like that: the Boccherini Minuet, the *Zampa* Overture—the so-called junk stuff. When we went through the *Zampa* Overture the first time in '43 he said he hadn't done it in years and it was fun—let's do it again; so we repeated it! Could he play the *Blue Danube Waltz?!* And how!

He knew all that stuff. Maybe it was at the rehearsal of *Zampa* that Mitropoulos was present; and when some of the men asked him how he liked the music, he said: "There is no bad music, only bad conductors."

Yes, the Old Man's performances did change: toward the end he knew he was getting old, and he was afraid of their getting draggy and heavy like Bruno Walter's. As for the greater energy you speak of in the performances of the first NBC years, *he* was younger, and everybody in the orchestra was trying and working like crazy. Also it was a better orchestra in those years—with some of the woodwinds and those strings. Some of the old boys in the Philharmonic still talk about the Old Man and are convinced he was much better when he was there than when he was at NBC; but I suspect these things grow in people's imaginations.

He hated recording. He would hate it even more the way it's done today; but in the 78-rpm days he hated it because of the business of stopping at the end of a side. He felt that he should conduct the performance and the engineers should worry about getting it on the record; that when he couldn't just think about the performance but had to think about stopping, it spoiled the performance. And besides, it never did sound right on the record. When tape came in, the difficulty was that once he started what was intended as a short test passage, he might keep going to the end of a movement and find out then that it hadn't been recorded.

He gave no interviews, accepted no honors: he felt he was merely doing his job of serving the composer, and nothing was owed him—everything was owed the composer. That was why he could conduct a Strauss waltz. He did nothing for show, nothing for himself; and that was why we worked. *He* was working like crazy for the composer; so *we* worked like crazy with him.

I remember when we did the *Grand Canyon Suite* he kept

57

asking Grofé if the tempo was right and so on: after all, Grofé was the composer, and the Old Man always felt the composer was much more important than the conductor. Every time he asked Grofé anything he called him 'Maestro'; and Grofé was just in heaven. When it was all over the Old Man called him up to the podium to ask him if everything was all right; and Grofé said yes and was so overcome as he backed away that he backed into the chairs and fell over them.

The Old Man just seemed more sincere than anyone else—trying to find what a man like Beethoven had put into his music. I remember what Hindemith said once: "Music has a face: leave it alone. If you don't like it, don't play it, but don't change it." The Old Man felt like that.

Alexander Kipnis

HAGGIN:

I wanted also to get to the singers who had sung with Toscanini. The record-reviewers who specialized in opera disapproved of his performances of Verdi's operas on records, in which he didn't permit the self-indulgent singing that distorted tempo and phrase. These reviewers objected to his "fast and rigid tempos" that "thwarted" the singers' attempts to sing "expressively"; and contended that he used only the inexperienced and inferior singers who would submit to his tyranny. What I heard was a beautifully and coherently plastic flow, created by a beat which was never anything but flexible in relation to the music, and was unyielding, in relation to the singer, only in compelling him to operate within that plastic flow. Moreover, Milanov, Albanese, Nelli, Peerce, Warren, Vinay, Valdengo and others were not inferior singers, but some of the best available to him at the time, and sang expressively with him. So did the famous singers of the past whom he conducted—Destinn, Fremstad, Hempel, Matzenauer, Rethberg, Kipnis. Had he conducted differently for these singers? Or had they accepted his tyranny? I couldn't ask Destinn, Fremstad, Hempel and Matzenauer, who were dead, or Rethberg, who didn't reply to my letter asking if I might see her; but I was able to ask Kipnis. A friend reported having met him at a party, where he had talked about Toscanini, mostly with admiration, but with strong objections to the 1937 Salzburg Magic Flute. These were something I decidedly wanted to hear; and luckily Kipnis was willing to tell me about them.

KIPNIS:

I sang for the first time with Toscanini in Bayreuth in 1930. I was one of the last singers to arrive for the rehearsals. Most of the singers came six or eight weeks before the beginning of the festival; but I had already sung in Bayreuth, and was allowed to come only two weeks before the beginning. Toscanini was very impatient; and I had a rehearsal with him as soon as I arrived. It was perfectly pleasant, and I was not nervous at all—perhaps because I knew my part well and had sung it at Bayreuth before. Yes, of course I knew Toscanini's formidable reputation; but I also knew what I could offer, and there was no reason for me to be nervous. One of the assistant-conductors played the piano, and I sang the entire monologue of King Marke from *Tristan*. Toscanini walked back and forth in the room; he didn't interrupt—he just listened; and once in a while he made a gesture as if he were going to conduct. When I finished he didn't say a word, but only grabbed me by my hand and took me down to where Siegfried Wagner was sitting in the *Festspielhaus*, and said: "Why don't *all* the singers sing like that? Your father wrote 'Muss es sein'; but on your stage they sing 'Mussssss es sein' with six s's." He was objecting to the fact that the singers gave more importance and emphasis to pronouncing the word than to singing the music.

No, I don't recall any further rehearsals. The rehearsals of *Tristan* were very long; and I didn't stay for all of them because King Marke has only two scenes. But I can say that Toscanini's manner of rehearsing was more or less routine, though a very painstaking routine. A singer, if he knows his responsibility, surely is nervous before each performance; but after he has sung several pages and knows that his voice is in good condition, all the nervousness disappears. And so it was with Toscanini: we all knew what he expected of us; and after the first fifteen or twenty minutes of rehearsing with him it became absolutely natural and we were colleagues: he was not Maestro Toscanini in the sense that he was someone we had to fear. And it was very pleasant. (The only time in my experience that he was not very pleasant was in Buenos Aires, when he was suffering from a terribly painful bursitis, which made it difficult for him to conduct, and he conducted with both hands, holding one hand with the other in order to be able to lift his baton.) Also, Toscanini could be a diplomat in his own way—or a realist. We had heard many stories about his calling in the manager of La Scala and demanding *"un altro baritono"* or *"un altro tenore"* because the baritone or tenor didn't sing well; but when I was with him in Bayreuth we didn't have *un altro tenore*; we had Melchior to sing Tristan, and Melchior was the best; so Toscanini was calm—he didn't break any batons or throw any scores.· (*1980: See note on page 275.*)

In his working with singers Toscanini was very expressive; and he demonstrated how a phrase should be sung with his hoarse voice and with his piano-playing, which was definitely not the playing of a pianist. I remember in Salzburg when he demonstrated to Milanov how to take certain phrases in Verdi's *Requiem,* and I wondered how she would do them; because even with his hoarse voice and his piano-playing the music sounded as if it were created at that moment. Milanov said: "I cannot do it because I haven't the breath support"; and Toscanini was very kind and smiled. I don't remember him being irritable or shouting at any time: in Salzburg he was as though in his own home. There was no excitement there; and I think he felt happier than in Bayreuth. I don't know what it was in

Bayreuth—maybe the atmosphere, the spirit, or the feeling that this was Wagner's place. There was still, written in chalk on the door of one of the dressing rooms, Wagner's invitation to the soloists to have tea that afternoon after the rehearsal; so you had the feeling that the spirit of old Wagner was still there (the Germans say, *"Der spukt herum."*). Also, though it never came out in public, there was the unpleasant situation with Muck and Toscanini on the same stage, in the same theater, in the same town: you could feel the jealousy of Muck. Until Toscanini came, Muck was the principal conductor and the king—the musical Amfortas of Bayreuth. When Toscanini came, they built a room for him—the so-called conductor's room; and it was embarrassing when Muck, with a bitter expression on his Mephistophelian face, shouted: "So many years we have been in Bayreuth without a conductor's room; but now we have to have a conductor's room for Mr. Toscanini!" That summer Siegfried Wagner passed away; and a few days after his burial we had a concert in the *Festspielhaus*. On the program was the *Siegfried-Idyll* conducted by Toscanini: it was the most beautiful *Siegfried-Idyll* I have ever heard in my life; and everyone in the audience had tears in his eyes from the sound of this music, and the thought that the Siegfried for whom it was written was no more. Then old Muck conducted the Funeral March from *Die Götterdämmerung*: it was so old, like a piece of parchment, a piece of dusty old scenery—in comparison with the unbelievably beautiful *Siegfried-Idyll*. A few days after that we had a benefit concert for retired elderly singers who were in need. Maria Müller and I were the soloists; and the concert was in a little old and beautiful theater, the *Markgrafentheater*. Toscanini and his family sat on the right side of the theater, Muck with his—I don't know if it was a family—on the left side; and they didn't look at each other. Oh yes, definitely, Muck started it. Toscanini had no reason to be jealous: he had his operas to conduct, and he was concerned only about his artists and rehearsing them so they knew their parts.[1]

You ask about the hypnotic power which some have spoken about—which they say caused musicians to exceed their capacities. I would say every singer tries to do his best in any case. The inspiration comes, of course; but we singers always felt great responsibility, and gave our best, with Toscanini or without Toscanini. I cannot say that when I sang with him I gave a hundred percent, and when I sang with another conductor I gave sixty percent or eighty percent.

I remember that singing a part with Toscanini—Sarastro, Rocco, the Landgraf—very often I made accents which Toscanini had not heard from other singers; and at such moments he would look up, but he didn't say anything—he didn't say, "Don't do that." For instance, in *Tristan*, when King Marke says: "*MIR dies? Dies, Tristan, MIR?*"—in this quasi-*parlando* outcry I diminished the tone on *mir*, going over to a slightly breathy quality; and Toscanini looked up, but he didn't say anything. He insisted on the *rhythm* being the way he wanted it; but he never told me anything about phrasing, and he never said anything about the phrasing or accents which represented my feeling. I remember one thing he insisted on: in Bayreuth the melodic turns in *Tannhäuser* were done in the German way, as part of the rhythm of the measure; but Toscanini insisted on the more graceful Italian way, in which they were delayed and sung as a quick introduction to the next beat.

Other examples of such Italian style or taste? I would say his *Tristan* was like an Italian opera; and curiously enough, some time before Toscanini came to Bayreuth, Siegfried Wagner said *Tristan* should be sung like an Italian opera. So when some of the singers and critics found fault with Toscanini's *Tristan*, saying: "It is like an Italian opera," I answered: "But Siegfried Wagner said very clearly that it should be sung like an Italian opera." And once, when Koussevitzky, who didn't care very much for Toscanini, said to me: "I heard *Tristan* with

you in Bayreuth. Don't you think it was like an Italian opera?",
I told him the same thing, and said that was the way *Tristan*
should be sung, because it was not a Teutonic opera.

The chief characteristic of Toscanini's Tristan was its lyricism, which the typical German conductor doesn't bring to this
work. The heavy staccato style in which Kurwenal sings in the
first act is suitable for the music of Kurwenal, but not for what
Isolde or Tristan or Marke sings, which has nothing Teutonic
whatsoever. I always loved the lyrical approach to *Tristan*,
which I heard many times from other conductors, but never
in such a degree as from Toscanini. We had a conductor in
Berlin named Leo Blech, who had a lyrical approach almost to
anything. And I sang in *Tristan* very often with Furtwängler,
who in this work was definitely not one of the Teutonic conductors.

Toscanini's *Tannhäuser* was different. Though the work is
not late Wagner, still it is a German opera, in a German style.
But Elisabeth, Venus, Wolfram, the March, the Hymn are
based on a lyrical approach: the only characters who are a little
dramatic are the Landgraf and Biterolf. And Toscanini's approach to every phrase was very soft. Of course he made the
ensemble of the knights, when Tannhäuser is sent away to
Rome, very dramatic, and also Tannhäuser's aria when he returns from Rome; but they were dramatic in the frame of a
lyrical picture. It was not Italian; it had its German character;
but in this character it was lyrical. Toscanini always insisted:
"Sing. Sing. I would like to hear a singing tone." Also it was
the first *Tannhäuser* in which the Hymn sounded like a hymn.
Usually it was taken so fast that what should be heroic praise of
Venus sounded like a little ditty. In Toscanini's slower tempo it
was a real hymn. Later, other conductors took over his tempo;
but they made it *too* slow.

Die Meistersinger I didn't sing with Toscanini; and I didn't
hear the whole opera from him in Salzburg, only scenes; but I

was very much impressed. My feeling in general was that Toscanini was a dramatic conductor—that his real element was the drama of Beethoven's symphonies, *Fidelio*, *Tristan*, *Tannhäuser*, *Parsifal*; although being a great musician he could also conduct a comedy or a purely lyrical opera. In performing *Die Meistersinger* he was concerned with the music, not with the comedy; and being guided purely by the music he, for example, avoided all exaggerated caricature—with Beckmesser, or with Kothner. He didn't want the usual exaggerated "*DER—SAENGER—SITZT!!!*"; he wanted "*Der Sänger sitzt!*"—sung, as it is written in the score. And the same with "*Fanget an!*"

Somebody said that it's not difficult to conduct Wagner; that it's more difficult to conduct Donizetti or early Verdi, because it doesn't guide you, it doesn't tell you much, whereas Wagner tells you clearly everything you need to know. Still, in spite of his clarity, a lot of good conductors make mistakes in Wagner. Whereas with Toscanini, something like the changes in rhythm—from three beats to four, and four to five—just before Isolde's entrance in the last act of *Tristan*—such a headache for the tenors!—with Toscanini it went just like that . . . As for his performance of *Die Meistersinger*, and the German criticisms you mention—that it was too transparent, too lyrical, not solid and German—I feel that its lyrical character was justified. Surely, it is a German opera; but it is not a Teutonic opera like *Die Walküre* or *Die Götterdämmerung*.

I come now to *The Magic Flute* in Salzburg. As I said before, in spite of his *Falstaff* my feeling was that Toscanini's real element was drama, not comedy. And we had the impression that he wanted to make of *The Magic Flute* something different from what he used to hear. He thought the German conductors had such respect and devotion for Mozart that they tried to make of *The Magic Flute* a bombastic opera, by making everything too slow: *Andante* was made *Larghetto*, *Larghetto* was made *Adagio*, *Allegro* was made *Andantino*. And he decided this was wrong—this was why *The Magic Flute* was not as successful as *The Marriage of Figaro* and *Don Giovanni*. That was in his mind when he came to the rehearsals. He knew the music well, and also the libretto: in spite of not being very fluent in German he knew every sentence, every word of the opera by heart. And his idea seemed to be that everyone in the opera had a little song to sing, which should be delivered in a fast tempo —except the service of Sarastro and the priests. Possibly he was right in some places; but the impression we singers received at that time was that the entire opera was upside down. He spent a great deal of rehearsal time with the Three Ladies—with their first entrance, which sounded magnificent, as I never heard it sound before. Even now, on a bad tape, it sounds good. But Papageno's entrance, *"Der Vogelfänger bin ich"*, was too fast; Tamino's *"Dies Bildnis"* was definitely too fast; the Queen of the Night's first aria, *"Zum Leiden bin ich auserkoren"*, was taken at such a speed that she could not follow the beat with her fast runs, and the orchestra and the singer were often far apart.[2] Then the presentation of Tamino's flute, the recitatives of his approach to the temple, his conversation with the Speaker —all were too fast. At the beginning of the second act, the entrance of the priests, Mozart wrote *Adagio;* and this was the slowest *adagio* I have ever heard. Sarastro's *"O Isis und Osiris"* was very slow: this was considered to be a service in the temple, not a little song. The Queen of the Night's second aria, *"Der Hölle Rache"*, was too fast. Sarastro's *"In diesen heiligen Hallen"*, which is marked *Larghetto,* was not very satisfactory—too fast. Pamina's *"Ach, ich fühl's"* also was a little too fast; the trio of Pamina, Tamino and Sarastro was much too fast; Papageno's *"Ein Mädchen oder Weibchen"* also went much too fast. The desire to drive this opera, to make it faster and faster, was felt all the way through; and it was not satisfactory. It's a heavenly, beautiful opera; and it cannot be changed. In spite of the fact that it is Mozart, it is a typical German opera—more

German, I would say, than *Die Entführung*.

After the first rehearsal we singers had a meeting. We realized that the opera might be a fiasco; and it was not only Toscanini's performance: it was everybody's performance. We had a fine cast, of singers who were well equipped and acquainted with the music; each of us had a position, and none of us was a 'prima donna' singer: we were all pulling together and in the same direction, and wanted a success not for this one or that one but for all. We realized that this might not happen; and we didn't know what to do. So we went to Dr. Graf, who was staging the opera, and asked him to speak to Toscanini. He said: "It is more possible to move the mountain behind the *Festspielhaus* than to change Toscanini's mind. If you want to sing the performance, and if you want us to *have* a performance, sing the way he conducts. If you want to change him, the best thing would be to quit." We had another meeting; and we decided to sing. The opera did not turn out as badly as we expected; but it was not a success. People don't talk about *The Magic Flute* with Toscanini as they talk about his *Tristan* or Verdi *Requiem* or *Missa Solemnis*. *The Magic Flute* is a forgotten thing: when one speaks with people who were in Salzburg *The Magic Flute* doesn't come up. You tell me you remember the audiences' enthusiasm;[3] but how could a performance with Toscanini *not* be received with enthusiasm, even if it were a *bad* performance? That is something to keep clearly in mind. No, *The Magic Flute* didn't have the Toscanini touch, the Toscanini fire. Also, not one word was cut in the dialogue; and I believe that with so much dialogue the music lost some of its impact. (Speaking of the dialogue reminds me of something I never experienced with any other conductor. Toscanini asked us to modulate the dialogue into the key of the aria which followed it. He asked me, for instance, to modulate into F major for the aria "*O Isis und Osiris*", and into E major for "*In diesen heiligen Hallen*".) (1980: *See note on page 275.*)

Fidelio also has a great deal of dialogue; but it has drama, which *The Magic Flute* doesn't have. And it doesn't need a sense of humor. So *Fidelio* in Salzburg was a different thing, because here Toscanini was in his element. We speak of a dramatic tenor or a dramatic soprano; and Toscanini was a dramatic conductor. No, we weren't aware that the tempos were faster than usual here too—or rather, we knew it was faster, but we didn't *feel* it, possibly because the drive of the drama was so strong, so immense. I was struck only by Toscanini's faster tempo in the finale of the first act, when the prisoners go back into the prison. The tempo in the score is very indicative —*alla breve*, very fast—but nobody does it in that tempo. Toscanini did, and he was right: in his tempo the drama came out very strong—even when the singing ended and the orchestra went on, and Rocco and Fidelio, loaded with their tools, started down to the dungeon.

Toscanini was completely absorbed in the music of *Fidelio*: I think he was not *there*, actually. He was like a high priest of this work: in what he did, it was as if he felt Beethoven was present; and we had a beautiful performance. At the first rehearsal with piano we started from the very beginning; and after each number we stopped and waited for corrections from Toscanini. He was brief and to the point; and we understood him very well, speaking some Italian, some German, and also some English. After Florestan's aria at the beginning of the second act there is the famous digging duet; and when the Fidelio and I finished it, we waited for corrections. Toscanini sat with his head bent down deep in his hands, and didn't say a word. After a few minutes he looked up at us and said, "What music!" At that moment the Fidelio—since you heard it you know who she was—went over to Toscanini and embraced him and kissed him on the mouth; and he was so embarrassed that he said loudly: "If you do that again I will not transpose your aria!"

In Salzburg one morning, after a rehearsal that had gone very well, I came out of the *Festspielhaus* and saw Toscanini sitting in his car. When he saw me he beckoned to me; and when I came to him he didn't say a word, but only patted my cheek! And I can tell you another story like that, about his kindness. In 1936 he came to Vienna to conduct the *Missa Solemnis* with the Vienna Philharmonic, the chorus of the Opera, and good soloists. In the *Benedictus* the long violin solo is played by the concertmaster of the orchestra; and this time it was played by old Rosé, who had been concertmaster for a generation—under Mahler, Strauss, and several others. At the rehearsal this little old man, with lots of white hair, stood up and stepped up in front near Toscanini, and seemingly was so afraid he might not please Toscanini that his face was pale and his hands trembled as he lifted his violin and started the long high note before the main theme of the solo. His performance wasn't bad, but it wasn't very good; and when he finished Toscanini bent down to him and patted him on the back!

I also remember something amusing that happened at the first orchestral rehearsal. After twenty years of service a member of the Vienna Philharmonic automatically acquired the title of Professor, just as a singer, who after twenty years might have a voice like the bark of a dog, acquired the title of *Kammersänger*. At Toscanini's first orchestral rehearsal the manager of the orchestra presented several players to him: this oboist was Professor A, this clarinettist was Professor B, this trumpet-player was Professor Z, and so on. Then the rehearsal began; and Toscanini corrected this and that, controlling his impatience for a long time; but finally he burst out: *"Tutti sono professori, ma non possono suonare!"* ["They are all professors, but cannot play!"] (1980: *See note on page 275.*)

I was not engaged originally for this performance of the *Missa Solemnis*. Toscanini didn't pick the soloists; and the bass, who was from Berlin, couldn't come for the first rehearsal. It was my first year in the Vienna Opera; and I was rehearsing in some opera when the Director came in and told me that the bass for the *Missa Solemnis* couldn't come, and would I be so kind as to help out only for this rehearsal. I said, "Surely." The rehearsal was to begin in about fifteen minutes in the *Grosser Musikvereinsaal*, which was very near the Opera; and I went there and greeted Toscanini, whom I knew from Bayreuth. He was very quiet and didn't say anything; then he started the rehearsal, which was with piano. Everything was all right; here and there he corrected a tempo; and I remember that he was very dramatic about the *Crucifixus:* he said he wanted it to be like hammering—"CRU - CI - FI - XUS!"—as if Christ were being nailed to the cross. After the rehearsal, as soon as I got to my hotel, I received a telephone call from the Director of the Opera: "Toscanini wants you to sing in the performance; he doesn't want the other man. Could you do it?" I said, "*Could I?!*" This was a renewal of our activities; but I sang with him in Vienna only in this *Missa Solemnis*.

I had sung in the *Missa* two years before in Vienna with Fritz Busch. He was a good, reliable conductor, but of an entirely different caliber from Toscanini: the burning of a volcano that there was always in Toscanini—there was no trace of this in Busch. And so the real feeling of the *Missa Solemnis* came to me only when I sang in it with Toscanini. This was an entirely different conception, an entirely different fanaticism—burning—expression—drama. The powerful rhythm of the opening chords of the *Kyrie!* And later, the *crescendo* to the *Christe:* the drive of this *Christe* I never experienced with any other conductor. I have on a tape the *Missa Solemnis* in which I sang with Toscanini in New York in 1940; and I think it is one of the greatest things he did.

But listening to this tape, I wonder why Toscanini allowed the soprano sometimes to dominate the solo quartet. It would be different if the soprano had the melody and the other voices

were subordinate; but in a passage where everybody is supposed
to sing *piano*, Toscanini allowed the soprano to sing so much
louder than the others. In the *Agnus Dei* too the mezzo-soprano
sometimes shouts so loud. I hear the beautiful voice of Bjoerling,
and I have a good voice, and we could sing loud; but always
Toscanini would hold up his hand to us, and the mezzo-soprano
would come out too loud. I hear the same thing in the Victor
recording of Verdi's *Requiem*. If somebody has the melody,
surely he should come out. But in the *Lacrymosa*, after the
mezzo-soprano sings her solo, the bass sings the same thing
while she sings only "ah - ah - ah - ah"; and though he has the
solo her "ah" comes out with such force that you can almost
not hear his melody. The same thing happens again when the
soprano sings the "ah".

I sang in the *Missa Solemnis* again with Toscanini in 1942
—with different soloists whose names I don't remember, including a young lady whose presence could be explained only
by Toscanini's eye for feminine beauty. Everybody was de-
pressed by that singer; and it wasn't possible to say anything:
none of us was on such terms with Toscanini that he could go
to him and simply say: "Maestro, you cannot let her sing." I
never tried to get close to Toscanini. Once we visited him in the
Hotel Astor; and he asked us why we didn't come to see him
more often, complaining that so many people came and bothered him, while the people he would like to see didn't come.

No, the *Fidelio* was not the revelation to me that the *Missa*
was. I had had so many performances—good, poor, mediocre.
And when you sing in opera you are not in such contact with
the conductor as in a concert: the orchestra and the prompter's
box are in between. Also you are performing a character—which
is not like just standing there and getting the music in your face.
So I can say the *Fidelio* was very good, and very strong, and
made a strong impression during the rehearsals; but it didn't
affect me as the *Missa Solemnis* did.

The Ninth Symphony was, in a way, a surprise for me. I expected Toscanini to take the recitative in tempo; but he made it very flexible, and didn't insist on having it go one, two, three, one, two, three. It was very simple; and it was easy to sing. The last phrase on the word *"freudenvollere"* is written to be sung in one breath; and when I sang it once with Bruno Walter he said: "Do me a favor and don't sing it in one breath." I asked why; and he said: "Because most of the people, instead of listening to the music, sit there wondering, 'Will he make it?'" At the first rehearsal with Toscanini I again broke the phrase—and he didn't say anything: I sang it that way. As for my impression of his performance, certainly it was different from others: it had more drive, more fire, more fanaticism; it was not what we used to call *sehr gemütlich*. And I remember the last section of the finale, which begins *Poco allegro* and accelerates *sempre più allegro*: if it is too fast it is banal; but in the tempo in which Toscanini began it and accelerated it, it was extraordinary.

In Oslo once the wife of a conductor there asked me: "What is it about Toscanini—what is it he does that my husband cannot do? Does he do something with his hands? Or with his eyes? Does he conduct faster? Or slower?" I answered what Gurnemanz answers Parsifal. Parsifal asks him: *"Wer ist der Gral?"*; and Gurnemanz says: *"Das sagt sich nicht. Doch bist du selbst zu ihm erkoren, bleibt dir die Kunde unverloren."* ["Who is the Grail?" "That may not be told. But if you are chosen for it, you will not fail to know."]

Even after Toscanini's death, when we hear a recording of his, the power of his conducting and of his conception of the music is still completely alive. The recordings of other conductors become mechanical transcriptions; a recording of Toscanini does not. When I hear the *Missa Solemnis* on the tape that I have, it is not mechanical music; it is to me as if he is standing there and still conducting. This kind of conducting, this kind of interpretation, is not a dead thing.

Nicolas Moldavan

HAGGIN:

More than one NBC player said that Nicolas Moldavan, who played viola in the Flonzaley and the Coolidge Quartets, was a distinguished musician who would undoubtedly have valuable things to say about Toscanini. When he opened the door of his apartment he turned out to be another of the NBC Symphony musicians I had said hello to at rehearsals without knowing their names.

MOLDAVAN:

I could hear Toscanini only occasionally while I was playing in the quartet, because I was always traveling. It was not until I went into the NBC Symphony that I began to know him really—to know what only a musician playing with him could know about him and about what made him great. In this transition from a quartet to an orchestra—particularly with a man like that—I was all ears. And I may say that had I played in quartets *after* playing with Toscanini—with what I learned in those twelve years with him—I would have understood much more about how to play quartets and how to approach music. In a quartet you have four individuals; and if I feel like playing this passage a little broader I take my time; and the cellist takes *his* time; and so the music becomes distorted. What Toscanini taught me was that a piece of music has a frame, and you phrase and build within this frame—any piece of music, a quartet—and if I were starting now I would approach music in the way I learned from him. Most musicians distort: if you listen to a recording you hear this bar is a little longer and this one a little shorter; and Toscanini showed that it wasn't necessary to take such liberties to make a piece of music beautiful.

This conception of music was one of the important things in his conducting. Other conductors we played with—good conductors (they were all good: these days you may not be great, but you have to be good)—it took those conductors half a page to know what they wanted to do, what tempo they wanted to take. Toscanini had the piece of music there like in a frame— in the right tempo, and with whatever he wanted—before his eyes when he started the rehearsal; and if he stopped and started again, it was the same tempo. That was one of his great gifts; and it was something which only those who played with him knew about—those who were able to understand; because there are all sorts of people in the world and in orchestras; and I am speaking about the conscientious, sensitive musicians, who had played a great deal and knew music and would notice things.

That whole picture was always before him. Other conductors work out details here and details there; with him it was the whole: if he got that he was satisfied. Things like up-bow, down-bow, he didn't bother with: he expected you to take care of them. You produced every note clean; the phrasing was up to him. And he did the phrasing—of detail within the whole— with his stick. There were no words: we knew his stick. When he did this or did that with it we knew what it meant: he didn't have to say anything. The build-up of a *crescendo*, for example. Nobody could build up a *crescendo* as he did—by holding you back—holding you—holding you. Other conductors don't know how to do that: they run away with you; and when it comes to the *forte* they haven't anything left. He knew how to build it up gradually. And he did it all with his stick. Other conductors use their tongue—which orchestra musicians hate, and which produces complete disruption and disintegration at a rehearsal. The musicians are used to being told with the stick; and the moment a conductor starts to explain things, they don't listen, and talk about their own business. Some conductors don't stop talking. Bernstein, for example: he can conduct anything—the 5/7 and 3/13 in the modern pieces is nothing for him; but when he comes to Brahms he doesn't stop talking. The musicians hate it: they have played the Brahms symphonies hundreds of times; what can he tell them about that music? Or Bruno Walter: he always talked; and Toscanini got furious and said: "He doesn't let them play!" With Toscanini it was "Watch my stick!", and he let you play. If you did it right he didn't bother you; if you did it wrong he would get angry and say: "Don't you see my hand?" Conductors talk because they don't have rehearsal technique: they know the music, they are good musicians, but they don't know what to do with an orchestra—how to handle it, how to get its attention, how to give it what they have in themselves. Whereas Toscanini knew all this. That was why a rehearsal with Ansermet, who was a fine musician and knew every detail but talked too much, was something you dreaded; but a rehearsal with Toscanini—or with Cantelli—was something you looked forward to. For certain players—the first oboe, the first clarinet, the first horn—who had very responsible and exposed parts, a rehearsal was a difficult time; but for most of us it was something to look forward to. Toscanini would accomplish in two and a half hours what the others with all their talking didn't accomplish in five; and sometimes his rehearsal would be finished in two hours.

Then another thing. An orchestra musician feels the personality, the authority of a conductor the moment he steps on the podium and takes his stick and shows what he knows. With other conductors you hesitated. With Toscanini there could be no hesitation, no question: you knew this was a genius standing before you; and you had confidence and respect. It was not because you were afraid of him—because he was the boss and could fire you—which he never did in all the years that I was there—not even one clarinet-player who drove him crazy because his playing was so cold. No, it was because you felt that this man standing there was a superior human being.

Also, you were affected by his intensity. There were times, in the playing, when everybody felt like giving, like going with him: those were the great moments. Or if he tried two or three times and it didn't go—the tempo wasn't right for him, or something else—then it was *"Andiamo!"*; and something in it—the fire in him—would communicate itself to us; we would feel it with him, and would go all together. This happened many times; and the only explanation was just magnetism, electricity.

Then there was the knowledge he had. No matter what it was—the quartet literature, the violin literature, the cello literature, the piano literature—he knew everything. It was most amazing. Others have great knowledge too: I remember when I was with the quartet in Los Angeles once, we had an evening with musicians—Feuermann was there, and Szigeti, and Szell—and we played quartets for our pleasure. And Szell sat down at the piano afterwards and played not only the quartets but each part separately. Though Szell leaves me cold as a conductor, he has this great knowledge. But Toscanini surpassed them all. To remember so many things—it was fantastic.

And his integrity. He always rehearsed the orchestra's part in a concerto without the soloist. How many conductors do that? To them it is an accompaniment; to him it was a piece of music, which had to be rehearsed. When the soloist came to rehearse with the orchestra, Toscanini never said a word to him if the playing was musical; and he followed one hundred percent. The last time Heifetz played the Mendelssohn Concerto with us, he began the Allegro of the finale in a much faster tempo at the concert than at the rehearsal; and the Old Man didn't try to hold him back: he—and we all—followed Heifetz through to perfection. With singers sometimes he had trouble: they held the phrase, or they mispronounced a word. He stopped Nan Merriman once because the Italian word had two r's and she pronounced only one. It was always *"Parole!"* and "Don't swallow the words!" and "Don't eat the music!" But he was patient with singers—provided they were musical. He never had trouble with Jan Peerce, or with any other musical singer.

For me his great gift, his genius, was that he kept the music always alive, so that people didn't fall asleep, as they often do. Particularly in a slow movement, where it's very easy to get sluggish, and it gets slower and slower, until the trend of the music is lost. When Toscanini felt that it was slowing down, he was able—without giving any indication, without anybody noticing it—to bring it alive. In a Haydn or Mozart symphony, for instance, those long slow movements, which were made so much longer by everybody else, and dragged out until they fell apart and were dead: with him they were always alive. That is the greatest test—not to conduct Strauss.

Speaking about Mozart, one year Bruno Walter, who was considered a Mozart specialist, conducted the G-minor Symphony and made it very graceful and gay. Toscanini was at the rehearsal; and we knew by the way he looked, and walked back and forth, and left the hall, that he was angry. A month later, or whenever it was that he came back to conduct us, he put on this symphony; and at the rehearsal he started the first bars and stopped: "No — NO — NO!!! Everybody imagines Mozart as a little boy with short pants! No! He was a man! This music must be *drammatica—molto drammatica! Arco! Arco!"* And the symphony became another piece—not a tiny thing, graceful and gay, but *molto drammatica,* with full bow. And it made sense, because it was done with conviction, as everything was by Toscanini.

You ask about his tempo in the Andante of the *Jupiter* Symphony, which was considered too fast. He felt that people played *andante* too slowly because they didn't understand that the word *andare* means to walk. And to emphasize the contrast he would exaggerate at the start; but then the tempo would settle down. As he got older he got a little faster: usually a man slows down with age; but with Toscanini it was always forward. And he would come to a rehearsal and begin by saying: "I listened to the record of our performance three years ago of this symphony. Shame on you!—and on me too! Was slow! Was no good!" And as a contrast, to show us, he would start with such a fast tempo—and then of course come down to the right tempo.

This illustrates that he was always listening to what he did before, and studying it, and thinking about it. He was full of music, and always searching in it.

There were great, great moments which I'll never forget as long as I live. One which moved me almost to tears was the *Götterdämmerung* Funeral March, because of the music itself, and because he particularly felt it. There was so much emotion, so much profundity—and power, yes—when he did it. This was one of the rare moments I'll never forget. I remember also Schubert's *Unfinished* Symphony—the rehearsal—not the performance. The performance was fifty percent less; and only the people who were at the rehearsal, who faced him there, could know this. At the performances he stood there and conducted and didn't give a damn—he even had a candy in his mouth: the real work was already done. His great moments were not at the concerts; they were at the rehearsals; and anybody who missed them, missed Toscanini. If you were there you were fortunate;

because that was where there were the moments of beauty and intensity that only Toscanini could achieve.

You ask about changes in the later years. I think he slowed down a great deal in his powers and his demands; and this caused the changes you ask about in the performances. Oh yes, I was aware of them—definitely. Particularly in recordings. With them he had the attitude that he didn't give a damn, because he could never get from the machine the sound which he had in his ears and his mind. Particularly with a piece like *La Mer*, which was a nemesis for him, because he couldn't get the color he thought Debussy meant. At a rehearsal he would somehow —but not on a record. And as you know, for many years he didn't accept the recordings of *La Mer*. It was in later years, when he was less demanding, that he said okay.

I'm a little man, talking about a great man, trying to say why he was great. There was his musicianship, plus a tremendous drive and force. And whatever he did, he did with conviction, with integrity—which was his greatest quality for me. He didn't compromise in anything: in dealing with music he was a man of one hundred percent soul, mind and integrity.

Robert Shaw

HAGGIN:

Robert Shaw didn't himself rehearse and perform under Toscanini; but as the one who prepared the chorus that did rehearse and sing under Toscanini, he could tell about anything of interest in that particular and special working relation. And what he recalled did add new and extraordinary details to the picture of the Toscanini powers and operation.

SHAW:

The first time I met Toscanini was in 1945, when the Collegiate Chorale was to sing in Beethoven's Ninth with him. I went up to check the tempo changes with him and to ask him about certain technical things. Because we were a little short of men's voices during the war years we'd been in the habit of using some altos occasionally in high tenor parts; and in the Ninth I thought it would be wise occasionally to use some tenors in low alto parts too. I asked Toscanini if this would be all right with him. He said: "Will it make the score sound?" I said: "Maestro, I think this is the only way it *can* be made to sound." And he said: "Anything which makes the score sound is right." Then he said: "You know, I have never had a good performance of this work. Sometimes the chorus is bad; sometimes the orchestra is bad; many times the soloists are bad. And many times *I* am terrible." It was this fantastic modesty that was part of the way he moved people. And I also think it was the thing that made his tantrums easy to take. They *were* childish; but they weren't "You are crucifying *me*; you are being cruel to *me*." It was "You're being cruel to Beethoven; you are being cruel to Verdi."

Toscanini was to come and listen and take the final rehearsal of the chorus before the orchestral rehearsals. Everybody was there an hour early for a brush-up. This was in the City Center, up on the fourth floor; and I was rehearsing when someone looked in through the doorway and said, "Maestro's here." He walked in with that slow, deliberate walk, and saw us and came over. We greeted each other, and I introduced him, which was unnecessary of course; and assuming that he would take the rehearsal, I said: "Maestro, where would you like to begin?" And he said: "No, you conduct. I listen." So I began, more than a little embarrassed; because although the group was very well disciplined, and I felt it was prepared for what *he* might do, I didn't know whether *I* could pull it off. What happened was that as I conducted he walked up and down in back of me. It was a long walk—if you remember that City Center rehearsal hall; and of course everybody's eyes followed him as he walked. They told me later that when we would get to a *fermata* or a change of tempo he would stop and stand still until we went on. When we finished he came—and it sounds silly— but he was crying, and he threw his arms around me and said: "It's the first time that I hear it sung." Then he started to walk away, and said: "I'll see you at Carnegie Hall." He didn't touch it at all. And in Carnegie Hall we just ran through it with the orchestra.

By the time we got to know him he was a legend, which prepared the young people of the early Collegiate Chorale—

who didn't ever expect to see him alive anywhere, let alone be in the same room with him—it prepared them, if he said, "Jump off the twenty-seventh story," to do that. As for our impressions when we worked with him, for me there was his incredible purity of motive—no showing off of technique or anything: he seemed to be quite unconscious of his technical virtuosity. And another thing was that he was always after the emotional or dramatic meaning of the music, rather than simply the right notes at the right time—though of course he wanted them too. I can think of first-class craftsmen who might take care of the cosmetology of the music, so to speak, and figure that if there's any soul it will shine through. But it was as though Toscanini would say: "Let's have none of this skin business; let's get down to where the thing really happens." So much so that in the last years I felt sometimes he was inattentive to much of what was going on—not just wrong notes but wrong rhythms—because he was hearing and conducting not the performers and the performance before him but something in his mind. I recall particularly a performance of Beethoven's Ninth in which the recitative had obvious roughness that didn't disturb him, as though he didn't really hear it. But then, of course, other things he did pick up and seize on—like those trumpets in the *Dies Irae* at the dress rehearsal of the Verdi *Requiem*.

The Verdi *Requiems* were the great moments for me. It seemed to me as though Verdi was conducting a Toscanini score: such identification of composer and performer I've never experienced. The Elisabeth Schumann or Lotte Lehmann identification with Schubert or Schumann—or Bruno Walter with Mahler—I don't think even that was as white hot as Toscanini's with Verdi. I had grown up with a modern Protestant disaffection for operatic religious music; so it wasn't until we did the *Requiem* with him that I realized how incredibly great a work it was. It was the heat he brought to it. You remember the incident at the dress rehearsal in 1951, where he came down off the podium in fury at the singer who had repeatedly made a wrong entrance. Then, you remember, he got back on the podium and stood there shaken and silent for a moment; and then he said: *"Dies Irae!"* He had asked me to go upstairs to hear the balances up there; so I could look down and see what was happening; and what I saw at that moment was that the faces of the chorus, which had been very red with the exertion of singing, were suddenly white. And the sound when they began the *Dies Irae* was unlike any sound I ever have heard out of voices: they were screaming with hysteria.

There was one other incident of that kind—the other time when he changed the tone of a choir of mine. I think it was in *Mefistofele*: he made one of his gestures—remember, where he would go like this? [Shaw leaned forward, his arm pointing down, and propelled it powerfully from side to side]—and in immediate response to his gesture the tone of the choir got richer and deeper and broader—a staggering thing which never happened with another conductor. In general, vocal sound, when it's in blocks of sixty people, remains what it is: you can't get a college glee club to change this tone just by gesture; you can do it by exercises or by telling them what you want. But with Toscanini the tone changed in immediate response to his gesture.

Another performance I remember was the *Falstaff*. It was my first acquaintance with the work; and Toscanini did it so wittily and with so much enjoyment that it was as funny as Shakespeare. I couldn't believe anybody could be this funny in music.

As for my general impression of Toscanini's work, I remember writing in one of my first family-style letters to the Collegiate Chorale about our experiences, that I had the feeling Toscanini sought expressive quality through dynamics or texture, not through tempo, which was the constant. And while in terms of inner pulse the tempo might be enormously fast, he retained clearly before him the point toward which he was heading; and this made it possible for musicians to articulate and singers to follow him even in his fast tempi. There was every reason to believe that the two fugues in the *Credo* of the *Missa Solemnis* simply couldn't be sung by human voices in his recorded tempos —but they were!

There is one episode with Toscanini I must tell about, even though it isn't about him as a musician. A group of forty of u_ were to do a broadcast of a Monteverdi *Magnificat* with Cantelli on Christmas Eve; and I phoned Walter Toscanini the day before and asked if we could come up after we'd finished the broadcast and sing a few Christmas carols for Maestro. He said it was a wonderful idea. So we rehearsed some of the carols on the record I'd made years before; and we went up to Riverdale. It was rather cold; and we expected to stand out on the porch and sing a few carols and then go. But Walter Toscanini must have been looking out the window; because before we could begin he opened the door and asked us to come in. We filed very quietly into the big central hall and stood on the stairs in the middle there and began to sing the carols. Maestro was in the television room looking at wrestling or something as he used to; and he came out, tears rolling down his cheeks. We must have sung ten or twelve carols; and when we finished, suddenly he went around shaking hands with everybody. Then a door was opened; and there was a table full of Italian cheeses and pastries and wines and champagne. And he went around and talked to everybody in the group—asked where they'd come from and so on—*each one*—which each of those forty people has cherished greatly, of course—so that we didn't leave until 3:30 or 4 in the morning.

He was always incredibly sweet and kind and inspiring.

Remo Bolognini

HAGGIN:

Nobody had to tell me Remo Bolognini was a distinguished musician whom I should talk to about Toscanini. There remained in my memory the delicacy and purity of his style in a marvelously light and winged performance of Mendelssohn's Violin Concerto that Toscanini conducted in 1933, when Bolognini was assistant-concertmaster of the New York Philharmonic. And when I went to see him I learned some of the background of that style: after he had been playing professionally a few years, a wealthy person had sent him to Europe for two years of study with Ysaye. It was immediately after this that Toscanini engaged him for the New York Philharmonic.

BOLOGNINI:

My father was a cellist—as well as a pharmacist and a calligrapher—and played eighteen seasons with Toscanini at the Teatro Colón in Buenos Aires; and my mother sang in the chorus. So even when I was not yet born I heard about Toscanini. The first time I saw him was when I was twenty years old and my mother took me to the Colón, where he was rehearsing something—I think it was the Prologue of Boito's *Mefistofele*.

85

It made a great impression of course. Then I didn't see him for many years; and I really came in contact with him in 1931, in Bayreuth. I was there to hear the festival. Toscanini had chosen Mishel Piastro as concertmaster of the New York Philharmonic, and was looking for somebody to be assistant-concertmaster; and Alfred Wallenstein knew I was in Bayreuth and wanted me to play for Maestro; so he sent him a telegram. I didn't know anything about it; and one day somebody knocked on the door, and it was a chauffeur, who said: "Mr. Bolognini?" "Yes. Who are you?" "I am Maestro Toscanini's chauffeur. I have been looking all over Bayreuth for you; because Maestro wants to see you." You can imagine my surprise. I went to see Maestro the next day at the theater; and he was suffering tremendously from bursitis: he could hardly move his arm; and that day he had to conduct *Parsifal,* no less! He was in great pain; but he was very sweet to me. He said: "I have heard so much about you—that you play so well, and have been studying with Ysaye." And many other things: he really was very sweet. Then he said: "I would like to have you as assistant-concertmaster in the Philharmonic, if you will accept." I said: "Maestro, for me it would mean a tremendous thing to be under your baton. But for my satisfaction, Maestro, let me play for you." He said: "Yes, any time." "But Maestro, I don't have an accompanist." So he called the chorus master; and we had a rehearsal; and I played for Maestro in the Villa Wahnfried. I played a Locatelli sonata arranged by Ysaye—a beautiful piece and a gorgeous arrangement. Then I played the Chaconne of Bach. Maestro was raving about it; and he said: "Do you play the Mendelssohn Concerto?" "*Yes,* Maestro," "Can you play the last movement for me?" "*Yes,* Maestro." So I played it; and he said: "Well, did you decide? Would you like to play with me?" I said: "Maestro, just one second." And I *dared* to tell him: "Maestro, you are so demanding. I don't know if I would be able to satisfy you." He said: "Why? What's the matter? You know the music; you play well; there's nothing to worry about." So immediately he sent a telegram to Van Praag, the personnel manager; and that was my engagement with the Philharmonic.

I stayed with Maestro four seasons. Then one day I was doing an extra job at NBC; and Mr. Spitalny, who liked me, called me and said: "Would you like to be a house man here?" And I don't know for what reason, I said yes; and I left the Philharmonic without even one word to Maestro—which he resented. After I was at NBC two years, he came there; so I was together with Maestro twenty seasons—which is my pride. It is my pride also to have been in contact with two giants like Ysaye and Toscanini—though there was contrast in their ways of thinking musically, and their personalities also were so different. In music, Ysaye was *"Laissez aller"*—"Let go"—whereas Toscanini wanted everything in place. But even with this contrast, they were two geniuses.

I don't remember the first Philharmonic rehearsal with Maestro; but I do remember when I had to play the Mendelssohn Concerto. As you know, the conductor always listens to the soloist privately, to see what they are going to do; so I went to Maestro, who accompanied me at the piano; and we talked, and he said at one point: "I am going to give you an advice. I have been conducting the Fifth Symphony of Beethoven for fifty years; but every time that I have to conduct it I look at the score, and I always find something." He was right: I looked— and I found something!

So every time he conducted something he would say: "We must play this piece better this time. Because last time we played it I was bad, the orchestra was bad." And he knew the score so well that it was impossible to fool him. I remember in the Philharmonic, we were playing *fortissimo* in some piece; and he stopped and said to one player—the second clarinet or someone like that: "Did you play this note? Because I didn't hear you." And the man said: "No, I didn't play it." Maestro had a tremendous ear.

But first of all he had—I don't know what to call it—an electricity, a dynamic. Even when he was in the audience at a concert or an opera, and the orchestra and the artists knew he was there, it changed the atmosphere. When he left the podium happy, everybody was happy; and when a catastrophe happened, everybody was in bad humor. He had something that I never experienced with any other conductor. Yes, there was a magnetism also in the great conductors you mention—Nikisch, Furtwängler, Cantelli (he was something remarkable, that boy; he had *every*thing—*every thing*!). But the authority of Maestro, nobody else had.

For me he was complete: perfect in the tempi, perfect in the expression. His tempo gave you the possibility to play every note. For example in the Overture to *The Flying Dutchman*, where there are difficult passages for the strings: other conductors take it so fast that it is impossible to play every note; but with Maestro we could. And I remember that when he conducted those operas by Wagner that are so long, the difference between two performances of an opera would be only one minute. In expression he made the right *coloriti*—dynamics, nuances, and everything that is written in the music. And what made him more angry to a player than anything else was if the player didn't sing. There was a wind-player who was very cold in his playing; and Maestro said to him: "My God, you're so cold, if I would be a woman I would never marry you. *Canta!* Put some blood in the notes!"

He had knowledge of things that were difficult for an instrument. But now I come to the peculiar psychology of this man. He hated—and fought—the musician who thought something in music is easy; and so when we had to play the *Traviata* Prelude, and he came to the podium already with the idea that the orchestra thought this was easy to play, he would make a tragedy, and then he would say: "You think it is easy to play, eh?"

One of the places that always produced a tragedy was the passage for the cellos in the first movement of *La Mer*. But the last few times that we played *La Mer* at NBC Frank Miller rehearsed the cellos apart; and these were the only times that Maestro was happy—or if not happy, he didn't make a tragedy about it. In general Debussy was very difficult: every note has a nuance or accent or something. And Berlioz's *Reine Mab* was one of the most difficult things—very, very delicate—difficult for the strings, the woodwinds, the French horn, everybody. And how beautiful it sounded with Maestro! And do you remember the rehearsals of the beginning of the *Pastoral* Symphony? So many conductors take it so easy; but for Maestro that entrance was something terrific. Before the rehearsal I would tell my colleagues what Maestro would say: "Remember, this is a boring symphony if you don't play it the right way. There are very long *crescendi*, very long *diminuendi*." Then Maestro came, and said: "*Pastorale!* Remember, there are very long *crescendi*, very long *diminuendi*. Watch the *coloriti*." And what do you say about the second movement—the turns in the melody, which were made so gracefully that they didn't disturb anything!

I remember that one of the performances that impressed me the most was the Prelude to *Tristan und Isolde*: that was really something remarkable. And also the Funeral March from *Götterdämmerung*. There he always had to fight for the exact rhythm:

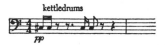

Because if that last sixteenth-note was not exact it changed completely the effect of the phrase. He used to say: *"Son passi di giganti*—steps of a giant." And one unforgettable thing in my life is when we recorded Beethoven's Ninth in Carnegie Hall. It was very late—twelve or one o'clock in the morning; and at the end of the first movement the orchestra was completely silent—nobody could say a word. But Maestro said: *"Così!"* I will never forget it. Especially in the first movement of the Ninth, there was another thing with which he used to take much care: did you notice that with him it was never boring, because he knew the places that were a little weak and would fall, and in those places he started to move—to animate a little. He did this also in the second movement of the *Eroica*, where it goes into the major: a little faster. And certain places in the second movement of Schubert's C-major.

When you ask about changes in later years—changes in tempi—I remember that in 1955 or 56, when I was assistant-conductor in Baltimore with Mr. Freccia, he rehearsed one day Rossini's *Semiramide* Overture in such a fast tempo; and when he asked me afterwards about the tempo I said that in my opinion it was too fast. He said: "It's Toscanini's tempo." I said: "No, Maestro, I am sure not; because I played it with him at NBC." He insisted; I insisted; finally we bet a hundred dollars, and he said: "Let's have lunch at my home; and then I'll play the record for you." And my God, when he played the record, it was that fast tempo! I wanted to pay the hundred dollars; but he said: "No, only five dollars." But that isn't the end of the story. When I was in New York I had a call from Walter Toscanini, who said Maestro would like to see me; so I went there; and after dinner we talked, and I told Maestro how he made me lose five dollars. He said: "Ah, but there are two records. One I made with the NBC; and one I made with the Philharmonic, when I came back from Italy angry because the stupid shoemakers, my colleagues, played it so slow it was a shame. I wanted to show that it had to have life; that's why I played it so fast."

Another time Walter Toscanini called me and asked me to come because Maestro wanted to play something for me. Imagine—for me! I went; and after dinner Walter went downstairs in the basement where they had records and tapes, and I was sitting with Maestro—Maestro and myself, nobody else—and he said: "You know, Bolognini, I wanted you to hear these records." They were *Le Donne Curiose* Overture of Wolf-Ferrari, the whole *El Amor Brujo* of Falla, Salome's Dance and *Death and Transfiguration* of Strauss. Well, to hear that music in that silent house with Maestro, and to observe him standing there—it was something I will never forget. And in *Salome*, in which the instrumentation is so heavy, so muddy, to hear every instrument—*every instrument*—it was terrific. After *Death and Transfiguration* it was such an impression that I was crying. Unforgettable!

The last time I saw Maestro it was on a Sunday afternoon; and I had to go back to Baltimore that evening, because I had to conduct a rehearsal the next morning. He said: "Stay for dinner." And I said: "Maestro, I can't, because I have to rehearse tomorrow morning in Baltimore, and I must take the train." He took my hands and said: "Oh, but please stay. Stay." Such a plea from a man like that: it was cruel to refuse; but I had to go. "*Vieni a vedermi. Vieni a vedermi.* Come to see me more often." I said: "Maestro, I would like to see you more often, but I am afraid to bother you." He said: "You never bother me! I know who bothers me! Come here any time you want!" One of the most unforgettable memories of Maestro. How I miss him! He was very, very nice.

Jennie Tourel

HAGGIN:

When Toscanini performed Berlioz's Romeo and Juliet in its entirety the first time—with the New York Philharmonic, in 1942—Jennie Tourel, then completely unknown, sang Strophes. In those performances, and in whatever I heard her do subsequently, she used her small but lovely voice with a musical taste and intelligence that I thought would make what she would have to say about her experience with Toscanini worth having. And I was interested also in how he treated a soloist who was not a celebrity.

TOUREL:

My meeting with Toscanini—in August 1942—was very interesting. It was when I came to this country and was struggling to get an engagement. Although I came as a leading singer from Paris, nobody knew me, nobody knew what I could do. Two friends—Friede Rothe and Mieczyslaw Horszowski—heard me sing in my home some Debussy. They told me that Toscanini was looking for someone who sings French, because he has to do *Romeo and Juliet* by Berlioz. And Horszowski said that he would ask Toscanini if he would be interested to hear

me. Toscanini said: "The name Jennie Tourel strikes a bell"—
that was what Horszowski told me—"all right; I will hear her."
It was like manna from heaven, because Toscanini for me was
someone unbelievably unapproachable. I heard him in '37 in
Salzburg conduct *Falstaff* and *Die Meistersinger*—no, I couldn't
get to *The Magic Flute*; I heard just these two performances.
And they were for me something that I couldn't even discuss,
because I was very young—and I was overwhelmed. And all of a
sudden I hear that I have to go and sing for him!

I went with Horszowski, who played the piano for me.
Toscanini was marvelous when we arrived; and his wife was very
sweet and very hospitable. We were talking, and he said what
did I sing in Paris; and I told him that I made my debut in
Carmen. Then he said, "*Ma*—now we'll go to the studio and
I'll hear you." When I was going up to the studio, which was
on the second floor, Mme. Toscanini said: "Wait a minute;
I'll give you a glass of water, because you have to sing for Maestro, and maybe you are nervous." And you know, I was *so* sure
of being able to sing for this great man; because it's always
much better to be in contact with a great man than with a
mediocrity, who has a chip on his shoulder. So I said: "Mme.
Toscanini, I really don't need water, because I'm not nervous.
When I have to sing for a great man I'm not nervous."

I went into the studio, and I started to sing. The first
thing I did was the Letter Scene from *Werther*; and after I sang
it Toscanini said to me: "*Brava. E bella voce.*" You know, I
was so taken with this that I said to myself: "Even if I'm not
engaged it doesn't matter: this gives me courage. If Toscanini
finds that I have a good voice, that gives me reason not to feel
frustrated or disturbed." Then he said: "Would you like to
sing something else?"; and I said: "I'll sing for you *Jeanne d'Arc*
of Tchaikovsky, because I sing it in French." When I sang it
for him he liked it very much. He said, "*Merci*," and took me
down back to the living room.

Now I *knew*—in my head—that he was looking for someone to sing *Romeo and Juliet*; I *knew* that there was a mezzo-soprano solo, but I have never sung it before. Then I had to be very smart. So when we came downstairs and he said: "I am going to conduct *Romeo and Juliet* by Berlioz with the Philharmonic. Do you know it?" I said, "Yes." He said: "There is one mezzo-soprano solo. I will give you the music. Could you come on Monday"—this was on Friday—"could you come on Monday and sing it for me?" I said, "Certainly." He gave me the music; he sent me back in his car; and he asked me to come on Monday. But he didn't say he was going to engage me; and this was torture for me, in spite of being very happy that he said I have a beautiful voice.

Well, I went home. Saturday, Sunday, and Monday—I worked like a dog, and I learned the music by heart. Monday I came to sing for him again. He played the piano for me himself; and he said: "Very good! You know it by heart!" I said: "Yes, I know it by heart." And he said: "Fine. Thank you very much." And you can imagine what it is—for somebody who already has hope and anticipation—not to hear that he's going to engage me. It was a let-down; but it was again a hope. I went home; and when Friede Rothe asked me what happened, I said, "Nothing." Because he didn't say anything—only that it was fine that I knew it by heart. But really, I can tell you truly, I wasn't upset. I was as a matter of fact quite happy. I told her: "It means that I do have something, if he approved. If not with him, then with somebody else: something will have to come."

That was on Monday. On Tuesday morning I was awakened by a call from Mme. Toscanini, who told me: "Congratulations. Maestro has engaged you to sing with him." And I almost fainted at the telephone. She said: "Do you know Bruno Zirato?" I said, "Yes, I do." "He's manager of the Philharmonic; and you have to go to him today, and he will talk to you." And so I signed a contract; and Zirato said to me: "Do you know what has happened to you? It is a great thing for you to be chosen by Toscanini." I said: "I know . . . I don't even have to say it twice."

Now I was very excited. A few rehearsals were in Toscanini's home; and he sent his car for me. And for some rehearsals he took me in his car to Princeton—to the Westminster Choir. My solo begins with the orchestra, and then the chorus comes in; and there are some other things I had to sing with the chorus; so he had me all the time at the rehearsals with the Westminster Choir. He used to come at eight o'clock in the morning to take me with him to Princeton. And the first time he asked me: "How often would you like to rehearse?" I said, "Every day." He said: "That's very interesting. Most singers don't want to rehearse at all; they just learn, and then they come to sing." I said: "Not me! I want to rehearse every day." He also told me he didn't like singers who put something around their mouth when they rehearsed so that they shouldn't get cold air in their throat. I don't believe in that too; I don't believe in mumbling in rehearsal: I rehearse absolutely full voice. It's like with the piano: you have to make your fingers work; and you have to make the place in your voice; then you can sing. And when we rehearsed with the orchestra he didn't like anybody to sit down, because *he* was standing; so we all had to stand. I understand that: why should I sit down when the conductor is standing?

What did he do when he rehearsed with me? You know—very little: he just played and listened when I sang; and he didn't ask me to do anything. My solo is really not very much to sing; and probably the phrasing was right, so he didn't change anything. And he never said a harsh word to me. Really, I can only tell you that no matter what I heard about him—you know, Zirato said I must not say anything to anybody until the announcement in the papers on Sunday; and when the news broke out on Sunday everybody began to call me and to say: "Be careful with Toscanini; he's very difficult; he's going to rehearse you every day; he's going to break your voice"—you have no idea how many people warned me against him. And I didn't feel it; I just did—not—feel it. I was in such awe before him. First of all, he was so handsome, his face was so inspired, that I stared at him all the time. And I felt terrific dedication to music in him right from the beginning, without even talking to him. All right, he was yelling at rehearsals; but he was yelling for a reason. He was the kind of person I admire, if the goal is perfection. And as you say, with a good musician he was quiet and reasonable: between us there was a great harmony.

He was a most perfect musician; and I was fascinated to watch him conduct the orchestra, and to listen to what he could do with a phrase. I still remember when I watched him rehearse the chorus: he was so meticulous. He rehearsed very, very much—and *very* precise. He didn't want the chorus to sing with music; and he was absolutely right, because when you sing with music you only read. The same thing with me: he wanted me to know it by heart; and I knew it so well that he could have put me on my head and I could still sing it! I remember that at the performance—it was the hundredth anniversary of the Philharmonic, you remember, and nobody knew me—when the reporters came to ask me, "Are you nervous?" I said: "No! I'm *not* nervous—but I'm excited. Look: to stand in the middle of the stage of Carnegie Hall for the hundredth anniversary of the Philharmonic—in front Toscanini, in back 250 people of the Westminster Choir, and knowing my piece— I can't be nervous; I can be only excited and exalted." I was absolutely aware of everything I was doing; and Toscanini knew that: he had terrific faith in me. At the dress rehearsal—oh, I must tell you that for the dress rehearsal I was told by Zirato to come at ten o'clock, and I came about 10 to 10. When I was walking up the stairs to Carnegie Hall backstage, Toscanini and Zirato were standing at the top of the stairs, and Toscanini— with the face of a *lion*—said to me: "TOO LATE!" I said:

"Maestro, I was called for ten o'clock." He said: "I WAS HERE AT 9:30; and *you* should have been here at 9:30!" I felt as if my heart dropped down. And he was right; because at 10 to 10 it means I rush in like a musician just to take his violin from the case and sit down; and instead there must be a certain composure. But it was all right. At the dress rehearsal, when I finished singing my solo, Toscanini said, *"Brava!"* Piastro was then concertmaster, and Joseph Schuster was first cellist; and they told me afterwards that as long as they knew Toscanini they never heard him say this to anyone; so that I should build a pedestal and stand on it. Toscanini said, *"Canta con espressione!"* And he was following me just like an angel.

I must tell you that all the hardship I had to go through in '41—leaving Paris, leaving a career, and everything I have collected, and what I have worked up to a certain point—did not matter at this moment for me. I don't make a melodrama out of it: I just very honestly tell you that it was one of the greatest things in my life. When I saw my name on the poster with Toscanini's it was unbelievable for me; and I couldn't think of anything else but to do this thing perfectly so that I would be approved by *him*. It was not only one of the greatest things in my life; as a matter of fact it was *the* thing that started me. I was a nobody here at that time; when I came to this country nobody knew what I could do; Toscanini was the one who heard me first, and recognized me, and gave me an opportunity. *After* that I sang with Koussevitzky, and made the premiere of *Alexander Nevsky* with Stokowski and the NBC Symphony.

I remember one day—I think it was before the third performance of *Romeo*—Toscanini always rehearsed my solo in the greenroom before the performance; and this time after we rehearsed he was playing the piano, and I said to myself: "This is not *Romeo and Juliet*, what he's playing; it's something different." So I said: "Maestro, what are you playing now?" He said: "I conduct next week Shostakovich; so I play it." His mind worked in perspective: when he was through with one thing he was already living further. My mind works that way too: when I finish a concert I am already thinking about something that I'm going to do next time. It's a marvelous thing, because you don't get stagnant in things that you repeat all the time. Hindemith, after he wrote a piece, wasn't interested in it anymore. He never came to hear my *Marienleben*; although he knew I do it very well, he said he's not interested to hear it—he's written it.

I had just that one contact with Toscanini: I never sang with him again, because when he conducted the operas I wasn't asked to sing, and when he asked me once to sing again *Romeo and Juliet* I was already busy. And I can't tell you very much about him because I wasn't one of those people who were in the entourage and always went and bothered him and asked him to do things for them—never! I only went when I was invited. I didn't even go to his rehearsals with the NBC because I just didn't want to bother him. I remember once during the rehearsals of *Romeo and Juliet* he took me out for lunch, because there was some free time; and I said to a friend: "At that lunch he was more a gentleman than any other man who took me out for lunch." He was such a—*chevalier*, to entertain me at this lunch: he was *Toscanini*, and he was seventy-five, and I was still a young woman! I adored his profile! I adored his hands! And I had a feeling of tremendous awe before this great man.

I once, though, did something after that. It was ten years after I sang with him, when he was eighty-five. I wrote him a letter; and I told him that I felt terribly nostalgic, because it was ten years since I first met him and since he opened wide horizons of my career: I called him the godfather of my career in this country. I would like so much to see him if it's possible, just to say hello to him. He called me immediately, as soon as he got the letter; and he said, "Would you like to come for dinner?"; and I said I would love to, naturally; and I went. He received me like a father, with open arms; and he said: "I'm so glad to see you, Tourel"—he always called me Tourel—and then he said, "How are you?" and I said, "I'm fine," and he said: "Oh, you're all right, I *know*; I always say to everybody, '*Canta con la testa.*' ['She sings with her head.']" When he offered me a cocktail I said: "Maestro, I drink for the ten years I know you, and for the next ten years that I'll see you again." And he said to me in French, "*Vous, surement; moi, peut-être.*" I felt so terrible when he said that; and as you know, a few years later he died. Even then, when he was eighty-five, he was handsome—and very *aware*, very *alert*, when he talked about things, about music. He asked me what I sing; and he wasn't in favor of my singing contemporary music: he said it's not very good for the voice. Whatever happened to him later—I wasn't here at the time—probably happened all of a sudden.

He was very nice, and very—human. In '44 and '45 I went to South America; and I called him, and he asked me to come to his home Sunday, when they had people. He said to me, "What are you going to do in South America?"; and I said: "I'm going to do operas; I'm going to do *Carmen* and *Mignon*; and then I'm going to do *Norma.*" And he said: "Give my regards to Gabriella Besanzoni; she was also a Carmen, and now she lives in Rio de Janeiro. O-o-h, she was a very, very vain singer; tell her that you know me." I said, "I will"; and he said, "She wears lots of diamonds." He was a marvelous *human being,* who talked about everything, not only about music. He always asked me how I was, am I happy, do I like my work, do I like what I do. This is so astonishing when you talk to a man who's so busy, so revered. You think such a man is unapproachable—but no! with Toscanini you could be just like I am with—with you, with anybody: he made you feel that way. He was a great man.

Did he say anything about composers and their works? The one he talked about with me was Bernstein. He heard him conduct; he talked with him; he liked him; he was impressed with him; as a matter of fact he said he was one of the greatest talents that came right now; and he wrote very warmly on a photograph that he gave him. He always sent me a photograph for Christmas. I have his and Bernstein's—they are the only photographs that I keep on the wall: these are my two conductors.

I remember at the time I sang with Toscanini he was trying to do the *Rhapsody in Blue* of Gershwin; but you know he somehow never had the flair for that kind of music; and also he was already not a young man. But with me he didn't speak very much about composers. Verdi, naturally; and Puccini: I remember him talking about them, but not what he said. He was not a very talkative man, not one of the people who always talk about themselves; he was much more a thinker than a man who blah-blahs about "I did this and I did that." When I asked a question, he answered in a short way. I do remember he loved Debussy—he loved *Pelléas et Mélisande*; and he always talked about a singer I knew in Paris, Fanny Heldy—that she was a marvelous Mélisande. He also spoke about Claudia Muzio, who sang with him. Actually he didn't speak about singers very much —only about some of the people in the past. And also, as I said, I wasn't hanging on his neck: he was too great a man for me to bother him. The only time—yes, this will be interesting. When I made *The Rake's Progress* in Venice, afterwards I took a plane in Milan, and the plane wasn't starting, and I wondered what happened. Then I found out that they were waiting for Toscanini. I was sitting in the back, and I saw Maestro with his son Walter coming on the plane; and they went to the front. I waited until we were airborne, then I walked down and said to Walter: "Hello, I saw you coming in, and I want to say hello to Maestro." He was already seeing very badly; and I said, "Maestro, this is Jennie Tourel." "Ah," he said, "wonderful!" I sat down next to him; and he said: "I heard you on the radio. Ah, Stravinsky was wonderful when he wrote *The Fire-bird* and *Le Sacre du Printemps*"—yes, *Petrushka* too—"but after that, no more!" And he said: "You had very good diction— very good diction. But *musica—*"—*that* he couldn't understand. I guess he had his favorites in composers; and *you* know how he felt about contemporary composers—Copland and all those. He did play Copland and other Americans? I didn't know about that.

I wish I could tell you more about him. One thing I can say is like a red light—that he was a great gentleman, and very polite—in spite of all the talk about him that he was rude, that he yelled, that he cursed. All right, everybody knew about his rehearsals: he cursed because he wanted to get what he wanted— that was all. He demanded from everybody exactly as I demand from everybody—that it has to come to perfection. We don't know *what* is perfection, but we *go* after it. And when things were right he was the happiest man—and very nice, and very human. I will never say anything like—"Oh—Toscanini never thought about anybody, because he was such an egomaniac." I don't think so; I really don't think so—not for the time I knew him. I can only praise him; and I can only say that he was a great influence in my life just for that one thing—that he de-manded discipline from everybody. In art, without discipline there is no art. I learned that from him. I wish I had more to do with him; but I have to be grateful for what I had.

I have his picture on my map of the United States, where it is a symbol that he opened this country for me. He was the first man who recognized me; and I am very proud that I was recognized by a great man.

Mieczyslaw Horszowski

HAGGIN:

Horszowski was, like Jennie Tourel, a musician of taste and intelligence; and though he was not completely unknown here when he played Mozart's Piano Concerto K.595 with Toscanini and the NBC Symphony in 1943 (he was the pianist with whom Casals had recorded Beethoven's Cello Sonatas Op. 102 before the war) he was not a big-time celebrity. For these reasons I was interested in what he would have to tell about his experiences playing with Toscanini.

HORSZOWSKI:

The first time I heard Maestro Toscanini was in 1906 in Montevideo—a performance of *Tristan*, which of course made a great impression. During the first world war I was living in Milan, where he conducted a series of twelve concerts for the benefit of the orchestra players; and I heard all of these concerts, of course. And he also conducted a season of opera performances at the Teatro dal Verme, which started with *Falstaff*, which was unforgettable, then *Pagliacci* with Caruso (this was his last performance in Italy), then *Ballo in Maschera*, *Forza del Destino*, *Manon* (of Massenet) and *La Traviata*. Then, when La Scala started again after the war, I heard nearly all the important operas conducted by Maestro Toscanini. I didn't hear his *Don Giovanni:* he rehearsed it, but when the tenor became ill it was postponed to the next season, and someone else conducted it. But I heard *The Magic Flute*—yes, Maestro Toscanini conducted it at La Scala before he did it in Salzburg. And I heard *Parsifal* and *Fidelio.* Then after the opera season he conducted every year two symphony concerts, which I heard. Also, I came here in the winter of 1926 and 27, and again in 1934 or 35, and heard him with the New York Philharmonic. And when I left Italy before the last war I heard him with the NBC Symphony.

It was Maestro Toscanini who suggested the performance of Mozart's Concerto K.595. I had played it with other conductors; but he hadn't heard me. He loved this concerto; it was his favorite Mozart concerto; and he had a photostat of the manuscript, which was given to him by Serkin, who had great difficulty in obtaining it, because it was for Maestro Toscanini and the Germans didn't want him to have it. (The manuscript was in the State Library in Berlin; they don't know where it is now.) When Maestro Toscanini received this photostat he was very happy; because in the published complete works the slow movement was in 4/4, but the photostat showed that in the manuscript it was *alla breve;* and he said: "I always was sure the slow movement is *alla breve.*" Also, in the photostat were seven bars in the first movement that were missing in the published edition.

It happened that I didn't have much rehearsal before the rehearsal with orchestra. Two weeks before, I became ill with bronchitis and had to go to the hospital. I told the doctor I had to play with the NBC Symphony; and he told me I would have high fever and he hoped for the best but didn't know how I would react to the sulfa drugs. The Tuesday before the broadcast, which was on Sunday, Maestro Toscanini came to the hospital to speak to me about the concerto. We went to a little room of the nurses, which had an upright piano; and he asked me to play my solo. So I started; and after listening a short time he said: "No, no. I don't need to hear you. We will find each other"; because he saw that I was not very strong at that moment. On Saturday I came to the rehearsal with the orchestra. Maestro Toscanini began with the orchestra's *ritornello*, in which he put all the details in order—this more *cantabile*, this more rhythmic; and this was at the same time a rehearsal for me, because in the *ritornello* were all the elements of the movement that I would play later just the way they were stated now. He had looked at the work from every side, to achieve his idea; and he was clear and firm about it. When *we* study something we have doubts; with him there was no doubt: everything was the way it had to be. So I could fit right in—into the tempo and everything else.

I remember one detail that will interest you. I know my weak points: I know I have a tendency to rush; and this worried me, because I knew Maestro Toscanini—I remembered his rehearsals of Rossini overtures: the strict tempi in the *crescendi* —no rushing. But when he arrived at this passage of rapid figuration—beginning here at bar 39—he said to the orchestra: "*Andiamo, andiamo! Non siamo a scuola!* More animated! We are not in school!" So I didn't have to worry about rushing the same passage when I would play it with the orchestra later, at bar 150.

I don't remember anything else at this rehearsal, which was short—just once through. But at the concert, just at the moment when we had to go out on the stage, Maestro Toscanini showed me this passage in the Larghetto, beginning at bar 100— a transition, a sort of cadenza, leading to the return of the principal theme—and said to me: "More animated, more lively; because in tempo it is dead. Then the theme in tempo again." He didn't say anything about it at the rehearsal: probably he thought of it afterwards. Or as you say, he may have read the score again that night, and decided the passage was too slow.

No, there was no special occasion for the Martucci Concerto. Maestro Toscanini always liked it; he performed it with Martucci several times; during the war he performed it with a pianist who came here; and he wanted to give it again. I heard this performance, and liked the work; so I didn't play it only because Maestro Toscanini asked me: it was something which appealed to me. The week before the performance I went to him three or four times to play it for him; and he showed me how he wanted many things; then we had at least two rehearsals with the orchestra.

At the rehearsal of the first movement he stopped here, and said he couldn't conduct with my tempo; and he was right. It's a dialogue; and the piano has to continue the same tempo as the orchestra, or the connection is lost; and I had played a little slower. Once this was corrected we went on until this second idea—a great solo for the piano, where he left me completely free. It's a very beautiful solo: people said it is music which comes from others; but it has the character of Martucci.

I did some things that were not to my own satisfaction: this passage, for example, didn't sound as full as I would have liked; but Maestro Toscanini didn't say anything, because the important theme is in the orchestra, and the piano is only reinforcement which is not to be heard as a virtuoso thing for itself. Then this beautiful big cadenza, where again Maestro Toscanini left me completely free. And this is very beautiful—a long cello solo, which was played so beautifully by Frank Miller. Look at the ornamentation for the cello with the piano. And in this recitative Maestro Toscanini made some correction; but would you believe it, I don't remember anymore what it was. Then the last movement: brilliant, as you can see. It reminds me of all the last movements of piano concertos.

Oh yes, his corrections and suggestions were always reasonable—always illuminating: something which I hadn't understood completely, but which now I saw clearly. And it was just more expression, and better form—these two things, always.

I couldn't see much of him when I played, because he was with the orchestra. When I had a long solo, he looked—he didn't conduct. I once saw the film, *Hymn of the Nations*, where you saw Maestro Toscanini's face; and it had a power you couldn't escape. This the audience didn't experience at a concert; and I didn't have this experience when I played. But I could feel that he was following every note in my playing—not as note but as part of the line of music; and that if I had made an unexpected retard or *rubato*—which of course was not possible in the Mozart —the orchestra would have been immediately with it. Sometimes playing with an orchestra—I must use a figure—is like playing with an overcoat: you are not quite at ease. Playing with Maestro Toscanini, you had wings.

Jan Peerce

HAGGIN:

As the tenor in the broadcast performances of Fidelio, La
Bohème, *Act 4 of* Rigoletto, La Traviata *and* Un Ballo in
Maschera *that were issued on records, Jan Peerce could say
whether Toscanini's dealing with a good singer and good musician in these performances was different from his dealing with
Kipnis in the Bayreuth performance of* Tristan und Isolde *in
1930.*

PEERCE:

Toscanini had heard me on the radio, and seemed to have
liked my voice; and when he was going to do Beethoven's Ninth
in 1938 he asked Chotzinoff if he knew me, and Chotzinoff
said yes. So Toscanini said: "I'd like to hear this boy personally";
and Chotzinoff called me and asked if I'd like to audition for
Toscanini. After I'd almost fainted and got up from the floor I
said, "Of course!" Chotzinoff was supposed to play for me at
the audition; and I waited in the lobby of the Hotel Astor,
where Toscanini was living, but there was no Chotzinoff. (He
later told me he was afraid because he didn't know how I would
do; but I thought the truth was he didn't want his presence to

influence Toscanini's opinion of my singing.) Finally I called the Toscanini apartment and was told to come up; and when the door opened after I buzzed, lo and behold, there was Toscanini acting as his own valet. He greeted me very cordially and shook hands; and he asked me if I had brought any music with me. I said: "Only the tenor part of the Ninth Symphony." He laughed and said: "Ah, I wanted to hear you sing something more—" more singable, shall we say. I said: "I'm sorry, but I don't have anything else with me." And he said: "Do you *know* anything else?" I said I knew some arias; and he asked which ones; and the first one that came to my mind was *"Una furtiva lagrima"*. "Oh," he said, "you know 'Una furtiva lagrima'. Come: I play for you." And he sat down at the piano—without music, of course—and began to play; and believe it or not, he made a mistake! One of the very rare mistakes that Toscanini made! As you know, the two stanzas of *"Una furtiva"* begin the same but continue differently; and in the first stanza Toscanini played the continuation of the second. He stopped; but I went on with the first stanza; and after cussing himself out he resumed playing, and we finished together. At the end, exclamations of *"bella voce!"*—he liked it very much—and he said: "Would you like to sing in the Ninth Symphony with me?" I said: "It would be the greatest moment of my life!" And he said: "All right, you sing with me," and told me the date. And that was how my association with him started.

Oh yes, I was at ease at the audition. The challenge was a challenge; but there's the animal instinct of self-preservation: you fight back. The first moment was what I had expected; but when we shook hands I found he was a human being who smiled and was very cordial and very sweet and very fatherly. I remember it began to snow as we were talking; and when I sang I was concentrated on what I had to sing—and on the snowflakes I could see through the window: Toscanini didn't matter at the moment. Till he made the mistake; and I guess he was impressed by the fact that I could keep going no matter what happened: it meant I was *some*what musical.

Leinsdorf prepared the singers; and by the time I came to the first piano rehearsal with Toscanini I knew the tenor part pretty well. What struck me was Toscanini's self-discipline, and the fact that when he sat at the piano the most important thing in the world for him was what was happening at that moment. If you pleased him by just doing the music—no matter what it was—*as written*; if you gave the notes the right values and the words their right pronunciation and flavor, he was the happiest man in the world; and every time you sang a phrase he liked you'd think he was finding a thousand dollars. And yet, I can tell you a story: in one performance of the Ninth Symphony— I don't remember which one and who the soprano was—he changed the music for the soprano. This man who kept saying, *"Canta come è scritto"* and "Is written this way; sing it the way is written"—this man changed the B-naturals in the last quartet for the soprano! Yes, I heard about his transposing *"Abscheulicher"* for Lehmann in Salzburg; but to change *notes!* I said to myself, "What's this?" And that was one time when I realized: "Look, he's a human being."

With him it wasn't just a piano rehearsal and then "Let's do the performance." You saw him for weeks—three times, four times a week, as often as he felt; and the day you had a rehearsal with him, that was it: you made no other appointments. If he called you for a three o'clock rehearsal, he might keep you till 4 — 6 — 7 — there was no telling. When we were through we used to love it when he was happy after a good rehearsal and would offer us a cup of tea or coffee and a piece of cake and we'd sit around; and Moscona, who sang with him many times, or Nan Merriman would know how to get him to talk: it was fabulous, the way he would give you his opinions on everybody and everything. I'll never forget: once the subject of coloratura sopranos came up, and he said: "Coloratura sopranos! If I had a daughter who wanted to be a coloratura soprano I would cut her throat!" Or someone mentioned a guy who said he had been Toscanini's assistant at La Scala. "That pig?! I wouldn't let him into my room!" He remembered—everything he remembered. With me he remembered tenors. Once he mentioned Paul Althouse: "Was very good—ve-e-e-ry good—good musician—good, good. Knew how to sing." Then he mentioned a tenor who wound up badly—the poor fellow died on stage—Aroldo Lindi, who toured with the San Carlo Company for years: Toscanini spoke in glowing terms of this boy in his early days. And that Italian, Pertile: he was musical—he knew what to do with a phrase. And of course, sometimes you'd mention a name to him, and it was "That pig!"

At the orchestral rehearsals he was so dynamic, so forceful, so fiery, that I couldn't take my eyes off him ever—and this was true even after fifteen years: I had to watch the expression on his face as he conducted, which conveyed his innermost feeling. And because he had this drive, this power, you just responded as if you had known exactly what he wanted. He had it not only over singers but over instrumentalists—the men in the orchestra. It was a great orchestra, and these boys had played with everybody and knew everything backwards and forwards; but the way they responded to this man was something! They *wanted* to please him: they knew he was so sincere in what he asked for that they were anxious to do the right thing. It's been said that musicians played or sang over their heads for him; but I don't think he made me do the impossible: that would be pushing the point a little too far. What I would say is that he got as much out of you as he could, and as much as you *should have given.* Though he didn't ask for anything but what was there in the score: in fact, I'm sure that if you had tried to *over*do something he would have said it was overdone and don't do it that way. He wanted passion, but passion from within; he wanted warmth, but not manufactured warmth. And he wanted you to know what you were singing. He always said: "Say the words correctly: the tone will come." And it's true: if you know what you're saying, the meaning of the words will bring out the quality of the tone—provided you have the tone in your voice.

People ask, was he acting or was he sincere; and my answer is, he was *he*. Once he got on that stage he was a different person —he was just the musician. He was an actor; but he acted what he felt. When we did *Bohème*, tears were coming down his face; and it wasn't put on: nobody saw it, just us. We singers were more fortunate than the public; because all they could see was his back and his arms waving, but we could see the man, and what the music meant to him, whether it was the Ninth Symphony or an opera.

That performance of the Ninth went off very well, and Toscanini was very happy. Of course, between you and me, what is there in the Ninth Symphony for the tenor? It's no aria: you sing sixteen bars, then the tenors of the chorus join you, and you're inundated—you're a thwarted man. I did it for the association: it was my moment of discovery, which led to other things with Toscanini. Also, it's a trying experience to sit there for those three movements, knowing you're going to have to open your mouth and sing. I'll never forget Pinza that first time: he kept clearing his throat, and finally he said to me: "I always promise myself I will never sing with that man the Ninth Symphony; but when he calls me I can't resist him." I said: "What's the matter?" And he said: "You have to sit for forty-five minutes, and then you have to start with 'O Freunde'." He was afraid of that frog in the throat—which never happened, incidentally.

I sang Verdi with Toscanini the first time in a Verdi program in January 1943: the Trio from *I Lombardi* and *Hymn of the Nations*. What he liked especially was my pronunciation of Italian; in fact, he found fault with the pronunciation of certain Italians, and asked me to demonstrate to one of them. I felt terrible, because this was someone who spoke a beautiful Italian, but for some reason didn't sing it well. No, there was no special problem with the musical style. You see, when you came to Toscanini it wasn't to learn something from the start: you were prepared by Trucco, and had a pretty good idea of what you were doing; so Toscanini didn't have to tell you much. He'd sit at the piano, and if there was something to tell you he'd say: "This is the meaning of this phrase." Or he'd ask, "You know the meaning of this?" and you'd tell him, and if you were right he'd say: "Yes. Now do it a little darker," or "Do it warmer," or "Do it with more heart." He had ideas for everything; and everything he wanted seemed right. They say he didn't let you hold high notes; but if you listen to the records you find you *held* high notes—you didn't *over*hold them and make the thing ridiculous. When I did *Bohème* with him I reveled in the sound, and he let me; and in *Rigoletto*—just the other day I listened to the Quartet, and I hold those B-flats—just enough—but I hold them.

The *Hymn of the Nations* was something Toscanini felt very close to, because he was a warmly patriotic Italian, very proud of his background, and the piece was by Verdi, and it was tied up with Garibaldi—it was written for a Garibaldi Day celebration. These things made Toscanini feel this was his piece of music—especially when he changed the words from "my beautiful country" to "my betrayed country"—"*mia patria tradita*". He made sure that when "*tradita*" came along you said it and meant it.

In another Verdi program in July 1943 we did the fourth act of *Rigoletto*, which we did again at the Red Cross concert in Madison Square Garden in 1944. I had already sung *Rigoletto*—I started singing it about 1940, before I was at the Met— but of course Toscanini's tempos and interpretation were different. I like the people who tell you he played something faster because he knew it had to fit on a record! He played it faster because he felt it *should* be faster. I'll never forget when we did *Traviata*—the fast tempos in some places. The *"Libiamo,"* for instance. He said: "This is a drinking song on a festive occasion; you can't go to sleep." Or the gambling scene. He explained what's going on—what's happening with the girl and the boy— he doesn't really want to gamble, but is jealous. Toscanini said: "Verdi meant it to be exciting; and [here Peerce imitated Toscanini's burlesquing of the usual tempo] *that's* not exciting." And he sang it as it should go [Peerce demonstrated Toscanini's faster tempo], singing everybody's part, getting the meaning, and making it live.

In the *Fidelio* of 1944 he worked us very hard. Mind you, he didn't speak German well, but he knew every word and corrected our German and made us enunciate it clearly. His tempos were fast; but he could explain every one of them. Some of the singers had done *Fidelio* at the Met; and everybody had ideas and feelings in the matter; and you could talk to him. "Maestro, is there any special reason for this? Don't you think we could do it a little slower?" And he told you why you couldn't—what would happen if you did. He said: "How should this man act? If you sing it slowly you will lose the intensity." But he listened to you: he wasn't the ogre he was painted. The only time he was a tough guy was when he got angry; and when would he get angry? When he thought you were betraying the composer— weren't doing what the composer wanted. If you made a mistake once, it was *nischt gefährlich*: he'd look at you; but if you made it again, or made more mistakes, then there was hell to pay. In *Fidelio* one day he lost his temper with a singer who made a mistake he had made the day before; and it was terrible: the man stood there crying because of the things Toscanini called him.

No, it was my first *Fidelio*: I learned it for Toscanini. He made me learn it; because I didn't want to: why should I learn a part I might never do again. He said: "You learn the part.

You please me." There were other things he wanted me to do which I wouldn't do. He wanted me to sing a Wagner program with him once; and I'm sorry to this day that I didn't. He wanted me to do the second half of the first act of *Die Walküre*. That was the first thing he heard me sing on the air when I was at Radio City; and what appealed to him, he told me later, was the fact that he was hearing a Siegmund who was not yelling—who was singing. I have a letter in which he wrote me, when I told him I was sorry but I couldn't do it: "Who told you that in order to sing Wagner you must not know how to sing?" That was his argument; but I refused; and even afterwards he said to me: "You should have done it." The other thing I refused to do was *Aida*. I was careful about my choice of repertoire, because I wanted to be able to sing for a long time, and if you give too much—especially in your early years, when you don't know as much about vocal technique as you do later— you can't last: by the time the technique is part of you, you say: "Where's the voice?" This is where the critics can be of service to a young singer: they can tell him he's on the wrong track. Instead of only saying "Great performance", they should question whether the guy should have done the part at all. I remember listening to a Toscanini broadcast of an opera while I was getting dressed for a concert in Cleveland, and saying to my accompanist about two of the singers: "They never sang like this before, and I predict they'll never sing like this again." They were fantastic; but they gave too much, and got into vocal trouble afterwards. Singing is like charity: you give—but you don't give everything, so that you have nothing left for yourself; you have to be a little selfish. So I refused to do *Aida*.

In *La Bohème*, in order to satisfy Toscanini, we had to undo a lot of things we'd learned from others. And I remember how he spent hours with the baritone who tells Marcello, at the end, that Mimi has died—"*Marcello, è spirata*"—how Toscanini spent hours to get this baritone, who was a great artist, a great actor, to speak the words the particular way he wanted—with a breathless quality that Cehanovsky just didn't dig at the beginning. "No—no—Cehanovsky, no—*caro:* 'Marcello [Peerce imitated Toscanini's croaking whisper]—Marcello'—" until he got Cehanovsky to do exactly what he wanted. The same with everybody: he had something to say to everybody, to give him the feeling for the interpretation of his part. The notes, he said —everybody knows the notes: the thing is to make the notes mean something. And even when he didn't say anything, when you just listened to the beginning as he zipped into it [Peerce sang the orchestral passage] you had to sing [Peerce sang the vocal phrase]: there was no other way of answering when your cue came. Or before *"Mimi è tanto malata":* just with the expression on his face this guy was giving you a message [Peerce sang the phrase].

In the broadcast of *La Bohème* he sang along with me—in the aria especially; and in the third act, my God, he helped me cry. You can hear it on the record; and there are some people who say, "It spoils the record." And I tell them: "Isn't that funny; for me it makes the record." Imagine hearing Toscanini —not planning it, just naturally singing faintly in the background [Peerce imitated Toscanini's croaking]—and knowing this guy's blood is on that record; and some shmo says, "That spoils it." They don't know what inspires people.

I suppose you know what happened at the end of the broadcast? No? Well, after Mimi's death there is one beat of rest, and it's a tradition that the conductor doesn't beat that rest. Toscanini had explained to the orchestra that he wouldn't beat the rest; but at the broadcast he was affected by the drama of the moment and was crying, and his hand made some sort of movement. Some of the brass thought he was giving them their first beat, and came in, but others didn't; and there was bedlam. Of course it didn't take Toscanini more than three beats to straighten them out; but for him the heavens fell; the world went black; he wouldn't take a bow; he cried; he carried on; he sent for the brass section: "What did you do? What did you do? You're sorry! What, sorry? *You* go home now with your wife and have dinner; what do *I* do?"

You asked whether it was true that the next time I sang *Bohème* at the Met I was told to forget some of the things I had done with Toscanini. Sure. *You* know: those petty jealousies. I antagonized some people at the Met once when I was interviewed on the air—I think by Tex McCrary—and he said: "Your association with Toscanini was marvelous, of course. But who do you think—at this time—is rising to take his place?" And I said: "No one!" He said: "You mean to say that of all the people—" And I said: "No! No one!" And I was very vehement about my no ones. And of course there were five different conductors at the Met who thought, "Why no one?" There was only one conductor—I mean it: if I were questioned today I would say it—only one, and the poor fellow died—Cantelli—who showed signs of that kind of greatness. Who else? Do *you* know anyone else? In another interview I said: "A lot of his imitators think that if they speak with a hoarse voice and cuss out musicians, that will make them Toscaninis. No, *that's* not Toscanini: you have to be a genius." So some of the conductors *don't* like me so much!

I've already told you a few things about the *Traviata*. I remember another example there of Toscanini's insistence that the notes must mean something. Merrill has a great voice, the greatest baritone around; but Toscanini wanted him to get a certain softness, a certain mellowness; and finally he said: "Merrill—Merrill—please—please, Merrill—be a father—don't be a baritone." He never yelled at me; but once I came near it—in a *Traviata* rehearsal. I made a mistake—I mispronounced a word. He looked at me and his hands dropped from the piano: "*Un altra volta.* Again." So I did the phrase again; and again—I didn't think of it; it was a small thing—I made the mistake. And

he dropped his hands: "Peerce! You too?!" I said to myself·
"There has to be a first time"; and I tell you, my heart sank: it
would have killed me, to be the butt of his anger.

At one *Traviata* rehearsal he gave the orchestra a **Ge-
schichte.** My wife Alice had never come to a rehearsal; and I
told her: "You're missing a lot if you don't come to the rehearsals. They're better than the performances." So she said:
"All right, I'd like to come." But she couldn't come any day but
Friday. "Oh, come on!" I said. "Friday is the dress rehearsal—
just a final run-through. Can't you—" No, it had to be Friday;
So I arranged it for Friday; and at the rehearsal on Friday Albanese said to me: "Oh, I see Alice." All week there had been
fireworks: Toscanini had really carried on; and I said to Albanese: "Today she comes, when he'll just run through it." So he
starts the orchestra in the Prelude to Act 3; and he stops them:
"*Piano!*" He starts them again, and stops them: "*Piano!!!*" And
the third time: "*Io voglio PIANO!!! PIANO!!!*" And *he* broke
his stick; *he* threw the score; *he* knocked over the stand; *he*
stamped his feet. I saw my wife looking at me; and afterwards
she said: "I *shouldn't* come Friday?" But the beautiful thing
was that finally he cooled off and began to play with his mustache and said: "Next season, anybody in this orchestra who
wants to play with me must have audition. Nobody can play
next year without audition." At that point he saw Mischakoff,
the concertmaster, looking up at him with that smile on his face
like a little cherub's; and he looked down at Mischakoff and
said: "You too!" Mischakoff had been with him ten years at
that time!

There was one broadcast in there that he wanted me for;
but I was booked for two concerts at some college that just
wouldn't release me; and I think that time he wanted to do
Lucia. He loved *Lucia.* Most people: you mention *Lucia,* and
they say, "Aaah—*Lucia!* Kukuraku, kukuraku [a term of ridicule
for coloratura singing]!" But when you mentioned *Lucia* to Tos-

canini he'd say: "*Lucia!* [Peerce imitated Toscanini's intake of breath] *Che bell' opera!*"; and if he was near a piano he sat down and played it for you. I said to him once: "You know, Maestro, I'd love to do *Lucia* with you—at least the Tomb Scene"; and he said: "Yes, yes, some day." And I think he wanted to do it at that broadcast.

About *Un Ballo in Maschera* I had a whole thing with him, which of course I didn't publicize at the time. I had been promised that *Ballo* originally—oh, yes, I had been promised it; but there was some management political business, and all of a sudden I *heard* that my friend Bjoerling was to do it. When I inquired, "Oh, yes, there was a change." "What do you mean, there was a change? I was *promised* this thing!" "Well, he had a change of mind." "*Who* had a change of mind?" And right away the people around him began to guard him: before that I could get to him any minute of the day; now I couldn't. I was heartbroken, because I worshipped this man: for me he was someone on a pedestal who could do no wrong; and when this happened I said: "I don't ever want to see this guy or talk to him, great as he is." And if it weren't for my wife I would never have done it—which would have been terrible, because *Un Ballo* is one of the best things I ever did with Toscanini, and one of the greatest things that ever happened to me. Walter Toscanini called my wife to ask her if I would talk to his father; and I refused at first; but she said to me: "What are you, crazy? Are you going to cut off your nose to spite your face?" So finally I said: "All right, I'll talk to him." So he got on the phone: "Peerce—Peerce—believe me, is not my fault." And I felt miserable; because I knew he had been victimized; and to have him, a man like that, whom I loved so, apologizing—I felt so miserable, I cried. I said to him: "But Maestro, I haven't done *Un Ballo in Maschera* in six or seven years, and I don't remember it." "Peerce, you will know it—you will know it." This was just a week before the broadcast; I had a concert on Sunday and a performance at the Met on Tuesday; and he wanted me

Wednesday for rehearsal with the orchestra. No piano rehearsal: I couldn't *give* him a piano rehearsal. He said: "You don't have to memorize it: you can hold the book." Well, I got to work with my accompanist and coach, and got the thing back in my system. When I came into Carnegie Hall for the rehearsal there was electricity in the air, with people who knew about all this wondering what was going to happen. I'd seen Toscanini upstairs for a minute; and he'd said to me: "Just sing. I follow." "I'll follow *you*, Maestro." "No, no, you just sing." We went through the first act without a mistake; and he called an intermission; but before that he jumped off the podium and threw his arms around me and kissed me. This was the side of Toscanini that seldom came out; and I felt just like a kid. And upstairs he said to me: "You afraid? You afraid? I told you: you just sing." I said: "But Maestro, I was worried about not satisfying you." He said: "Don't worry. Just sing." And it was a fabulous success. The fire he gave to it![1]

About a year ago a friend called me and said: "They've just announced they're going to do the Toscanini *Bohème* on WOR." So I turned it on and sat listening to it; and what it made me think was that at this late date—with the new sound, and stereo, and shmereo—this was still the greatest recording and made the greatest sound—greater than what you have on all the new ones. You get the quality of that extemporaneous performance: you know you're listening to a real show. You didn't walk into a studio where someone said: "We'll start at letter D and make twelve bars; then we'll cut and make fourteen bars after letter K"; you didn't make one note here and one note there—*you* know the way they make records these days. No—you went in and did a show. So you had to remake an ending or something; but it was a living thing; and that's the greatness of the performance. And I can feel proud of my singing in it; because it isn't a patching together of one note here and another note there in the recording studio: it's the real singing I did that day.

Sol Schoenbach

HAGGIN:

In addition to the recollections of the musicians who played with Toscanini for years in the New York Philharmonic and the NBC Symphony, I wanted those of musicians who played with him only a few times, when he made guest appearances with their orchestras—specifically musicians of the Philadelphia Orchestra, which he conducted in three of its Friday-Saturday pairs during the season of 1941-42, another pair in November 1942, and a pension fund concert in February 1944. I was unable to talk to Marcel Tabuteau, the orchestra's first oboe in that period, and one of its great personages, who after retiring went back to France; or to William Kincaid, its first flute and another great personage, who I was told was ill. The first horn, Mason Jones, whom I did see, claimed to have nothing to tell. But the first bassoon, Sol Schoenbach, was able to tell me a great deal that he remembered.

As the men of the orchestra had stood smiling behind Toscanini after the performance of Schubert's C-major, at the concert of November 15, 1941, their smiles had seemed to me evidence of how much it meant to them to be playing again under a great conductor (Stokowski had just left the orchestra), and one who was in addition a great musician. But I now discovered that it had meant less to them than I had thought. Schoenbach—who, I gathered, could be taken as speaking for his fellow-musicians in the orchestra—recognized, certainly, that Toscanini was an extraordinary conductor and musician; but had reservations and criticisms concerning objectives and methods that the Philharmonic and NBC Symphony musicians did not have.

SCHOENBACH:

I was raised in New York; and my teachers were Benjamin Kohon, first bassoon of the New York Philharmonic, and for the major portion of my studies Simon Kovar, the second bassoon. And so all I heard about was Toscanini, and from the inside: they used to bring home the music and discuss it; and I was very well steeped in that tradition. Also, my sister gave me a subscription to the Saturday night Philharmonic concerts, which I heard from the top balcony from the time I was a little boy. So when I got to the point where I myself played with Toscanini, I had enough background; and at the first rehearsal I was full of respect and awe.

I found that Toscanini never quite explained himself. He would make all kinds of remarks and shout; but it wasn't clear what he was driving at, unless you yourself knew what the problem was. The conductors I had worked with were quite articulate; but though Toscanini was voluble he wasn't articulate. (I guess the language was a problem.[1]) So when he was dissatisfied he couldn't say exactly what to do about it. He would say "Sing!"—which was a wonderful suggestion; but when you 'sang' and it didn't quite fit into his idea of the phrase, he just got furious. Oh yes, he did sing it for you; but that didn't help, because he sang in this half-voice that was out of tune, and when you listened to it, you couldn't relate it to what he said he wanted. He had something in his mind; and he did the passage over and over until he got it as he wanted it; but he couldn't tell you specifically what he wanted. So it wasn't just being in an exposed position that kept me from feeling at ease, but not knowing what was going to happen, when he was going to erupt. Fortunately Marcel Tabuteau had had his previous experience with Toscanini at the Metropolitan, and could relay to us in the woodwind section what the problem was— which prevented some shouting. Also, I had this background through my teachers, which was helpful. And the Schubert C-major doesn't have a very exposed bassoon part. So I escaped his wrath.

Another thing that caused trouble was that we had an approach to the music down there, best presented by Tabuteau. In addition to being an instrumentalist he was a very great musician, who had made an analysis of all that goes to make music—how rhythm is put together, and how the line of music is derived from the harmony, and so on. He gave this to all his students at the Curtis Institute, and not just his oboe students, because he had the woodwind class. I went to Juilliard, where Barrère was our woodwind teacher; and when I came to the Philadelphia Orchestra I noticed that there was something special going on. I set about analyzing it, and asking Tabuteau questions; and I began to participate in it. Toscanini wasn't acquainted with this approach; and many times we got into trouble because he thought of music as starting from beat 'one', where we thought of it as starting with the preparation for beat 'one'.

I don't think he made any such theoretic studies: he was concerned with preparing the piece that had to be played. An orchestra was just an instrument for him: as a pianist would say: "Deliver me a Steinway," Toscanini would say: "Deliver me an orchestra." Whether it was French or German or American or the BBC, he set out to make the music come from that orchestra the way he heard it from the score: he wouldn't change it by one iota to suit the players he found in the particular orchestra. Every player was—not an enemy, but someone who had to be taught to do the thing right. Toscanini was in full possession of the facts; and we were all just instrumentalists who had to be beaten into shape so that we played the music right. And he never gave us much credit for brains. He seemed to regard orchestra players as inferior; and *he* had to get them up to a professional level. But I will say that he wasn't like some conductors who, when they're not satisfied, try to get rid of the man and get someone else. He worked with what he had, whether it was the greatest or not so great. He wasn't the most patient man; but he didn't say to the player: "Go home, and we'll get someone else."

As for what he wanted in the playing of a wind instrument, his first consideration was the singing quality: he kept shouting *"Cantare! Cantare!"*; and he wanted the instrument to sing out. Another thing he cared a lot about was intonation. Then rhythm; and here I'll say there was another thing I observed with Toscanini, for what it's worth (it's easy to sit here and talk about the giant he was!): he was so preoccupied with rhythm all the time that very often he made a rhythmic problem terribly complicated when it wasn't. Anything that involved a dotted figure—for example the beginning of the Allegro in the first movement of the Schubert C-major:

almost before anyone even played it he'd say the eighth-note was too early, and he'd begin to carry on. All these common little rhythmic things that musicians are familiar with seemed like an obsession with him: you hardly had played before he'd stop and say it was wrong; and then it usually did get wrong, because it wasn't clear to us exactly what he wanted. We did the Mendelssohn *Midsummer Night's Dream* music—you know what transparent music that is—and he fussed so much about the tempo and the rhythm, the tempo and the rhythm, that after a while you had trouble with something you never had trouble with before. We began to feel that he had a complex about this—that he was so afraid *he* might be wrong, that he assumed *we* were wrong—though many of us didn't find any problem. And I remember once when there *was* a problem he didn't settle it. Knowing how fussy he was about everything like that, I went to him and asked about a triplet figure in the first movement of the Beethoven *Pastoral*, which in the exposition came to an eighth-note, but in the recapitulation came to a quarter-note, with no logical reason for the difference. He went into a long discussion about the original manuscript that he had seen in the British Museum or some other library; but he never answered the question—because I don't think there *was* an answer.[2]

To get back to that first rehearsal: I remember the Schubert C-major vividly. He was concerned with the movement of it, the flow of it; and he tried to make everything clear—he didn't want anything muddy. One of the other pieces on the first program was Debussy's *Ibéria*; and there is a bridge passage from the slow movement to the last movement—a distant-sounding passage in which the bassoon plays with the flute and violin. I played it all the time; but he sent word that he didn't want me to play it for the recording; and when I asked him why, he said *his* score—a revised version suggested by Caplet—didn't have it. I don't remember whether I did play it or not for the recording, which I never heard: those recordings never came out; they were supposed to have been damaged.[3]

I'll never forget the Tchaikovsky Sixth on one of the later programs. It starts with a bassoon passage; and because of Stokowski's and Ormandy's training, it was my custom to play this opening passage in one breath—which took a lot of doing. At the first rehearsal with Toscanini I presented him with my great accomplishment—and he didn't like it! He didn't say anything at the time; but I could see that he wasn't really in accord. Either he sent for me or I went to him; and in his dressing room he asked me why I played the passage all in one breath; and I told him this was what I had been trained to do. He said no, he preferred that it be segmented; and he proceeded to sing in that voice of his: "I-ee love you; I-ee love you—" this mournful Tchaikovsky Sixth in that voice! I had all I could do to keep from laughing; but I played it his way. Then, later in the movement, just before the development section, there's a passage that traditionally is begun by the clarinet and ended by the bass clarinet, although the last notes are scored for the bassoon. He absolutely refused to have those last four notes played by the bass clarinet. He said: "It's in the bassoon part; and you must play it," And I—*tell*—*you*: to play that! I think it's marked six *p*'s; and with Toscanini it became twenty-six *p*'s; and it became the biggest feat in the world: I filled my bassoon with absorbent cotton and handkerchiefs and socks!

As a wind-player I can say it was a privilege to play with Toscanini. All the conductors I've played with were fascinating; but he was one of the greatest. You ask how he differed from the others. One difference was that whereas Stokowski was engrossed in colors—he'd even ask you to change your reed, because he thought your instrument was too bright for the gray he wanted—Toscanini was more interested in the lines: all he saw was this melody moving like that; and it had to move just right: he wouldn't permit one note to get in the way of another. But the chief difference was Toscanini's drive, his intensity. Everything was intensely felt; and he burned with white incandescence. When you started the piece you knew you were going to the end, and you felt swept along. He never dawdled, never went on any side excursions: it was unrelenting. Sometimes the music didn't lend itself to this: his strict observance of tempos didn't help the Tchaikovsky Sixth, which I felt needed a little more expansion in space and time. You thought it was marvelous? Well, one gets used to certain conceptions: Stokowski and Ormandy used to give it more space.

With Toscanini it's the drive and intensity that I keep coming back to. Though he didn't have the greatest technique with the stick, it certainly was adequate for everything that had to be done. But I think it was his personality more than his technique that enabled him to hold huge forces together in concentration. A conductor has to be a personality, has to have something in him that's dynamic, that makes him a leader whom men are willing to follow even if they hate him. And Toscanini had that.

I would say a concert with Toscanini was not as exciting as the rehearsals. There *was* excitement, of course, at the concert, and the feeling that everything had to go or else; but you also knew there wasn't much he could do if something went wrong except show you his displeasure; and mostly it went off like a preconceived affair: he never did anything but what he had asked for at the rehearsal. However it didn't have, for me, the excitement that the rehearsal had, where I didn't know what was going to happen to whom, and where he was going to blow up.

I don't think this complete autocracy, and these tantrums, could happen today—that the union and all the other forces today would put up with it. I don't think it could even get started. Toscanini was an established figure; and the situation was very different in the thirties; so the men in the New York Philharmonic were living in terror when he was putting the orchestra together; and when he took it to Europe with programs that were already studied and well rehearsed, I remember the fear that my teacher exhibited, which was shared by all the other men in the orchestra. Or take the Philadelphia Orchestra.

When Stokowski comes back now to conduct it he's mellow and it's "Dear Old Stokie"; but in the days when I first came to the orchestra the men used to sit on the edge of their chairs and go absolutely white when he came on the stage. People will not put up with that kind of abuse today. When Cantelli came to the Philadelphia Orchestra and started to throw some abuse—yes, in Italian—someone who understood got up and said he wouldn't have him talk like that in front of the ladies in the orchestra.[4] I don't see how those fellows in the NBC Symphony can say Toscanini was sweet and wonderful after the way he demolished people. Of course a conductor should have the right to have things done his way; but he should also say what his way is, not call people names.

But to get back to Toscanini's work: I remember one incident that showed something very extraordinary about him. You remember that during the war he did the Shostakovich Seventh with the NBC Symphony. Well, a couple of years later, at a reception after a pension fund concert he conducted for us—which I'll tell you about in a minute—there was a secretary of the Russian Embassy present who said to Toscanini: "You played Shostakovich's Seventh; and we in Russia are very grateful. But how is it you never have played the Fifth Symphony of Shostakovich?" Well, it was a fantastic experience for me when Toscanini told him why he hadn't done the Fifth; because it turned out that he had studied it just as much as if he *had* played it. The average person knows what he has to know; and what he doesn't have to know he doesn't bother with. But Toscanini had made a thorough study of the Fifth; and he explained to us that if you observed the metronome markings in the score, you arrived at the exposition at a certain tempo, and that played this way the music was boring, and he wouldn't play it. Other conductors ignored those metronome markings; but not Toscanini: what was printed was like from God; and if that's what it said, that was what he would do. The

man from the Russian Embassy said: "Maybe the markings are
wrong. I happen to live in the same apartment house as Shosta-
kovich; and I will ask him personally." Some months passed;
and back came a recording of the Shostakovich Fifth conducted
by Shostakovich and played exactly as the score had it, with a
statement by Shostakovich that the score was correct. This
proved to Toscanini that he had been right to think it was
boring and not to play it. I found out that there were other
scores that he had studied and absorbed even though he hadn't
played them; so that when you asked him why he didn't do
them, he knew why, and could tell you why.

About that pension fund concert in February 1944, which
was the last time Toscanini conducted us. I guess it was in 1943
that I was elected to a small committee to organize a pension
plan for the men; and I came up with the plan that is now in
operation, called the Pension Foundation. One important part
of it was to raise money through concerts; and we had a marvelous beginning with Piatigorsky and Milstein; then we had
Lily Pons and Kostelanetz; but we weren't getting the kind of
money we needed to really establish the plan. Someone suggested getting Toscanini—which was a challenge, and which I
thought was a good idea. I got in touch with Walter Toscanini,
and found that the family would be delighted to have me come
over and talk with Toscanini; because the dynamic Maestro
wanted to conduct more than his season with the NBC Symphony. So I saw him at NBC, and he consented to put on a
Beethoven concert. It was quite a program: the *Egmont* Overture, the Sixth, the Septet, and the *Leonore* No. 2. I couldn't
say to him that we didn't want such a wonderful program; so I
tried to intimate that it was well above the union limitations
on the length of a concert. He flew into a fury in which he
denounced all the officials of the union, living and dead, and
carried on like a maniac; and I thought I'd leave it alone. But
he kept on fighting: "People think that I'm old, that I'm sick!

I'll show them! I'll conduct more than two men!" So we ended up with an enormous program.

When he came for the rehearsals we put in a supply of champagne; and at the first rehearsal Tabuteau made a speech in French and Toscanini answered in his bad French. Every rehearsal was just wonderful—a love feast—until the last one, when he blew his top. It was in the Septet. When I had asked him why he wanted to do the Septet, he had said it was the first score he had bought with his own money: he hadn't eaten lunch for a week to save up the money for it; and it was still his favorite piece. In the last movement the violins have a passage—a series of triplets ending in two eighth-notes—which is very difficult because the two eighth-notes are high E-flats, which are followed by a huge leap down to a low B-natural; and because of that leap the violins rushed the two eighth-notes. As I said before, rhythmic exactness was an obsession with Toscanini; and the rushing of those two eighth-notes irritated him. His irritation used to start at his feet and rise from there; and by the time it reached his mouth it was like a volcano erupting. And on that Sunday morning he just blew up completely. I had been a hero for the orchestra because I had persuaded him to come and conduct for nothing for our pension plan; but now after he insulted everybody, they were angry with me.[5]

The concert was fantastic, all of it: the usual Toscanini treatment of everything showed up. After the concert there was the reception I mentioned before; and I came in late. Toscanini was sitting and eating by himself—he hadn't eaten before the concert, and was quite hungry—and he insisted that I sit down and talk with him, which consisted mostly of listening to him. He was very happy, and was already making plans to come back the following season, when he would do the Beethoven Ninth. It never took place; and I don't know what the reasons were, because I went into the army. But I'll never forget: in the course of the conversation he told me how he was at the

Metropolitan and got fed up with just conducting opera and went to Gatti-Casazza and said he wanted to do the Beethoven Ninth. Gatti-Casazza put him off, until it got to the point where Toscanini said: "Either I conduct the Ninth or I quit"; so Gatti-Casazza said o.k. Toscanini told me the soloists he had—those great voices, the golden voices you hear about—and the fine chorus, and the orchestra; and he said that before the performance he took his pulse, and it was just right; so everything was just right. But, he said, "the next day the *critica* wrote in the papers: 'Who does this man think he is, conducting Beethoven? He should stick to Verdi and Puccini.'" Gatti-Casazza said: "You see?"; and Toscanini was furious. Then, years later when he was conducting the New York Philharmonic he performed the Ninth; and the soloists weren't up to it, the chorus wasn't up to it, the orchestra wasn't just so, and, he said, "before the performance I took my pulse, and it was terrible—I must have had a fever. But the next day the *critica* wrote: 'At last we have heard the Beethoven Ninth as it should be.'" This was to show me how little it all meant; because, he said, the Metropolitan performance the critics had condemned was much better than the Philharmonic performance they raved about.[6]

As he was entertaining me and telling me this and that, all of a sudden he began to tell me about a performance of *Carmen* he had conducted, and about a chord which involved an oboe and three trombones, and how the oboe in those days had an almost trumpet-like sound so that it matched those brass instruments. And while telling me this story he got angry all over again about something that had happened in that performance thirty years before: he blew his top and banged the table and knocked over the dishes. Everybody came running up and asked: "What did you say to him?"; and I said: "I didn't say a word."

But that Beethoven concert! I'll never forget Tabuteau after it was over: he said, "Now I can die." That program was absolutely the end as far as every detail was concerned. It was prepared with great heat, and presented with great illumination; and everything went right. Sometimes, no matter what you do, something goes wrong; but not this time: this one was incredible. I think this was the greatest performance he did with us. The others I don't remember as being special, though they were very good. The Mendelssohn *Midsummer Night's Dream?* Yes, that was marvelous. It had such transparency: he really worked on that; and of course he wouldn't settle for less. Somebody else would get tired and say "What's the use?" or "Let's go on"; but not he: he'd go over and over and over it. Also, I'll never forget his correcting the English of the singers: he had a fantastic ear for that sort of thing. The *La Mer?* Terrific! I remember in the first movement how he worked that cello passage over. Also in the last movement, where the flute and oboe play the theme over the harmonics in the violins—how carefully he had that whole thing worked out to get the feeling of the long shadow, and that sound almost like the wind up there above the sea. I was carried away almost to the point where I'd forget to come in and play.

Well, it was a great privilege for us, hm?

Josef Gingold

HAGGIN:

One of the young violinists who gave up a concert career to join the NBC Symphony in 1937 was Josef Gingold. Two years later he played in a quartet of NBC string virtuosos headed by William Primrose (Oscar Shumsky, Gingold, Primrose, Harvey Shapiro), which made an exciting first public appearance at a New Friends of Music concert with a dazzling performance of Mozart's Quintet K.614 (with William Carboni, second viola). When I began to attend Toscanini's rehearsals at NBC in 1942, Gingold was one of the musicians I enjoyed talking to about the things that happened—the one who spoke with the greatest enthusiasm and warmth. It was he who, after an extraordinary rehearsal of La Mer, exclaimed: "You can quote me on this: we come here to go to school!" And he spoke about Toscanini with the same warmth and an additional fervor twenty-three years later.

GINGOLD:

My first rehearsal with Toscanini—for the first NBC Symphony broadcast in 1937—I think was the greatest musical experience of my life. I had of course heard Toscanini many times

132

with the New York Philharmonic: he was my favorite conductor; and that was why I joined the NBC Symphony: I wanted to make music with this giant. I was a little apprehensive because of what I had heard about his temper; but I thought I'd try it for a season and see what happened.

That Sunday afternoon in 1937, a week before the broadcast, when he raised his stick to begin the Brahms First, there was electricity in the air; and the first chord gave me goose flesh. I don't think I've ever been as thrilled as I was then; and I'm still thrilled when I speak of it now, thirty years later. He went through the entire Brahms symphony with very little comment,[1] apparently pleased with the orchestra; and we responded to his conducting by not only playing our hearts out for him but playing over our heads. After the Brahms we played the Mozart G-minor; and it was a marvelous performance, a marvelous experience. I have still to hear a Mozart G-minor as great as Toscanini's: in it Mozart emerged in a new light. Toscanini made it a great drama; and I will never forget the opening phrase—the pathos it had with the inflection he gave it. He kept saying to the violins: *"Molto arco! Molto arco! Non tedescho! Italiano! Molto arco!"* [Gingold illustrated with big movements of his bow arm as he sang the opening phrase in an impassioned manner.] It was *his* Mozart; and it was wonderful![2]

We also did the Vivaldi Concerto Grosso in D minor, which opened the broadcast on Christmas Eve; and I recall that at the broadcast, I don't know what happened, but Toscanini's first beat in the Vivaldi was very indecisive, so that we almost didn't get started together. For a moment the orchestra was a little shaken; but somehow we did get into it, and then it was all right. (I don't remember his making any mistakes— though I did see him balled up once, in Copland's *El Salón México*, by the constantly changing meter. Even so, I believe Copland said it was one of the best performances he ever had.[3])

I remember in those first weeks a wonderful experience in

the two movements of Beethoven's Quartet Op. 135, which Toscanini played with string orchestra, and in which I've never heard any quartet approach him. The way he worked out every detail in the Largo! And the fire in the Scherzo! And those complicated string crossings that he worked out with the first violins alone! I wish he had done all the Beethoven quartets: for me they are the greatest masterpieces in the quartet literature; and where can you find a first violinist who is a Toscanini? He also did the *Moto Perpetuo* of Paganini, which was a lot of fun for the violinists, who practiced their parts and were well prepared.

It was in our second season that we played Tchaikovsky's *Pathétique* the first time; and it was quite a revelation to us, and gave us a bad morning. He came to the rehearsal with the preconceived idea that the orchestra was set in its way of playing the symphony; and he was right. We came to the second subject, the D-major melody which traditionally—for I don't know how many years—we had all played with a *ritardando* on the first three notes. When Toscanini began to conduct the melody in tempo, the orchestra took it away from him and slowed down the first three notes. He stopped: "*Signori, perchè?* Why? Is written so, eh? *Ancora!*" We started again; and again we made the *ritardando*: it was so ingrained in us that we couldn't help it. And he threw a fit. "*Si, tradizione!* The first *asino*, the first jackass, did it that way, and everyone follow him!" Then he pointed to the score: "*This* is my *tradizione!* So play like this!" Toscanini's logic was unanswerable: if Tchaikovsky had wanted a *ritardando* he would have written it in the score: "Is very easy to write *ritardando*, no?" So we played the three notes in time; and from then on we played everything as Tchaikovsky wanted it. This was the way we played it at the broadcast; and for the first time musicians and music-lovers heard the music as Tchaikovsky wrote it; but a great many of them didn't like it, because it was different. And today I hear the Tchaikovsky *Pathétique*

played again in the "traditional" manner. I won't say by everybody: George Szell, for instance—who, incidentally, was a great
admirer of Toscanini; oh yes, he had a tremendous admiration
for him[4]—Szell, who treats the classics with the utmost respect,
tries to follow in Toscanini's footsteps with a personality of his
own. I never heard Cantelli, unfortunately; but except for him,
Toscanini didn't have the great young disciples to continue
what he achieved.

I remember marvelous performances we gave in Buenos
Aires. We were having a beautiful trip; we were rested; we were
playing nothing but symphonic music, and not one broadcast a
week but a concert every other day; Maestro was in fine spirits.
And one performance of the *Tristan* Prelude and Finale in the
Teatro Colón was *UN-FOR-GETTABLE!*

Certain performances of Toscanini's I don't think will ever
be equalled by anyone else. The *Enigma Variations,* for instance: I don't think anybody did it as well. I don't think there
will ever be a *La Mer* like his. The time he spent with the cellos
and violas in that passage in the first movement! Also the
Beethoven Ninth. The first movement: it was classic; it wept;
it was operatic! The slow movement! And the recitatives of the
basses in the finale! Berlioz's *Queen Mab*: the magic of it! The
Rossini overtures: impossible to duplicate! The Wagner: no one
conducted Wagner like Toscanini—*no one!* And of course
Verdi: who will ever hear Verdi played like that? Even the
accompaniments in performances of the arias: never banal,
always with dignity, grandeur. Nothing was too small; everything
was important. A little miniature like *Queen Mab*: how he
worked on it! Twenty batons must have been broken to achieve
it! Or the little Martucci pieces: with what grace and charm he
did them! And I played with him at that Chatham Square
benefit—in that little orchestra in which Heifetz played, and
Milstein and Adolf Busch and Feuermann, with a few NBC
men; and Toscanini conducted the *Moment Musical* of Schu-

bert, the *Musical Joke* of Mozart, the *Perpetual Motion* of Reis, and a piece called *Loin du Bal* by Gillet, which you hear on Muzak and used to hear in hotels. Even though it was supposed to be a jamboree, we had a rehearsal, and the Old Man conducted as if it were a concert or broadcast: everything was done perfectly. And what he did with this little piece, this trifle, *Loin du Bal!* It came out like a wonderful jewel! Whatever he played, he played as though it was the greatest work.

I think he was the greatest recreative artist of this era—certainly as a conductor; and the explanation of how he did what he did has to begin with the unexplainable—that he was a genius. One can say he was a masterful conductor, who knew what he wanted and knew how to get it; one can speak of his tremendous knowledge, his thorough preparation, his ear, his baton technique. But I think that in the final analysis it was his genius that really won out: he was a genius blessed with all these things he needed for realization. It was not just one of them, but the combination of all of them.

From a purely technical viewpoint he had the clearest beat of any; but it wasn't the beat of a specialist in virtuoso conducting; it was the beat of a musician who had a stick and could show whatever he wished with it. And he never did more than was needed. He once quoted Hamlet's directions to the actors: "Suit the action to the word, and the word to the action"; and he himself made the motion that was suited to a *forte*, a *piano*, or any dynamic. He once said to the violinists, in a *pianissimo* passage where we were using too much bow: "Watch my hand. If my motion is small, your bow must be small; if my motion is large, your bow must be large." And the marvelous way he could conduct a slow tempo—the control! He is the only conductor I know who conducted the *Parsifal* Prelude in four instead of the customary eight; and he didn't give the silent downbeat most conductors give to assure perfect unanimity at the very beginning. He said: "Is no cadenza *per me*: I start to beat when we start to play." And he did, and the violins came in together! Also, he beat it all in four, and with his superb stick control it was always together. (To say nothing of the mood, the magic that he got in this piece.) Also the second movement of *Ibéria*, which is written in two, but which everyone does in four. Toscanini said: "I know is conducted in four, but I cannot do it so"; and he did it in two—and the control was marvelous. He was like a human metronome: a *human* metronome, I say, because I mean that his sense of rhythm was so marvelous. We played the *Eroica* one year; and the next year he varied by five seconds in a work which takes forty-eight minutes.

And yet he was smarter than some conductors who are *Kapellmeister*—who always hold the reins: he would run with a running horse. We did a performance of the Haydn No. 88; and we heard later from the people who were backstage after the performance that the Old Man came up beaming and said: "Did you hear the beautiful tempo *primi violini* took in finale?" They laughed at the idea of the violins taking a tempo; and he said: "*Si,* they took the tempo." Of course it was his tempo; but within hairsbreadths it could be a tiny bit on the fast side; and once it started there was nothing he could do; so, smart man that he was, he took what he got—which happened to be perfect—and played along with it. And he was so delighted! So many times he walked off the stage cursing—disgusted with the orchestra or with himself. He was very tough on himself: many times he said: "*Stupidi—anch' io!*" Even when something was good he was sparing with his praise: when he said "*Non c'è male*—not too bad" that was a real compliment.

Which reminds me of an extraordinary incident the first time we played Wagner's *Faust Overture*. The piece starts with a solo for tuba; and when our tuba-player, William Bell, had played it, Toscanini stopped and said: "*Ancora.* Again." So Bell played it again; and this time Toscanini went on; and we in front heard him say under his breath as he conducted: "This is first time in fifty-five years that I hear this solo played correct. Bravo, tuba, bravo, bravo." This was extraordinary; but so was the rest of the story. Since Toscanini said it so softly, only those of us around him heard it; and each of us assumed one of the others had told it to Bell, who sat too far away to hear it. Well, Bell and I now teach at Indiana University; and last year, when we were reminiscing about the Old Man, and I referred to Toscanini's terrific compliment to him, he didn't know what I was talking about. It turned out that no one had told him at the time; and when I told him what Toscanini had said, he was just as thrilled now as he would have been in 1938.

To get back to the other things about Toscanini's conducting: the score and parts of the Shostakovich Seventh arrived here at the last possible minute; and Toscanini had no more than two weeks' preparation before calling the first rehearsal. The work is about seventy-three minutes long; and when Toscanini began that first reading he knew the entire work by memory. Now we were playing from the parts of the Leningrad Philharmonic or whatever orchestra had played it in Russia—if not conducted by Shostakovich, certainly supervised by him—and not just one performance, but I believe twenty or more. When Toscanini had run through the first movement he said "*Da capo*"; and pretty soon he stopped and said, either to a trumpet- or a horn-player: "What you play there? You play *si bémol*, eh? I think should be *fa*." The player said: "But Maestro, I have a B-flat in my part." "No, *caro*, I think should be *fa*." And in his myopic way he peered at the score; and he was right. He was right the first time; he was right the second time; and I believe he must have found thirty-five or forty mistakes in the parts, that Shostakovich himself hadn't heard in twenty or more performances. The same thing happened when we played Roy Harris's Third Symphony. I think we had the parts from which the Boston Symphony had played it and recorded it under Koussevitzky. Roy Harris was at the rehearsals; and I imagine he must have been at the Boston Symphony rehearsals; and Toscanini kept finding wrong notes in the parts and turning to Harris: "Eh, Maestro, you don't think should be this note?" Poor Harris had to look at the music; and of course Toscanini was never wrong.[5] There was a contemporary piece—I can't remember what—that he programmed, tried once, and took off: he couldn't take it; it was too dissonant for him. He came to that rehearsal knowing the piece by memory; and as we were reading it we came to a terrific discord: it was so dissonant that we actually had to look at the fingerboard to see where our notes were. And he stopped: "Eh, *terzo corno!* Third horn! *Re!* I didn't hear!" The man had had a few bars' rest and had cleaned his horn, and hadn't been able to get it up again in time to come in. Toscanini couldn't see that far, and didn't see that the man wasn't playing; but he heard that the D was missing.

Then there was his knowledge—not just of symphony and opera, but of everything in music. I don't think he ever forgot anything. This background of all-round knowledge came into the playing, no matter what particular work he was doing. One felt it.

And then there was the spell which his genius cast over the men. My wife likes to tell the story about the day I had some bug and wasn't feeling well enough to go to a rehearsal, but there was something on the program that I wanted to play, so I said: "I'll bundle up and go, and I'll play that one piece and then come right home." I went there feverish and in no condition really to play; but once Maestro began the rehearsal, I became so absorbed in what we were doing that I forgot I was sick, I forgot about myself entirely; and at the end of the rehearsal I was feeling completely well. This was the effect Toscanini had: when you were playing with him your mind never wandered for one moment; you were completely absorbed in music-making and at one with him and with the composer. And also, no matter what you were playing, you were convinced, at that moment, that this was the only way it could be played.

It was the spell of his musical personality; but it was also what he gave of himself. From the moment he began the rehearsal it was music-making plus a workshop; and it was never "Let's take it easy and save ourselves for the concert": he never spared himself, and he expected his musicians never to spare themselves. How could we help responding to this man who worked harder than everybody else (there was a pool of water around him after a while), for whom music was a religion, and who made us feel the same way? We adored him; and we *tried* at least to give as much—and not only for him but for the music's sake. And let me say this: the concerts were of course a marvelous thing to have; BUT—THE REHEARSALS! As much public acclaim as he had in his sixty years as a conductor— and for me it wasn't enough; he should have had even more— only the musicians who were in the workshop with him really knew how great he was: they saw aspects of his art that one couldn't see at the concert. The concert was a finished thing; and sometimes one had a feeling, not that he didn't care, but that the work had already been done, the concert had to take place, so let's go through with it. *Some*times; I wouldn't say always. He was always inspired; but the rehearsals were incredible: he was as inspired at them as most conductors are at concerts. It was the wonder of wonders, the things you saw this man do, whereas you had difficulties playing just one line. You felt like a little nincompoop in the presence of a god.

A great, great genius—one in a lifetime: there will never be another one like him—not in our time. And the impact he had on all of us who played with him was such that our whole musical being was altered for the good—for the best. Music was a religion for him; and it rubbed off on all of us who came into contact with him. He instilled a love of work, a devotion and respect for music, for the composer. He taught us to look carefully at the composer's indications on the printed page—to see, for example, what he wrote *after Allegro*. He would say: "Is not *Allegro*. Is *Allegro ma—*" or "*Allegro con—*" Every word meant something. In *Allegro giusto* you had to pay attention to the *giusto*; in *Allegro vivace*, to the *vivace*. When we played an Andante he would say: "*Non marcia funebre! Andante!*"

But the statement one often hears—that one of the great things about him was that he played everything as it was written—those who say this are uttering a mere empty phrase. To play what's written is quite easy; what people don't realize is that Toscanini, being a great musician, read between the lines, and this was what gave the music the life it had in his performance. And very often he did change dynamics—because he had to. In a Beethoven symphony, for example, you will find that Beethoven wrote double-*forte* throughout a passage; and if you played it exactly as written it would sound poorly balanced and blurred. So Toscanini made certain changes in the dynamics for clarification, to enable certain voices to emerge. Where the violins had to fight against all the brass he changed the double-*forte* to *mezzo-forte* for the brass and left the double-*forte* for the violins, so the violins could be heard clearly without having to force.

His ideas of clarity, of voices always emerging clearly—there has never been anything like it. He would take just, let's say, the second clarinet and third horn and violas—inner voices—and make them play alone. And always "*Cantare! Cantare!* Sing! Sing!" He made these voices sing as if they were thematic, and then incorporated them with the rest of the orchestral texture. And how beautiful the whole thing became!

One thing he did that occurs to me is his beating in circles. Musicians I knew would ask me: "How do you know what he's doing?" The perspective was different for someone *in* the orchestra. He did the circular movement when he felt that the music called for expansion, for excitement, which he achieved by getting away from the square one-two-three-four beat. He always was making music; and as far as we were concerned the beat had been established. It was difficult for an outsider to understand; but we understood it perfectly.

As I said before, working with this man we felt that we were in the presence of a god. That's why when he would throw fits and would insult people—though it wasn't very pleasant, I must say, and we wished he had acted differently—we understood and accepted it. Sometimes we accepted even when we didn't understand. Chotzinoff once gave me the explanation of an incident which baffled us at the time. He sometimes came to a rehearsal with a preconceived idea about what was going to happen. I told you about the first time we rehearsed Tchaikovsky's *Pathétique*; and in this case it was the first time we were going to do the *Leonore* No. 3. At the end there is that famous violin passage, which we prepared in advance: we practiced it individually, and together; and as you know we had a marvelous violin section. The day of the first rehearsal, Chotzinoff told me, the Old Man was pacing back and forth, back and forth, in his room. Chotzinoff asked him what was the matter. "*Tutti violini di NBC son stupidi!*" "But Maestro, you seemed satisfied at the concert on Saturday." "Eh, but you will hear *Leonore*. They cannot play. Is *male, male!*" At the rehearsal, we sensed that he was in an unusually bad mood; but it wasn't the first time. When he came to the difficult violin passage he stopped, pointed to the last four violins of the section, and said: "Last four violins play alone." They played very well. "Next four." They played very well. Down the line: everyone played well. Then the whole section: it was marvelous. And he was so angry that it went well, because it was contrary to what he had expected, that he began to scream: "You are *dilettanti!*" We just looked at him: there was no use trying to figure out what this was all about.

But he could be very understanding and patient when

something was difficult. And he could be wonderful to people. When the orchestra manager once wanted to fire a musician, Toscanini said: "He stay." And when one of the men was killed in South America and Toscanini found out about it, he locked himself in his cabin and wept for hours, because he felt that if he hadn't made the tour this man would still be alive.

I myself had a wonderful experience with the Old Man. None of us ever approached him personally: we were asked to keep away from him when the orchestra was organized. So when I resigned from the orchestra in 1943 to become concertmaster of the Detroit Symphony, I handed in my resignation to the personnel manager, not to Toscanini. But a notice appeared in *The Times* on the day of one of our Sunday afternoon broadcasts; and Maestro read it. After the broadcast Chotzinoff said: "Maestro wants to see you." I didn't associate it with the notice in the paper, and didn't know what it was about. For the moment I was stunned, and thought: "My God, what did I do?" I recapitulated the entire broadcast in my mind; but as far as I could remember I had played as well as I could, and hadn't spoiled anything. So I went in to see him; and he looked at me and said: "*Caro*, you don't like Maestro anymore?" I said: "Maestro, I adore you!" "Then why you leave?" "Well, Maestro, I've always wanted to be a concertmaster; and of course one has to start in a smaller orchestra to realize this ambition." "*Ma*—is good orchestra here, and good maestro. Why you leave?" This was the first time he had shown any awareness of my existence: until then I had thought I was just another number—but not at all. He then invited me to visit him in Riverdale; and we spent a whole afternoon with him that was just terrific.

We debated whether to take our boy, who was then four years old. My wife didn't think we should; but I said he was old enough to be able to remember it and say he once shook hands with Toscanini; so we decided to take him along. Tosca-

nini was wonderful to him—gave him cookies, and took him out
to a swing or something in the yard. We were alone with the
Old Man the whole afternoon—four hours. He was sniffling
and sneezing, and said: "I have terrible cold"; but my wife
whispered that she thought it was hay fever, because *she* had it
and it was the season; and we found out later that he did have
hay fever. Well, he asked me about myself—with whom had I
studied? I said: "With Ysaye." "Ah, is great violinist. He play
with me innnnnn—Scala. Was innnnnn—April—eighteennnnnn
—ninety-six. *Mi-maggiore* Bach—and Mendelssohn." Just like
that; and if the Old Man said it was April 1896, it was so. "He
play beauuutifully. Beautiful *rubato e cantabile.* A beautiful
artist." And then he said: "You know, Sarasate play with me in
Italy first time Lalo *Symphonie Espagnole.* Is not very interesting, but beautiful technique. He play like—like lady."

It was lovely: he reminisced, and I asked him questions. I
asked him about the great days at the Metropolitan when he
was there. I said: "It must have been wonderful when they
had singers like Caruso and Scotti." He said: "When I am
young man I admire certain singers. And people say: 'You think
these are good. You should have heard *Rubini!* You should have
heard *Grisi!*' Is always so. Now in twenty-five years you will
say: 'Singers today are no good. You should have heard *Peerce!*'
Were not such golden years."

He spoke about Chaliapin, for whom he apparently at one
time had great admiration. He said that they were going to do
Mefistofele at La Scala and were looking for a suitable bass;
and it so happened that a very dear friend who went on a
business trip to Russia heard Chaliapin there. This friend was
not a musician, but he knew opera, he knew singers; and he
told Toscanini about this young Russian bass who he said was
wonderful. So Toscanini sent Gatti-Casazza on a special trip to
hear Chaliapin; and Gatti signed him up. It was the first time
that Chaliapin sang outside of Russia; and Toscanini said that

when he came to rehearse, "Was *molto bene, molto modesto.*
He did some things not *perfetto;* but we worked. Everything I
tell him, he say: *'Si, Maestro, si.'* And he did a wonderful
Mefistofele. Correct! CORRRRECT!!!" You know what a compliment this was from Toscanini. Everything was done beautifully; and it was a great success. At last, Toscanini thought, he
had a singer who not only had a marvelous voice and was a
wonderful actor, but was modest and took direction. They
engaged Chaliapin again for the following year; and meanwhile
he was engaged elsewhere: he sang in London, he sang everywhere, and always with great success. Then reports came to
Toscanini that Chaliapin had already had a fight with the conductor somewhere—that in the middle of a performance he
signalled to the conductor—you know: "*Via, via, via!*" And
Toscanini said: "No, no, you make mistake. Is *molto, molto
modesto.* No, no." Then he had to go to Paris; and in Paris he
saw in the newspaper that Chaliapin was singing in *Mefistofele.*
So he went; and he said: "Was *porcheria! Male*—bad—bad
taste—everything distorted! I went backstage, and I said to
him: 'Chaliapin, you must restudy the whole thing when you
come to La Scala! We must work again!' *'Si, Maestro, si.'* "
Then, he said, about two weeks before Chaliapin was scheduled
to return to La Scala, they got a telegram that he was sick, so
they postponed the performance. Then they got another telegram that he couldn't come for some other reason. And finally
it was evident that he didn't want to come. Toscanini said he
was disappointed that this man didn't want to be corrected.
To find a great artist like that, and not to be able to do anything with him! He was so disappointed in him!

Later that afternoon Toscanini played a recording of
Harold in Italy, which Koussevitzky and the Boston Symphony
had made with Primrose; and he listened, tugging at his mous-
tache, and said: "Poor Primrose. *Poor Primrose!* Next year he
come to play this piece with me again; and he must play correct!

This is not correct! This Koussevitzky play very good double bass, you know? *Molto bene.*" And he said it was a wonderful orchestra, but Boston always had good orchestras. "I remember Karl Muck. He play the Beethoven First"; and the Old Man imitated Muck conducting the Allegro of the first movement in a dragging tempo. "He did not make the first repeat: *was boring also for him*, no?!" And we couldn't laugh as you and I are laughing now; because the Old Man couldn't take a joke, and to him this was serious: he didn't think it was funny at all.

He was in great form that day. He recalled that when he was at La Scala, Ricordi came to him and told him that a composer named Leoncavallo, who was associated with them in some way, had written an opera, and they wanted Toscanini to do the premiere. So he looked at the score of *I Pagliacci*, and said: "*E porcheria.*" ["It's a mess."] And he said: "I didn't want to do it; but Ricordi, who was a good friend, begged me. He said: 'Do it just once. This man Leoncavallo is so poor.' And I don't know why, but I say: '*Bene, bene.* I do this *porcheria.*' And you know what success had this piece! It went all over the world for fifty years! But you know, *caro, anche* today is *porcheria!*"

It was a wonderful visit. A few years later—I don't remember exactly what year—I listened in Cleveland, over the radio, to an incredible performance; and I sat down and wrote a Christmas card to Toscanini. I wrote him: "I was just listening to your broadcast. It was absolutely sublime. Maestro, I wish you a Merry Christmas and a Happy New Year." That's all I wrote. On Christmas Day, at eight o'clock in the morning, a special delivery; and there was an envelope addressed in Toscanini's hand, with a bold "Special Delivery" at one side, and inside a card with a photograph of himself in it, and a handwritten inscription: "Thank you, my dear Gingold, for your very kind words. My very best wishes to you for a Merry Christmas and a Happy New Year." He went to the trouble—he probably went to the post office himself to send it! He never forgot a former musician.

And I had a lovely visit with him—it was the last time I saw him—when the orchestra played in Cleveland on the transcontinental tour. They played in the Public Auditorium, to 10,000 people. I went to the concert, and tried to get backstage afterwards; but there was a police guard at the stage door, and I couldn't get in. The next day some of the men came to my house for lunch; and I told them: "I tried to see the Old Man, but I couldn't get in. I feel so terrible: I wanted to tell him what a wonderful concert it was." And one of them said: "Call up Walter Toscanini; because the Old Man was expecting you, knowing you are here." So I called up Walter Toscanini; and he said: "But Father left word with Walker to let you in." I said: "I couldn't even get to Walker." He said: "Come to the train. We leave at midnight; and Father will be there about ten o'clock." I did, and had about two hours with the Old Man on the train—a beautiful visit. He wanted to know all about the concerts in Cleveland, and how I was doing. He told me I was getting too fat. And I must tell you this wonderful story. He was having trouble with his knee; and they had a railing around the conductor's podium, so that if his knee gave way he could hold on. In Cleveland he conducted the Brahms Fourth; and the Scherzo was as energetic as ever; but at the end of it, the three *forte* chords came out *forte—forte—pianissimo.* I was taken aback, but thought maybe because of the acoustics I didn't hear right. When I saw him he said: "You notice something in Scherzo of Brahms, eh?" And he looked at me with those eyes. I said: "Well, Maestro, I noticed the last chord was *piano.*" "*Si, caro,* was *piano.* You know, I have trouble with my knee. And I start to make *energico* the last chord; but my knee is going to break, eh; and I could not make the last chord big as should be. I make *piano;* and the *stupidi musicisti*—they follow me!"

I had brought him a little present—a book containing the programs of the Bonn Festival of 1892, which included programs of the Joachim Quartet. It was a very rare book; and when I gave it to him he was very happy: he looked through it thoroughly; told me he had heard the Joachim Quartet play; and spoke about them. I also had brought along the memoirs of Arditi. He's the man who wrote *Il Bacio*; and he was a well-known conductor in his day. I brought the book because Arditi has in it a story of how Rossini once and for all settled the question of a note in the English horn solo in the *William Tell* Overture. Arditi asked Rossini which is it: E D B C B G or E D B C A G? And Rossini took out his visiting card and wrote on it E D B C A G and his signature. Arditi writes in his memoirs that now when English-horn-players ask him, he shows them Rossini's card; and he has a photograph of the card in the book. I showed it to the Old Man; and he said: "*Si*, is Rossini's writing. But is *banale* like this. Rossini sometimes write this way, sometimes another way. No, *caro*, is wrong—is *banale*. Is *banale* also for Rossini!"; and he shut the book *molto energico*.

It was a beautiful visit. And do you know what amazed me? When I left I embraced the Old Man; and he had the skin of a baby! I noticed also that he had all his teeth—and this was a man who was then over eighty! And the most beautiful eyes I've ever seen in my life! Incidentally, when he would look at the first-violin section, when he got angry, his eyes covered everybody: everyone thought he was looking at *him*—whereas he was looking at the whole section.

And that was the last time I saw the Old Man. He emerges today greater than ever—though I don't know whether his influence is very great now. The things he fought for are being distorted again—the tempi in Brahms's symphonies, for example: *allegros* are played as *andantes*, *andantes* as *adagios*—the very things Toscanini fought against. And if you question the conductors about this, their answer invariably is: "Well, that's the tradition." But there is hardly a day—when I am teaching, or practicing, or playing—that his image isn't before me, and that I don't recall some remark or idea or other reminder of his genius. I thank God for giving me those seven years of playing with him; because my whole life has been enriched by my contact with this great, great musician. And I am sorry that others didn't have this opportunity. In my twenty-five years of symphony playing I have played with great conductors and wonderful musicians; but there was only one Toscanini.

Hugo Burghauser

HAGGIN:

In addition to conducting the New York Philharmonic, in the thirties, Toscanini conducted in various places in Europe. Kipnis told a little about this; and a great deal was added by Hugo Burghauser, who after 1940 played bassoon in the Metropolitan Opera Orchestra for many years, but who before the war was the chairman of the Vienna Philharmonic during the several years that Toscanini conducted it in Vienna and Salzburg. Not only could he speak about what he experienced with Toscanini in those years, but as a member of the orchestra for fifteen years before that, he could place this experience in the context of what he had experienced with Nikisch, Weingartner, Richard Strauss, Furtwängler and Bruno Walter.

From Kipnis I had got the impression that the performance of Beethoven's Missa Solemnis in which he sang in 1936 was Toscanini's very first performance with the Vienna Philharmonic. I said something about this to Burghauser; and he began by correcting my wrong impression.

BURGHAUSER:

Before the Missa Solemnis, Toscanini conducted in Vienna

the Verdi *Requiem,* which was important for very special and sensational reasons. After his very first appearances with the Vienna Philharmonic in Vienna, in the fall of 1933, he was—on my initiative as chairman of the Vienna Philharmonic—invited to appear for the first time at the festival in Salzburg in the middle of August 1934. Two weeks before he was to arrive, Dollfuss, the Chancellor, was murdered. Naturally all the foreigners left Salzburg; and in spite of the fact that Mussolini saved Austria politically, it was like after an earthquake, and everybody was in fear and despair. And then Toscanini—contrary to all expectation, and keeping his word courageously—did appear and conduct at the Salzburg Festival the two Philharmonic concerts which repeated the programs he had conducted in Vienna in '33. Because of this connection of the Philharmonic with Toscanini, the government of Austria asked me to ask him if he would conduct the Verdi *Requiem Mass* for the murdered Chancellor. To this—again to our surprise—Toscanini readily consented. And so in the fall of 1934—two years before Beethoven's *Missa Solemnis*—Toscanini conducted Verdi's *Requiem* in Vienna; and with his great reverence for Verdi it meant a great deal to him that he conducted it on the very same spot, in the Vienna State Opera, on which Verdi himself had conducted it sixty years before. Only, Toscanini conducted out of piety for the murdered Chancellor—which proved again how strongly Toscanini felt: he shunned official politics; but this was a political act against Fascist Germany and the Fascist murder. That obviously was his attitude and his reason for conducting the *Requiem.*

And when he conducted Beethoven's *Missa Solemnis* in '36, again politics got involved and made difficulties. We had engaged a great basso—I forget whom—from Germany; but on the very day before the first rehearsal he was forbidden by the Third Reich to come to Vienna. We were at that time with Toscanini in Budapest for a concert; and when I heard by phone that our German basso was forbidden to come to Vienna, I arranged with Kipnis, who was then the leading basso in Vienna, to be ready. When Toscanini first heard there was no basso, he realized there might be no *Missa Solemnis*; but when we both came from the airplane after the flight from Budapest to Vienna, Toscanini couldn't believe his eyes: there with my secretary was his trusted basso Kipnis ready for the rehearsal, which was to take place immediately.

But now I go back to the beginning. In 1933 Toscanini consented for the first time to conduct the Vienna Philharmonic. It happened that I was then the newly elected chairman of the orchestra; and Toscanini accepted my invitation. As a result there was a collaboration of five seasons in Vienna and Salzburg. Just last week, on the occasion of my seventieth birthday, the Vienna Philharmonic wrote me a congratulatory letter, in which they said that in connection with their wishes for my birthday they must mention that after 120 years of the orchestra's existence—from Nicolai to Hans Richter, Karl Muck, Mahler, Nikisch (I played in the Vienna Philharmonic with Nikisch fifty years ago: I was then, after the first world war, a newly engaged member, and had the great advantage of playing with this great man when he made his last appearances with the Vienna Philharmonic two years before his death)—in their letter the Philharmonic told me that—looking back, in historical perspective—they could now say this was the greatest, the real climax of the historical achievement of *any* European orchestra, but especially of the Vienna Philharmonic: to have had Toscanini those five consecutive years. And I can accept credit for it; because I had the initiative, and also very big luck. I quote now Napoleon, who when he promoted an officer—say from colonel to general—naturally because of his ability to be a general—always asked also the question "And does he have luck?" And I can say that I, as a sort of general of the Vienna Philharmonic, did have the most important, absolutely essential, mystical gift of luck. Because Toscanini—for ten, fifteen, twenty years—had been invited to Vienna, but had never accepted. He came once with La Scala for two evenings, and with the New York Philharmonic, and that was wonderful; but it was not what we wanted: we wanted him to lead *us*, if possible in a continuing and growing activity. And it so happened that to my invitation he accepted—which was sheer luck—though I did put in just a little diplomacy too, which my predecessors may not have done. In my letter to Toscanini, my very first letter as the elected chairman of the Vienna Philharmonic, I invited him as my predecessors and other people had done; only, I added that we as musicians realized his high standards and his inexorable demands; and as we were, besides the Vienna Philharmonic concertizing society, also the State Opera Orchestra, we had duties—rehearsals during the day, performances in the evening—which might, from his viewpoint and also in reality, limit our ability to rehearse with him; therefore, since whatever program he would choose—and he always chose chiefly what we call the Vienna *klassische Schule*: Haydn, Mozart, Beethoven, Schubert, Brahms; and then of course his beloved Debussy and Verdi—since this would be such an enormous task for him and for us, I suggested: if there was not enough time during the day, we were ready, after every performance at night, to have rehearsals with him after midnight as long and as arduous as he wanted. I suppose such a suggestion was never made to him; and later when I got to know him very well and intimately, I learned that such an appeal and such a suggestion psychologically overwhelmed him. When he saw such an ardent desire, such a zeal—it was a sacrifice, after all, for people who played opera every night till eleven or twelve o'clock, to be then ready to rehearse with him—then he was willing to come. This little piece of psychological diplomacy, so to speak—and of course I meant it seriously: after all it was our word, and it would have to be fulfilled—played a great role in Toscanini's decision: "This time I'm willing."

When he arrived, his first program was Beethoven's Seventh, the Brahms *Haydn Variations*, his most beloved Mozart *Haffner* Symphony, and the *Meistersinger* Prelude. I said: "Well, Maestro, we have four, five mornings, and of course nights." Toscanini, smiling as he looked at the program, said: "*Ma—per* Beethoven, Brahms and Mozart, *credo* we will not need more than possibly three, four sittings?" "All right, Maestro, we start. Whatever you want." After the first rehearsal—of Beethoven and Brahms—he said: "All right—not more than two more." And when he finished the second rehearsal, he said: "That's all we need"; and there was no third rehearsal. But although I had known the orchestra more than twenty years—fifteen years as a member, and many more as a young student—I never had lived through the phenomenon of such a superhuman concentration as it showed at these rehearsals. This was such a breathtaking experience: Toscanini was by then sixty-six years old—of course a mythical figure—I would say quite a bit mellowed, contrary to his awe-inspiring reputation, and with the utmost simplicity. And the orchestra, in my time from Nikisch to Richard Strauss—who was an extraordinary, not sufficiently recognized, grandiose conductor, one of the greatest, but so self-effacing in appearance that in spite of the greatest effect people were not aware how great a conductor he was—so, the orchestra, which had been day in, day out with Strauss, Weingartner, Bruno Walter, by then also Klemperer, with this ensemble of the greatest talent of the world, still unsurpassed in spite of all the Karajans!!!—the orchestra, with Toscanini, realized this was the climax of every musician's experience. Not only because he was superior to other conductors —which was taken for granted; but because he made us *superior to ourselves*—which was the phenomenon that was practically unexplainable. This I call magic; and you can call it Indian fakir—hypnosis—telepathy—whatever you want—but a phenomenon clearly, realistically unheard of and unexperienced. This was the essence; and also that the effect with the old Beethoven Seventh, which every one of us knew in his sleep, and with the Brahms and the Mozart, was that they were *as newly created for us*. This was the greatest surprise; and it remained so for five years. And then again, while everybody was transported to some higher sphere, at the same time Toscanini was in educational method a sort of martinet of a country teacher—severe, inexorable, overlooking nothing, to the point of pedantry, yet with geniality.

From then on it was every year a matter of about a dozen concerts. Opera we played with him only in Salzburg; but in 1936 when Bruno Walter took over as artistic director of the Vienna State Opera after Weingartner—who was quite a great man in his time—Toscanini, as a gesture to his friend Walter, opened the season by conducting in Vienna a few performances of *Fidelio*—with Lotte Lehmann and others and the set from Salzburg. His first operas in Salzburg in '35 were *Fidelio* and *Falstaff*. It was what you call a *conditio sine qua non*: he said, "All right, *Fidelio*—but only on condition that I conduct also *Falstaff*." Now he would conduct *Falstaff* with an Italian ensemble, which was never done in Salzburg even with Mozart, whose operas were mostly written originally in Italian; and it was unheard of that in a German town like Salzburg, three miles from the border of the Third Reich, an Italian should come, an anti-Fascist, who publicly declares, "I make war on Mussolini, and I throw Bayreuth in the teeth of Hitler," and should establish there the first Italian performance of *Falstaff*. There were a lot of objections and difficulties;[1] but it was done— and of course done beautifully. And so *Fidelio* was done also; and this *Fidelio* was, so to speak, transplanted to the Vienna State Opera a year later, when Toscanini opened the season in

September 1936 as a courtesy to Bruno Walter.

He was also very often a listening guest in Vienna; because whenever he was going to conduct an opera in Salzburg—say *Magic Flute*, or *Meistersinger*, which was a dream—he listened before in Vienna to get acquainted with the style of the performance. Of course it turned out that he did it quite differently; and though we all believed ours was the highest standard, *his* standard afterwards made us realize ours was not always such a high standard until he took over. Fifteen or twenty years later, here in his house in Riverdale-on-Hudson, somebody played for him a recording made from the broadcast of his *Meistersinger* in Salzburg. It was by no means a perfect recording (there was never a regular recording of the performance); but when he heard the second act he was touched in just the same way as when he conducted it in Salzburg. He said then: "It's a heavenly dream." And here, when he heard it fifteen years later, he was moved to tears—this man who was hardly addicted to sentimentality, to show sentiment; he was moved to tears, such was the power of his own conducting. And of course for all of us also.

You ask how he achieved what he did, and how he differed from others. Speaking as a very old professional—a craftsman who has been playing now for fifty years—what I must say of Toscanini is that he was able to *project* whatever was in the score and in his mind. The *conceptions* of great interpretation, of what it should be, can quite often be found in fine artistic minds; but to *project* such ideas into the orchestra *unmistakably*, by technical means that are absolutely convincing—which Toscanini did—this is the sort of miracle which I can explain in part only as a result of a real capability of telepathic communication; and in fact he rarely used words to communicate what he wanted. Of course he exhibited the best conducting technique, an unfailing ear, gesture and facial expression which made so clear the intention of any dynamic nuance, that you knew—without his saying a word—that it meant not *piano* but *pianissimo*, not *forte* but *mezzo-forte*. This was perhaps, in the work situation, his greatest ability: to show unmistakably, unfailingly, even to a musician of medium-caliber mind, what is going to happen. And another almost unheard-of ability, which some of the *best* conductors did *not* possess: when he was conducting, especially in a performance, in a medium tempo, say an *Allegretto* or an *Andante*—about half a bar before the occurrence of a detail in the music you saw already on his face and in his gesture what he was coming to and would want. This was extraordinary: the parallel conducting of what was going on now and what was coming the next moment, so that the musician felt he was being guided through the polyphonic complexity of the music, like Theseus led by Ariadne's thread through the labyrinth. It was an entirely unheard-of ability, almost like the clairvoyance of a seer. And again it was a communication not with words.

Toscanini was in fact a poor linguist. Though he knew of course by heart the words of all the Wagner works, he wasn't able to pronounce one German word correctly. After five years of intimate acquaintance he still could not say 'Burghauser' but said 'BurgAHHHser'; and he could not say '*Meistersinger*', which he conducted in heavenly manner, but said '*Mashters-INNNger*'. Yet when a Hungarian chorus from Budapest sang with us—after Kodály's *Psalmus Hungaricus*—Beethoven's Ninth Symphony in German, and began to sing not "*Freude! Freude!*" but, being Hungarian, pronounced it "*Freide! Freide!*", Toscanini at once interrupted and shouted, "Not '*Freide!*' It is '*Freude!*'" So, although he was himself not able to speak fast correctly another language, he was aware of every wrong nuance in pronunciation—in *pronunciation, diction*, mind you—forget about the music. And of course again the psychological effect: a foreign-speaking chorus, standing here in Vienna and singing Beethoven's Ninth; and there is an Italian maestro who can only shout and curse in Italian, but who is all of a sudden a master in German pronunciation and diction! This creates such concentration and awe that people achieve beyond their usual capacity—not because they want to, but because they are elevated spiritually.

And another thing about Toscanini, in which he was different from others. Suppose a conductor makes a mistake—say when he is conducting variations, and by mistake jumps from the second variation to the fourth—which can happen. When he gives the down-beat or the up-beat for the fourth variation, then probably out of the hundred musicians, ten, maybe twenty, will begin with him this wrong variation. But Toscanini happened to conduct with us *Pictures at an Exhibition* by Musorgsky-Ravel in Budapest, after we had produced it in Vienna; and it happened that he started—instead of *Tuileries*—*Bydlo*. I say 'started': I mean he gave the down-beat for *Bydlo*. And a phenomenon occurred which not one of us, and hardly Toscanini himself, ever experienced: *not one musician started to play!* It was ghost-like, a little like a nightmare: Toscanini conducted in the air, and not one sound occurred! Toscanini, for a tenth of a second, was flabbergasted and stony-faced: how come nobody plays? But in another tenth of a second he realized that instead of *Tuileries* he had conducted the beginning of *Bydlo*, which was very different in dynamic character. And with an almost undiscernible nod, he gave the right dynamic sign for the beginning of *Tuileries*, and then the orchestra, most harmoniously, as if nothing had happened, started to play. Afterwards he said: "This is the greatest compliment an orchestra can pay me: *I* make a mistake, and the orchestra at once realizes I am wrong." Why? Because his *Zeichengebung*, his gesture for communication and conducting, is so unmistakable in its one possible meaning that you cannot take it as meaning anything else; and you say: "Sorry; he's mistaken; I don't play." But that a *hundred people* should have this immediate mental contact—this happened with no other conductor in my fifty years of playing.

Conductors make mistakes; but the orchestra usually goes with the conductor into the mistake; and of course they get out of the mess; but it is never entirely avoided. With Toscanini it was avoided—because of the magical power of this man. It's not enough to explain technically—to say his down-beat for *Bydlo* was clearly different from his down-beat for *Tuileries*. Because if another conductor gave this clearly wrong down-beat, ten or twenty musicians out of the hundred would make the wrong entrance. Consider that among the hundred people playing, say ten to fifteen were tired, not too bright, even if they were good technicians; how could you expect them to be alert like seers? Yet on that evening in Budapest everyone was; and that is what I call surpassing themselves.

Of course, usually conductors don't produce such miracles. Let's say the great Nikisch and Furtwängler, or even Bruno Walter and Klemperer, conducted a mediocre orchestra; then they were mentally, spiritually much better than the performance they produced, because the orchestra was not able to follow them in the higher sphere of art. This is quite understandable: how can a mediocre musician play better—with better intonation—than his physical equipment makes possible? And with other conductors even a bad orchestra plays better than the conductor conducts—which I say is the usual situation. After fifty years' experience I say truly and sincerely: in a good fifty percent of performances the orchestra plays better than the conductor deserves and *is able to do*. You can believe me: I have no axe to grind. Every evening, in the opera—any opera, from the Metropolitan to Vienna—the orchestra, on the average, plays essentially better than the conductor conducts. And this is a condemning shame for the conductors' profession. Unfortunately they are more phony than ever. What is phony? A wrong beating technique; no ear: sometimes an ear in the middle register, never in the high octave, rarely in the low octave: the contrabasses can play anything they want—wrong by inches on the string—

and the conductor's ear is utterly unaware of it. This means they are not gifted enough; but then they pretend to be maestros; and this I call phony. Contrary to all this phoniness going on in the realm of music, Toscanini was the outstanding rarity; and during his lifetime half a dozen—maybe a dozen—came near to him, and were gifted and sincere. But you have *hundreds* of conductors in the world; and they really depreciate and deprive and pervert the whole musical business—every day, every evening!

I tell you this to show what Toscanini really was. *Tja*—a deity! Not as a human being: he had all his faults and his shortcomings and his extravagances which were sometimes hard to bear. I talk about music, and the sense for music. After all, we know Beethoven threw a chair at his housekeeper, yet his Ninth Symphony was holy, and he even spoke about his feeling close to God. And Schopenhauer, the greatest philosopher of Buddhism and compassion, could be very cruel in life. So with Toscanini, we can say, we musicians, that among conductors within our fifty years' experience he was the nearest to a deity. And we can say—we are old enough—that before him the one predecessor of such quality was Nikisch. Though by far not so universal; because Nikisch would not have conducted Verdi and Bellini and Donizetti as he conducted Wagner's *Ring*; whereas Toscanini—with in-a-lifetime unheard-of universality—did conduct a *Meistersinger* as perfect as a *Butterfly*, and a *Götterdämmerung* as grandiose as any—almost you could say ascetic Brahms *Requiem*. Maybe Nikisch would have been able, but he did not have the opportunity; whereas Toscanini could prove his universality. I can say he did not make *The Magic Flute* as heavenly, as naive, as perfect-fairy-tale-like as Richard Strauss did: Strauss happened to love it like a child.[2] But from *Falstaff* to *Fidelio* to *Trovatore* to *Walküre* Toscanini achieved perfection. Strauss conducted a perfect Wagner, and a perfect Bizet, a perfect Boieldieu, mind you, and a *Barbier* not of *Seville* but of *Bagdad*, by Cornelius, to unheard-of subtlety: this was the greatest German master of my time. But Toscanini proved he could do the same, and also Verdi, Bellini and Donizetti. I did not find any other conductor who could do all this. And again a confession about the others: I found Italians who conducted Italian operas terribly; and Germans who mistreated their German music; and American boys who conduct terribly all the repertoire!

Toscanini, when we carelessly played just one phrase in routine manner—say in a Brahms symphony, which we thought we *possessed* (because many of my colleagues played with Brahms himself; and even in the thirties when Toscanini was in Vienna there were still a few violinists in the orchestra who had played with Brahms, who died in the nineties, and who was a good conductor)—Toscanini, when this happened, what did he say, what did he do? He did not correct us. He said: "*Ma, signori, è vostra musica!* It's your music! And you play it not right?" With Italian music it was different: it was *his* music; and "You are going to follow *me*, or I crucify you!" But when it was Brahms or Mozart or Beethoven, he said: "*Ma vergogna!* Shame! Your music! And it's not as good as it should be?" He was such a moralist, and he made such a moral appeal, that you were overwhelmed by the mere morality. Not intonation, not dynamics, not rhythm—which were of course all necessary; but like a Moses with the Ten Commandments he stood there and said: "This is the law, not of me: it is *Beethoven* who demands it!" So we found out what Beethoven is: nobody else made such an appeal to us. It was tragic; because after this we could never enjoy other conductors. I have clippings from Viennese papers which say: "It's now finished for good after this performance of the Verdi *Requiem*; because it never will be the same, and we never will be able to enjoy another performance, good as it will be. After this we are spoiled." You have an affair with Greta Garbo; what else can afterwards happen to you as a man?

I remember that Toscanini once said about a phrase in a love duet: "You play this as if you would say [Burghauser's voice dropped to a murmur] 'I love you.' Who ever believes you? In the first place not the girl! You must say [Burghauser's voice rose to a roar] 'I LOVE YOU FROM THE HEART!!!' " You can call it a gimmick; but he didn't do this often: he talked very, very little. When he conducted Beethoven's Seventh the first time—the second movement, which starts with an A-minor chord *fp*—we played "WHAmm: *FORTE—piano*." He said [Burghauser's voice became reproachful]: *"Ma signori!"* And he put both hands to his heart: "BEE-THO-VEN!!!" Without another word he said "Again!" We played "Bai": the chord had a different quality.

What I tell you is for me like repeating a dream; but it was everyday reality. And it didn't need months or years: it was at the first rehearsal, from the very first hours. The contact was immediate. And with others too. I was with him once in Monte Carlo, in 1936: from an orchestra which played on the esplanade every day a little Bizet, a little Auber, you cannot expect much; but he conducted Debussy and Haydn's *Clock*; and it was amazing. I had never seen him conducting a poor what we call *Kur* orchestra, which played out of tune and had little technique, but usually played in the open air anyhow, so it didn't matter. Of course they were all trying hard; but you cannot change the basic ability in intonation and technique and bowing; yet after ten minutes it was amazing to hear what happened: the orchestra sounded what I would call galvanized; the playing had a coat of sheen and shimmer. He would not have been so patient earlier—when he was thirty or forty: then he was cold, and insisted, and was often brutal. But later he mellowed; even Bruno Walter then said: *"Er ist wie ein Heiliger.* He is like a saint." So you couldn't say anything against what he did. A saint can even curse and condemn people to hell—which he did occasionally; but the orientation, the direction, let us say, was heaven-like. Truly, it was out of this world, though we played on strings, we blew, we snorted, and we had the music before us, the Viennese classics with which we had a lifelong acquaintance—Beethoven, Schubert's Ninth—the great C-major, and we said: "But it's our old Schubert, with which we have grown up from the time when as children we sang the masses in the church; it's the oldest acquaintance of every schoolboy in Vienna, the choir boys, the singing boys. How come that with him it's entirely different?"

Do you know that when as an experienced opera conductor he conducted an orchestra in his very first symphony concert in Turin in 1894 he played the Schubert C-major? This shows how strongly it had impressed itself on his mind; because seventy years ago, in the middle of Italy, it was unheard of to play one of the longest, the "heavenly longest" of symphonies, which usually bores people because it is unending. It was only many decades later that they performed the *Missa Solemnis* in Italy, and *Fidelio*; and Schubert also was not known. And this little shaved conductor, as he was called—because among the bearded conductors at this time, in the 1880's and 90's, like Nikisch and Richter, Toscanini was the one who shaved—this little shaved conductor played the Schubert C-major—quite a daring thing to do. Well, what struck me when he played it with us in Vienna was the introduction of the first movement, before the transition to the Allegro. This is always what Toscanini called *pasticcio*— a sort of what we call *Brei*, like mashed potatoes or cereal; because it is not very discerningly, very discriminately instrumentated: the tender melodic instruments—oboe, bassoon in its highest register—are always covered by the big, thick sound of the strings. And what Toscanini did was to keep this beautiful, voluptuous sound of the strings down, so like little flowers which usually have been hidden in the deep grass, the oboe and bassoon flowered out. This introduction was miraculous. Then when the Allegro came it was clear sailing. And I can say that we in Vienna, with our Schubert, the only one born in Vienna —never before did we hear this symphony so discriminately, with such finesse of different shades, projected into *Akustik,* realized acoustically.

And the Andante with its oboe melody. Here there is the great danger that it becomes unending; and Toscanini always said—in *Magic Flute* also—he was desperate and in his exasperation he shouted: *"Ma signori, andante è caminare! Andante* means walking. Maybe we Italians walk a little faster than a heavy German; but I don't call *this* walking [Burghauser imitated Toscanini's plodding]! *This* is *andante* [Burghauser imitated Toscanini's brisk stride]!" So when he conducted the great G-minor aria of Pamina, *"Ach, ich fühl's".* The orchestra started in six-eighth time: [slowly] ONE — two — THREE — FOUR — five — SIX — ONE. And he said: "But this is *adagio,* what you play. It says *Andante:* [briskly] ONE—two— —THREE—FOUR—five—SIX—ONE. So you can put in the expression, and you are sure there is enough breath." You could call it simple to the point of primitive, yet so subtle that all the Furtwänglers and Bruno Walters did it wrong.[3] Not Strauss: Strauss in tempo and technique was in my lifetime's experience the nearest to Toscanini; and to my great regret and sorrow this was hardly realized, even among musicians.

So the Andante of the Schubert C-major was flowing, relaxed, not dragging—like a healthy, elastic man, instead of one who is old and feeble: [Burghauser sang the oboe melody in dragging tempo]. That way everything is lost. Toscanini, even when he stepped up a staircase at eighty!—that was the way he was able to realize even a slow tempo. Whereas other people were boring even when they conducted fast! It's a tragedy I lived through half my life. I had those five years of festivals with Toscanini; and before that there were the years with Strauss. But I played fifty years! And at the Metropolitan where I played twenty-two years, the last ten I experienced the poorest musicianship in my life! Not because these young American conductors are not brilliantly gifted; but because they are utterly untrained and therefore unmatured. An old musician cannot consider them professionals: they are brilliant amateurs. An amateur can be trained to become a professional; but they are spoiled: instead of being trained they start at the top, as generals. And what musical perversities they commit, what technical shortcomings! It's a great pity!

You ask how Toscanini's Schubert C-major was received by Viennese musicians. We heard this symphony in Vienna, in the *Musikvereinsaal*, in the *Philharmonie*, at least every second year —from Furtwängler, Bruno Walter, Weingartner—one of the greatest in his time—Fritz Busch, Strauss and so on. It was conducted by these men with few differences; and of course it had the deep, genuine sentiment of Schubert melancholy and *Lebens-freude*. And now there came an Italian firebrand, who conducted it absolutely differently: with greater dynamic emphasis, greater *Steigerung*—which meant technically more *crescendo*, more *diminuendo*, more accentuation, the *sforzandi* more *marcato*, sharper, and immediately more *piano*, with greater contrast. No soft contrasts, like Bruno Walter's, which were very lovely and fine. Toscanini made in the *Plastik* stronger contrast: instead of half-relief—bas-relief, as you call it—he carved a little deeper and sharper, with the shadows blacker. You could say it didn't have the good old *gemütliche* Viennese sentimentality, which was true; but it was fascinating. Some critics said—quite rightly and to the point—Toscanini's Schubert C-major was nearer to Beethoven than to the Kahlenberg and the *Wienerwald*. It is remarkably true that the great Schubert just before his death was nearer to Beethoven than to the young Schubert. Absolutely true. This was the novelty with Toscanini that really was completely new to Vienna: a Schubert which was not traditional Viennese, not traditional Schubert. But since Schubert never heard his own C-major Symphony, where can you say that a

Schubert tradition for this symphony exists? It does *not* exist. And if it had existed in the beginning, since there was no gramophone it would perhaps have been lost. We had our Viennese style for Schubert; but Toscanini showed us a new style, a new Schubert. In the C-major Symphony; not in the *Unfinished*: this he conducted and interpreted in the perfect Viennese tradition, as if he had learned it in Vienna. Of course the powerful accents, the dramatic *fortissimi*, the more clearly defined contrasts were there; but the tempi, the flow, the expression, the lyricism were entirely what the Viennese were acquainted with. Not so the C-major: this was a surprise. And my Viennese contemporaries said: "We have never heard it that way. But how grand it is in effect!" I hardly expected Vienna to accept anything in this symphony that was not entirely traditional. But though they were aware that Toscanini's C-major was so different that it was debatable, they said: "It's not our Viennese Schubert; but it's done with true Beethoven character. It has a majesty which we're not used to, and which we don't believe even that Schubert meant; but it's convincing." But how can you put in majesty when it's not there?

You ask about the coda in the finale—whether he distended the four unison C's at the climax. I will tell you first about the coda in the first movement. The final *reprise* of the first theme, in *allegro* tempo, is always conducted—though it's not written that way—broadly, majestically, which is *andante con moto*, you can say, but not *allegro*. Toscanini, without saying a word, kept the *reprise* in strict tempo without the slightest modification; but he made us hundred men put in such intensity—not loudness, not three *fortes*, but intensity—that it was *as if* he had broadened it, though he did not broaden it an iota. (He did the same thing with the chorale in the finale of Brahms's First: the first time, at the beginning, it is *piano*; in the *reprise*, in the coda, it is *fortissimo*, and is always broadened very effectively and convincingly. Not by Toscanini, who made it impressive and convincing *without* the modification of tempo. And of course he was right: the *reprise* should have the same face, the same appearance as the original statement; and the changed tempo changes its face.) Now in the finale of Schubert's C-major, at the beginning of the last *Steigerung—Aufbau*—build-up in the coda, Toscanini said: "*Signori, bacchanale di Vienna Prater.*" You could call it rhythmically exciting; but "*bacchanale*"! Of all the orchestra, no one had ever heard this word. You say 'bacchanale' in *Tannhäuser,* in *Samson et Dalila;* but he said in Schubert's C-major "*Bacchanale di Vienna Prater.*" Well, it was unearthly in achievement, really metaphysical. When it came to the climax –the four unison C's—Toscanini got such a demonic expression on his face that you saw something of an awful power behind it, which made us play with an intensity that another conductor couldn't have achieved, couldn't have got out of us. And the effect was *as if* he broadened, though in reality there was no modification in tempo. (Weingartner also achieved this, by the way, with different means. He was really grandiose in this way, especially with the Schubert C-major. Whereas he usually conducted conventionally, with absolute clarity and geometrical regularity, at the climax of the coda in the finale he began to stab the four C's like with a rapier—which was very effective and also made us play with great intensity.)

So Toscanini's Schubert C-major was a surprise for Vienna; and this was true with Brahms also for us who *lived* with Brahms, *in Brahms* all the time. Toscanini, in the first place, did not start with the First Symphony, or the Fourth, or the Second: at his second concert in Vienna he conducted the *Third,* which is for Viennese the least spectacularly effective. This was a subtle surprise: there comes the greatest star; and he plays first the Beethoven Seventh, which is of the biggest caliber—you could even say more popular than the Ninth; but after that he plays the *Haydn Variations* of Brahms, and then the Third Symphony: this was almost daring for a newcomer. But what an effect it made! What I call *musikalische Plastik*—truly three-dimensional in plastic reality—this was what Toscanini gave us with this symphony—as he did with the Schubert C-major, which also we had never experienced. This Brahms was new, unheard of; yet it fitted into the tradition: it was only taken out of the everyday routine—noble routine, since Brahms is always noble, and yet smoothed down at the corners, at the edges; whereas Toscanini made it sharp and fresh again. And with the Fourth Symphony—the first movement, and the passacaglia, Bach-like, severe, ascetic: people said, "How wonderful to hear once in your life an Italianized Fourth Symphony. It's not our Nordic Brahms; but it's a nice Brahms." And there was no debate; whereas with the Schubert C-major there were debates—spoken, printed.

So the word 'plastic' *is*, absolutely, a most significant word for Toscanini and his interpretive art; and the Schubert C-major was an example very much to the point. Toscanini was a man of few words, and hardly any explanation; but when you were, as a musician, well acquainted with him, he relaxed and unbent and confided; and so I learned that after he established the basic tempo with the very first phrase, what he was most aware of, in lifelong incessant search of, and like with a divining rod hoping to find, was the right *transitional* modification of the tempo in what followed. In the *Haffner* Symphony, after the first proclamation, *forte*, comes a pensive continuation, *piano*; and there has to be this little modification of tempo, which you cannot fix with a metronome, but which is clearly different. Toscanini broke his head and his brain to achieve a nuance of difference which would be just enough and not too little—and convincing. When he was aware that he was not sure—which he expressed quite openly—or when he *thought* he knew, and the playback showed him it was wrong—then it was disastrous. So he played the *Eroica*, and after the first theme and the second theme there was a transition which did not have just this proportion that he wanted, this slight difference in tempo un-noticeably going into the next phase of the *plasticus*. And when the machine reproduced this to him: "Oh, what *stupido cretino son io!*" First despair and hopelessness; then anger: he took the record and smashed it: "*Tu bestia—canaille,* you are the witness of my insufficiency!" But say in ten times he missed—a near miss —once or twice; the point is that eight times he hit the bull's eye. Yet he was aware that it's always like with a tightrope-walker: you can't be sure; there is no net that catches you; and you may fall to your destruction. It can be wonderful—or it can be no good at all. He was always aware of this—for any one of us— and for himself. Yet it didn't upset the work. If another con-ductor were afraid, he would be inhibited. Not Toscanini; and this was another thing about him: his powerful spirit.

One peculiarity of his working method which occurs to me is that when he was working with one group of the orchestra by itself he often sang with this part the parts of the rest of the orchestra that was not playing. And I remember also that forefinger going up near to the tip of his nose in warning and caution for a perfect balance in a chord or an even *pianissimo* in a passage.

You ask about the Salzburg *Meistersinger,* which some musicians said was too fast. In reality it lasted five whole hours! His *Parsifal* in Bayreuth was the longest ever: no Richard Strauss or Karl Muck or Furtwängler conducted such a *largissimo Par-sifal.* He could be slow if it had to be slow. And his *Meistersinger* lasted fully five hours; but it *seemed* fast because it was so lively in expression. For example, at the beginning of Act 3, in the scene of David and Sachs, he made us play with a much lighter tone than we were accustomed to produce. He said: "*Com' una commedia, non tragedia.*" And this new lightness of the tone gave the *impression* of faster tempo, though in reality it was not faster. The peculiarity of the performance was that he illuminated the work from the inside, and it became plastic and alive. This we found remarkable. Because it was taken for granted that his *Falstaff* should surpass all others—even the best of other Italians, like de Sabata, who conducted at La Scala a *Falstaff* which was wonderful. But that Toscanini should conduct such a *Meistersinger!* Of course he had Lotte Lehmann and his Kullman, who was excellent.

The first and third acts, you could say, were of course the highest standard, but well-known standard, no surprises—convincing, and yet what we were well acquainted with—except for the scene of David and Sachs at the beginning of Act 3, which I mentioned. This I dare to say. *But—the second act—*was the literally unheard-of! The poetry of what went on with Sachs and Eva! And Beckmesser! Our Wiedemann sang Beckmesser; and Toscanini—who did not often write such outspoken inscriptions—wrote on his photograph for Wiedemann: "To the best Beckmesser of all my life as conductor." And again those subtle modifications of tempo! In the dialogue of Sachs and Eva the subtlety, the tender polyphony in the orchestra! By then I had heard *Die Meistersinger* for twenty-five years, and had played it, as a member of the State Opera, for fifteen years; but this second act was an entirely new experience for me. In sound and dynamics, in clarity, in expression—this was the ultimate. And afterwards, when we ran up to Toscanini's dressing room, I never saw him as he was then. He said: *"Com' un sogno.* Like a dream. It's a heavenly dream." In such a dream he could speak in an emotional way that was unusual for him: usually if you said something was good, he made a deprecating gesture and said: *"Si, si, va bene, va bene.* It's all right." But this second act —that's when he cried fifteen years later, when somebody played the recording: he looked transported, you could almost say paralyzed: "This happened!" It was the fulfillment of a dream.

And as with the Schubert C-major in concert, he started twice as director of La Scala with *Meistersinger*—in Italy, mind you, with this work which is even today not entirely understood and entirely accepted there. It's too heavy, too *Teutonic*—not German—*Teutonic*. But Toscanini—just like with the Schubert C-major—had the great audacity to play it. Just as during World War I, when the Austrians and the Germans were at war with the Italians, he gave concerts for the benefit, say, of the invalids; and what did he conduct? The Funeral March from *Götterdämmerung* by Richard Wagner! The concert was of course sold out; but all the people walked out of the hall, and he was alone with the orchestra. This showed the sort of conviction—spiritual conviction—that probably gave his interpretations such power, in addition to their charm. This combination was another thing he had: he could be powerful like a giant—like a Michelangelo— and full of tenderness and charm. This was unique: show me another example.

You ask also about the Salzburg *Magic Flute*. Before Toscanini finished it he said: "My belief is that this piece is usually in Germany, and in Vienna too"—where he heard the standard performance—"such a bore that it is a pity and unbearable. And I am going to make it *entertaining*." (He said in German *"unterhaltend"*, and in Italian *"con amore e con piacere"*.) This meant in the first place: never drag. And not only with Papageno: even Tamino is sometimes gay and passionate; and Toscanini put in really moving passion. But of course the traditionalists said: "An Italian, who takes different tempos from Schalk and Bruno Walter. It's all fast, and too fast." They forgot about Strauss, whose tempi in *The Magic Flute* were like Toscanini's. And of course the tempi were not all fast and too fast. But people were used to the great Walter, who put in his heart's blood, and in this way made it so emotionally gripping that it was even sentimental. With Toscanini it was *not* sentimental; and people were not mature enough for this. For this reason—because it departed entirely from the traditional and conventional—it was not a success—the only thing Toscanini conducted in Vienna and Salzburg that was not an acknowledged success. But of course it was delightful. It could not be otherwise: after all, his heart was in it, and his great understanding and everything else. And such an ensemble: the lovely Novotna, who sang Pamina so sweetly; and the great Scandinavian tenor, Roswänge, with a splendid voice for Tamino, and of course first-class interpretation; and a fine Sarastro, Kipnis. It was beyond any performance nowadays anywhere in the world. Yet for the general public the great Toscanini was in this performance least remarkable—which was a great irony.

But I must tell you what had great success. Once Toscanini, all of a sudden, said: "BurgAHHHser, next time I have in mind to conduct the *Liebesliederwalzer* by Brahms." By then I had been playing in Vienna with the Philharmonic and the Opera for twenty-five years, and chamber music all over; and I had never heard a public performance of the *Liebesliederwalzer* of Brahms. Well, Toscanini came to a rehearsal of the State Opera Chorus—sixteen people, each voice in four. It was in the choral rehearsal room, a little amphitheater; and Toscanini's eye was caught by the yellowed old posters on the wall, of operas in the 1860's: a new production of *Der Freischütz*, prepared, staged and conducted by Richard Wagner; the first production of *Lohengrin*, prepared and conducted by Wagner. Toscanini began to read the names of the singers through the pince-nez which he held before his eyes, and became so absorbed that he forgot what he was there for. But then he listened while the Viennese sang for him Brahms waltzes. *Tja* . . . The choral director had prepared the piece well; the chorus knew it perfectly: it was *theirs*—after all it was *Hausmusik*, everyday music, loved. Then Toscanini went to the piano and said: "I don't ask for any new ideas—only a few things, in tempo and *Agogik*"—he didn't say that word—"flexibility." Of course he wanted more than a few things—some tempi much faster, and much faster articulation to produce clearer diction: ta-ta-ta-ta-ta, like *staccato* between the teeth and the tongue. And then he conducted this piece in the Vienna *Musikvereinsaal,* where never a Hans Richter or Furtwängler or Bruno Walter ever conducted such a simple music, however subtle (after all, it's Brahms). There is always a complete quiet at these concerts: people sit there with a sort of religious concentration and devotion. But after one of the waltzes Toscanini made what we call *eine Atempause,* a very short intermission to take breath; and you heard in the entire hall an exhalation, "Ha-a-a-ah." The people had been sitting pent up, holding their breath in fascination. This was the greatest applause I ever experienced. Mozart says in a letter to his father: "I appreciate most the silent applause, when I enter for my *Magic Flute* performance, and people receive me concentrated and quiet." What we experienced this time with Toscanini was almost a demonstration.

By the way, since it just occurs to me, I tell you this: In Christmas '56, Toscanini's last Christmas, I went with Jonel Perlea—one of our greatest conductors, unrecognized and now very sick, but he still conducts—I went with Jonel Perlea, who had been at La Scala and the Metropolitan, to see Toscanini in Riverdale-on-Hudson. He was practically blind; but he reminisced about Salzburg and *Falstaff* and talked about the short-comings of Walter and Furtwängler and this and that—how it's never *all* good and therefore it's really *never* good: it's good enough, but never perfect, so it's *not* good. But there was one who was good: Nikisch. And Ernst von Schuch in Dresden: "I heard things—I was transported. He was never a star: he was a star in Dresden, but never international." So Toscanini admitted always: there *were* conductors; but they are not here now; and those who are here now—sorry, it's good enough, but not really good. He reminisced so happily, this time, that when his daughter, after an hour, hinted that maybe *"padre è un po' stanco"*—that it was too much for him—he said: "Oh no, stay here. I want to go on talking." And what did he talk about at the end? He said: "Preparation for my ninetieth birthday on

March 25—exactly three months from now. They tell me they prepare something nice; and I am going to enjoy it." He was utterly sure, optimistic. Whereas when he was seventy and we celebrated in Milano, he said: "I am now an old man. And who knows: every new day is a gift of heaven, which I cannot even expect and hope for. I am not sick, but after seventy where are you? Should I even go out and conduct?" But when he was three months less than ninety he said: "I am going to enjoy it." It was one of the gayest of Christmases; and three weeks later it was all over. So I am glad to have been, with my friend Jonel Perlea, among the last to see him. It was so moving, and not only in personal sentiments, which are not important for others, but in the thought that the loss was irreplaceable: where in the world today do you find an Arturo Toscanini?

I can say that we in Vienna, who had a succession of the best, finally had the experience of being lifted to a new height by Toscanini. A few years after the last war I visited my homeland, and listened again to opera in Vienna and Salzburg. One evening I wanted to hear one of the greatest artists of former years, Maria Jeritza, in *Salome*; and as I could not obtain a ticket I took a place with the orchestra in the pit, where I sat enthralled by the flood of sound and the still remarkable dramatic singing of Jeritza. It came to the point where Herod says about Jochanaan: "*Er ist ein heiliger Mann. Er ist ein Mann der Gott geschaut hat.* He is a holy man. He is a man who has seen God." And at this moment an old colleague in the orchestra, with whom I had played for many years, including the years with Toscanini, turned around to me and said: "*Auch wir haben Gott geschaut.* We too have seen God."

Alfred Wallenstein

HAGGIN:

At the opening concert of the New York Philharmonic's 1929-30 season Toscanini presented the orchestra's new first cellist, Alfred Wallenstein, in a performance of Strauss's Don Quixote. He stayed with the orchestra until Toscanini left it; then he left to become a conductor himself—first of an orchestra at WOR, later of the Los Angeles Philharmonic, and more recently of other orchestras here and abroad. It seemed to me that having sat directly in front of Toscanini during seven seasons, he must have a great deal to tell; and it turned out that he did.

WALLENSTEIN:

The first time I heard about Toscanini was in 1921, at a rehearsal of the Leipzig Gewandhaus Orchestra, where Nikisch said: "Gentlemen, I have just come from Milan, where I heard a performance of Siegfried conducted by a man named Toscanini that was the greatest performance of opera I have ever heard. Remember this name; because you will hear much of it." And since I was young and impressionable the name stuck with me. In 1927 my wife and I were in Europe, and got to Milan, and picked up a paper, and saw that Toscanini was conducting *Ariane et Barbe-Bleu*. It was the last performance of the season; and we were fortunate in getting the last two seats there were, in the last row downstairs. I remember I went to the performance with my mind made up that I just wanted to hear the opera, because I didn't know it; but I found myself fascinated by one person, Toscanini, and didn't know what took place on the stage because my eyes were riveted on him. I was first cellist in the Chicago Symphony at that time—from 1923 to 1929—and came back raving about Toscanini; and in the summer of 1928 I said to Papi, who was conducting opera at Ravinia Park, and who had talked about Toscanini: "There's one thing I want to do. I want to play with this man." Papi said: "You wouldn't like it. He's very difficult to play with." I said: "I don't care how difficult he is. I've played with everybody else, and I want to play with him; because this is the first time I've heard honesty and truth in music, and I want to have this experience." So Papi said he would arrange an audition; and in January 1929 I came to New York, to the Astor Hotel, to play for Toscanini. I played about five minutes; he asked did I play this, did I play that—and that was it. He couldn't have been more charming; and I was absolutely spellbound: he had this marvelous face, and one of the most beautiful smiles any man has ever had. I mention these things because the personal experiences are the most important in one's life, and Toscanini became not only a conductor for me, but also almost a father in all ways—an amazing man.

You asked about my first experience playing with him, which was the first rehearsal with the New York Philharmonic— of *Don Quixote*. I had arrived in New York with a bad sore throat, which I had during that whole first week; so I had a high temperature and was unable to speak. But after the first rehearsal I came home and talked without stopping until 3 in the morning, telling my wife about Maestro. Everything I had experienced until now was undone by this one experience with him. And contrary to Papi's prediction, I found him the easiest man I'd ever played with—the easiest in all ways—assuming you knew your instrument and could play and had taste. During the entire time I was with him in the Philharmonic—until he resigned; and the same day *I* resigned—there was never one word that he said to the cello section, or to the horn section (Bruno Jaenicke was the leader of the horns). Whenever there was anything difficult I'd get the section together to go over it with them alone. That would be hard to do today; but it was possible then; and we wanted to do our best. So he might say play loud or play soft; but he never had to correct notes or balances. And naturally, when you find that the harder you work the more appreciation you get, it instills confidence and love of the man.

As for what it was like to play with him as a soloist—I think the first season, in addition to *Don Quixote,* I played the Boccherini Concerto and the Brahms Double Concerto—I went beforehand and played the work with him at the piano; and it was never a technical thing he wanted, but mostly a matter of dynamics; and he was very literal: if it said *pianissimo* he wanted it played really *pianissimo*. It was all done here beforehand; and at the rehearsal with the orchestra he didn't say anything to me. Playing with him was unique in one respect: every time I looked up at him, if I was playing an up-beat, it looked to me as if he was on the down-beat—which was a little disconcerting. I remember that once many years later, in Riverdale, Walter Toscanini played an off-the-air recording of the Brahms Double of 1935; and Maestro said: "It's a little fast, don't you think?" And I said: "I'd say it's damned fast!"

It was the same with outside soloists: everything was discussed and settled beforehand; and at the rehearsal with the orchestra nothing needed to be said. I do remember one rehearsal, though, where Ernest Schelling was playing a piece of his for piano and orchestra. Maestro had got the score only two days before—I know that—and was of course rehearsing from memory; and Schelling, who was playing wrong notes, was embarrassed when Maestro stopped and said: "You are not playing what's in the score." And I can give you another example of his perceptiveness in listening. It was in *Don Quixote*—in the windmill variation. There are conductors who happen to know there is a mistake in a part at a certain point, and who stop at that point and tell the player: "You played this note, which should have been that one." But Maestro actually heard: with the *fortissimo* going in that windmill variation he stopped the orchestra and said to the second bassoon: "Weren't you playing B-flat?" "Yes, Maestro." "It's B-natural." I was sitting only three or four feet from this player, and I didn't hear it; and I don't think anyone else did. Only Toscanini did; and when a man shows this kind of perceptiveness you are drawn closer to him.

And I do remember one rehearsal, when Rethberg was singing in some German work, and at one point Maestro corrected her pronunciation. She is a German, and her diction is wonderful; and she said to me: "Can you imagine him telling me? And he's right!" This was true with every language, including English, though his own spoken English was far from impeccable. I really think that if he had spoken English as well as he did French or his own language he wouldn't have had occasion to blow up as much as he did. I think it was the impediment in communication that caused many explosions here that wouldn't have happened in Europe. They happened there too, but not to the extent that they happened here—which gave rise to the idea of him as a tyrant and so on. He was anything but that. Once after the war he was conducting a Wagner program in Milan; and at the rehearsal he was so sweet to the orchestra that afterwards I asked him about it. "Everybody was playing out of tune, and you didn't say anything. If it were New York you would be on top of them—as a matter of fact you would walk out." And he said: "Because in New York I know they can do it, but here I know they cannot."

The main point of Toscanini's efforts was very simple: to be honest in music, to give the truth in music as he saw it. He came to the rehearsal knowing the score, knowing exactly what he wanted out of it, because it was in his mind and in his heart. That was it, and what the orchestra had to do; and he got the orchestra to do it by explaining and repeating over and over again. First all the winds in right relationship: the leading voice a little louder, the third horn a little softer, the second bassoon a little more, and so on. Then the strings. Then together —and so you had the whole with perfect balance. But it was all in his mind and heart before he started rehearsing; it was something that had to be achieved; and it was when they didn't get it that the tantrums came. The same with what he wanted in a musical phrase. He was patient going over it twice; but if they didn't get it the third time, then he would lose his temper. And he wasn't satisfied even when it came out right: it could have been better. Yes, *"Non c'è male."*

But he came with knowledge of more than the score he was conducting. I've never known anyone with the range and completeness of knowledge Maestro had. Not only of the operatic literature—many times he'd sit down at the piano at the beginning of the evening and play through operas that aren't heard anymore, singing all the words—but the chamber literature: he knew all the quartets, and sat down and played them all. And the violin literature: once I asked Zimbalist to play some old concerto, to see if one could trick Maestro; and Zimbalist played it, and played some of it wrong; and Maestro said: "That's wrong," and played the whole thing. Then he said: "Let's see what *you* know," and began playing concertos that none of us knew—the *Concerto Militaire* of Kreutzer—that kind of thing. He had the same knowledge of the song literature, and, strangely enough, the poetry of Shakespeare, Shelley, Keats and Byron: not alone that he knew them, but that he could turn to the page of the book for the point he was making.

That reminds me of the time in Bayreuth, during a rehearsal of *Tannhäuser*, when Elisabeth entered for *"Dich, teure Halle"* and the stage was darkened. Maestro stopped and asked: "Why is the stage so dark?" And Siegfried Wagner said: "That's what Father wanted." And Maestro said: *"Father* wanted?! You have the writings of Father?" They had, of course, at Villa Wahnfried; and one person Toscanini didn't want to see was Cosima; so they went straight into the library, and he took down the particular volume he wanted, turned to the exact page, and said: "Here! Read!" And Wagner said that for Elisabeth's entrance there should be the brightest lights possible. There were thousands of incidents like that: it might involve only a rest or a grace-note; but he wouldn't be satisfied until he had seen the source material. Whatever he did he did with this tremendous knowledge of the background of the music. But he also had an instinct, and taste, and an ear. When he reduced the orchestra for a Mozart concerto it wasn't because of what Mozart did or what the musicologists said: it was because his taste, his ear for balance told him one flute couldn't take care of eighteen first violins, sixteen seconds, and so on. Or if there was too much wind sound he would add strings. And I remember that in the first movement of Beethoven's Eighth, at the beginning of the recapitulation, where the first theme returns, there are just the cellos and basses playing against the full orchestra, and it's impossible to hear them in the hall; so he added tympani (but when he recorded the Eighth he took them out!). Those were the changes he made: nothing that would change the character of the music; only reinforcement of something that should come out but didn't come out.

I remember the time when I had given Maestro some scores by young American composers to look at, and I took one of the composers up to see him. Maestro went to the piano and said: "In this passage you have written so; but tell me"—and he showed the composer a manuscript page on which he had re-scored it—"isn't *this* what you really meant?" The composer was completely taken aback: it *was* what he really meant; he told me later it was absolutely uncanny. This was a kind of criticism of composers' work that Maestro did on many occasions, and that was enormously interesting.

The truth he was after started of course with the right tempo. I would go home after rehearsals and check tempos for which there were metronome indications, and find they were right on the head—and not just the first time but every time the passage came back. This didn't mean the performance was metronomic: it had freedom and flexibility and grace and elegance. Also it had the utmost of lyricism—the word he used constantly was *"canta!"*—and it was full of sentiment, but never sentimental. In his feeling for music it was the lyrical line that was important: he thought horizontally, not vertically—that was why Bach wasn't very close to him.

I remember when we got to Berlin on the tour, Maestro as always scheduled a rehearsal to hear the sound in the hall. Just before the rehearsal I was in the Bote & Bock music store, and ran into a well-known conductor who said: "How can I hear a rehearsal?" I knew that Bruno Walter and Furtwängler and Kleiber were coming; so I said: "Simple. Why don't you just come down?" So he did; and later on I happened to run into him again. He said: "Tell me, what does he do to make that piece [it was *Death and Transfiguration*] sound that way?" I said: "You know, I really can't tell you. All I know is that he just has the notes played the way they're written and gets the right balances." He said: "There must be more to it than that." I said: "No, there isn't more to it—just that." And I was telling the truth up to a point: it was true that everything in the part was played just the way it was, so you didn't even have to look at Maestro to find out where you were and what to do (*I* looked

at him simply because it was fascinating to watch what he did).
But it was true that you were bound to be affected by his complete dedication—the fact that he was a man who loved music
above all in life, for whom life *was* a *life of music*. And you were
always on the *qui vive*; you knew you had to be *there* at every
moment, concert or rehearsal. Although the eyes didn't see you,
the ears heard. So anybody who played with Maestro was made
to play better than he *would* play—not physically or technically
better, but emotionally better.

One thing people don't realize is how hard he worked even
here. And when he was head of La Scala he would start at 8 in
the morning with lighting, or rehearsing singers individually;
then he would rehearse with the orchestra from 10 to 1; then
rehearsals again from 2 to 6; then if he had a performance he
conducted that; and after the performance he would go home
and study until 8 in the morning. He did this every day.

Speaking of his Scala years reminds me of the time we were
driving somewhere, and he was tired and had his eyes closed,
and my wife asked Mme. Toscanini: "Who was the greatest
artist among the singers Maestro ever worked with?" And suddenly he came to: "Chaliapin!" Just like that! And this in spite
of what he had told me about Chaliapin years before. He had
Chaliapin do *Mefistofele* at La Scala, and worked and worked
with him; and it was a very good performance. But two months
later he was in Paris and went to hear Chaliapin in *Mefistofele*
at the Opera; and he had forgotten everything and was doing
what he had done at the first rehearsal. You had to stay on top
of these people all the time, he said; then it was all right. But
he still considered Chaliapin by far the greatest.

Yes, I do recall the performances in the Philharmonic years
being more relaxed and spacious and greater: they really were. I
remember especially the last performances—the Mozart G-minor,
which I thought was as near perfect a performance—and yes,
the Schubert C-major at that concert—as I've heard. I think

almost any professional would agree that one can count on one's hand the performances that have completely satisfied one from beginning to end. I can remember only three, really; and those three were with Toscanini. (I'm talking only about the Philharmonic, not about NBC.) One, certainly, was a performance of *Ein Heldenleben*: there were individual flaws, but not collective ones; and it was a great performance because it had tremendous momentum, and none of the sentimentality which the piece itself has already and doesn't need to have dragged out more. Maestro didn't cheapen anything: he had fabulous taste. The others? Well, one was that last concert in April 1936. And one was a concert in Berlin with the *Eroica* and *La Mer*. I remember these as times when everything went right—when every player in the orchestra was just right, and the balance and the sound and everything—the occasions you hope and work for. Oh, I remember another one—Elgar's *Enigma Variations* in London. I've never heard it like that in my life: it was the last concert of the tour; and it was the *most impeccable* playing and performance I've ever heard. It was fabulously beautiful; and the audience just went wild. Now, thirty years later, you find the English saying it wasn't good. I've found a few players in the BBC and other English orchestras who were at that concert and still talk about how wonderful it was; but the majority of the people, who weren't even there, tell you from hearsay that it was too fast, it wasn't English, it wasn't this or that. Hell, it was what Elgar wrote; and the sad thing was that Elgar, who was still living and should have been there, wasn't there. But I remember one rather elderly lady who was there in the first row of Queen's Hall, and got up and came close, applauding and calling out "Bravo, Maestro! Bravo, Maestro!" I wondered who she was; and it turned out that she was Melba. She came backstage; but Maestro had already gone.

If Toscanini had been a composer, the music would still be there; but the unfortunate thing about a great performing musician is that when the man is gone, everything he achieved is gone. There are the recordings: there is the *Falstaff*, one of the great recordings of all time for him. But some of his greatest performances didn't get recorded;[1] and some of the performances that did get recorded give a wrong impression to someone who doesn't know all his work. I don't think he was well served by his recordings—on the basis of sound and other things. The sound of the Philharmonic on 78's was better than anything they got in 8H—yes, the sound of the Philadelphia on 78's too.[2] I wish he had been more attentive to quality of sound; but he wasn't interested. For him recording was the most difficult thing in the world; because it made him tense. Any audience didn't disturb him; but the microphone did; and so the performance he recorded was sometimes a little fast, sometimes a little slow.[3] But whether he was fast or slow, the intensity was always there, and he made a right thing out of the performance. And the people who heard all his work are not misled by these fast or slow performances on the records, and never say, "He did this too fast" or "He did everything too fast," as the people say who know only the recordings. In this way the recordings do him a great disservice; and another disservice is for one of these people who didn't hear the performances and know only the recordings to write a book about him—about what was good and what was bad—on the basis only of the recordings: I find no excuse for such a book.[4]

But as you say, even the recordings are being withdrawn, and most of the Philadelphia Orchestra recordings are still not issued. And I think this is a great disservice not only to Maestro but to music.

Also, I think the engineers can be blamed for the loss of some recordings we might have had. I was present at a recording session at which Maestro began to rehearse at 9, and had a fabulous performance at 10:30; and they said: "Maestro, are you ready to record?"; and he said "No" and went on rehearsing.

By the time they did record, he was tired and the tempo was too slow. They should have taped what he did all along, and pieced it together—which everyone does today—and we would have had that fabulous performance.[5]

When I look back I think that those of us who were privileged to know and work with Maestro and benefit by his all-round knowledge were the luckiest people in the world; and the years in the Philharmonic with him were the happiest years of my life. And as I said at the beginning, he remained as a father and a sort of father confessor. In my early years of conducting on WOR, when I had some technical problem I could call on him and his knowledge of all those problems: "Oh yes, you mean the place so many bars after this theme. Watch out, because you feel this and you must do that." And after the broadcasts he'd call up to tell me this was fine but that wasn't good. Later, when I was conducting in Los Angeles, he came out in 1945 to do a pension fund concert, and stayed with us; and when he got back he wrote us a letter about the visit that was wonderfully warm and sweet. It also contained one extraordinary statement. Mussolini had been dealt with as Maestro felt he deserved; and Hitler had just done away with himself; and as you can see he writes: "No one will find his body," which I think was extraordinarily prophetic. I was in New York when certain well-known people and friends asked him to come back to Salzburg in 1938; and I saw the cable he sent them telling them how mistaken they were and how little realization they had of what was happening, and that he would never go back to any place with a dictator. I also was present when he did the same thing about Stalin—oh yes, they wanted him to go to Russia—there was a big to-do about that. I think he loved freedom more than anybody in the world.

Giovanni Martinelli

HAGGIN:

Giovanni Martinelli could tell me whether Toscanini's dealing with the famous singers at the Metropolitan was different from his dealing with Kipnis, Tourel and Peerce. He was a little reluctant to talk to still another writer; but his good nature won out; and he gave me a little time which was enough for him to tell me what I was interested in knowing.

MARTINELLI:

You ask did Maestro make it difficult for the singer or easy. Difficult—because he wanted singing to be as precise as if you had an instrument. And at rehearsal he used to say: "Do what is written—what the composer wants. If the composer wants *piano*, do *piano*; if he says *pianissimo*, do *pianissimo*." But sometimes it was difficult for the voice to do this. For a singer it is much easier *forte*, loud, than *piano*, fading out, especially with phrasing—beautiful long phrasing.

You mentioned Beethoven's Ninth Symphony. This was very difficult for me because the music was not in my character, and I had to sing in German. What happened? I adjusted the voice and did it. Especially I had to adjust in the passages in very quick tempo. Of course I studied it before; but I didn't realize what Maestro wanted: such precision—to stick to the principle to do what the composer wants, so you do I won't say a hundred percent but a good ninety percent what he wants.

We did wonderful work—especially when we prepared a new production of *Il Trovatore* in 1915. As you know, everybody says *Il Trovatore* is just a blah-blah-blah-blah; but it's not so; and Maestro wanted to show *Il Trovatore* was a beautiful opera and deserved great consideration. I knew my part, because I sang *Il Trovatore* before; but it was entirely different when the rehearsals started with Maestro. He changed everything—especially the precision of the tempi and the long phrasing. He wanted when was written *Adagio*, do *adagio*; and as well, when was written *Presto*, do *presto*: don't accommodate the tempo to the voice. He obtained beautiful results with the orchestra, and as well with the voices. He told us: "Do what the composer wants. He knew the singers can do it; otherwise he wouldn't have written like that." So we did it: we didn't add anything, and we didn't take away anything. And we knew—I say we, plural, because my colleagues, the soprano, the baritone, everyone—knew that the result would be great, something different than usual, but not extravagant. Toscanini said: "Let's demonstrate that *Trovatore* is a wonderful, wonderful score, a wonderful opera." And we did it: we gave it a beautiful edition, a wonderful edition. So it was a great loss for me when Maestro left the Metropolitan in 1915, my second season, because I was still young. But I had the opportunity to do *Tosca, Madama Butterfly, Aida, Il Trovatore* and *Madame Sans-Gêne* with him.

Before the Metropolitan I worked with him in Rome, in *Girl of the Golden West*, in 1911. That was my first experience with him. *The Girl of the Golden West* was to be done in Rome for the first time after they gave it here at the Metropolitan with Caruso. The tenor in Rome was Amadeo Bassi, who would sing only the first performances, because he had to go to London; so they prepared another tenor—myself. I was very, very green. I was just out of school—only six months from my debut; so you can imagine how green I was. Certainly I was frightened; especially because the score of *The Girl of the Golden West* departed very much from the first melodious operas of Puccini— *Manon Lescaut,* for instance. And of course from Verdi, which I had been singing: I started with *Ernani,* my debut, and then *Ballo in Maschera.* I learned these two operas in ten, twelve days, because the phrases go so easily in your mind. But *The Girl*—except for two short arias—is short phrases with other singers—difficult to go in. And that was the moment when I found myself in great difficulties with Maestro; because he tried himself to give me the cue, but he was not in the right pitch, so I gave the wrong pitch! So Puccini took off his coat and went to the piano to teach me the opera; and then with a couple of orchestral rehearsals I was already well prepared when Bassi went to London. Yes, Maestro was patient; because he knew— first of all that I understood the difficulty, together with the great honor and joy to be associated with such authority. At first it frightens you; then you feel different. It's not exactly fright: your conscience bothers you, are you doing well, are you doing wrong?

In Rome we did also Verdi's *Requiem*—three performances. That was another work! With the *Requiem* I began for the first time to learn and to understand Maestro Toscanini's religion for Verdi—for this Verdi repertoire which I loved myself afterwards. As I said before, I already knew *Ernani* and *Ballo in Maschera*; and now I learned the beautiful phrasing in the *Requiem*—especially the tenor solo, "*Ingemisco*", and then the famous solo in the *Offertorium,* "*Hostias*"—that was really beautiful. We considered that the *Requiem* is a sort of opera, because Verdi put in melodies that could be in *Don Carlo, Ballo in Maschera, Forza del Destino.* There was the same outpouring of beautiful feeling as, for instance, in "*O terra, addio"* in *Aida,* where we poured the melodious voice together with the feeling of the words. But the *Requiem* is a sort of oratorio that has to be treated religiously, not as you sing a phrase in an aria. The phrase has to be correct, without any— what we call, permit me to say—Neapolitan colors. I don't mean like Mozart or Beethoven, but with correct voice, without exaggeration in *portamenti,* without sobbing, without that *pulsus* which Italian singers have when they sing in opera. Correct and precise. This was what Maestro wanted. He wanted to obtain the best, and always what the composer wrote: "Don't do what *you* feel to do."

But Maestro felt phrasing; he felt Verdi's phrasing. When we sang "O *terra, addio"* with Maestro there was a little suspension, a little elasticity—not a stop, but elasticity in the phrasing. The composer could not write this; it had to be in the feeling of the interpretation; and we did it. Or in the third act, when the tenor sang *"Abandonnare la patria"*: he couldn't sing straight, "A—*ban*—*donn*—*are*—*la*—*patria"*; he had to sing with *espansione,* "Aban—*donnare*—*la patria".* Maestro said: "Is a little slower than we start; then we catch up."

Beethoven's *Missa Solemnis* I sang here later with Maestro. That too has wonderful, beautiful phrasing; and it was easier for me than the Ninth Symphony because it was in Latin. But very difficult for me was to subdue the voice, to tame the voice, in certain passages: no *pulsus.* Oh yes, I was able to do it. For the Maestro—especially for the Maestro, the big Maestro.

It was a great pleasure to sing with Maestro—very great. Because he knew what we can do; he was patient; he tried again, worked again, tried again. They say he was ferocious—cruel with singers. It was not so—no, no. He might shout; he might break a baton; but it was not anger; it was just for the result. And after the work he was a good friend. As I told in the NBC broadcast—the few items—the teasing about my haircut. So he was human like everybody else.

[Martinelli is referring to his story of an incident during the break of a rehearsal at the Metropolitan. Holding the hat which he usually put on at this point, Toscanini went to each singer, who put some coins into it. Then, proffering the hat with the money to Martinelli, he said: "Here. Go have your hair cut." In this broadcast Martinelli summed up his experience with Toscanini in the statement that he had learned "the joy to sing, the joy to work, the joy to know . . . the beautiful interpretation of what the composer wanted that Maestro was passing on to us."]

Felix Galimir

HAGGIN:

Though he was for many years an orchestral musician, Felix Galimir in recent years has limited himself to chamber music, part of the time as leader of the Galimir Quartet, part of the time with other groups. And the viewpoint of a chamber-music-player appears on occasion in what he said about Toscanini. Unexpectedly he provided an account of Toscanini's activity with the orchestra that is known as the Israel Philharmonic.

GALIMIR:

I heard Toscanini when he came to Vienna with the Scala in 1929—*Lucia* with Toti dal Monte—a fantastic performance. That of course created great excitement; and they tried to get him in Vienna for a long time; but I think he demanded some fantastic amount of rehearsals, which of course the Vienna Philharmonic thought it didn't need, or didn't want to give him. Until finally they broke down and granted his demands for so many rehearsals; and he came in 1933. There were terrible blow-ups at the rehearsals, because they didn't play well: I mean the Vienna Philharmonic was a wonderful orchestra, but in the rehearsals they took it easy and said: "Tonight we'll play"; and they did play—if there was a good conductor. But Toscanini wanted them to play in the rehearsals; and it took a long time for them to get used to it; and until then there were quite a few blow-ups—I don't remember if he walked out or not. We heard in the conservatory that it was something special; so we tried to sneak into the rehearsals; and I got into one. And *before* the rehearsal—this was a historic event—all the violinists of the Vienna Philharmonic were actually practicing their part—which had never happened since Gustav Mahler left! And at the rehearsal really it was something fantastic: basically the sound was wonderful, and it was *so* precise! We had never heard the orchestra like that, and we probably *will* never. They rehearsed the *Meistersinger* Prelude: I know because I remember the passage of the first violins [Galimir sang it]—high A, which just didn't come and wasn't in tune! And then there were the Brahms *Haydn Variations*; and THAT — WAS — PHENOM-ENAL! It always was probably Toscanini's best piece: there was that variation with the winds—the fifth variation—so fantastic: that we'll never hear again. Years later, in Palestine, when we had a dinner for him, and I told him that I had heard this rehearsal, he said very proudly: "You know, Rosé came to me and said, 'Maestro, Brahms would have been pleased by this.'" He really liked that: he must have felt that Rosé—well, Rosé was quite a personality. That rehearsal of the *Meistersinger* and the Brahms was the only one I heard; and I didn't hear the performances: they were too expensive! (1980: *See note on page 275.*)

My next experience with Toscanini was in Palestine. The orchestra was formed by Hubermann; and Toscanini was the first conductor; but before he came we rehearsed about two weeks with Steinberg. The orchestra was of course picked very carefully, and consisted of very good players—and some *excellent* players; but there were a few weak spots, because the players had to be Jewish, and in Europe there just were no Jewish brass. The horns were excellent; the trombones were good; but trumpets didn't exist; and double-bass-players—very few. Steinberg was very meticulous; and there was a rehearsal every day. Of course the closer it came to Toscanini's arrival, the more nervous we got; and everybody told stories of how terrible he was, how he threw shoes at musicians, and murdered them, and so on— you know those exaggerations. Then Hubermann came, a few days before Toscanini: he was just as nervous, and wanted to see if it was worth having Toscanini come or he should wire him not to come. He found that there were a few weak spots, but thought it would be possible.

Then Toscanini came. And of course everybody was prepared for big speeches, or for *some*thing; but he came on the stage and he didn't say anything—not even good morning— nothing! He said, "Brahms"—the Second Symphony of Brahms. We started to play the first movement, and he didn't interrupt once; and at the end of the first movement he said: "*Bene. Andiamo avanti.* Good. Let's go on." And everybody was terribly disappointed: was this the great conductor?—because they expected blow-ups. And in the second movement also, at the end —he corrected a little something, but again, "*Bene.*" Then in the third movement, in the beginning, there was one of our weaker moments with the woodwinds; and he didn't like it and got a little angry and said: "Why don't you sing?!" And now everybody looked around and said: "Ah! that's it." After this run-through he started really to rehearse; and at each rehearsal he went a little more into detail; and it was very beautiful—it was a real Toscanini rehearsal. And the concert was a fantastic success: people went completely overboard. They climbed on the roof to get in—it was a small hall—it was incredible.

It happened that at one rehearsal of the Brahms, in the third movement, the first trumpet overlooked the marking "third movement *tacet*", and began to play the fourth movement in the third movement. Toscanini gave him a look; but it was only a rehearsal, and it was a little mistake that could happen. But we repeated the same program many times: we played it two or three times in Tel-Aviv, two or three times in Jerusalem, and then in Haifa. And after so many times it starts to become a little routine for the player; he doesn't pay attention; and so in Haifa the trumpeter made the same mistake at the concert. You remember the fourth movement starts very *piano*, with the trumpet playing just one note: ta. And the trumpeter played that one note at the beginning of the *third* movement. Toscanini got furious: while he conducted he cursed, he threw dagger-glances at the poor trumpeter, who was dying with fear; he continued to curse all the time while we played the rest of the symphony; he got faster and faster; he didn't hold the *fermata*; he ended in a fury, *prestissimo* and *fortissimo*. The audience, which of course didn't know what was going on, never heard such fire and such sounds; and there was tremendous applause. But Toscanini rushed out, kicking over the music stands—*you* know that exit—and didn't come back on the stage again. The intermission lasted an hour and a half: he didn't want to continue. Hubermann came; everybody came; nothing helped. Finally he did continue; and then the opposite happened. He was completely disheartened and didn't want to conduct; and he conducted almost without any motions. The orchestra went from *pianissimo* to fantastically loud: he didn't move. And the public reaction was: what fantastic technique of this conductor who practically doesn't make any movement, and the orchestra plays like that! Apparently it made a very good impression on Toscanini also; and he conducted a second pair of concerts and was very happy there, actually. The trumpeter? He was through. A cellist who was also a trumpet-player had to play second trumpet, and the second trumpet, who was not too good, had to play first trumpet, for the rest of the concerts. So that was the first real taste of Toscanini.

We played in Egypt; and Toscanini came back to us the second year. After the second year I left, and came to America at the end of 1938. I met Toscanini here; but I don't know whether *he* mentioned me to Chotzinoff, or Steinberg, or who did. I played at NBC for Chotzinoff—and yes, of course, for Spitalny; I substituted once or twice; and in the fall of 1939 I was engaged as a regular member of the orchestra. And except for two years in the army, I stayed until the end.

Let me say this. I've played with many conductors—great conductors—Furtwängler, Walter, Klemperer—I really have played with most of the so-called great conductors of that time. (No, not with Strauss. I heard him of course. His *Don Giovanni* was—in Mozart he was really fantastic. And you know what also? *Tristan.*) With every conductor there were great moments; and maybe one conductor did this particular piece better than the others. But I would say the greatest experience, *playing* with a conductor, was with Toscanini. There was something that electrified you to a point where you had the feeling you played better than you can play. I know that at *any concert* with him —maybe even a concert that did not sound so well outside—the players themselves on the stage, most of them, gave everything; and you came out saying "Ah!" You were proud of the way you played when you played with him; because you could not do anything but give your best: you always were enticed to give your best. And it was not because of fear that you lose your job, or because he was a mean guy—that had nothing to do with it; there were meaner conductors. You had only to look at his face: he was so inspired, that he had to inspire *you.* There was the knowledge he had—the knowledge of the instrument: he knew exactly what can be played and how it can be played—which some really great conductors sometimes either didn't know or didn't care about, but which made it possible for any player to play any note—and every note—in any composition. In Strauss's compositions, for example—you remember the famous rehearsal of *Till Eulenspiegel*—he wanted every note to be played cleanly; and I'm sure Strauss, if he had heard the performance, would have said, "It's too clean." But to play that clean was a pleasure that you can't imagine. An orchestra player felt wonderful. This made it a great experience for any orchestra player to play with him: there was never any possibility—or necessity—to play badly with him.

Then there was something else about this man. He conducted the NBC Symphony how many years?—seventeen years; in those seventeen years he conducted the same composition many times; and every time he tried to do better what he thought was not so good the last time. There was never the slightest possibility of a routine performance—that he would say: "Oh, we've played this many times." I remember an incident in Palestine: when we played for the radio in Jerusalem, they were not experienced in the set-up for the broadcast, and asked him if he would try it for a half-hour; and he was very co-operative, and rehearsed for a half-hour. He played one passage of the Schubert *Unfinished* Symphony—the big climax in the first movement—about twenty times; and not once did he get less excited about the *fortissimo*. He never could think: "Well, let's take it easy now." And this he demanded also from the players—which was very good.

Then another thing. I had a teacher who said: "You should play so that a blind man can see the score." This means that you hear all the notes. And with Toscanini there was never a possibility that you had to fight the trumpets to come through— which very often happens. This, again, made it so pleasant to play: you did not have to force. That didn't mean the climaxes were not perfect: they were always perfect. This was because of another wonderful thing—the proportion. The sense for proportion of this man was really incredible. In Europe, when we played, let's say, the Beethoven Seventh, we used to play the second movement very slowly. Toscanini came and decided it said *Allegretto* and must be *allegretto*; so suddenly you played it very fast; and this was a great shock, after you had played it for

ten years very slowly. But after you were through with the movement the very first time, you had to say to yourself: "Yes, I think
it's right." The sense of proportion was always correct with him;
and this made the Rossini overtures so wonderful. I've never
heard in a Rossini overture the *crescendi* drawn to that point—
when it got loud, louder, always louder, and you thought it
couldn't anymore, but it *still* got louder, until the moment when
it was supposed to be the loudest! And the same in Wagner. In
everything—it was immaterial what—the way the proportions
were made was fantastic: this was one of his best qualities. Yes,
in the shaping. This was an incredible thing. It seems obvious:
you have *piano,* and then *fortissimo,* and you have to go from
one to the other; but *how* you go—and how that face got redder
and redder, and still redder; and you thought now he's going to
burst—but no, it went on! And that made you play.

Aside from the fact that it really was a beautiful thing to
watch him. He had a very expressive beat. I've seen conductors
with more *facility* in the beat; but the *expressiveness* of his beat
was incredible: you really could see everything he wanted in
that beat: the *staccato,* the *legato,* the *espressivo*—everything
was in it. You really had only to look at him, not at the music.
That's why he got so angry when he showed and they didn't do
what he showed. Actually he got angry only when—*either* he
felt one was not prepared, or was negligent; *or* when he felt one
was inattentive, so that he showed something and one didn't
respond. I understand that; and I think he was right: he always
was justified when he blew up—sometimes a little overblown,
but always justified. There was never any doubt what he wanted;
but you had to know your part very well. He always said: "*I am*
prepared; why aren't *you* prepared?" And he was right. In the
rehearsal one should work to make the musical phrases and
details, not to learn the notes.

Another part of his technique was that he always looked at
the players; and with all his nearsightedness I think he saw every-

thing that went on. And what a fantastic look: he could stone you to death with that look! It was a very fiery look! And it was very necessary to get that look sometimes: it inspired you. Of course sometimes it was very disagreeable when he looked at you angry: you got scared. But for inspiration that look was something fantastic. Of course every good conductor always looks at his players; but there was something in Toscanini's look that made it special: it lifted you up and made you do something extra. And contact, yes—incredible contact.

So let's see. A conductor, first of all, must be a big personality: he was. He must have a very good ear: he had a wonderful ear. He must have a tremendous authority: he had. And he must be very musical: he was. A conductor has to be a combination of all the qualities a musician should have; and he had *all* these qualities to a degree that made him great. Another conductor might be greater in one particular quality; but I don't know anybody who combined *all* these great qualities to such a high level as he did.

And the honesty! He was so honest—musically honest, and with himself honest. When he conducted badly, he said it—not at that rehearsal—he couldn't admit that he made a mistake that day—but at the next rehearsal: "I was not good"; and he said it *very often!* When we played the piece the next time he said: "*Anch' io sono stupido*. I didn't do it well. We do it better this time." Which is very nice: it gives you a feeling that you trust a man, when he doesn't only bawl you out, but bawls himself out too.

He always studied the work, and always found something new. And it's true, as you say: only what he did now was right, and what he did different before was a mistake, *stupido*. When the orchestra went to South America, on the boat they heard the short-wave programs that RCA broadcast; and once they heard a performance of the *Semiramide* Overture. Toscanini was cursing: "What stupid players! What bad conductor! Bad!

Bad!" Then the announcement came: "Arturo Toscanini and the New York Philharmonic." A marvelous performance, I know. But he said: *"Stupido! Bruto! Anch' io!"* And as you say, he felt the same way when he listened to someone else. It's natural: when you are so convinced—which every musician must be: before you go on the stage you have to be convinced that what you do is the only possible way of performance—if somebody else performs in any other way you have to disagree. It's very difficult to find something is played differently than you think, and still is good. And very rare.[1]

You ask about the characteristics of his performances. The two great qualities were—one, the shape, that fantastic sense of proportions in the work; the other, the clarity, which made any piece of music, even *Die Götterdämmerung,* sound like a string quartet: you heard every note that it was necessary to hear— which *I* enjoyed very much. And he had a natural sense of style. A man who actually, when he started to conduct symphonic music, was an opera conductor—how quickly he adjusted. This is a very difficult change which takes real understanding, superior talent—particularly to go from *Italian* opera style to a Beethoven symphony. Yes, actually it was the Schubert C-major that he did first. And he conducted it *very* well, *very* beautifully. The charm! Really, he had everything: he had this charm—personal, for instance: the charm of this man was incredible!

And when it came to Mendelssohn—the delicacy—yes, the elegance—fantastic! Looking back, there are so many great moments. It's a long time ago; but how many great moments there were, particularly in rehearsals with this man, that I cannot get out of my memory. In French music, for instance: there was a rehearsal of *La Valse* by Ravel—and what went on with his hands to get the flavor was incredible: I can't describe it. There was once *Ibéria*—the second movement, *The Perfumes of the Night*: I swear I smelled the perfumes; and I was not the only one. Not to speak of *La Mer*. And—*well,* the Italian operas!

Otello! After that I got tickets to hear *Otello* at the Metropolitan. It was a very good conductor, and it was supposed to be
one of the superb performances at the Metropolitan; but really
you could not listen to it—after the *Otello* that we did. In fact
any Italian opera sounded trivial after his performance. Those
opera performances you don't forget—you can't. The nicest part
was when *he* sang—not the singers with their beautiful voices,
but he with his hoarse voice. There was such expression in his
singing: you felt the whole drama was *in* it. Those were some of
the great performances: I think I will never hear anything like
that *Otello.*

Then German music. His Wagner was absolutely great:
you couldn't imagine better than that. Yes, that *Tristan* which
we recorded—wasn't it wonderful? And Brahms! The Third
Symphony of Brahms! He struggled with it for a long time: I
think he was never really happy with it. But when we played it
the last time, in Carnegie Hall, he was *so* happy. Everybody was
happy. I think he *found* it—he had the feeling "That's it." That
was a wonderful performance: I think it was the greatest Third
Brahms I ever heard or played; it's one of the things I won't
forget. And Beethoven! The *Eroica!* That moment in the Funeral March when he always screamed *"Terribile!"* Yes, the
climax of the *fugato.* That was the most *terribile* thing—I think
everybody among the dead people was scared by it. But there
were so many things that it's impossible to think of all: on every
program we had, there were some things.

As for the change in the later performances which you
speak of, I felt different.[2] I felt that there was a time when it
sounded a little tense, and there was this fear—"Don't make a
retard. Don't slow down"—and it tended to be a little fast.
There's a recording of the E-flat Mozart Symphony where it's
really much too fast and tense; and there were quite a few other
performances like that. There *was* a period of tension; but at
the end I thought it was very relaxed and beautiful. Of course it

was also that Toscanini felt much happier in Carnegie Hall because of the sound. That 8H sound was very clean; but it was not an ingratiating sound;[3] and when we went to Carnegie Hall the playing started really to sound. And I felt that the orchestra itself was a little tense in performances—not in rehearsals—in performances, in the earlier years, but there was a general feeling of relaxed music-making at the end in the performances: "Ah! *now* it's relaxed!"

The things you were told about in the last *Don Quixote* did happen. Toscanini was a little absent-minded; he forgot; he made a few mistakes—in tho performance. There was even one bad mishap, which is not on the record: they must have replaced it from the rehearsal. But look: at the age of eighty-five it was very possible that he forgot sometimes a little bit. When he was good he was just as good as ever; but there were bad moments—that was true. Even earlier he made mistakes: I remember the *Bohème* performance—which was in 1945—where he made a bad mistake. It was his fault: I don't know if he forgot, or what happened; nobody knew. Everybody can make a mistake; mistakes happen. His became more frequent only in the last year; and I would not be surprised if it was because he was told it was his last year. I can't possibly make a judgment; but I'm sure this must have been responsible. Anybody would feel *very* bad to be told that; and for a man like Toscanini to get what is it called?—the pink slip! How did we know? Through the grapevine: it was a rumor, and finally it was a fact. It was in the air: we felt it was going to happen.[4] And it was very sad. Because I'm convinced that he would have conducted still another few good years—very good years. And maybe he would have been in better physical shape than he was at the end if he didn't have to stop. When you took away the baton, you took away the thing that kept him young.

Frank Miller

T.H.–1988:

Frank Miller was the principal cellist of the NBC Symphony Orchestra from 1939 until the disbanding of the orchestra in 1954. Afterwards he was the principal cellist of the Chicago Symphony until he retired. He was a conductor as well, and a wonderful player of chamber music, with a commanding and expressive tone and an extraordinary sense of timing. (Haggin recalled hearing a superb performance Miller gave with the Budapest Quartet in the nineteen-forties of Schubert's String Quintet in C major. When they played it together a second time, and Miller's playing seemed more constrained than before, Haggin asked him what had happened; Miller replied: "Oh, they sort of sat on me.") Miller was also the player Haggin mentioned on page 236, who withdrew his contribution from this book before it was published after a bad experience with one conductor—one of the many conductors who considered admiration for Toscanini, when it came from former NBC players now in these conductors' orchestras, as an affront—led him to fear further incidents if he put his opinions on public record. After Miller died his widow gave permission to publish his recollections of Toscanini at last. They appear here exactly as Haggin first wrote them out, with the passages he softened later in an effort to relieve Miller's doubts given as he and Miller had first put them down.

MILLER:

I remember my first experience with Toscanini—my very first rehearsal—so clearly. It was in November 1930, when he came to conduct the Philadelphia Orchestra for two weeks while Stokowski conducted the New York Philharmonic. The work was Beethoven's Fifth; and when Toscanini conducted the first two bars—nobody could play them! The men were accustomed to playing them to Stokowski's beat of two in the bar: | OOM da DA da | DA |. And when Toscanini beat one in the bar: | OOM da da da | DA | nobody could play them! After a few attempts Toscanini went into a rage and broke his baton over his knee—and stuck out his hand. We wondered at this, until Bruno Zirato [Toscanini's long-time friend, who had been hired by the New York Philharmonic to look after him in North America] came out on the stage with another baton and put it into Toscanini's outstretched hand. This happened three times; and in one solid hour Toscanini couldn't get the orchestra to play those first two bars. Finally, after he had broken three batons, the men got the idea of one in the bar and were able to play; and after that things went all right. I might add that it was a great Beethoven Fifth.

That was my first season with the Philadelphia: I was only seventeen and still a cello student at the Curtis Institute. And it was nine years later—five with the Philadelphia and four with the Minneapolis Symphony as first cellist—that I had my next experience with Toscanini. This was when I came to the NBC Symphony as first cellist in the fall of 1939; and this time, sitting right up close to him—I was hypnotized! I saw this famous man with his beautiful face working in front of me so beautifully: it was a magnificent spectacle; and I forgot about playing and sat there staring at him. No doubt I did play; but I didn't know it.

At this time I could appreciate the purity, honesty and sincerity of Toscanini's conducting, and its greatness. There are good conductors, and there are good musicians; and it's when you get a great conductor who is a great musician at the same time that you get a Toscanini. For me he was the finest musician who conducted.

His musicianship began with his infinite knowledge of the musical score and his honesty in performing it. He would say: "Play what is written." How he knew the score! And how he interpreted it—so beautifully, so classically—with the simplicity that is the hardest thing to attain, but the most wonderful in the end. But though he revered the composer and stayed close to the letter of the score, he wasn't rigid about it. Some of Beethoven's metronome markings, for example, are simply too fast; and Toscanini changed them. Also, he knew that in balancing our big orchestras of today we have to modify the markings in the scores for the small orchestras of the past. And he would say: "No two beats are the same; no two bars are the same. I am not metronome; so follow me." (What he really said was "Fol-LOW me.") In other words he did put himself into the performance: he revered the composer and stayed as close to the score as he could, yet he knew it was he who had to make the performance.

You learned music by playing under Toscanini. You couldn't help learning if you kept your eyes and ears open and were receptive to what this great man had to give and what he gave. I *thought* I knew something about music before I came to him; but really I knew very little, and I learned a tremendous amount from him. And musicianship is of course the highest part of playing. The technique and facility in both hands are only the beginning: to play an instrument, to play a certain concerto, you have to have enough facility to play the instrument and the notes of the concerto. But if you have ten times the facility it won't help you to play the piece better. What will do that is fine musicianship—the ability to turn the musical phrase. And that was something you learned from Toscanini. His treatment of the phrase was plastic and free within the bar, but each bar was exactly as long as the next; and that was its greatness— the freedom within the bar that didn't destroy the continuity of the bars. Casals in his prime did the same bending of the phrase within the bar; and his phrasing still remains very beautiful. I don't know whether he ever played with Toscanini; but he has more of what Toscanini had than any cellist I can remember.

It wasn't only the men in the orchestra that Toscanini taught how to phrase. You remember those operas we did in concert form. He would sing for the soloists, and his croaking voice would come out in double stops sometimes; but the way he sang the phrase and the feeling he put into it, they with their beautiful voices couldn't duplicate. They never knew such greatness as Toscanini showed them. Those performances will never be duplicated: and I have never played in opera as great as that. It was all the more great because there was no scenery and no action—just pure music; and we were doing pure music with the greatest master of that music. Earlier Toscanini had played programs of popular Verdi arias and instrumental pieces; and musicians have said to me he did them so classically that they became great pieces. The same with the "pop" numbers he played: this musician could make the smallest—what we consider the most trivial—of them sound like classic pieces. It wasn't the technique: many orchestras could play them technically as well, maybe better. It was the musicianship, the phrasing: that was the outstanding thing.

I have been talking about Toscanini as a musician; now I want to talk about him as a conductor. First there was this ability to balance the orchestra. Nature gave him weak eyes, but the most accurate and sensitive musical ears we have ever known, which enabled him to hear in a big orchestral tutti the wrong note of the third bassoon or a string-player in the back of a section. With his infallible ear for intonation and balance he would have the winds repeat a chord until he had balanced it perfectly.

Then there was his actual conducting of the orchestra to achieve what he wanted. He used to say: "Look at me," meaning "Look at my baton" [here Miller's left hand pointed to the tip of the index finger of his right hand]. He said: "When I beat strongly, play loud; when I beat softly, play soft." Many conductors do their work not by conducting but by talking; at a rehearsal they stop after a bar and tell you what they want you to do. Toscanini was the essential conductor who did everything with his conducting: he spoke with his baton; and its movements told you all you needed to know—you didn't have to hear him talk. I should add that at concerts his movements were more restrained than at rehearsals and showed less what was happening. But that beautiful beat kept on going!

And behind the movements was a personal force which carried the whole orchestra along with him: as he moved, so the orchestra played. I can't say that of any other conductor. Many of them, at a concert, wave their stick, but don't really say or do anything with it; they count on you to do what they told you and what you wrote on your part at rehearsal. Toscanini was so different! And his players became so spoiled! The personal force spread itself across the stage to every player and held him in a rapport that never stopped. At rehearsal you couldn't let yourself sag or think about something else: this man had you tied to him as though with a string, and you were with him, on the edge of your chair, watching and ready, every second of the time. This shortened the rehearsal. Often, even though an orchestra knows the Beethoven or Brahms symphony, the conductor will rehearse note after note, rehearsal after rehearsal, until the two and a half hours are interminable, and you are ready to die. Not Toscanini; we seldom rehearsed much with him because it wasn't necessary—because with this control that kept us on edge every minute, this rapport that never stopped, his rehearsal was so concentrated that we often finished ahead of time.

I said a minute ago that the beautiful beat kept going; and I want to stress how important that was. With a great orchestra like the NBC Symphony, and with a conductor who set a tempo that was exactly right—that had the right feel and got the right response—and that was kept constantly going—the whole thing, the whole performance went off beautifully. Toscanini had this more than anybody I've ever played with. Some conductors wait and think to get the tempo before they begin a movement; but Toscanini didn't have to: he began immediately, and as he began you felt the tempo and responded right away. And so I've been shocked on some occasions when I've spoken about tempi in Toscanini performances to musicians in the Middle West who never heard him, and they have objected impatiently and haven't wanted to hear about it. I might add that there were times when we recorded Beethoven symphonies and were listening to the playbacks and were shocked to hear how fast the tempo seemed. While we had played, Toscanini had had us absolutely convinced that it was the right tempo. This was the force the man had.

You ask whether Toscanini was equally effective in all music. He played almost no Bach; and the reason was simply, as he told us time and again, that he never understood Bach. And if one can say he did anything poorly it would be something like Debussy's *Afternoon of a Faun*: he did this piece too straight, conducting it in three right from the start; and it didn't have the freedom we have come to expect in it. And yet the same composer's *La Mer*: just fabulous! As for the beginning of Ravel's *Daphnis and Chloë* that you mention—the exactness he tried to get from the woodwinds in this atmospheric passage—he himself gave it up. I remember the rehearsal at which he tried to conduct all the beats in the bar, and tried and tried; and it just didn't work. So he gave up and conducted three in the bar instead of subdividing them. But these few things are the only ones I recall. The English critic's criticism of his Mozart that you tell me about, I cannot agree with: I remember performances of Mozart that were just beautiful! I can remember how he conducted the G minor, especially the first movement: how he bent forward and conducted with his arms low swinging from side to side [here Miller, singing the opening phrase, demonstrated the impassioned manner in which Toscanini conducted it]. How his movements got you to do that! And yes, the Divertimento: what a performance that was! But I agree that parts of the E flat Symphony were too fast.

In those later years he didn't do new contemporary works. But who can even live to eighty, much less perform at eighty? And at that age we want from a man all the knowledge he has stored up in the past; it would be unreasonable to expect him to start again with new compositions.

As for whether his performances changed with the years, one thing that stands out in my mind is that toward the last he said to us his Brahms had been too fast, and we did Brahms in slower tempi—whereas his Beethoven was getting faster. Yes, many of his performances got faster and less expansive with the years; and it is true on the other hand that there were other exceptions besides the Brahms—one of them being the *Tristan* Prelude. I remember this one because the opening of the Prelude and a great deal after the opening is especially for the cellists, and we felt the broadening in tempo because it required us to do different bowing. Yes, I remember the holding back and broadening later in the piece too. And I remember another performance that changed. (How great this man was!) At the beginning of the Funeral March of the *Eroica*, the double basses always played the little grace notes *on* the beat; but in the last years Toscanini said: "I must be crazy: should be *before* the beat." This great man, after all these years, told us he was crazy to have done it that way, and now at the culmination of his career changed it!

That *Eroica*! I think we played it twenty times on the 1950 tour, and eighteen of those times it was just tremendous: people told me they had never heard an *Eroica* like that. On the tour Toscanini didn't rehearse, except for ten minutes perhaps to hear the sound of the hall; and outside of the three or four concerts a week it was a vacation. And so, playing concert after concert, week after week, the orchestra blended into a beautiful instrument—something difficult to do with one concert a week over the radio. The last concert of the tour in Philadelphia—you heard it?—what a concert! The *La Mer* was one of the greatest I ever played with Toscanini.

I also remember the wonderful day in Sun Valley on the tour. Toscanini was like a little boy: he went with us on the ski lift, and he was sparkling. The fact is that off the platform he was as kind a person as you would want to meet; and to people he liked especially he was marvelous. Not that one got to know him closely: I think he lived in a world of music and didn't have time to spare for anyone outside to get close to him. And of course when he stepped on the platform all hell could break loose. He heard everything, and nobody got away with anything: he spared no one. No matter how good you were—if one day you played badly he told you. He was so sensitive to the very finest that he wanted perfection all the time; and after all, given such a conductor, with a superb orchestra in front of him, why shouldn't he have as close to perfection as possible? I heard it said that his outbursts were a psychological means to achieve his end; but I don't know whether that was so. I do think that sometimes they were related to things in his life outside. And I felt badly about them—I must say it. I felt badly for the people who were getting the impact of the anger; and I felt badly that Toscanini should have to display it. But I also felt that one had to see beyond a great man's little faults, and had to accept Toscanini as an entity. How could this man burst into storm in his music if he didn't do so in his speech sometimes?

There were a few men in the orchestra who felt differently, and who took exception to those faults. Some of the hardboiled old-timers sneered at his outbursts; and you might hear one of them say: "Who does he think he is?" But even those who objected to the personal unpleasantness never said anything about the work. I've known men in other orchestras who didn't like to exert themselves; but not in the NBC Symphony. Everyone in the orchestra fully appreciated Toscanini and was proud to be able to say he played with him.

The fact that Toscanini had been a cellist meant that sometimes he would tell us what bow to use or make some other technical point. As for my experiences with him as a solo cellist, the first time I played in Strauss's *Don Quixote* it was only after the first rehearsal with the orchestra that Toscanini called me into his room and said that in the long extended solo [of Variation 5] I had played too freely for him, and that he wanted it played more within the meter. And there were a few details of phrasing that he wanted me to do a little differently. I had played the solo part for him at my audition; and maybe he remembered that. I don't know; but at any rate he didn't go over it with me before the first orchestral rehearsal.

I remember an amusing incident at the first rehearsal of the Brahms Double Concerto, which I played with Mischakoff a couple of times. Near the end of the last movement there is a place marked *poco meno*—a little slower. Toscanini's tempo for the entire movement was a little fast; and the *poco meno* wasn't at all slower—it was the same tempo [Miller demonstrated his struggle with the rapid passage-work in the fast tempo]. At this rehearsal it was so fast that I stopped. Toscanini stopped.

"What is the matter, *caro?*" he asked.

"Maestro," I said, "I think it's too fast for me."

"Ah," he answered, "you can play it in any tempo."

So—I played it in the fast tempo (I worked at it!).

I would like to say that the performance of the Brahms on the Victor record is from the broadcast, which took place in Studio 8H, with the orchestra and soloists all on one microphone; so the balance is poor. And one bad mistake in the last movement I didn't have a chance to correct.

That reminds me of the Brahms B flat Concerto with Horowitz—the cello solo in the third movement. It was my first year with the orchestra; and I've been trying to live it down ever since. There was no microphone for the solo cello; and they couldn't pick me up where I was sitting with the section. Eventually after several tries they set up a microphone for me; but Toscanini was not in the center of the stage—he was off behind the piano; and I had to turn away from the microphone in his direction. Even then I couldn't see him; so we couldn't get together. My playing was not good; and I didn't have a chance to re-do it.

But I'm grateful for those few experiences. If I had never played after Toscanini, they would have been enough to last me forever.

I also benefited as a conductor from my years with Toscanini. After Toscanini's retirement, I was engaged to conduct an orchestra in Florida. Unlike Sam Antek [another member of the NBC Symphony who had become a conductor] I never had an opportunity to talk with Toscanini about details in scores. But the Italian school of conducting, of which he was the greatest member—there was also Cantelli, a great talent; and there is Giulini, another fine talent—that school—its musical ideas, its movements—was and is, for me, the finest. And so, while I'm certainly far from being a great conductor, the style of my conducting came to be that of Toscanini.

And that brings me to my last experience with him. There was a doctor who made his batons for him; and when Toscanini, after his retirement, heard I was going to conduct in Florida, he had this man make eight batons, which he presented to me!

Milton Katims

T.H.—1988:

Milton Katims is the distinguished violist whose recordings of the Mozart String Quintets with the Budapest Quartet Haggin admired above all others. From 1943 to 1954, in addition to conducting and playing chamber music, Katims played at the front stand of the NBC Symphony Orchestra viola section. Haggin interviewed him in 1963— by which time Katims had become the conductor of the Seattle Symphony—for the purpose of including his recollections of Toscanini in this book. However, when Katims read the monologue Haggin had put together from his spoken words, he asked permission to rewrite it. Haggin refused to allow him to do more than substitute preferred expressions or words here and there. As both were adamant, the chapter was never published. (Katims is the musician "who doesn't speak in this book" whose stories about a horn-player and about Toscanini's occasional use of his temper as a shock tactic Haggin relates on page 238.)

After Haggin's death I asked Katims if he would write out for me the alterations he had wanted to make. This he kindly consented to do. In his revisions he elaborated and clarified some points he felt he had stated inadequately; he restored a few anecdotes Haggin had omitted;

214

and he and I, working from the transcript of the original interview, restored a few others that seemed more revealing now than they may have in 1963, when the memory of Toscanini was still vivid in many people's minds. Otherwise, Katims kept largely to the sequence of recollections and observations Haggin had established, and the revised version which follows differs from the original mainly in its style of expression, which is closer to Katims's manner of writing than to his manner of speaking. The statements themselves remain unchanged in all their essentials, and they concern several matters that are not touched on by anyone else in this book.

KATIMS:

As a school-boy I used to attend the New York Philharmonic concerts in the late nineteen-twenties and early 'thirties, when Toscanini was the conductor. My sister and I sat up in one of the high balconies—the "Family Circle"—in Carnegie Hall, and from up there, Maestro and the orchestra were about the size of the picture on a nine-inch T.V. screen. One night after a concert, I felt that I had to have a closer glimpse of this wonderful conductor—my idol. My sister and I went backstage and worked our way into the reception room. Toscanini was talking animatedly in Italian with a group of friends and admirers. Even if I had known how to speak his language, I would have been tongue-tied. All I was able to do was hold out my program and a pencil. He stopped talking, pushed things aside on a table, and autographed my program for me.

When I was a bit older and had been studying the violin for a few years, I used to sneak into Carnegie Hall during

Toscanini's rehearsals. I would lie on my stomach in the very front box just over the stage, where I could hear everything he said without being seen. My most vivid recollection is of a Beethoven Ninth rehearsal, and of his singing at the top of his lungs. In the fourth and fifth bars of letter A in the first movement, the first violins and violas have a downward rushing figure, and when these players did not give him the furious quality he wanted, he shouted "*Leóne! Leóne!*" (—Like a *lion!*). The way his voice roared through that empty hall, I could easily have heard him up in the Family Circle. Even in later years, when he was in his seventies and eighties, I was impressed by the tremendous voice that came out of this barrel-chested little man.

My mother and sister sang in the chorus of the Schola Cantorum, which was engaged by the New York Philharmonic for choral works like the Beethoven Ninth. For years I had been watching Toscanini's conducting from the back and the side. Now I was dying to see what his musicians saw from the front. I tried to substitute in the chorus for an absent tenor at a Sunday concert, but the secretary of the Schola spotted me and threw me out. However I didn't leave the backstage area but stood watching Maestro from the wings with a few other people during the performance. What a revelation! His face was electrifying. Every facet of the music, every fleeting emotion, was reflected in that photogenic face—in his eyes, in the expression around his mouth, in the way he darted a glance at a player or a section of the orchestra, not *when* they played, but just *before* they played, not merely to cue them (which he didn't need to do), but to let them know the *way* they were to make their entrance, the *way* they were to play. The musicians couldn't help but come in with the particular quality of playing the "Old Man" wanted for that particular moment. It seemed impossible for one man to be in so many places at one time.

As for my recollection of his performances at that time, sitting way up there in the balcony, I was very impressed by the visual element—his use of the baton, the expressive use of his left hand, the upper half of his body. I could literally see the music in his motions as if he were choreographing it with his movements. If the orchestra had suddenly been silenced, I think I would have been able to hear the music despite the loss of sound. (I once said that to him many years later, and for some reason I never really understood, he became furious.) As for the musical aspects of his performances, I think I appreciated most his molding of phrases, the orchestral balance and ensemble, the tremendous dynamic quality of the electrically charged performances. But more complete appreciation of what I responded to instinctively and with admiration did not come until many years afterward, when I was a professional musician striving for the same things myself.

I never met Toscanini before I began to play in the NBC Symphony in the fall of 1943. I had been solo violist and assistant conductor at WOR (Mutual Broadcasting System) for a number of years and at the same time played in a string quartet with Erica Morini, Josef Gingold and Frank Miller. Both Joe and Frank played in the NBC Symphony. One evening, after a quartet session, Joe told me that William Primrose had resigned from the orchestra. Joe suggested that although I was conducting at WOR, if I really wished to learn something about conducting, I should be playing in front of that fantastic Old Man. I wholeheartedly agreed, and the very next day I applied for the Primrose chair. The personnel manager said he would let me know when Maestro could audition me. (You can im-

217

agine how I felt.) The next day the manager phoned me to tell me that there would be no need for an audition. Toscanini had been tuning in on a Sunday series of viola-piano recitals I had been playing for over a year, and he wanted me to join the orchestra.

At the first rehearsal I sat next to Carlton Cooley at the first desk of the viola section waiting expectantly for Toscanini to appear. When he stepped on the podium at precisely 10 a.m., I was overwhelmed, not so much by the realization that I was to be playing with him at last, but by the overpowering amount of Italian cologne with which he had doused himself. He was most fastidious about his person, and he perspired profusely when he conducted. At the end of a rehearsal there was literally a large wet spot on the stage in front of him. (During the eleven years I played for him, I never ceased to be fascinated by the way the beads of water would form high on his forehead, roll down his face, hang for a few seconds at the end of his nose, and then drop to the floor. Sometimes they'd get into his eyes and sting; then he'd rub them, and they'd be red with irritation. His son Walter solved that by covering Maestro's eyebrows with mustache wax, with a bridge across the top of his nose. After that the beads of perspiration would bypass his eyes and come down his cheeks.) Immediately after a rehearsal or a concert he would slip into a terry cloth robe, and if he hadn't had time to do so, he would be very embarrassed about anyone coming too close to him, because he was conscious of being soaking wet.

Although I soon became accustomed to the strong cologne, that first whiff had me reeling for the next half hour. When I recovered, and before I could think of being nervous playing with the legendary Toscanini, I was so excited and absorbed in making music with him that I felt as if I had been playing with him all of my life. (That happened only one other time, when I first played with the Budapest String Quartet. I had been nervous about that, too, but when I sat down to play, before I knew it, I felt as if I'd been playing with them for years.) Toscanini's way of making music was so compelling and so right that I had no difficulty fitting in quickly. He had the uncanny ability of drawing a performance from a player. I remember a horn player telling me about his being quite nervous during a twenty-bar rest. Like many players he counted in reverse, the same as a count-down for a space lift-off. The hornist's count-down was at three bars, two bars, and then one bar before his entrance he'd look up and find Maestro looking at him, and before he knew it he was playing—as if some unseen hand had drawn the music from his instrument.

That brings me to your question of how Toscanini achieved what he wanted from the orchestra. A doctor friend of mine, also a close friend of the Old Man, said to me once, "Toscanini is a biological sport—a freak of nature." And I would say that he was one of those rare men with tremendous personal magnetism of a sort that occurs only once in centuries. Alexander the Great and Napoleon probably possessed it; great religious leaders like Jesus and Moses must have had it. I put Toscanini in the same category. When he stepped on the podium you couldn't help feeling the power of that magnetism—those piercing eyes, his whole bearing as he began to conduct—persuading you to do exactly as he wanted. It was this gift which enabled him to inspire, to draw from his players and from his soloists (singers or instrumentalists) performances over their heads. Every musician has a qualitative level at which he operates when he is doing his best. Maestro was able to lift musicians above that level.

As for his behavior on the podium, he used every trick in the book—and some tricks not in the book—to get what he wanted from the orchestra. He exhorted, he demanded, he browbeat, he was bitingly sarcastic, he cajoled, he pleaded, he begged. On that famous occasion when he wanted a passage played as *pianissimo* as if it were coming from Brooklyn, he was on his knees before the orchestra. He used visual illustrations, as when he took out a large white silk scarf and threw it into the air. As it floated gently to the stage, he said *"Comme ça"* to show the ethereal quality he sought in Debussy. And he also illustrated by singing in his cracked voice, but giving the phrase in question the most beautiful expressiveness I've ever heard. This made playing opera with him an unforgettable experience. During a rehearsal of *La Traviata* Jan Peerce sang an aria and Maestro was unhappy with the way the orchestra had played. He said to Peerce, "You rest, save your voice. I sing". And we went through the aria with him singing every word. Despite the croaky voice the musicality was unmistakable. (I remember one time we were recording something, and after one of the takes he asked Richard Mohr, the RCA producer, "Well, how was?" Dick, very haltingly, said, "Maestro, you were singing." Toscanini clapped him on the back—I thought the poor man would fall to his knees—and said, "With Toscanini tenor, you sell more records!")

He had a fantastic baton technique, and when he couldn't get what he wanted and had to resort to talking or singing, he would become furious with himself. He would hit the stick, call himself stupid and on more than a few occasions would break the baton. It wasn't merely a stick technique in the usual sense: it was really a translation of his mental aural image into a visual physical motion. Of course, there was always a definite downbeat at the beginning of each bar. You knew where the beginning of each beat was and where it ended, but it was what went on from the beginning of that beat to the beginning of the next that was the important thing. The number of things he could indicate simultaneously was simply fantastic. I was playing the viola part, which only occasionally carries the leading voice. Most of the time it plays a subsidiary line; nevertheless, somewhere—in his elbow, his shoulder, the movement of his head—I could discern the viola's rhythm. It was uncanny!

When we did *Aida*, I was in charge of the off-stage chorus and band. It was the third of his performances to be televised. I asked the producer for a T.V. monitor back where I was. "When I'm to conduct," I said, "you turn the camera on Toscanini, even though he doesn't conduct in that part. I'm positive he'll be moving with the subtle rubato he wants from my chorus." So the producer did, and I followed Toscanini precisely. Afterwards he was amazed. I never told him how I'd done it.

This translation of his mental musical image into visual physical movement was completely instinctive. I'm sure he was not consciously aware of what he was doing. Only once when we discussed a score that I was going to conduct did he pick up a baton to demonstrate a point. He went through two or three beats (without an orchestra, of course) but stopped abruptly when he became self-conscious. He said, "Isn't this a stupid thing for a grown man to be doing?" (It reminds me of the time I had to be late to one of his rehearsals because I was conducting another program. When he was told what I was doing, he said, "Conducting? Why should such a fine violist want to conduct? Anyone can wave a stick!")

Maestro was instinctively a very good psychologist, without ever having taken a course or read books on the subject. He certainly knew the psychology of rehearsing an orchestra. He was very aware that orchestra musicians resented having their time wasted, and he knew how to get the maximum results in the shortest period. There are conductors who use up a great amount of time talking instead of having the musicians play. I was sitting with Maestro once during a guest conductor's rehearsal with the NBC Symphony. (I was in the unique position at NBC of playing in the orchestra only when Toscanini conducted. The reason for this was that, when I began conducting at NBC, the union didn't want me playing in the orchestra anymore. I explained that I had joined the orchestra expressly to learn conducting by sitting in front of that wonderful man. So they made an exception: I could play, but only under him.) This guest conductor kept stopping constantly to make observations. He would play two or three bars and stop to talk, three or four more bars and stop to talk. Finally Toscanini couldn't stand it any longer. He slapped me on the knee, stood up and said, "I go! He talka too much!")

Obviously Toscanini never learned scores at rehearsals. He came knowing every note and exactly how he wished it to sound—with the music alive in his mind. He started a rehearsal with an almost fierce determination to achieve immediately that perfect performance he had in his head. Instant perfection! At times I almost thought that he looked upon the orchestra as an adversary—a cage full of lions who had to be overcome or tamed. If he sensed in the orchestra anything less than an immediate springing to life with an intense concentration equal to his, he would remain with the same three or four bars until he sensed that he had reached the limit of the orchestra's endurance; at that point he would go on. He never repeated a section or a phrase merely to play it again. There had to be a reason: either a correction or an improvement. If he explained what he wanted, the explanation was rarely, if ever, an intellectual analysis: he was too instinctive a musician for analysis, and his concern was for the life of the music. His way was to sing what he wanted or to illustrate it in a similar fashion. Of course, with the NBC Symphony he was dealing with excellent players who responded and could achieve his goals. I doubt if the Old Man would have had the patience to be a teacher and conductor with a lesser group of players.

Toscanini was amazing in his ability to anticipate what might go wrong. I don't think the well-known story about Maestro and the French horn players is apocryphal. Supposedly, while on tour with the New York Philharmonic, he was studying a score on the train, singing parts, conducting and giving entrance cues. At one point he cued in the imaginary horns, and after two or three beats he shouted—NO! NO! He knew the capability of almost every player in his orchestra extremely well, so he could anticipate whether one of them would have difficulty with a particular passage. He could anticipate whether the dynamic level of an instrument was going to be what he wanted, or whether it might need to be bolstered in some way. With an orchestra like the NBC Symphony it was more likely to be the limitations of the instrument rather than of the player. In certain passages and instrumental combinations, the bass clarinet, and also the bassoon, not possessing very strong voices, would probably need help, perhaps some doubling. The Old Man's ear for exquisitely balancing a chord was quite incredible. The orchestra would play a chord and he would stop us and pick out precisely what needed adjustment in dynamic level—the second bassoon a bit more, the third horn a bit less, etc. We would then play the chord again. The difference was like night and day.

Many people believe that Toscanini played just what was on the printed page—literally stuck to the letter of the score. Nothing could be farther from the truth. In his constant search for the composer's true intentions, he made changes in phrasing, in dynamics; he even added instruments. The listener was never aware of these changes unless he was following the performance with a score. Even then he would have difficulty spotting them, because they were very subtle and made with great musical intelligence and taste. Let me give you one or two examples. There are four bars in the last movement of the Brahms First Symphony where the composer includes trumpets, trombones and timpani the first time this passage occurs (bars 176-179); but the second time (bars 360-363), when the music is in a different key, Brahms omitted these instruments because of the difficulty of changing the tuning of the timpani quickly (there were no pedal timpani at that time). But no such obstacles exist today, and Maestro did not hesitate to add these instruments. Another instance of his genius for recreation, for improving on the composer's original orchestration with taste and intelligence, is to be found at the beginning of Tchaikovsky's *Manfred*. He bolstered the sound of the clarinets and bassoons by adding muted horns in unison with them, achieving a darker sound with more substance. I believe the composers would have approved heartily. The ones who were alive in Toscanini's time certainly did—Debussy, for example, gave his permission to change some things in *La Mer*.

Changes like these enabled Toscanini to achieve what the composer hadn't fully realized. It also enabled him to take a piece that wasn't very good, really, and make it seem important. It enabled him to make us feel—and this, for me, was the greatest facet of his conducting—that no matter how many times we had performed the music at hand (be it the Schubert *Unfinished*, the Dvořák *New World*, or the Beethoven Fifth) that *this* was really the first performance, *this* was the first time we were really playing it—the first time we were really *hearing* it. There was always the freshness, the spontaneity of a first performance. That was how he approached every score he conducted. He was constantly restudying it, no matter how many times he had performed it. When we recorded the Beethoven Ninth, after the final take of the last movement we were waiting for the recording engineer's technical okay to wrap it up. Maestro stepped over to where I sat, put his hand on my shoulder, and said, "You know, young conductor, I have played this symphony for fifty years—fifty years—and finally I think I understand something!"

Unquestionably, this was why his performances were vividly alive, not merely another reading. This was why each piece of music he touched appeared to be revealing its joys and wonders for the first time, as if it was being created at the moment of performance. This was the greatest part of the genius of Toscanini!

His expectation that the orchestra should produce the perfection he had in his mind almost at once resulted at times in the now legendary explosions of temper. However, he also had the patience of Job. If he felt that musical intelligence was in use, that a real effort was being made, and that if a mistake was made, the player was aware of it, he would ignore it. (I'll never forget the time, in the Beethoven Fifth in Carnegie Hall, when I made a wrong entrance all by myself. Toscanini whirled around and quickly gave me a glance, saw how furious I was, and never said a word about it to me.) He had absolutely no patience with stupidity, and he couldn't abide laziness. He was always giving unstintingly of himself, and if he felt that *we* weren't giving *him* as much as he was giving, he became furious. "Don't zleep!" he would shout. "Look to me! Give of yourself! I give everything!"

But I must add that sometimes I felt that an explosion was really manufactured—that it was really one of his methods (a sort of shock tactic) to get what he wanted. (I'm sure that if standing on his head would have led to a more perfect performance, he would have done just that.) He had a habit, when we were nearing the end of a long movement and he wanted to go over it again, of exploding over something—anything, in order to be able to say, "*Da capo! Da capo tutto!* From the beginning!" I remember his picking up on something wrong near the end of the long first movement of the Schubert C major and exploding. He really was angry at something—it wasn't an act—but at the same time you sensed that he'd been looking for something like this in order to have a reason for going back to the start. Finally he said, "*Da capo!* Beginning!" He was facing the violas as he said it, and behind him one of the first violinists, exasperated, expelled his breath with a flutter of his lips. The Old Man whirled around: "Who make like a horse!"

Even an explosion for cause could turn into one for effect. Near the beginning of Tchaikovsky's *Manfred* there is a crescendo in which one group comes in after another, ending with the brass followed by the cymbals a beat later (at letter C). Once when we were rehearsing this symphony, the cymbal player came in with the brass instead of after them. This happened not once, but twice. That's all Toscanini needed. "After the *trombe!*

After the *trombe*!" he yelled. "Not with the *trombe*! Is the first time you play this music?" And he went on and on. "You think I enjoy to conduct? No! I hate to conduct—I suffer too much!" After many minutes of this tirade he stopped, and looked at each of us sitting near him to see what effect this was having. We sat with poker faces. And then his eye encountered the face of one player who seemed to have a half-sneer around his mouth, an expression he'd been born with. He couldn't help it. Maestro stopped and looked at the hapless player in complete silence for almost a full minute, while the unfortunate fellow's face grew redder and redder. Finally, the Old Man said: "You look at me? You are astonished? You believe I am crazy? No! I am sensitive and intelligent—do not look at me that way."

With all of his efforts to recreate the music in his mind and his heart and to mold an orchestra's will to his, his conducting was not completely the kind that required every note to be played precisely in his way. No, a player was permitted plasticity of expression as long as he fit within the framework of Maestro's concept. This was also true of singers in performance of opera. However, here he was constantly returning to the score and insisting that the composer's intentions should be followed more closely rather than continuing certain traditions which, across the years, had been established in the opera house. His definition of tradition was "the last bad performance".

There was a perceptible difference between his conducting at rehearsals and at performances. Most conductors take it comparatively easy at rehearsals and come to life at the performance, doing many things which they didn't do before. It was almost the reverse with Toscanini. He conducted every rehearsal as if it was a performance. And then when it came to the actual concert for the audience, he relaxed a bit and seemed to be saying to us, "I've shown you exactly what I want—now go on and do it." We now were more responsible for the drive and energy that he had expended at all of the rehearsals.

Other characteristics of Toscanini performances? Enormous clarity—clarity of line, of contour of phrases, and clarity of texture which revealed not only the inner voices but revealed every note to be seen in the score. If the clarity wasn't there, he would say, "Is dirty—we wash!" No matter how complex the score, everything that was there to be heard had to be heard; and if necessary, he would change or add to achieve the clarity he sought. How many times did we hear the word "*cantare*"— the singing quality of every instrument was of utmost importance to him. Another word we heard just about as frequently was "*vita*"—all his music-making had constantly to have life. When he began to conduct a work, he seemed to have a total concept of the music—in the case of a symphony from the beginning of the first movement to the end of the final movement. The propulsive element in his conducting was naturally conducive to the unfolding of the music to its inevitable conclusion. For him each composition was very much like the topography of a landscape with its valleys, foot-hills, small mountains and a high peak or two—the high point of a piece of music toward which he shaped his performance. There was an increasing intensity toward a certain point, then a relaxation away from it—like breathing in and out. I think he did this instinctively, and as a result the music seemed literally to breathe. He gave it the logic of speech. And lest I forget, there was his instinctive sense of theater. Timing was of the essence. I always marvelled at the natural way he would delay a beat ever so slightly in order to heighten the dramatic effect.

A number of people have been critical of Toscanini's fast tempos in his later years. I played with him in those later years, and I never felt that the tempos were too fast—it was always possible to play every note. His having been a cellist himself, I'm sure, had a good deal to do with his selection of tempos that were never beyond a musician's capabilities. There is also the belief that he played everything strictly in time, as if with a metronome. Wrong! He played with a rubato so subtle, as natural as breathing, that it was the naturalness you were most aware of, not the freedom. Once when I was discussing a score with the Old Man, he said of a particular passage, "This must be *assolutamente preciso*—like with a metronome. Here, I show you." He reached over and selected the appropriate tempo on his electric metronome and began to play the passage in question. But after only a few beats of the metronome he was no longer with it. He shut it off and said, "But you can't be a machine!" And another time, when I suggested that one of the guest-conductor's playing of the "Perfumes of the Night" movement of Debussy's *Ibéria* was dull because he played precisely what was on the printed page—nothing more, nothing less—Maestro insisted that that was what he did! I brought the score over to the piano and asked him to play that section. As he played I pointed out the slight *stringendo* he made here, the *poco ritardando* he made there, his rubato in another spot, etc.—none of which was in the score. Again he protested that it wasn't possible to be a machine.

When I began to guest-conduct the NBC Symphony I had the rare privilege of conferring with him about the scores on my programs in his home in Riverdale. On one of my visits, I posed the following question: "After you have carefully examined all of the tangible evidence the composer has left you on the printed page, how then do you determine the true tempo, the true character of the music?" He replied, "My dear, you must rely on your musical instinct and your good taste. If you have, you find. If not, don't make music—*mend shoes!*" He attended my rehearsals in Studio 8H, too. I can assure you, I had no need for a rear-view mirror to let me know when he walked into the studio. Every player in the orchestra would straighten up just a bit more. The first time I guest-conducted his orchestra, Maestro questioned me after one of the rehearsals about something I had done in Mendelssohn's *Scotch* Symphony. I told him that I had been uncertain about that section, and so I had listened to an air check of his performance of two years earlier. He interrupted me and exclaimed, "And I did that?" I nodded. "If I did that," he went on, "I was stupid—*stupido!*"

After all that I have said about Toscanini the great artist I revered, I must say something about the warm human being, the man away from the podium. Backstage, before my first NBC Symphony guest appearance, he hovered over me like a mother hen, arranging my pocket handkerchief and adjusting my tie. When I asked, "Maestro, where are you going to sit during the broadcast?" he said, "I have no ticket." (I felt like saying, "Are you kidding?") But then, Al Walker, a member of the NBC Public Relations staff, came back and escorted him to the balcony and sat with him. At the end of the performance, when the Old Man was applauding and noticed that Walker wasn't, he poked him and said, "Applaud! Applaud!" Afterwards he came back to my dressing room and embraced me. All I could think of were all the little mishaps, but he said, "Oh, my dear, something always happens." One of the greatest moments of my life was when Maestro embraced me after that broadcast.

Anyone who visited him at Riverdale will agree that he was a warm and wonderful host. He usually greeted you at the door, he was attentive to your every wish while you were his guest, and when you were ready to leave, he would always escort you to your car. In all the years my wife and I knew him, we always talked about music except just once, when we visited him one summer on his island in Lago Maggiore. It was at the time Dwight Eisenhower was running for the presidency, and Toscanini expressed a negative reaction to the idea of a military man becoming our president.

To sum up—Arturo Toscanini was the most incredibly gifted musician I have ever known, a conductor concerned with every note in a score, and concerned with bringing all music he touched to life. I feel enormously grateful to have had a close musical association with him.

There was a poignant coda to that association: Our final visit to him was shortly after he had finally retired. We were about to leave New York for the Northwest where I was to become the conductor of the Seattle Symphony. As we arrived, Virginia, as always, greeted him with, "Good morning Maestro, how are you?" He stepped back and replied, "Do not call me Maestro, I am no longer a Maestro."

Postscript and Notes
by B. H. Haggin

Postscript

On an NBC broadcast a year or two ago one heard Toscanini describing the historic incident in Rio de Janeiro in which —a nineteen-year-old cellist in the orchestra—he took over the conducting of a performance of *Aida* after the conductor had been booed from the podium by the audience. Then one heard the description of the incident which the impresario of the company had given to his son; and finally the description of it by a man who had been in the theater that evening. And the three descriptions differed irreconcilably on a number of details—even on what Toscanini wore.

There is nothing surprising in this; nor is it surprising that a few instances of such differing recollections of a happening occur in the foregoing monologues. In some of these instances the differences can be accounted for; but in any case they are concerned with what is unimportant. Thus, one can accept Burghauser's recollection that he arranged by telephone from Budapest that Kipnis replace the bass from Berlin in the *Missa Solemnis*, but can think he may be mistaken in recalling that Kipnis was waiting at the airport when Toscanini returned to Vienna, and can believe Kipnis's recollection that he was asked, during a rehearsal at the State Opera, to substitute for the

Berlin bass at that day's first rehearsal of the *Missa*, that he went to the *Musikvereinsaal* where he found Toscanini ready to begin the rehearsal, and that after this rehearsal he was told of Toscanini's request that he sing in the performance. But the important thing is not what preceded Kipnis's participation in the rehearsals and the performance; it is what he experienced at the rehearsals and the performance when he got to them.

The musicians who speak in this book are of course only a few of those who could speak; but they seemed to me a sufficient number to achieve the book's purpose. Since some may wonder at the absence of certain leading players of the NBC Symphony, I will say that I asked a few of them, but one didn't answer my letter, one accepted so reluctantly and unpromisingly that I proceeded no further with him, and one did record what he had to say about Toscanini, but, when I sent him the monologue I made of it, decided not to allow it to be published, for reasons that are worth telling. He wrote that his reverence and love for Toscanini had already got him into difficulties with one conductor, and he feared that the published monologue would get him into difficulties with all conductors—not because of the way he would play for them, but because of what they knew he had said about Toscanini, and what this might lead them to suspect he thought of them. As it happened, another musician wrote at this time to request the elimination of a conductor's name here and the change of a dangerous word there in his monologue, explaining that "the conductors who were adumbrated by Toscanini's brilliance have never forgiven him his greatness; and this creates a continuing professional problem for those who worked with the Old Man." He illustrated this by describing his experience with a conductor for whom he auditioned, who said to him: "You will of course have to forget you played under Toscanini." The player felt obligated to answer: "I certainly will respect and co-operate; but I can hardly forget that I played under Toscanini"; and he didn't get the position.

And further illustration was provided by the Szell-Lang conversation described on pages 255-7.

In addition to Schoenbach of the Philadelphia Orchestra, I
saw Mason Jones, the orchestra's first horn when Toscanini conducted it in 1941-42. In 1949 he came to my home with my
friend Gordon Kahn, ostensibly to hear my copy of the test
pressing of the unreleased recording of the *Midsummer Night's
Dream* music, with his marvelous playing of the horn solo in
the Nocturne, but really, it turned out, to ask me to try to get
Toscanini to autograph a photograph of him rehearsing the
orchestra in 1941. I inferred from this that playing with Toscanini had meant something to Jones; and agreed to try. The
next time I visited Toscanini I took the photograph with me;
and I watched the formidable operation that the autographing
of it proved to be: the search for the bottle of white ink, then
for the pen, and then the making of each stroke of the inscription with an intensity that was awesome and moving. Though
Jones consented to see me now, he said he didn't have much to
tell me; and it turned out that playing with Toscanini had meant
very little to him. He said he had been very young (only twenty-
one, if I remember correctly), with knowledge of how to play
the horn, but no knowledge of music; that being in his second
year as first horn, he had thought only about making good in
that position—which had meant delivering whatever Toscanini
asked from his instrument with no thought of anything but that
task; and that he had been too busy with this to be impressed
by Toscanini, who, he added, had been no hero for *him*: on that
stage he had been a Stokowski and Ormandy man. My first reaction was to find it extraordinary that even a young player, and
even one so intent on the task of playing his instrument, and
even one who was a Stokowski and Ormandy man, should have
been completely unaffected by the powerful personality and
musicianship that impressed everyone else. And my further reaction was that if Jones had spoken with the same candor in

1949 I would have spared Toscanini the labor of autographing a photograph for someone who wanted it only as an impressive decoration on his wall.

One member of the NBC Symphony who doesn't speak in the book thought that once in a while a Toscanini explosion was just another of his many different ways of getting the orchestra to produce what he wanted—a way of shocking the orchestra into producing it. And he told me something a horn-player had told him once: that when this player had a number of bars' rest which he was counting in reverse—increasingly nervous as he counted "five, four, three"—at one bar before his entrance he would look up and find Toscanini's eye on him; and then he would simply find himself playing, as though Toscanini's hand had reached out and drawn him in.

And I add one item which the players who recalled Toscanini's repeated *"Cantare!* Sing!" failed to mention—the variant on one occasion: *"Cantare! Non solfeggiare!"* ("Sing! Don't do *solfeggio* exercises!")

Notes

[1] (*from page 36*):

It is interesting to read the late Samuel Chotzinoff's account of this incident in his book, *Toscanini: An Intimate Portrait* (Knopf, 1956). Toscanini's demands, he writes on page 108, sometimes interfered with the operations of the commercial programs that earned the cost of the NBC Symphony broadcasts. When it was not working with Toscanini the orchestra was assigned to those commercial programs, of which it could play only a few in any case, since seventy-five or eighty percent of its working time each week was required by Toscanini's rehearsals and broadcast. On one occasion Chotzinoff scheduled the usual two-and-a-half-hour rehearsal for a performance of Verdi's *Requiem* in Carnegie Hall at 4, to make sure that if Toscanini ran over the two and a half hours there would be ample time for thirty of the men to get to NBC at 8 for the commercial program they had to play. But after three and a half hours, Toscanini—who "knew nothing about the '*commerziale*' and would have cared less . . . had he known"—gave no sign of ending the rehearsal; so Chotzinoff had to instruct the personnel manager to signal to the men to sneak out. And

239

though Toscanini made a scene when he discovered what was happening, the next day he recognized the men's need of the extra income from the commercial program, and all was well again.

Every detail in Chotzinoff's account is untrue—including the one that Toscanini knew nothing about the commercial program. It wasn't in his mind while he was rehearsing the *Missa Solemnis;* but he did know about it and did care about it. As Shulman says, it had taken him some time to discover that the men of his orchestra had to play in other programs, and he had disliked it when he discovered it. Chotzinoff not only had foreseen that he would dislike it, but had feared that he might even refuse to come, if he knew, and had therefore been careful to conceal it from him—as he is careful to conceal it from the readers of his book until his mention of it in connection with the rehearsal incident on page 108. On page 79 he writes that he told Toscanini in Milan that NBC "would build him a great orchestra"—which conveyed to Toscanini what it conveyed twenty-five years later to Eugene Lyons, who in his recent biography of David Sarnoff writes that Chotzinoff told Toscanini NBC "would create a great orchestra especially for him."* Chotzinoff's further statements on pages 84-86—that on his return to New York he "started to put together an orchestra"; that a symphony orchestra is not built in a day, and "we had only ten months in which to assemble one"; that by November 1937 "we had assembled a superb body of men"—these statements imply that, starting from zero, he engaged for NBC all the members of an additional new orchestra for Toscanini. And he makes the implied claim explicit on page 86: when Toscanini cabled his withdrawal from the project because he had heard it was costing some NBC men their jobs, Chotzinoff cabled in reply that far

---

*And the letter of resignation that was prepared for Toscanini to sign in 1954 contained a statement about the invitation seventeen years earlier "to become the Musical Director of an orchestra to be created especially for me."

from costing even one man his job, Toscanini's engagement
had caused NBC "to take on . . . a full symphony orchestra . . ."

In all this there isn't the slightest hint of the true facts that
were given in an article on the NBC Symphony broadcasts in
Fortune of January 1938: that NBC's contract with the musicians' union for 1938 had required it to increase its staff orchestra
from seventy-four to 115 men; that the ninety-two men con-
stituting the NBC Symphony were part of that staff orchestra
of 115; that those ninety-two comprised thirty-one men retained
from the 1937 staff orchestra, and sixty-one men whom Chotzinoff had engaged as higher-caliber replacements of members
of the 1937 staff orchestra (who *had*, then, lost their jobs) and
as additions for the 1938 staff orchestra; and that of the thirty
hours which the ninety-two were obligated to work during the
week, only fifteen were allotted to Toscanini's rehearsals and
broadcast, and the remaining fifteen went to other NBC programs, sustaining and commercial.

This fact—that the orchestra built "for him" was actually
playing half its working time with other conductors—Chotzinoff,
as I said earlier, had concealed from Toscanini because he had
known Toscanini would dislike it, and why he would dislike it:
the other conductors were unable to hold the players to his
technical and musical standards of performance, so that his
work in disciplining and teaching the orchestra was constantly
being undone; and many of the men came to his rehearsal on
Friday after several hours' work with Walter Damrosch for that
morning's music appreciation program and with Frank Black for
that evening's Cities Service program. The result of Chotzinoff's
concealment was that week after week Toscanini was baffled and
frustrated and exasperated by the strange fact that the orchestra
which delighted him with its youthful energy on other days
played "like tired old men" on Friday. Only after some time
did he discover why; and it was his growing anger about it that
boiled over in response to the crowning outrage at the *Missa*

rehearsal. And far from all being well again the next day, it impelled him to absent himself from NBC the next year.

What may have contributed to this action, Hugo Burghauser thinks, was another incident at this time. Though a Catholic who could have remained in Vienna after Hitler's takeover, Burghauser chose—"as a matter of conviction and taste"—to leave, going first to Toronto and then, with the advent of war, to New York. "I thought I had left intrigue behind me in the city of Metternich," he says, "but found it going on around Toscanini at NBC among the bureaucrats who tried to control not only administrative but artistic matters." Toscanini even earlier had invited him to play in the NBC Symphony; and he now recommended him for a position in the orchestra that happened to be vacant. As an experienced player Burghauser assumed he would be considered competent for the position; and he assumed further that with Toscanini's recommendation he would be engaged. But to his astonishment Leopold Spitalny, the union representative who was personnel manager at NBC, growled: "We don't want you here." A violinist who knew Sarnoff mentioned the incident to him; and Sarnoff asked Chotzinoff to look into it—which Chotzinoff did by summoning Burghauser to his office, telling him with cold anger: "I'm seeing you because my boss told me to," and informing him that Toscanini could of course suggest a player but had only the power to say no, while the power to say yes lay entirely with Spitalny and Chotzinoff, and that they had exercised this power to say no to Burghauser. In public Toscanini gave no sign of the outrage and fury that he expressed in private over this humiliating treatment of him, which Burghauser thinks may have contributed to his decision to absent himself from NBC the next year.

[2] (*from page 37*):

Again it is interesting to read Chotzinoff's account of this incident in his book. As Shulman says, when Toscanini's memory failed him and he stopped conducting, putting his hand to his eyes in an attempt to remember, the orchestra's first cellist, Frank Miller, kept the performance going, Toscanini began to beat time again, the piece was completed, and the audience applauded. But Chotzinoff invents a more dramatic conclusion: when Toscanini stopped conducting "the men stopped playing and the house was engulfed in terrible silence."

[3] (*from page* 37):

Photo-copies of the Toscanini letter of resignation that Shulman refers to, and the Sarnoff reply, were sent out by NBC and, I believe, reproduced in some newspapers. And the alleged circumstances leading to the exchange were described a couple of years later by Chotzinoff in his book as follows: Only a few days before the first rehearsal of *Un Ballo in Maschera*, in January 1954, Toscanini informed Chotzinoff that he no longer remembered the words of this opera and therefore requested him to cancel the project; then a day or two later he informed Chotzinoff that he remembered the words and would prepare and conduct the performance. This in fact he did. But, says Chotzinoff, it was now clear to the Toscanini family that the time had come for him to stop; Toscanini himself agreed, frowning on any suggestion that he return for another season; at his request a letter of resignation was prepared; and though weeks passed without his signing it, during the week of the final broadcast "he summoned the resolution to put his name to it and send it off."

Though Shulman's doubts about the letter and what it embodied were shared privately by others, the first and only public contradiction of them was the statement on page 213 of Filippo Sacchi's book, *The Magic Baton* (Putnam, 1957): "Only two months after [*Un Ballo in Maschera*] he was informed that the N. B. C. had decided to disband the orchestra, and that they could therefore dispense with his services." The importance of this statement was that Sacchi was a personal friend of Toscanini, who could be presumed to have received the information from him. Moreover, this public statement repeated what had been told privately to a friend of mine by Cantelli, who had seen Toscanini constantly during much of the season of 1953-54, when he was here conducting the NBC Symphony and New York Philharmonic—except that Cantelli had said it was in the late fall of 1953 that Walter Toscanini had told his father of NBC's decision to discontinue the broadcasts and disband the orchestra at the end of that season, and of Chotzinoff's suggestion that his father might, for appearances' sake, wish to resign.

Cantelli's mention of the late fall of 1953 recalled to me that it was at this very time that Walter Toscanini had written me no one would henceforth be admitted to his father's rehearsals, and it was soon after this that I had begun to hear about Toscanini's occasional confusion at rehearsals, which had provided a possible reason for the exclusion of outsiders. And I had myself heard instances of this confusion at two of the rehearsals for the final broadcast, which I had listened to as they came over a telephone line from Carnegie Hall. At that time it had looked as though Toscanini had begun to exhibit occasional failing of his powers; and that this had made NBC unwilling to risk another season.

But in the spring of 1966 another person in close touch with the situation—a friend of both Toscanini and Sarnoff—told me what Sarnoff had told him at the time: that Sarnoff and Chotzinoff had gone up to Riverdale to offer Toscanini a contract for the following season, but had been intercepted by Walter Toscanini, who had requested them not to offer his father the contract and had told them he wouldn't let his father sign it. At first I was at a loss whether to believe Sarnoff or Cantelli; but a friend pointed out that I could believe both:

Sarnoff could have been dissuaded by Walter Toscanini from offering his father the contract; and Toscanini then could have been told what Cantelli said he was told—that NBC would discontinue the broadcasts at the end of that season.

This certainly could be what happened. But if Sarnoff was ready to offer Toscanini a contract for the following season, Toscanini cannot have exhibited any failing of his powers; and one must assume that Walter Toscanini's reason for requesting Sarnoff not to offer his father the contract was the family's belief that conducting another NBC Symphony season would make too great demands on Toscanini's diminishing physical strength. What this failed to take into account was Toscanini's mind. Felix Galimir is not the only one who maintains that it was not the lapses of memory and the confusions that necessitated discontinuing the broadcasts, but the shock of the discontinuing of the broadcasts that caused the lapses of memory, the confusions and the mistakes of the last year—among them the mistakes that one musician remembered in the broadcast performance of *Don Quixote*.

FOR WILLIAM CARBONI'S STATEMENT

¹ (*from page 54*):

Carboni is referring to Toscanini's absenting himself from NBC during the season of 1941-42 because of the rehearsal of the *Missa Solemnis* at which thirty-five men of the orchestra had to sneak out to play a commercial program. It must be pointed out that he returned to NBC after that year's absence. And it must also be pointed out that he acted as he did in 1941 because he had discovered what Chotzinoff had concealed from him; but that he didn't discover it every time.

In July 1947 the time of the NBC Symphony broadcasts was changed, for the season of 1947-48, from Sunday at 5 to

245

Saturday at 6:30. (NBC had been unable to get a commercial sponsor for the NBC Symphony, and Ford wanted to buy Sunday at 5 for another program.) I pointed out in my *Music on the Radio* column in the Sunday *Herald Tribune*—which Toscanini read—that the new time was one when people were busy with their children and their dinners and therefore unable to listen; and a few weeks later I published objections to the new time from readers all the way to the west coast. The change was made in October for the last few broadcasts of the NBC Summer Symphony; and a couple of weeks before the start of Toscanini's series in November I visited him.

After we had been talking for some time he said suddenly: "Is very interesting: they say only 7,000,000 listen to NBC Symphony on Sunday, but 11,000,000 listen on Saturday."

Since nobody could be listening to his broadcasts that hadn't even begun, I asked: "How do they know that?"

"NBC make investigation," he said.

Again, NBC couldn't have "investigated" how many people were listening to the broadcasts that hadn't begun; so I asked: "Who told you that?"

"Chotzinoff."

In its July announcement of the change of time NBC had stated that "a number of additional stations are expected to carry the broadcasts" (which, I had written, they would do because not enough people listened at 6:30 on Saturday to make the time commercially valuable); and NBC probably had derived from the number of stations a total potential audience of 11,000,000. If Chotzinoff had been pinned down, he undoubtedly would have said this advance estimate was the "investigation" he had referred to; but he had apparently given Toscanini the impression that NBC had conducted a real survey of a kind which had definitely established that 11,000,000 people actually were listening. And so Toscanini had accepted the change of time which cost him part of his audience, and which he would have objected to, and might have refused to accept, if he had known the actual nature of the "investigation" Chotzinoff referred to.

[1] (*from page 63*):

In Bayreuth in 1928, Nikolai Sokoloff, who had played under Muck in the Boston Symphony, visited him one morning and took me along. Muck was greatly changed from the dark-haired, vigorous, proudly erect man I had seen walk out on the stage in 1917: he was gray, shrunken, wrinkled, with a ghost of a smile flickering over his face as he talked pleasantly. I discovered that he conducted the Hamburg Philharmonic in the winter; and I went to Hamburg in November to hear his performance of Brahms's Third. He allowed me to attend the rehearsal, where he spoke as quietly as he conducted. And after the rehearsal he talked with me in his room pleasantly—not at all the terrifying person one had heard about in his Boston Symphony days.

When I mentioned Toscanini he said: "Toscanini is a fine musician, very serious and earnest; I honor him. I knew him in Italy, and we made several voyages together. He never went to concerts; but he came to every concert in Boston." Evidently this friendly attitude could not survive his displacement as reigning monarch in Bayreuth by Toscanini in 1930.

Twenty years later Toscanini revealed that he had gone to the concerts in Boston only to hear the superb orchestra. Muck, said Toscanini, "was terrible! . . . Everything so slow! Muck was Beckmesser of conductors!"

[2] (*from page 66*):

In the performance of Toscanini's 1937 Salzburg *Magic*

247

Flute that is preserved on records it is the Queen of the Night's second aria that Toscanini performs in an unusually fast tempo, in which nevertheless the singer sings it perfectly. The *Allegro moderato* section of her first aria he performs in the usual moderately fast tempo; and it is not his tempo, therefore, that causes her to go to pieces in the florid passages.

[3] (*from page 67*):

Kipnis was answering the statement in our conversation in which I pointed out that *The Magic Flute* itself was not an opera which people talked about as they did about *Don Giovanni* or *Die Meistersinger* or *Tristan*; but I ventured the guess that if *The Magic Flute* had been one of the operas Toscanini performed here with the NBC Symphony, the performance would be one that people would be talking about as they did about the *Otello*, the *Fidelio* and the *Traviata*. Actually, I added, I *had* talked about Toscanini's enchanting *Magic Flute* ever since 1937; and so had the English critic Spike Hughes in his *Toscanini Legacy*. This had been on the basis of our memories of it; but recently I had been able to hear a recording of the performance, and had again found it enchanting. And my recollection, finally, was that at the dress rehearsal and the performances I heard in 1937 the audience every time had been tremendously enthusiastic.

FOR JAN PEERCE'S STATEMENT

[1] (*from page 119*):

Again Chotzinoff tells it differently—and again with the caricaturing malice of his entire book. On page 138 he has Toscanini—about to fly to his dying wife in Italy, overcome with grief, answering no, his life is finished, to Chotzinoff's reminder of the *Ballo in Maschera* planned for next season—

still weeping as he says to Chotzinoff: "*Addio, caro,* I pray you to engage for *Un Ballo* Bjoerling . . ." And on page 142 he includes "a last-minute substitution of Jan Peerce for the indisposed Bjoerling" among the difficulties he ironed out before the first rehearsal of *Un Ballo* the following season. According to Chotzinoff, then, Bjoerling was Toscanini's first choice, and his replacement by Peerce was a routine matter handled by Chotzinoff.

FOR SOL SCHOENBACH'S STATEMENT

[1] (*from page 121*):

Alfred Wallenstein agreed with Schoenbach, saying that Toscanini would try to find English words, and then would resort to Italian words, which most of the men didn't understand; but that the men of the New York Philharmonic and NBC Symphony—as against the men of the Philadelphia— knew enough about the kinds of things he talked about to be able to understand what he was trying to say.

[2] (*from page 124*):

Toscanini once said: "Beethoven is very exact—but even Beethoven sometimes write different"; and he cited the *pizzicato* note that Beethoven wrote now as an eighth-note, now as a quarter, now as a half.

[3] (*from page 124*):

Each pair of concerts in which Toscanini conducted the Philadelphia Orchestra in 1941-42 was followed by recording sessions, in which they recorded Schubert's C-major, Mendelssohn's *Midsummer Night's Dream* music, Berlioz's *Queen Mab.* Tchaikovsky's *Pathétique*, Strauss's *Death and Transfiguration*, Debussy's *La Mer* and *Ibéria*, and Respighi's *Feste Romane.*

None of these was issued by RCA Victor until 1963, when at last the recording of Schubert's C-major was released. Several months before the release it was broadcast by WFMT in Chicago and WRVR in New York, with an introduction by the music critic of the Chicago *Sun-Times* professing to give authoritative inside information on the history of the Philadelphia recordings, the reason why they hadn't been issued, and the reason why the Schubert C-major was now being released. He had, he said, heard the test pressings Toscanini received; and they "were really pretty horrible: the noise level was as high as the levels of the music in the pianissimo passages"; but the new tape processed from the original masters conveyed "all the familiar warm, round sound of the Philadelphia Orchestra." In other words, the beautiful sound that couldn't be heard because of the noise from the original test records—this sound was made audible by the new tape. Actually the *Sun-Times* critic was merely embroidering the Victor account in the brochure accompanying the Schubert recording when it was released: that the recording hadn't been issued in 1942 because wartime processing had resulted in "mechanical imperfections [i.e. noises] which neither the Maestro nor the company could accept"; and what made its release possible now was the engineer John Corbett's "[restoration of] the recording to its original state" through "750 hours of work and through the miracles of new electronic transfer techniques"—the result being, according to Roland Gelatt of *High Fidelity*, the revealing of "glories in the groove that were never suspected in 1942."

After the WRVR broadcast of the recording I told the musical director of WRVR that the *Sun-Times* critic's introduction had been incorrect in what it said and had left a great deal unsaid; and he asked me to prepare a correction. I did; but a few days after I recorded it he informed me that he had shown it to Walter Toscanini, who had requested him not to broadcast it, and that he had acceded to this request. I published some of the facts in my review of the recording; and I give all of them—or rather, all known to me—here.

In September 1942 I listened with Toscanini to test pressings of the 12-inch 78-rpm sides of Strauss's *Death and Transfiguration*, Debussy's *La Mer* and Berlioz's *Queen Mab*. All of these begin very softly; and even in those soft passages there was no unusual, obtrusive noise from the records that prevented us from hearing the musical sound, or that even disturbed us. (My recollection of this is confirmed by the account of the occasion in a letter I wrote to a Victor engineer named Sinnott on September 26, 1942: there is mention of the magnificent sound from the records, but no mention of noise.) What caused Toscanini to reject the sides he did was not their noise but the imperfect balance in the sound—either as performed or as recorded—that caused him not to hear this or that instrument he expected to hear. Thus, at the end of the first movement of *La Mer*, his face registered his delight as he exclaimed: "Is like reading the score!"; and he approved those two sides. But a moment later, listening to the second movement, he cried out in anger and stopped the record when he didn't hear one of the woodwinds; and this side he rejected.

At this time it was expected that Toscanini would remake the rejected sides with the Philadelphia Orchestra; and there was the same expectation about the sides which Victor itself rejected because of mechanical defects. But at this very time the president of the musicians' union, James Petrillo, ordered its members not to do any recording until the record companies agreed to his demands; and this prevented the remaking of the sides. It was not until two years later that recording was resumed; and by that time the Philadelphia Orchestra had transferred from Victor to Columbia. The orchestra would have been available for the correction and completion of its Victor recordings with Toscanini; but Walter Toscanini told me at that time that Victor wanted the Philadelphia Orchestra recordings abandoned and new ones made by Toscanini with the NBC Symphony, and that "we are trying to get Father to forget the Philadelphia recordings." He didn't say why Victor wanted this; and one could only conjecture that it didn't want Toscanini's name to promote a Columbia orchestra, and rather than have this happen preferred to sacrifice recordings which documented the collaboration of this great conductor and great orchestra in some of the greatest performances Toscanini ever put on records; and that for Victor's purposes one Toscanini performance was as good as another, a performance of *La Mer* with the NBC Symphony as good as one with the Philadelphia Orchestra. The argument that the Philadelphia was now a Columbia orchestra wouldn't have counted for much with Toscanini; and Victor could hardly argue that the performances were poor; but it could, and did successfully, argue that the Philadelphia Orchestra recordings were mechanically defective beyond hope of remedy.

Quite possibly, Victor, in persuading Toscanini, also persuaded itself that the recordings were atrocious—in particular that the musical sound couldn't be heard because of the noise—and that therefore they couldn't be issued. But it wasn't true: the surface noise was stronger than the usual surface noise from 78-rpm records; but it didn't prevent one from hearing the musical sound: one's ear separated it from the musical sound, which was clearly audible and marvelously beautiful. In the statement I recorded for WRVR I demonstrated this with passages from vinylite and shellac test pressings of several sides of the Schubert C-major—including one especially noisy side, on which nevertheless the quiet opening of the second movement could be heard. What Corbett's skillful and patient work had achieved was not to make audible a sound that had not been audible before, but to reduce the accompanying noise as much as it could be reduced without loss in the sound.

What I have said about the Schubert recording is true

of the others: the noise doesn't prevent one from hearing the beautiful sound and marvelous playing of the Philadelphia Orchestra in Toscanini's great performances.

[4] *(from page 127)*:

I had been told of other incidents at Cantelli's rehearsals with the Philadelphia Orchestra, but not of this one. I asked David Walter if Cantelli had misbehaved in this way with the NBC Symphony; and his answer was "Never."

[5] *(from page 129)*:

After the Saturday morning "love feast", at which Toscanini had rehearsed Beethoven's *Pastoral*, Gordon Kahn of the viola section remarked: "I'm a little surprised at the things he's letting pass," referring to flaws in execution which his orchestra player's ear had noticed. I mention this because of the explosion the next morning: I had the impression that Toscanini was raging not just about what had gone wrong in the Septet, but also about all the things he had let pass in the symphony.

[6] *(from page 130)*:

Actually, Richard Aldrich of *The Times*, in his review of the Metropolitan Beethoven Ninth, credited Toscanini with the qualities of a great symphonic conductor and described with evident approval the unbroken melodic line, the plastic shaping of phrase that did not lose sight of the proportions of the whole, the rhythmic vitality of a performance which rose to heights of eloquence. And in the 1927 Philharmonic performance not only was the orchestra finer but the soloists were Elisabeth Rethberg, Louise Homer, Richard Crooks and Fraser Gange.

¹ *(from page 133)*:

As against Gingold's statement that at this first rehearsal Toscanini took the NBC Symphony straight through the Brahms First, leaving the work on detail for subsequent rehearsals—his usual practice in this situation, as appears in Felix Galimir's account of his first rehearsal with the orchestra in Palestine—Chotzinoff, on pages 92-3 of his book, writes that after playing through the first movement of the Brahms, Toscanini said, "*Da capo!*" and began to rehearse it "in earnest"; and Chotzinoff then gives a picturesque description of the hour and a half of work on detail that happened—like the performance of the *Tannhäuser* Bacchanale coming to a halt in a hall "engulfed in terrible silence" at the last broadcast in 1954—in Chotzinoff's imagination.

² *(from page 133)*:

In conversation after the interview Gingold said: "Bruno Walter came to conduct us and began with an all-Mozart program. He did one of the big divertimenti, the D-minor Piano Concerto, in which he played—and the G-minor Symphony. Toscanini had come for the rehearsal. We saw the Old Man there, and remembered his wishes; and we played for *him*: with *molto arco*. Walter stopped us and said: 'Gentlemen, gentlemen, please, please, I beg you. Not so much bow, not so much bow. [Gingold imitated Walter singing the opening phrase delicately.] Little bow, very short. Once again, please.' Again we played with *molto arco*; and Walter stopped us and said: 'Gentlemen, gentlemen, please, please, I am unhappy. Do me the favor: short notes, please; little bow.' The third time; and again we played for Toscanini—which, I must say, was not right. Finally, the fourth time, some of us had the courage—the conductor asked for it, and we had to do it—we played as Bruno Walter asked us to. At that, Toscanini yelled something, banged his fist against the wall, and rushed out of the rehearsal. Walter knew exactly what was going on behind him. He was very calm, and said: 'Let's start once again'; and we played it exactly as he asked. The rumor was that they never spoke to each other after that. But I don't think the Old Man acted very nicely."

[3] (*from page 133*):

I had hoped Copland would tell me about Toscanini's rehearsal of *El Salón México*; but he said that for some reason he wasn't there. As for the performance, which he did hear, he would say it was o.k. That is, it seemed a straightforward performance of a piece in which Toscanini didn't feel at home. The continual change of meter made him nervous and unhappy; and he deprecated the performance when Copland spoke to him in the greenroom. Copland thought it was because he was unhappy about the performance that he didn't play the piece again; but I told him that most of the American pieces Toscanini played in the forties he did only once.

[4] (*from page 135*):

The surprise and doubt Gingold saw on my face when he spoke of Szell's tremendous admiration for Toscanini was caused by my recollection of the highly qualified admiration Szell had expressed on two occasions. One was a radio interview, on the anniversary of Toscanini's death, in which Szell began with the astonishing statement that the first Toscanini performance he heard, in 1927, was, unfortunately, one of "the Verdi operas he conducted least interestingly—to wit, *Aida*." More generally, Toscanini's performances "were always most impressive, and in most cases very instructive, partly in the positive, partly in the negative way . . . There was very often a tendency to rigidity and to a relentless drive even when the music wanted to breathe a little more freely" (this from Szell!). But he credited Toscanini with having "put a definite end to the arbitrariness of a whole generation of conductors before him." Thus his performances were "an education in discipline"; yet because of the rigidity the Toscanini influence could be "murderous for the one who went along blindly, and without any discrimination and any sense of criticism"; and Szell "could think of very remarkable performing musicians who were permanently or temporarily damaged or inhibited by too strong a Toscanini influence." Asked what distinguished Toscanini from other great conductors, Szell replied: "His relentless sense of continuity . . . Everything was pulsation and life from the first to the last note." This was interesting to recall a few months later at one point in a conversation between Szell and Paul Henry Lang in *High Fidelity*. Lang complimented Szell for his not excessive attention to detail, as against "the recording by a very distinguished conductor of advanced years who brought out every little detail with the utmost clarity—to the point where eventually it seemed mere meaningless precision"; and Szell replied in agreement: "Because probably the big general line was lost" (which, if true, would have made this performance unique among Toscanini performances). But the high point was Szell's reply when Lang asked who he thought were the great conductors of the past. After speaking glowingly of Nikisch and Strauss, Szell added that a man like Toscanini could not be left unmentioned—but not, it turned out, because of his performances. "Whatever you may think about his interpretation of a specific work," said Szell, with the implication that the specific interpretations offered much for men of superior taste like Szell and Lang to shake their heads over in pained disapproval, "that he changed the whole concept of conducting and that he rectified many, many arbitrary procedures of a generation of conductors before him is now already authentic history."

⁵ (*from page* 139):

Moldavan, who went to Bayreuth for Toscanini's performances of *Tristan* and *Tannhäuser*, told me that the German musicians there had resented the intrusion of an Italian in this shrine of German art where hitherto only Germans had performed—until Toscanini's first rehearsal of the orchestra, when he reduced them to stunned silence by detecting in their playing mistake after mistake in the orchestral parts that had for years gone undetected by the German conductors.

FOR HUGO BURGHAUSER'S STATEMENT

¹ (*from page* 155):

Burghauser later told me some of the details of these "objections and difficulties". After Toscanini conducted his orchestral concerts in Salzburg in 1934, the administration there—which was part of the administration of the State Opera in Vienna—asked him to conduct opera in Salzburg the following summer; and the agreement was reached that he would conduct *Fidelio* and *Falstaff*. But in Vienna the previous year, the enormous excitement over Toscanini's appearances—and even such a detail as the special 'Caruso' scale of prices for them—had been regarded rather sourly by certain eminences of the Viennese musical world, who had felt their own public image to be adversely affected, and had begun to plan a behind-the-scenes counter-campaign. Early in the fall of 1934 the Musical Director of the State Opera, Clemens Krauss, announced a new production of *Falstaff*, to be conducted by him. It was entirely legitimate for him to do so; and for Toscanini the announcement had no significance or importance; but those connected with the State Opera and the Salzburg Festival, who knew that it was customary for productions in Vienna to be transferred in their entirety to Salzburg, saw at once that Krauss's intention to conduct the new *Falstaff* in Vienna was in effect an intention to conduct it also in Salzburg the following summer, and created a conflict with the agreement that the opera was to be conducted by Toscanini. He was asked if perhaps he would be willing to conduct another opera with *Fidelio* in place of *Falstaff*, and answered: "No *Falstaff*, no Toscanini." After which the authorities, in Viennese fashion, did nothing further, hoping that, with almost a year until the festival, something would turn up that would remove the difficulty. (The chief authority, the general Administrative Director of the State Opera, could not act against Krauss, because it had been Krauss who, astutely, had had him appointed to his position the year before.)

Meanwhile Toscanini was in Vienna for his concerts with the Vienna Philharmonic and the performance of Verdi's *Requiem* for the murdered Chancellor Dollfuss. And a series of incidents almost wrecked the *Requiem* project and delayed the performance several weeks. In the *Musikvereinsaal*, where the Vienna Philharmonic gave its concerts, Burghauser, as its chairman, arranged everything connected with Toscanini's rehearsals, watched over him, anticipated or smoothed out difficulties;* but in the State Opera, where the *Requiem* was to be performed, he was merely a member of the orchestra, and as

---

* On one occasion when something had gone wrong, Burghauser rushed upstairs to the librarian of the Society of Friends of Music and said: "Quick, give me the manuscript of Mozart's G-minor!" With the manuscript he rushed back to Toscanini's dressing room, and said: "Most unfortunate, I agree. But I thought you would like to see this, which I have to return in a few minutes." At the sight of Mozart's writing on the manuscript, Toscanini, forgetting his anger, became transfigured; as he began to read, and discovered what, strangely, he hadn't known—that Mozart had scored the work originally without clarinets, and had later rewritten the woodwind parts to include them—he exclaimed: "*Che meraviglia!*"; and when he came to the end he kissed the manuscript reverently before handing it back to Burghauser.

such had to obey Krauss's orders that in the opera house he was to remain with the orchestra and have no contact with Toscanini. On the day of the first orchestral rehearsal, therefore, Burghauser sat with the waiting orchestra, while Toscanini walked alone from the Hotel Bristol across the street to the stage entrance of the State Opera, where the man at the door asked him what he wanted and—being told *"Ho una prova"*—answered: "No stranger may enter here!" So Toscanini returned to the hotel, while the orchestra waited in the Opera. After a time a search party was sent out, and found Toscanini in a fury in his hotel suite, where he now refused to return to the Opera for the rehearsal. So it was agreed that he would from now on rehearse in the *Musikvereinsaal*, where he felt at home and would, it was thought, be in no danger of further hostile acts instigated by powerful persons.

But his first piano rehearsal with the solo soprano at the *Musikvereinsaal* was wrecked by another such act. The co-repetiteur from the State Opera who should have been there to play the piano did not arrive (because, it turned out later, he had not been notified of the rehearsal). So Toscanini himself had to sit down at the piano, put his pince-nez on his nose, and begin to play for the soprano. He had said: "Give me a good Aida"; and she was the company's Aida, with an excellent voice, said Burghauser, but without commensurate intelligence. Soon after they began, Toscanini stopped and asked her to sing a phrase in one breath, instead of breaking it to take breath; and she answered that she was accustomed to doing it her way, and showed him her score in which Bruno Walter had marked it to be sung that way. Toscanini, still quiet, told her she would have to sing it as he asked. There were a few more such exchanges, increasing the danger of a storm; and then an abrupt movement of Toscanini's head caused his pince-nez to fall off his nose to the floor. Before Burghauser could get there, Toscanini was on the floor groping nearsightedly for the pince-nez, which he found; and sitting down again he put it back on his nose, only to discover that he could see nothing because the lenses had fallen out. In exasperation and fury he jumped up and stamped his feet; and at the terrible sound of the lenses being crushed, the soprano burst into tears and fled from the room. It took more than a month to find another suitable soprano who was willing to follow Toscanini's directions; and it was not until November 1 that the performance of the *Requiem* took place (in gratitude for which, the Austrian government gave Toscanini a first edition of the early version of *Fidelio*, with Beethoven's inscription to his landlord: *"Seinem werten Freunde, Baron von Pasqualati, vom Verfasser, Ludwig van Beethoven"*).

Back now to *Falstaff*. When the time came that something had to be done about the conflict created by Krauss's intention to conduct in Salzburg the *Falstaff* that it had been agreed Toscanini would conduct, and the administration of the State Opera still did nothing, there was only one recourse left: to inform the new Chancellor, Schuschnigg, of the situation and ask him to take action. He was, in the first place, a genuine music-lover who could recognize the artistic importance of Toscanini's participation in the Salzburg Festival; but in addition he recognized its financial importance, and the disastrous financial consequences if Toscanini withdrew. And so he decided that the agreement between the Salzburg administration and Toscanini would be fulfilled and Toscanini would conduct *Falstaff* at the festival (which caused Krauss to withdraw from the festival, and the next year to resign his position in Vienna and go to Berlin).

But the "difficulties" didn't end at that point. At the first orchestral rehearsal of *Falstaff* in Salzburg, Burghauser found a young, inexperienced substitute in the chair of the first oboe, who was "ill"; and his inadequate playing caused Toscanini to walk out after a few minutes. Luckily the missing first oboe was located and was in his chair at the next rehearsal. But disaster threatened as late as the first stage rehearsal. In Vienna the preceding fall, the last choral rehearsal for the *Requiem* had taken place at the State Opera; and on the way to the rehearsal room Toscanini had had to pass through the auditorium. The stage rehearsal of the first scene of the third act of *Falstaff* was in progress; and inevitably Toscanini stopped to listen and to look through his pince-nez at the stage. What he expected to see was Falstaff sitting outside the inn, shivering after his immersion in the river, warming himself in the last rays of the sun, and sipping hot wine; but what he saw instead was Falstaff in his room, in bed under a mass of bedclothes. Outraged, Toscanini turned to Burghauser and exclaimed: "Criminals! They should be put in prison for daring to change what Boito and Verdi did so well. If they want something different let them write their own *Falstaff* and leave the *Falstaff* of Boito and Verdi in peace. If this scenery appears in Salzburg I walk out of the theater!" Burghauser reassured him, and subsequently impressed on the administration the necessity of having the correct outdoor set for Toscanini the following summer. But in Salzburg, when the curtain rose for the first scene of the third act, there again, to everyone's consternation, was the bedroom set; and Toscanini, infuriated, rushed out of the theater. Miraculously, a correct set was produced overnight; and after that *Falstaff* proceeded without further "difficulties" to its marvelous realization in Toscanini's performance.*

[2] (*from page 160*):

When I told Burghauser about having heard Strauss con-

---

* In his book, Chotzinoff has Toscanini objecting to the set of the interior of Ford's house. "Do you call *that* . . . an Elizabethan house!". . . When, on the following day, the curtain went up on the new interior of Ford's house, the Maestro said triumphantly: *"Ecco!"*

duct not only *The Magic Flute* but *Così Fan Tutte*, in which he improvised delightfully witty accompaniments on the piano for the recitatives, he said: "In 1949, the year of his death, I had some hours' conversation with him in Montreux; and I said to him: 'I have one request.' He asked what it was; and I begged him to write out those enchanting accompaniments for the recitatives in *Così Fan Tutte*. But he pointed to the *Vier letzte Gesänge* and the Duettino for clarinet and bassoon, which he had to finish. So the accompaniments for *Così* were lost."

[3] (*from page 164*):

Burghauser described what happened at Novotna's first piano rehearsal with Toscanini for *The Magic Flute* in Salzburg. The pianist failed to appear; and before Toscanini could go to the piano himself, Bruno Walter, who was present, offered his services. The opening chords of *"Ach, ich fühl's"* enabled him to set his exceedingly slow tempo, in which Novotna had to continue when she began to sing. Toscanini paced back and forth impatiently, and after a few moments interrupted, exclaiming: *"Ma, caro Walter,* is *Andante,* and you play *adagio!"* Walter, embarrassed by the presence of Novotna and Burghauser, said: "My dear Maestro, you know I am always in agreement with you; but in this case I differ with you and think my tempo is correct." To which Toscanini answered heatedly: "And I, my dear Walter, am never in agreement with you!"

Years later Toscanini talked about the tempo of Pamina's aria. Clasping his hands as he acted her agitation, he exclaimed: "Pamina say, 'I lose my Tamino! Where my Tamino?!' Must be *andante,* but is always *adagio!*" And on another occasion he said: "When I conduct *Flauto Magico* in Salzburg I am afraid about my tempi; but Rosé [the old concertmaster of the Vienna Philharmonic] say once, 'At last!' I tell Bruno Walter, 'You will not like my tempi in *Flauto Magico*.' He say, 'Is very interesting'; but afterward he make again slow tempi."

[1] (*from page 184*):

Wallenstein is referring to certain great concert or broadcast performances which, as he says, were not recorded by RCA Victor on those occasions. They include the Mozart G-minor and Schubert C-major at Toscanini's last Sunday afternoon Philharmonic concert in 1936, which Wallenstein spoke of earlier; and to these can be added the 1936 Beethoven Ninth with the Philharmonic, the 1938 Strauss *Don Quixote* with the NBC Symphony (and Feuermann), which was superior to the 1953 broadcast issued by Victor, the 1940 Verdi *Requiem* and Beethoven *Missa Solemnis* with the NBC Symphony, both far greater than the later ones issued by Victor, the 1942 Berlioz *Romeo and Juliet* with the Philharmonic, the incandescent Haydn *Clock* Symphony and hair-raising Funeral Music from Wagner's *Die Götterdämmerung* at the 1945 Philharmonic pension fund concert. But as it happens, all of these except the Berlioz *Romeo* were recorded, though not by Victor. Because the 1936 Philharmonic performances were broadcast by CBS, they could be, and were, recorded privately off the air; the NBC performances were recorded by NBC itself; the 1945 Philharmonic performances were recorded by the recording company in Carnegie Hall for Walter Toscanini. They could be issued by Victor; and all—even the early ones with poor sound—should be.

But there is another sense in which it is true that Toscanini's recordings don't give us his best performances. Almost all the performances on Victor records today date from 1944 and thereafter, with a few Verdi excerpts and 'pop' numbers recorded with the NBC Symphony from 1939 to 1943 and the Schubert Ninth recorded with the Philadelphia Orchestra in 1941, but with none of the performances recorded with the New York Philharmonic in 1929 and 1936 and with the BBC Symphony from 1937 to 1939 (some of which are to be had on imported Odeon records). The significance of this is that the performances before 1944 were in Toscanini's earlier performing style—relaxed, expansive, articulating and organizing and shaping the substance of a piece with much elasticity of tempo, and inflecting the phrase with much sharply outlined detail; whereas the performances roughly from 1944 on were in the later simplified style that was swifter and tauter, setting a tempo that was maintained with only slight modification, and giving the phrase only subtle inflection. And while the performances in this later style are great performances, the ones in the earlier style are even greater. One discovers this when one listens to the 1941 Schubert Ninth after the 1953 performance, to the 1936 Rossini *Semiramide* Overture after the 1951 performance, to the 1940 Verdi *Requiem* and Beethoven *Missa Solemnis* after the 1951 *Requiem* and 1953 *Missa Solemnis*. Moreover the years from 1944 on include a period roughly from 1945 through 1947 when many of Toscanini's performances were tense and driving—one example being the 1948 Mozart Symphony K.543 on LM-2001, another the 1945 Sousa *Stars and Stripes Forever* on 11-9188 and VCM-7001 as against the relaxed performance broadcast in 1943. And as Wallenstein points out, the recording microphone disturbed Toscanini, made him tense, impelled him to set a faster tempo than that of the performance at the concert.

2 (*from page 184*):

Even worse than Studio 8H was Studio 3A, in which (on the insistence, I was told, of an NBC executive that some use of the studio appear on the NBC books) Victor had Toscanini record Mozart's *Haffner* and Haydn's *Clock* in 1946-47, producing two of the most atrocious-sounding Toscanini recordings ever issued.

And actually a few excellent-sounding recordings were made in 8H—on the occasions when the microphone was placed at the optimum location for the studio that had been determined by an engineer named Johnston, and the chairs were pushed all the way back to increase the studio's resonance. These things were done at one session in 1945 for Gershwin's *An American in Paris,* and made its recorded sound spacious, warm, clear and clean. But at the same session Sousa's *Stars and Stripes Forever* was recorded with a microphone on each side in front of the orchestra and one in the rear of the hall—which is to say, with none at the Johnston location; and the result was coarse *tuttis* without depth and spaciousness and textures not cleanly defined in quiet. The superb Debussy *Ibéria* of 1950 was achieved by placing the microphone at the Johnston location and pushing the chairs all the way back; the lessened sharpness of presence and impact of the *La Mer* recorded the day before was the result of placing the microphone a few feet back of the Johnston location and pushing the chairs only part of the way back.

Nor were all the poor recordings made in 3A and 8H. In Carnegie Hall Victor produced in 1940 the excellent-sounding Brahms Piano Concerto No. 2, but in 1941 a Tchaikovsky Piano Concerto No. 1 that was thin, shallow, harsh and noisily clouded with reverberation, and in 1947 a Tchaikovsky *Pathétique* without luster and spaciousness because the microphone was placed too far back and the side boxes and parquet were covered with draperies, a Mendelssohn *Midsummer Night's Dream* even dimmer and weaker because the microphone—for this lightly scored music!—was placed even further back. As late as 1952 Victor produced a Beethoven Ninth without the spaciousness and luster of the *Pastoral* it had made a few months earlier; as late as 1953 a *Missa Solemnis* in which the chorus predominated over the orchestra and soloists because their microphone (the principal microphone behind Toscanini) was placed too far away.

What all this means is that whereas it would have been unthinkable that anyone should change what Toscanini produced at a concert, when he produced the performance for a recording Victor's supervisor of the recording could change its sound by his placing of the microphones and his other decisions affecting the acoustic characteristics of the hall; and the mistakes of a number of supervisors did alter and damage the sound of many of the performances imprinted on the records. Nor did it end there. When it happened that a superb facsimile of the performance—of Beethoven's Eighth, of Musorgsky's *Pictures at an Exhibition,* of Bizet's *Carmen* Suite—*was* imprinted on the tape, and Toscanini had approved it, then a Victor music editor—assigned to make from this original the tape master used in the processing of the metal parts for the final disc records—could, and did, make the changes that resulted in the ear-piercing, raucous *Pictures at an Exhibition* on LM-1838, the harsh Eighth on LM-1757, the shallow, blowzily 'brilliant' *Carmen* Suite on LRM-7013. The worst of these editors went so far as to inflict on the clear, bright, solid Debussy *La Mer* already issued on LM-1221 successive doses of 'enhancement' by echo-chamber resonance that produced the glossy, blurred and blowzy *La Mer* on LM-1833. And the transfer of 78-rpm recordings to LP provided this editor and others with the opportunity for various forms of electronic 'enhancement' that spoiled good recordings and made poor ones worse—an atrocious example being the 1964 version of the 1946 Tchaikovsky *Romeo and Juliet* on LM-7032, *Toscanini Concert Favorites,* in which the solid, bright, clear sound of the original 78-rpm recording was deprived of its solidity by a cut in bass, of its brightness by the treble-filter used to eliminate surface noise, and of its clarity by the addition of echo-chamber resonance.

[3] (*from page 184*):

But there were exceptional occasions when Toscanini produced a better performance at a recording session than at the concert or broadcast. One instance was the Haydn Symphony No. 88 he recorded in 1938, with a slow movement even more overwhelmingly powerful than the one he broadcast. And another was the Beethoven Ninth he recorded in 1952, whose first movement was controlled, steady and powerful, as the first movement he broadcast had not been.

[4] (*from page 184*):

Wallenstein doesn't name the author of this book, but he can be referring only to the abominable Marsh book; and he nodded recognition and agreement when I pointed out in addition that Marsh had brought to his evaluation of the recorded performances no adequate or accurate critical perception and judgment (the recorded performance of the Prelude and Finale of *Tristan und Isolde,* he writes, "is over-refined, the antiseptic souvenir of passion rather than its full-blooded actuality . . . [This] is easily understood when we see that these two pieces rank fourth and fifth in frequency [of performance] in Toscanini's repertory: they have had all the life played out of them"; and one phrase in the Finale is "played in a cool, polished and unfeeling manner, more appropriate to Verdi . . ."). Also that he had, to my knowledge, never heard Toscanini conduct the NBC Symphony in a hall before the last season of 1953-54 and never been present at a working rehearsal, but had felt able to make statements about what he hadn't experienced that one NBC Symphony musician pronounced untrue or nonsensical and others contradict in their monologues ("He would rush a work rather than run the risk of letting it go slack even for a moment . . . In general, as he grew older he tended . . . to grow nervous when confronted with long stretches of music in a slow pulse pattern"; "In his later seasons there must have been times when the only thing that saved Toscanini from disaster in some performances was the phenomenal virtuosity of his orchestra, which could play anything at virtually any tempo"; because of his language difficulty, Toscanini, "with his American orchestras . . . did not talk a great deal [at rehearsals]: they simply played for many minutes at a time, going over works again and again until the Maestro was satisfied"). Also that he had certainly never heard Toscanini conduct the New York Philharmonic, or heard Mengelberg do so before him, but had felt able to make statements about them which I was in a position to pronounce untrue ("A peer of these great ensembles [Stokowski's Philadelphia Orchestra and Koussevitzky's Boston Symphony] was the New York Philharmonic . . . under Willem Mengelberg, to which Toscanini came as a guest conductor in 1926 . . . Although it always responded to Toscanini with sensitiveness and fine playing [it] apparently did not begin to take on all of the characteristics it was to exhibit under him in later seasons until 1927-28, when he led it for a longer period"—the facts being that under Mengelberg the Philharmonic was not a peer of the Philadelphia and Boston Symphony, but that from its first performance with Toscanini in 1926 it exhibited the dazzling sonorities and execution that made it the peer of the other two). Also that he had never exchanged a word with Toscanini, but had felt able to make statements about him as a person without any basis of first-hand knowledge ("Toscanini brooks no peers"; "Young conductors were able, under certain conditions, to make friends with the Maestro and enjoy a pleasant relationship with him until they became potential rivals, after which the friendship abruptly ceased"—the examples being Rodzinski and Steinberg, whom nobody else has ever thought of as potential rivals of Toscanini).

⁵ (*from page 185*):

It was not the engineer who asked Toscanini if he was ready to record, but the man supervising the recording session—the producer, as I believe he is called nowadays.

FOR FELIX GALIMIR'S STATEMENT

¹ (*from page 199*):

Preparing, in October 1944, to broadcast Beethoven's *Eroica* in November, Toscanini listened to his performance of November 1939, and—he told me—blushed at what he heard. The 1939 performance was in his earlier expansive style marked by great elasticity of tempo; and by 1944 there had been the change to the later simpler style involving only slight modification of the set tempo. But for Toscanini this was not just a change from one way of playing to another: it was a change to a right way, to the only right way, and from a way, therefore, that had been shamefully wrong. And I had suggested to Galimir that this habit of mind, rather than the jealousy Toscanini was accused of, was responsible for his unfavorable comments on other conductors: his intense conviction at a particular moment that *this* was the right way to play something made any other way—his own in the past, another conductor's now—appear to him wrong. Actually, it was not true that he spoke only ill of other conductors, out of jealousy. He spoke well to me of Nikisch, of Schuch, of Ansermet; he told me I must come to Cantelli's rehearsals, where I watched him nodding and smiling in approval of what he was hearing. And when he spoke ill of a conductor to me, it was because of something he had heard the conductor do that was wrong: Muck's excessively slow tempo in

Beethoven's First; Beecham's in Haydn's No. 99; someone else's whipping up of the tempo of the finale of Berlioz's *Symphonie Fantastique* for excitement; Koussevitzky's coming to the *fermata*, the rest and the trill near the end of the Adagio of Mozart's Divertimento K.287, and failing, through sheer ignorance, to interpolate the cadenza which they indicated.

² *(from page 200)*:

[2] *(from page 200)*:

Our minds failed to meet at this point. By early I meant the last New York Philharmonic and first NBC Symphony years, say through 1943, in which Toscanini's performances were unhurried, expansive, spacious, and shaped and articulated by modifications of tempo (e.g., the 1940 Verdi *Requiem* and Beethoven *Missa Solemnis*, the 1941 Schubert Ninth with the Philadelphia Orchestra). And by late I meant the years from 1944 on, in which the performances were swift, taut, smoothed out, with only the slightest, subtlest modifications of tempo (e.g., the 1951 *Requiem*, the 1953 *Missa Solemnis* and Schubert Ninth). The performance of the Mozart E-flat which Galimir speaks of was done in 1948; and what he thinks of as early is the period roughly from 1945 to 1947, in which there were performances as fast and tense as the one of the Mozart E-flat—as against the relaxed performances of the fifties.

[3] *(from page 201)*:

In the months preceding the first NBC Symphony broadcast, when the orchestra was being drilled by Rodzinski, Chotzinoff—operating as NBC's musical ear, and hearing the dry, flat, hard sound of the orchestra in acoustically dead Studio 8H—was in a position to insist that the studio was unsuited to orchestral performance. But on this subject he is not known to have said a word in private or in public; and so for several years Toscanini's performances went out over the air with this unnatural sound, which in addition was made airlessly tight by the audience that filled the studio. In 1941-42 Stokowski had a shell installed, which changed the unfilled studio from acoustically dead to harshly reverberant; but with an audience the sound still was flat and tight—as against the orchestra's normal spacious, warm, luminous sound at the occasional benefit concert that Toscanini conducted in Carnegie Hall. And his performances continued to go out over the air with this "not ingratiating sound" until the broadcasts were moved, in 1951, to Carnegie Hall.

4 (*from page 201*):

Galimir is referring to the threat to the NBC Symphony program during those last years from the belief of NBC's head, Sylvester Weaver, that this program should, like every other, pay for itself. The suitable comment on this was made by NBC itself repeatedly in the fall of 1946, when it kept informing listeners to the NBC Symphony broadcasts that their cost was being borne by the network itself out of revenue from commercially sponsored programs, and that they were thus part of "a balanced service of the world's finest programs" which, "sponsored directly or not," were "all dependent on the sound American plan of financing radio by advertising revenue." Which is to say that in 1946 NBC rightly considered its expenditure on the NBC Symphony broadcasts a fulfillment of its part of the bargain of the American system of broadcasting —the bargain that in return for the use of the public domain to make money, the broadcaster undertakes to spend part of the money for programs of public service. That was NBC's position also in the early years of the NBC Symphony broadcasts, when, if I remember correctly, it declared them to be unsuitable for commercial sponsorship. And it should have been NBC's position in 1954, when it discontinued the orchestra and its broadcasts because it couldn't get a sponsor for them without Toscanini: under the American system NBC had an obligation to the public not only to continue them with Toscanini as long as he wished, but to continue them without him—with Cantelli, with other gifted younger conductors, with some of the older men.

Actually, moreover, the cost of the NBC Symphony broadcasts was not money spent on a public service program, but money spent to acquire for NBC and RCA the prestige of Toscanini's name, which NBC profited by in its sale of time and programs to advertisers (as CBS profited by the prestige of the New York Philharmonic), and which RCA profited by in its sale of radios, phonographs and records, including those Toscanini made with the NBC Symphony. It was, in other words, an investment which right from the start brought a financial return even with the broadcasts unsponsored. The *Fortune* article of January 1938 spelled this out: with the amounts paid to Toscanini and the other conductors, and the amounts above contract minimum paid to higher-caliber players, the entire excess cost of the NBC Symphony program for performers came to $250,000. With fifteen of the orchestra's thirty hours of work each week available for other programs, unsponsored and commercially sponsored, *Fortune* estimated that the sale of the orchestra in various groups to advertisers would by itself recover the extra $250,000 by the spring of 1938. The network time, Saturday from 10 to 11:30, had a nominal value of $47,000 on the NBC rate card; but *Fortune* pointed out that few advertisers wanted to buy time on America's night out, and that in fact no advertiser had had to give up time for the program. And *Fortune* also pointed out the possible financial benefit of Toscanini's prestige to NBC and RCA that I have mentioned. All this at the beginning, when the Toscanini broadcasts were not commercially sponsored; and in later years there was the additional financial return from commercial sponsorship. I haven't cited this in disapproval: one must be glad when a broadcasting company operating under the American commercial system chooses to invest in the program of a symphony orchestra and is rewarded by financial return on its investment. What I contend is that even when there was no such financial return, and the program didn't earn its cost, NBC, under the American system, had in 1954 the obligation to offer the program that it acknowledged in 1946.

Concerning those NBC statements in 1946 about the "world's finest programs . . . dependent on the sound American plan of financing radio by advertising revenue," one could say then that the British plan of financing radio by license fees from owners of sets had proved equally sound and had given the British public even finer musical programs—the BBC's systematic presentation of the entire musical literature, as against the American networks' programs limited almost entirely to the big-name orchestras and soloists and the Metropolitan Opera. Specifically the BBC, solely out of regard for music, had set up its BBC Symphony ten years before NBC, with regard for the commercial value of Toscanini's name, set up the NBC Symphony. And today one can point out that the BBC Symphony still exists and enriches the musical life of the British public, whereas the NBC Symphony does not.

In his recent biography of Sarnoff, Eugene Lyons writes about his efforts on behalf of high-quality music on the air, which attained their climax for him in Toscanini's broadcasts with the NBC Symphony. Lyons reports how Sarnoff had to defend the program to his associates by pointing to the return in prestige and profits to NBC and RCA from their association with Toscanini. But he contends that while those arguments had validity, "they were also rationalizations. . . . No matter how logically he justified superior programs, he was in fact responding to his own hungers for beauty, music, culture . . ."—hungers which appear to have ceased in 1954.

273

Additional Notes — 1980

For page 61:
Five years after this account of how unintimidating and pleasant his experience with Toscanini had been, Kipnis—in a *New York Times* interview occasioned by his 80th birthday—recalled that he hadn't had any arguments with conductors but "Muck and Toscanini were the hardest to get along with."

For page 67:
In the *Times* interview five years later Kipnis recalled Furtwängler as the conductor who "asked me to end [the dialogue before '*O Isis und Osiris*'] on an F."

For page 69:
Kipnis claims to have witnessed this incident at the first orchestral rehearsal of the *Missa Solemnis* in 1936; but Toscanini's first rehearsal with the Vienna Philharmonic occurred in 1933, with Kipnis not present; and he is, therefore, merely relating an anecdote which Burghauser, the orchestra's "manager" at that time, vehemently characterized as a fabrication.

For page 192:
If Burghauser's recollection of only two rehearsals for the

first concert in 1933, on p. 154, is correct, then Galimir must have sneaked into the second one after hearing about the first one with Toscanini's "terrible blow-ups . . . because they didn't play well." Burghauser, in his account of these two rehearsals, says nothing about blow-ups and the Philharmonic's customary rehearsal behavior that Galimir says it took time and blow-ups for Toscanini to change, producing the "superhuman concentration" Burghauser reports.

Endnotes

T.H.—1988

(Throughout the book:)

The Italian word *sì* should be accented to give it its correct meaning.

(Page 3—Further relevant dates in the Toscanini career:)

1901, 1903, 1904, 1906—Principal conductor at the Teatro de la Ópera in Buenos Aires; 1912 principal conductor at the Teatro Colón.

1932-38—Guest conducted orchestras in The Hague, Stockholm, and Paris.

1937-38—Returned to conduct the Palestine Symphony.

1952—Conducted at La Scala for the last time—an orchestral concert.

(Page 21, line 10—Erratum:)

than, not then

(Page 25—The first concerts of the NBC Symphony:)

Monteux conducted the first two concerts, and Rodzinski conducted three more before Toscanini came.

Endnotes

(Page 85—Toscanini in South America:)

Actually, Toscanini conducted only five seasons in Buenos Aires, between 1901 and 1912. Only the last was at the Teatro Colón, which was not built until 1908. The others were given at the Teatro de la Ópera.

(Page 144—Toscanini and Ysaÿe:)

Toscanini's only performance with Ysaÿe of which there is any historical record took place in Turin, not Milan, in March of 1897, and the work was the Violin Concerto by Beethoven, not concertos by Bach or Mendelssohn.

(Page 146—Erratum:)
   È porcheria

(Page 163, line 12:)
   1896, not 1894

(Page 175—Nikisch's report about Toscanini:)

Toscanini's last performance of *Siegfried* took place in 1905. Nikisch must have been speaking of another opera or of a different occasion.

(Page 180—Toscanini and Cosima Wagner:)

Toscanini cannot have been worried about encountering Cosima Wagner the summer he conducted *Tannhäuser* at Bayreuth, as she had died several months before.

(Page 184—Availability of Toscanini's recordings:)

All of Toscanini's Philadelphia Orchestra recordings were issued by RCA on LP in 1976. As of 1988, it is RCA's intention to remaster most of Toscanini's commercial recordings from the original master discs and tapes and to reissue them on Compact Disc.

(Page 187, second line from the bottom—Erratum:)
Amedeo

(Page 189, middle—Erratum:)
abbandonare

(Pages 192, 193—Errata:)
Huberman

(Page 199, line 3—Erratum:)
brutto

(Page 201, line 17:)
1946, not 1945.

(Page 209, bottom—1950 NBC Symphony tour:)
Actually the *Eroica* was played only eight times on the tour.

(Page 211, top—Players who were not awed by Toscanini:)
Some of those hardboiled old-timers gave their views of Toscanini in Jerome Toobin's book, *Agitato*, about the Symphony of the Air.

(Page 223, line 9—Toscanini's methods with lesser orchestras:)
He could on occasion be patient with orchestras of less than virtuoso caliber. After a rehearsal with the orchestra of La

Scala, Wallenstein remarked to him that he would not have let the NBC Symphony get away with the things he had let pass that day. He replied that in New York he knew the players could do better; here he knew they could not. *(See: pages 178-79)*

(Page 236, line 17:)
The musician who withheld his recollections of Toscanini because he was afraid they would get him into difficulties with other conductors was Frank Miller.

(Page 238, second paragraph:)
The musician who spoke about Toscanini's temper, and about a horn player, was Milton Katims.

(Pages 243-245—Toscanini's resignation from the NBC Symphony:)
For a revision of this account of Toscanini's resignation, see Haggin's *Conversations With Toscanini*, Da Capo, 1989.

(Pages 248-249—Chotzinoff, Peerce and Un Ballo in Maschera:*)*
Sachs points out another discrepancy in Chotzinoff's account: Chotzinoff has Toscanini flying off to Italy in 1954 to be with his dying wife, even though she had died two and a half years earlier in the summer of 1951. Either Chotzinoff combined two separate stories—intentionally or by mistake—or else he invented most of what he purported to remember of this episode.

(Pages 249-253—Toscanini's Philadelphia Orchestra recordings:)
See as well my comment in *Conversations With Toscanini*, Da Capo, 1989, endnote to page 28.

(Page 264—The quality of Toscanini's recordings:)

The later history of the NBC Symphony recordings is recounted in *Conversations With Toscanini*, Da Capo, 1989.

(Page 271—NBC broadcasts moved to Carnegie Hall:)

Haggin says here that the NBC Symphony's broadcasts were moved to Carnegie Hall in 1951; in *Conversations With Toscanini*, he says the move occurred in the fall of 1950. The apparent discrepancy arose because the first NBC season in Carnegie Hall began in the fall of 1950, but the first concert Toscanini conducted himself took place in January of 1951.

Additional Endnotes

T. H. — 1988

(Page 68:)

The Leonore in the Salzburg *Fidelio* was Lotte Lehmann.

(Page 180 — Toscanini's tympani doubling in Beethoven's Eighth Symphony:)

In fact Toscanini retained the tympani for his first recording in 1939, and only removed them for the later recording of 1952.

(Page 239:)

The rehearsal at which NBC players were compelled to sneak out to fulfill other commitments was for the *Missa Solemnis,* as Haggin states on the following page, not for Verdi's *Requiem,* as Chotzinoff recalled.

(Pages 248–249: Chotzinoff's assertion that Toscanini's first choice for Manrico had been Bjoerling, not Peerce:)

This may be true. According to Arthur Fierro, a preliminary cast list in Toscanini's handwriting gives Bjoerling's name before Peerce's.

Index

Index

Index

Index

145, 146, 153, 170, 173, 182, 191, 277, 279–80
Schalk, Franz, 171
Schelling, Ernest, 177–78
Scherchen, Hermann, 30
Schoenbach, Sol, 237, 249
Schola Cantorum, 216
Schopenhauer, Arthur, 160
Schubert, Franz, 46, 82, 153; performance traditions, 165–66; *Moments Musical*, 135; Quintet for Strings **Op.163**, 202; Symphonies: **No.8** (*Unfinished*), 78, 166, 196, 225; **No.9**, 42, 90, 120, 122, 123, 124, 170, 182, 199, 226, 249, 250, 252, 263, 264, 270
Schuch, Ernst von, 173, 269
Schumann, Elisabeth, 82
Schumann, Robert, 82
Scotti, Antonio, 144
Shumsky, Oscar, 132
Schussnigg, Kurt von, 260
Schuster, Joseph, 97
Seattle Symphony Orchestra, 214, 231
Serkin, Rudolf, 103
Shapiro, Harvey, 27, 132
Sharrow, Leonard, 33
Shostakovitch, Dmitri, 44, 97; Symphonies: **No.1**, 31; **No.5**, 31–32, 127; **No.7** (*Leningrad*), 54–55, 127, 138
Shulman, Alan, 240, 243
Sinnett, Mark, 251
Smetana, Bedrich: *The Bartered Bride*, 41
Society of the Friends of Music (*See:* Musikverein)
Sokoloff, Nikolai, 247
Sousa, John Philip: *The Stars and Stripes Forever*, 33, 264, 265
Spitalny, H. Leopold, 51, 87, 195; overrode Toscanini's artistic

decisions, 242
Stagliano, Albert, 25
Stalin, Josef, 185
Steinberg, William, 192, 193, 195, 268
Stoessel, Albert, 25
Stokowski, Leopold, 26, 36, 97, 120, 124, 125, 126, 127, 203, 237, 268; Toscanini's disapproval of his performance of Franck's Symphony in D minor, 26–27 (un–named); has acoustic shell installed in Studio 8H, 271
Strauss, Johann, Jr., 57; *Blue Danube* Waltz, 56
Strauss, Richard, 29, 51, 77; as conductor, 69, 150, 154, 160–61, 164, 165, 169, 171, 195, 256; improvises *Così fan tutte* and *Magic Flute* recitatives, 261–62; *Death and Transfiguration*, 30, 91, 181, 249, 251; *Don Juan*, 17–18; *Don Quixote*, 175, 176, 177, 178, 201, 211, 245, 263; *Duettino* for Clarinet and Bassoon, 262; *Ein Heldenleben*, 43, 55–56, 183; *Four Last Songs*, 262; *Salome*, 3, 91, 174; *Till Eulenspiegel's Merry Pranks*, 48, 195–96
Stravinsky, Igor, 18; *The Firebird*, 101; *Petrushka*, 31, 44, 101; *The Rake's Progress*, 100; *Le Rossignol*, 32; *Le Sacre de Printemps*, 101
Symphony of the Air, 279
Szell, George, 76; comments about Toscanini, 135, 237, 255–57
Szigeti, Joseph, 76

Tabuteau, Marcel, 120, 122, 129, 130

Index

tour in **1950**, 21–22, 33, 34,
147, 209–10, 279; NBC
Symphony's first rehearsal
and broadcast with Toscanini
in **1937**, 25; incident at rehearsal in **1940** that caused
him to absent himself from
NBC for a season, 26, 35–36,
54, 239–42, 245, 282; resignation in **1954**, 37, 201, 240 n.,
243–45, 280; Toscanini's artistic decisions at NBC over-
ridden by others, 242, 248–49,
282; orchestra disbanded,
243–45, 271–73; Toscanini
exploited as commercial
property, 272–73
And New York Philharmonic:
38–49, 176–80, 182–83, 268;
incident with New York Philharmonic harpist, 44
In Vienna and Salzburg: 65–69,
150–64; Toscanini's performance of Schubert's Ninth Symphony, and the Viennese
public's reaction, 163–68;
"Caruso" prices for Toscanini's
concerts, 257
Rehearsal practice: 96, 169, 220,
254; force of his knowledge,
54, 76, 87, 177–78, 188, 204;
corrects Siegfried Wagner's
stage direction, 180; knowledge of entire musical literature, 76, 127–28, 139, 179–80;
knowledge of instruments' capacities, 19, 20, 88; this knowledge enabled him to set judicious tempos, 195; able to anticipate what might go wrong,
142; expected that some players thought certain music was
easy, 88–89; incident of imaginary horns, 223; made no

daunting demands of competent musicians, 86–87; rehearsals hardest on exposed
players, 75; un–heard compliment to tuba–player,
137–38; approach was the
same with every orchestra,
122–23; had tempo and shape
in mind before rehearsal
started, 40, 52, 54, 74, 179,
222; efficiency, 22, 27, 51, 52,
154, 222–23; conviction about
what he was doing, 78, 79,
104, 171, 198–99; his conviction made his interpretations
convincing to players, 78,
139–40; did not stop and start
repeatedly, 27, 52; his way of
working on details, 43, 52, 74;
efficiency made talk unnecessary, 52, 74–75, 162, 207,
223; used his baton instead of
talking, 39, 48, 156–57, 206–7,
197, 208, 216–17; instinctive,
not analytical, 30, 122; limited
English, 22, 121–22, 123–24,
157, 249, 268; poor English
resulted in outbursts of temper, 178; demonstrated outline of a piece by singing, to
make players sing on their instruments, 51; Tchaikovsky's
Pathétique Symphony: "I–ee
love you...," 125; incidents of
silk scarf and *pianissimo* "from
Brooklyn," 30, 220; intensity
of his concentration affected
the musicians, 19–21, 22, 24,
28, 41, 42, 46, 47–48, 52, 57,
76, 96, 101, 110–11, 115,
139–40, 157–58, 182, 192, 196;
obtained better than normal
playing, 154–55, 182, 219;
perspiration, 218; consistent

292

from one rehearsal to next, 39–40, 74, 56, 88, 126, 137, 196; stopped less for corrections in last years, 36, 79, 82; method of rehearsing with soloists, 177–78, 211; with singers, 60–61, 95–96, 109, 112, 113; his piano–playing, 61; as accompanist, 97, 76–77, 103–6; rehearsals greater than the concerts, 28–29, 56, 73, 78–79, 126, 140, 227–28; Berlioz's *Romeo and Juliet,* 96–97; Brahms's First Symphony, 133; *Till Eulenspiegel's Merry Pranks,* 195–96; *The Magic Flute,* 65–67, 262; *Fidelio,* 68; *Missa Solemnis,* 69–70; Wagner's *Tristan* and Verdi's *Requiem,* 60–61, 63; Vienna Philharmonic rehearsals, 154–55, 157–58, 162, 191–92, 258–60, 275–76; Vienna Philharmonic considered these the high point of its 120–year history, 152; subsequent conductors eclipsed, 161; combined every quality to a higher degree, 198; "You were proud of the way you played with him," 195–96

Personal magnetism: eyes obtained complete communication with whole orchestra, 30; galvanizes salon orchestra, 162; hornist drawn in unconsciously, 219, 238; eloquence of his expression, 55, 96, 106, 110, 115, 204, 216, 219; Kipnis felt no magnetism, 63

Temper: 12–13, 21, 22–23, 27–28, 39, 55, 75, 96, 101, 117, 121–22, 126–27, 129, 142, 178, 179, 189, 191–92, 197, 210–11,

214, 216, 225–27, 253, 259–61, 276; cause not always apparent, 40–41, 178; frustrated by failure to realize ideal in his mind, 39; inability to accommodate himself to outside realities, 46–47; impatience with anything unexpected, 47; anger at what was done, not to him, but to composer, 81; impatience with stupidity or carelessness, 52, 113, 226; podium behavior genuine, not an act, 101, 111; outbursts that were calculated, 226–27; restraint at concerts, 55; one instance of the opposite, 194; no personal animosity, 43, 55, 123

Players' response to outbursts: 23, 210–11; harder on individuals than on sections, 52–53, 75; "If he hadn't been right I'd have told him off," 23; quieter atmosphere would have made performances even better, 42–43; experience was rewarding but trying, 42–43, 44, 45–46; even those who resented him put out more than for other conductors, 53; mellowed in his sixties, 154, 162; outbursts have been made too much of, 22

His patience: 28, 76, 142–43, 162, 188, 189, 225–26, 279–80; no recriminations for mishaps in concert, 42; patient when music was difficult, 52; patient with singers who were musical, 77; "In New York I know they can do it, but here...they cannot," 178–79

Index

Beat: 122, 126, 136–37, 169, 177, 199, 203, 220–21; impossible for players to go wrong, 20, 30, 39, 48, 51, 52, 156–57, 158, 197, 206–7, 208, 216–17; beauty and eloquence of his beat, 39; economy, 136; beat reflected line, subdivided seldom, 51; gave the meter, and within the meter was delineative, 51–52, 141–42; ability to conduct simultaneously what was happening and what was about to happen, 157, 216–17, 221; players' response to his beat was immediate, 51, 52; changes choir's tone with a gesture, 82–83; trouble beating changing meters of some twentieth-century music, 133; incident of orchestra that was not accustomed to him, 203; instances of his giving wrong cues on occasion, 115–16, 133, 147, 158–59

Tempos: 112–13, 117, 184, 207–8, 209, 211–12, 262; "You play *funebre*, I want *marcia!*" 16; flexibility, 29, 52, 104, 137, 168–69, 181, 204, 229; flexibility within context of overall shape, 59, 63, 227; tempos that permitted every note to be played, 29, 55–56, 83–84, 88, 195, 229; Mozart's Andantes, 78; effect of broadening tempo achieved by expression, 166–67; effect of fast tempo by lightness of tone, 169; transitions, 168–69; tempos according to the score, 181, 196–97; recordings vs. concerts, 264

Form and structure: 18, 19, 29, 52, 73–74, 105–6, 186, 199, 228, 253; concerned more with line than with color, 125; classicist, not impressionist, 18; thought horizontally, not vertically, 181; forward movement with repose, 29, 55, 124; forward movement in context of overall shape, 48, 52, 125–26; details related to the whole, 74; propulsive beat gave outline and direction, 228; the expression of one phrase implied the right expression of the next, 115; continuity with freedom, 205; sense of proportion in shaping climaxes, 74–75, 196–97

Rhythm: 17, 29, 137; timing, 228; changing meters, 31, 41, 65, 133, 255; obsession with rhythm caused difficulties occasionally, 123–24, 129

Expression: lyricism, 29, 30, 79, 88, 123, 181, 217, 228; "*Cantare! Non solfeggiare!*" 238; *Tristan und Isolde*, 63–64, 65; intelligence and taste, 29, 177, 180, 183; delicacy, 199; simplicity and restraint, 43, 44, 65, 110, 112, 154, 204; restraint occasionally inhibited him, 43, 48; integrity in the face of tradition, 49; animation, 77, 79, 90, 125–26, 166–67, 169, 217, 228; unique capacity for both power and charm, 171; imagination, 18, 46; youthfulness, 21–22; energy of early NBC years, 24; wanted more than the right notes, 82; in *Die Meistersinger* more concerned with the music than with the

Acknowledgments

I am indebted to

The musicians who speak in the book, for their generous and patient co-operation.

William H. Youngren, for his critical reading of what I did with the material they gave me.

Roger Dakin, for the editorial advice I asked on several matters.

Margaret Nicholson, for, among other things, her suggestion of the introductions to the musicians' statements.

B. H. H.